SEO Warrior

SEO Warrior

John I. Jerkovic

O'REILLY®

Beijing · Cambridge · Farnham · Köln · Sebastopol · Taipei · Tokyo

SEO Warrior

by John I. Jerkovic

Copyright © 2010 John I. Jerkovic. All rights reserved.
Printed in the United States of America.

Published by O'Reilly Media, Inc., 1005 Gravenstein Highway North, Sebastopol, CA 95472.

O'Reilly books may be purchased for educational, business, or sales promotional use. Online editions are also available for most titles (*http://my.safaribooksonline.com*). For more information, contact our corporate/institutional sales department: 800-998-9938 or *corporate@oreilly.com*.

Editor: Mike Loukides	**Indexer:** Lucie Haskins
Production Editor: Sarah Schneider	**Cover Designer:** Karen Montgomery
Copyeditor: Audrey Doyle	**Interior Designer:** David Futato
Proofreader: Sarah Schneider	**Illustrator:** Robert Romano

Printing History:

November 2009:   First Edition.

RepKover™

This book uses RepKover, a durable and flexible lay-flat binding.

ISBN: 978-0-596-15707-4

[M]

1257456253

Table of Contents

Preface

I was compelled to write *SEO Warrior* for many reasons. Every day, thousands of sites are born in the hopes of making it big. Most of them will fail before achieving their goals. Many site owners create their sites blindly, without conducting proper research. Many site owners do not even know what search engine optimization (SEO) is and what its benefits are. Although this approach might work for some sites, it is hardly the case for popular and successful sites. The goal of *SEO Warrior* is to make you, the website owner, successful!

The topic of SEO is one of my passions. SEO—when considered right from the start—will give you an edge as well as an improved return on your investment. Although nobody can guarantee your site's rankings, if you do the things I discuss in this book you will greatly increase your site's chances of doing well in Google. If you follow the same approach, you should also do well in all of the other major search engines.

Everything happens for a reason. In 2001, I was hired as a consultant to work at Tucows.com, which was (and still is) one of the top-tier domain name registrars. It was one of the first to be accredited by the Internet Corporation for Assigned Names and Numbers (ICANN). During my stay at Tucows.com, I had the opportunity to work on the popular OpenSRS domain reseller software, which proved to be the catalyst of what was to come.

Not long after finishing my contract at Tucows.com, I was inspired to create my very own international web hosting company, with offices in North America and Europe. During this time I became interested in search engines and search engine algorithms. This experience provided me the opportunity to work on several hundred sites over the past several years.

I did many things during this time, from managing the business to providing different services including web hosting, web design, SEO, and search engine marketing (SEM). I worked on many different types of sites, including blogs, community sites, news portal sites, small business sites, and big corporate sites. This book represents the knowledge and experience I gained in working on many different websites over the past 15 years of my career.

Who This Book Is For

I wrote *SEO Warrior* with a diverse audience in mind. This book is aimed at webmasters, web owners, IT professionals, savvy marketers, and anyone interested in the topic of SEO. I cover many tools and concepts, all of which can help bring your site to the next level. This book is different from other SEO books in its breadth and depth of coverage.

Getting to the top of search engine results often requires multiple factors to work in your favor. SEO is not a one-time thing. If you are thinking of creating a new site, read this book before making your move. If you already have a site, you may want to do the same or just skip to your particular area of interest. Accordingly, you can read *SEO Warrior* from cover to cover or use it as a reference. I recommend going with the first approach and then coming back to the book as you see fit.

How This Book Is Organized

SEO Warrior takes a holistic approach when it comes to SEO. The book comprises 18 chapters. Here is a rundown of what you'll find in each:

Chapter 1, *The Big Picture*
: Examines the various parts of the SEO landscape, including SEO benefits and challenges. It also stresses the importance of formalizing the entire SEO process in a way that will help you track your SEO progress.

Chapter 2, *Search Engine Primer*
: Provides an overview of the search engine landscape. It covers the most important search engines (Google, Yahoo!, and Bing) while observing some of the lesser-known alternatives. It also examines search engine algorithms, including Google PageRank, as well as search engine bots.

Chapter 3, *Website Essentials*
: Examines domain name and hosting options, custom software design, and third-party software, along with website usability and web accessibility. This chapter provides the most fundamental building blocks for creating your online presence as well as the underlying infrastructure in an SEO sense.

Chapter 4, *Internal Ranking Factors*, and Chapter 5, *External Ranking Factors*
: Cover the various SEO factors that influence a site's rankings. Instead of just stating what those factors are, I actually prove them. The proof comes in the form of a Perl script that is available in Appendix A as well as on the book's companion website, *http://www.seowarrior.net*.

Chapter 6, *Web Stats Monitoring*
: Examines different web stats monitoring tools, including the most popular ones used by shared hosting providers. It also examines the NCSA Common log format

in detail. Understanding what goes into web logs is important for you to gauge your website traffic, no matter what tool you use.

Chapter 7, *Google Webmaster Tools and Google Analytics*
Goes into detail regarding these two platforms. Both tools are helpful in SEO. The bottom line is that you will need to use several tools to ensure proper tracking and monitoring.

Chapter 8, *Search Engine Traps*
Examines the kinds of scenarios that will prevent your site from being crawled. It examines each scenario in detail, with many code examples.

Chapter 9, *Robots Exclusion Protocol*
Discusses Robots Exclusion Protocol in detail. Coverage includes *robots.txt* and its associated directives, HTML meta directives, the *.htaccess* access control method, and the HTTP Header X-Robot-Tag(s). This chapter provides a solid foundation in terms of ensuring proper crawling and indexing of your site.

Chapter 10, *Sitemaps*
Highlights the benefits of Sitemaps. Google and others encourage site owners to create Sitemaps to help them index their sites. The chapter explores the creation of several different Sitemap types, including plain-text URL listings, HTML, XML, RSS/Atom, video, and mobile Sitemaps.

Chapter 11, *Keyword Research*
Covers one of the most important activities in SEO: keyword research. The chapter discusses ways to find keywords, a basic strategy and process, and timing and trending factors. It also covers several tools and how you can use them to find keywords.

Chapter 12, *Link Building*
Goes over the different link-building strategies you should use. Link building is one of the most important activities in SEO. The chapter discusses the topics of link bait, social bookmarking, and many others.

Chapter 13, *Competitor Research and Analysis*
Examines ways to find, analyze, and track your competitors. It also provides details on many of the tools you can use to perform these tasks properly and efficiently.

Chapter 14, *Content Considerations*
Covers many details related to website content. It discusses different concepts, including how to become a resource, short-term content, and long-term content. It also covers content duplication and content verticals.

Chapter 15, *Social Networking Phenomenon*
Discusses the importance of social networking and social media, and how to leverage the different social platforms and communities including Facebook, Twitter, and Digg. It also covers social media strategy and methods for automating social media interactions. You will create a Twitter scheduler application that you can

use as part of your Twitter strategy. The chapter also covers the concept of real-time search.

Chapter 16, *Search Engine Marketing*

Teaches ways to complement and improve your SEO efforts by utilizing SEM methods. Specifically, the chapter covers how to use Google AdWords to forecast SEO results, and it provides an overview of two of the most important Google platforms: Google AdWords and Google AdSense.

Chapter 17, *Search Engine Spam*

Discusses things you should stay away from to ensure that the search engines do not penalize your site for spam propagation.

Chapter 18, *Industry Buzz*

Covers three of the most talked about SEO topics as of this writing: Bing, Search-Wiki, and the `nofollow` link attribute. The chapter also discusses the Keyword Dashboard tool, which can help you compare search results in Bing, Google, and Yahoo!.

Tools come and go, but some of the most basic SEO tips will always be applicable. Most of the significant programming scripts mentioned in the book appear in their entirety in Appendix A. Even if you do not have any technical knowledge, you should still benefit from reading this book.

Conventions Used in This Book

The following typographical conventions are used in this book:

Italic

Indicates new terms, URLs, filenames, and file extensions

`Constant width`

Indicates variables, method names, and other code elements, as well as the contents of files

`Constant width bold`

Highlights new code in an example

`Constant width italic`

Shows text that should be replaced with user-supplied values

 This icon signifies a tip, suggestion, or general note.

 This icon indicates a warning or caution.

Using Code Examples

This book is here to help you get your job done. In general, you may use the code in this book in your programs and documentation. You do not need to contact us for permission unless you're reproducing a significant portion of the code. For example, writing a program that uses several chunks of code from this book does not require permission. Selling or distributing a CD-ROM of examples from O'Reilly books *does* require permission. Answering a question by citing this book and quoting example code does not require permission. Incorporating a significant amount of example code from this book into your product's documentation *does* require permission.

We appreciate, but do not require, attribution. An attribution usually includes the title, author, publisher, and ISBN. For example: "*SEO Warrior* by John I. Jerkovic. Copyright 2010 John I. Jerkovic, 978-0-596-15707-4."

If you feel your use of code examples falls outside fair use or the permission given here, feel free to contact us at *permissions@oreilly.com*.

We'd Like to Hear from You

Every example in this book has been tested, but occasionally you may encounter problems. Mistakes and oversights can occur and we will gratefully receive details of any that you find, as well as any suggestions you would like to make for future editions. You can contact the authors and editors at:

O'Reilly Media, Inc.
1005 Gravenstein Highway North
Sebastopol, CA 95472
800-998-9938 (in the United States or Canada)
707-829-0515 (international or local)
707-829-0104 (fax)

We have a web page for this book, where we list errata, examples, and any additional information. You can access this page at:

http://www.oreilly.com/catalog/9780596157074

To comment or ask technical questions about this book, send email to the following, quoting the book's ISBN number (9780596157074):

bookquestions@oreilly.com

For more information about our books, conferences, Resource Centers, and the O'Reilly Network, see our website at:

http://www.oreilly.com

Safari® Books Online

Safari Safari Books Online is an on-demand digital library that lets you easily search over 7,500 technology and creative reference books and videos to find the answers you need quickly.

With a subscription, you can read any page and watch any video from our library online. Read books on your cell phone and mobile devices. Access new titles before they are available for print, and get exclusive access to manuscripts in development and post feedback for the authors. Copy and paste code samples, organize your favorites, download chapters, bookmark key sections, create notes, print out pages, and benefit from tons of other time-saving features.

O'Reilly Media has uploaded this book to the Safari Books Online service. To have full digital access to this book and others on similar topics from O'Reilly and other publishers, sign up for free at *http://my.safaribooksonline.com*.

Acknowledgments

SEO Warrior represents roughly two years of work. I would like to thank many people who have assisted me in many ways during this time. First, I would like to thank my wife, Adriana. Without her, this book would not exist. She took care of our three little children (Drazen, Fernando, and Angelina) while providing me with her timeless love and support.

I will always remember my aunt, Blanka Jerkovic, who passed away April 4, 2009 (while I was writing this book). She is one of the people who have made a profound mark on my life in many ways. I am forever grateful to her. I would also like to remember Jasen Drnasin, my fallen friend and real-life warrior, who was one of the most phenomenal people I have ever known.

Furthermore, I would like to thank all of my extended family, including my mother, father, and Jana Lubina. There are also many friends and colleagues (they know who they are) to whom I would like to extend my humble gratitude and a big Thank You for all of their support.

I am also grateful to O'Reilly Media for giving me the opportunity to write this book. I want to take this opportunity to thank the editor, Mike Loukides, for all of his help and support over the past 12 months. I also want to thank the entire O'Reilly production team for their assistance in bringing this book into your hands. This includes Audrey Doyle, copyeditor; Rachel Monaghan, senior production editor; Sarah Schneider, production editor; Lucie Haskins, indexer; Rob Romano, illustrator; Jacque Quann, editorial assistant; and Laurel Ackerman, marketing director.

Furthermore, I would like to thank Soren Ryherd of the Working Planet Marketing Group (*http://www.workingplanet.com*) for taking the time to review the book. I am grateful for your time and all of your comments. I am also grateful to Matt Cutts (of Google.com) for reading *SEO Warrior* while providing many great comments.

Most importantly, I want to thank each and every reader of *SEO Warrior* for buying the book in either the electronic or printed version.

Everything good in life requires sacrifice, patience, and hard work. May this book bring you one step closer to all of your online aspirations.

## CHAPTER 1

The Big Picture

Often, search engine optimization (SEO) comes as an afterthought, and not everyone is always fully aware of its long-term benefits. Depending on the situation, SEO may involve both the IT and marketing departments. In a small business, just one (or very few) individuals will be doing everything. Other times, companies will hire specialists to help them with their SEO needs.

SEO can be defined as an aggregate of all the work necessary to produce a high volume of referral hits from search engines, web directories, and other websites, with the ultimate goal of making the website popular. SEO involves internal and external website analysis, including link building, proper website architecture and development, competitor analysis, keyword research, content development, and many other tasks.

SEO is partly about building appropriate content and partly about getting people to link to you. Your content is essential, but Google's ability to count incoming links, in addition to content, was considered a major breakthrough.

Search engine marketing (SEM) refers to the utilization of pay-per-click (PPC) advertising such as through Google AdWords. Although some elements are common to both SEO and SEM, PPC advertising is much easier to implement and can achieve immediate results, usually in the form of getting visitors to see your website in a matter of minutes. Marketers will often ignore (or confuse) SEO in favor of (PPC) SEM, but by doing so they are ignoring great opportunities. SEO is about as close to free as you can get. It takes work, and work costs money, particularly if you hire a consultant. But you won't have any advertising bills coming in. SEO work brings long-term value.

If you operate your website for hobby or profit, SEO can be an important tool in making your website popular. SEO is not rocket science (or anywhere close to it). But it certainly can get as technical and detailed as you want to make it.

One could argue that the deceptive SEO practiced in its early days is long gone. Today it takes a lot more effort for sites to be ranked well. Ranking well does not necessarily translate to relative site popularity or sites meeting their objectives (desired conversions). SEO gets the visitor to the door. It is up to your site's content to welcome and retain that visitor.

Optimizing just for search engines may not be enough. Social media websites along with social bookmarking should be considered as well. Today's web user demands more from websites. This evolution in site usability and interactivity, coupled with ever-changing search engine technology, brings with it additional demands for the website owner.

SEO Benefits

SEO provides numerous benefits. These include greater search engine results page (SERP) real estate, a historical trust factor, and a lower cost of ownership. SEO benefits are typically long lasting. The following subsections explore these benefits in more detail.

SERP Real Estate

Figure 1-1 shows the typical layout of a Google SERP. Sponsored (PPC) links appear on the far right as well as at the top (just below the Search box). Product results, local business results, book results, news results, and so forth may also appear just under the top Sponsored Links section. Moving farther down we find the SEO-based organic search results.

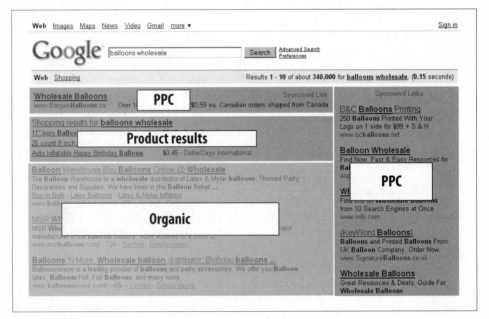

Figure 1-1. Google SERP

When looking at the SERP real estate in totality, you can see that organic results occupy most of the screen real estate. This is abundantly clear for the less popular keywords that have fewer sponsored links in the search results.

Popular keywords

When searching for popular keywords, search results are usually mixed with Blended Search results, as shown in Figure 1-1. This is perhaps the worst-case scenario in an SEO context. How do you stand out in all of the clutter? Typically, part of the answer is by targeting less popular keywords.

Niche keywords

Not all search results are cluttered. Searches for niche keywords often produce 100% organic results. Figure 1-2 is one example (for the keyword *electrodermal testing sensitivities toronto*). As you can observe, nobody is bidding for this keyword.

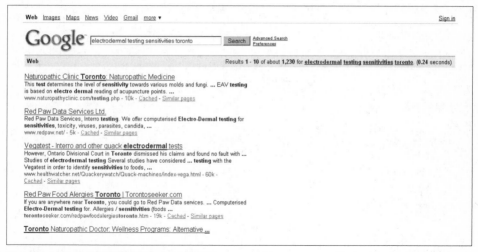

Figure 1-2. Google SERP: Niche keywords

Optimizing for niche keywords helps to attain greater conversion rates. To fortify their brands, the big industry players will also optimize their sites for the more (broad) popular keywords, irrespective of the conversion rate.

The Trust Factor

Most people trust organic search results. According to a survey by iProspect (*http://www.iprospect.com*), more than 60% of users click on organic search results. The percentage is even higher for individuals with more Internet experience. The full report is at *http://www.iprospect.com/premiumPDFs/iProspectSurveyComplete.pdf*.

Another study, titled "Paid search rates by industry" and conducted by Hitwise Intelligence (*http://www.hitwise.com*), shows a wider gap in favor of organic search results. The only exception to the rule is that of the insurance industry, with 45% of traffic coming in via PPC campaigns. The full article is available at *http://weblogs.hitwise.com/robin-goad/2008/09/paid_search_rates_by_industry.html*.

It should be very clear that if you are solely using PPC as your conduit for search engine traffic, you are missing out on the broader picture. Organic search results have traditionally enjoyed more trust, especially among more experienced and Internet-savvy people. And if these people are your demographic, you need to have your SEO in order.

The Golden Triangle

In an eye-tracking study conducted by Didit (*http://www.did-it.com*), Enquiro (*http://www.enquiro.com*), and Eyetools (*http://www.eyetools.com*), 50 participants were observed while browsing through Google search results. The results of this study uncovered what is termed the "Golden Triangle." This refers to the screen area (in the shape of the letter *F*) that 100% of the participants viewed, as shown in Figure 1-3.

Another interesting finding of this study included an analysis of the percentage of people looking at specific search result(s) as well as the percentage of people looking at specific paid results. Table 1-1 shows the breakdown. For more information, visit *http://www.prweb.com/releases/2005/03/prweb213516.htm*.

Table 1-1. The Golden Triangle findings

| Organic results | | AdWords results | |
Rank	Percent viewed	Ad position	Percent viewed
1	100%	1	50%
2	100%	2	40%
3	100%	3	30%
4	85%	4	20%
5	60%	5	10%
6	50%	6	10%
7	50%	7	10%
8	30%	8	10%
9	30%	Note: there are only eight ads per SERP	
10	20%		

Lower Cost of Ownership

Contrary to popular belief, SEO is not free. At the very least, it takes time to implement. From a long-term perspective, it does provide for better ROI when compared to PPC or other marketing methods.

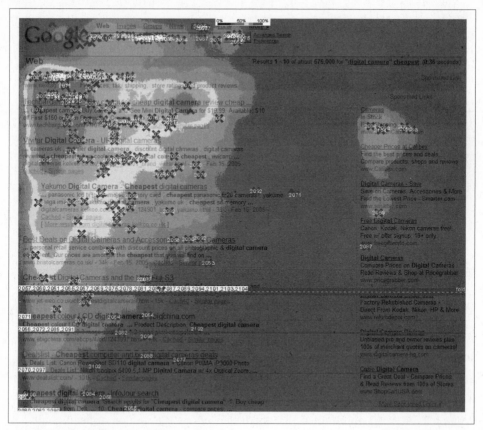

Figure 1-3. The Golden Triangle

Getting free hits from organic results can minimize or eliminate the need to use PPC campaigns. Well-ranked sites (utilizing only organic SEO techniques) can significantly reduce marketing expenditures. The added benefit of SEO is that it is long lasting, provided that it is content- and web user–centric. For companies on a budget, SEO can make all the difference. Investing some time in early website setup (mindful of SEO) can make a big impact on the future growth and visibility of such companies' websites.

Making provisions for SEO from the very beginning pays dividends in the long term, as less rework will be required to achieve specific SEO goals. If time is not a factor, that's all the more reason to use SEO. Once a company adopts SEO as part of its online strategy, everything becomes easier. Web designers, developers, web server administrators, and marketers now carry the same vision, with SEO being the norm. Table 1-2 provides a summary of the advantages and disadvantages of SEO and PPC.

Table 1-2. SEO and PPC summary

	SEO	PPC
Advantages	• Lower cost (time)	• Instant traffic
	• Sustained long-term benefits	• Easier to implement
	• Fosters natural website growth with reliance on compelling content	• Easier to manage
	• Trust	
	• Higher click-through rate (CTR)	
Disadvantages	• Initial results take time	• Can drain budgets quickly with low conversion rates
	• Requires more effort	• Highest positions go to highest bidders
	• No guarantees (but has proven to work time and time again)	• Historical distrust
		• Traffic stops when you stop paying

SEO Challenges

SEO does have its quirks and is a long-term commitment. Some of these challenges are not related to the technology. Some are just out of your control. The following subsections discuss some of these challenges, including competition, no guarantees, ranking fluctuations, time factors, and organization structure.

Competition

In June 2008, VeriSign reported that there were about 168 million domain name registrations across all of the top-level domain (TLD) names. You can find the report at *http://www.verisign.com/static/044191.pdf*. According to another survey, conducted by Netcraft in April 2009, there were approximately 231.5 million websites across the globe (*http://news.netcraft.com/archives/web_server_survey.html*).

Although these numbers are staggering, it is likely that the true number of all websites is even higher. As each domain can have numerous subdomains, websites realistically number somewhere in the billions.

It's almost inconceivable that you are the only person in your niche. At the same time, many sites don't do any SEO, and so it's relatively easy to gain mindshare and search engine rankings, particularly if you are serving a niche market.

No Guarantees

Nobody can actually guarantee the top spot on Google, Yahoo!, or Bing. It is simply impossible to do so. Though many have certainly tried, too many variables are involved.

However, the benefit of SEO is real. If you do your SEO due diligence, rankings and popularity will come in time—provided you have relevant content. Many sites are taking advantage of SEO. It would be foolish not to utilize SEO as part of your overall online marketing strategy.

Ranking Fluctuations

The motive of any business is growth. If you don't grow, you could be in trouble. This is especially the case with businesses that depend solely on their websites for revenues. For some, the Internet is one way to expand and increase their business. For others, the Internet is their lifeline and the core of their business model. With tens of millions of domains all competing for popularity, trying to stand out in the crowd can be a daunting or even frightening prospect.

With continuous improvements in search engine technology, search engines are using hundreds of different ranking factors. Sometimes all it takes is for one factor to change for your site to sink in the rankings or (even worse) be wiped out of the index completely.

Although nobody knows the exact ranking formula, each search engine has its own take on ranking factors. "Positive" ranking factors aid your rank. "Negative" ranking factors (such as having duplicate content) penalize your rank.

If you could illustrate this concept, it would look similar to Figure 1-4. The positive weights would represent the factors aiding your rank, while the negative weights would represent the factors working against your rank. The cumulative total (of all weights) would represent the relative rank weight that search engines could use in establishing the relative page rank for a particular keyword.

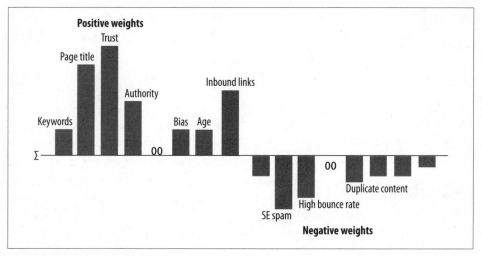

Figure 1-4. Ranking factors

Note that the bar height is only for illustration purposes. Every search engine will have its own weight formula.

Time Factors

Each site is different, so the SEO strategy applied to each site will also be different. There are so many factors that it would be naïve to put an exact time frame for SEO to show desired results.

SEO is not finished when you start seeing results. Even if you get to the top spot on the Google searches that you care about, your job isn't done. You need to make sure you stay on top of these searches. Your competitors will want to take your top spot away from you.

SEO fosters the natural, long-term growth of a website, and once you achieve its benefits, there is usually a ripple effect where you'll be getting traffic from sources other than search engines by means of other websites linking to yours. If you have the content or product that people want to see, it is only natural to attract inbound links.

Organizational Structure

Organizational structure can play a significant role in SEO. Big companies can sometimes be difficult to navigate. It may be unclear who is responsible for SEO. Having no ownership typically means no work gets done. Smaller companies can be faster paced, but also carry their own troubles.

Big companies and organizations

Although big companies have large marketing budgets, they too can benefit from receiving (almost free) hits. When it comes to large departmentalized organizations with marketing (or e-business) and IT departments operating in isolation, it can be difficult to adopt a common SEO vision.

Typically, large organizations have complex, dynamic websites. In these cases, marketers depend on IT (usually web development and infrastructure teams) for publishing their content, for site maintenance, and so on.

Most software developers or web server administrators do not think about SEO. Most marketers today employ SEM (PPC) and do not know all of the technical details of SEO. This is where a bit of education and training is essential.

Virtual teams. Forming virtual teams comprising members from each department can help solve these problems. This is often necessary because the best SEO is attained from expertise derived from multiple disciplines.

Adopting an early strategy and identifying roles and responsibilities can make a big difference. Most developers are not proficient copywriters. Most marketers do not understand what the HTTP response codes are.

Outsourcing. Sometimes an in-house approach may not be the best choice simply because no in-house expertise is available. Even when you have in-house expertise, sometimes it is good to get second opinions. Other times your key people may be involved in other projects and you just don't have enough resources.

Large, complex sites

Industry giants can run hundreds of different websites with millions of web pages. Having so many web pages (typically) manifests many unique challenges. Some of those challenges include:

- How to optimize many thousands or millions of pages
- Poor indexing of deep pages
- Determining which pages are preferred entry pages
- The quality of most inner pages
- Duplicate content
- Making changes to many pages at once
- Archiving

Small companies and individuals

Many small-business owners often struggle with the concept of the Internet, web design, and SEO. A smaller company generally means a smaller budget. With this in mind, SEO can become the most important tool for gaining online traction and eventual sales leads. Many free tools are available on the Internet, including content management system (CMS) portals, blogs, and forums—with built-in SEO. Leveraging these tools can significantly lower the total cost of SEO ownership while achieving most of the benefits. Refer to Chapter 3 for more details.

The SEO Process

The SEO process can be broken down into six general phases. These include research, planning and strategy, implementation, monitoring, (re)assessment, and maintenance. Figure 1-5 shows the phases connected with arrows. Note that the SEO process is highly iterative. Each phase constitutes its own body of knowledge.

Also note that Figure 1-5 uses arrows to indicate the relative order of each phase, and loops to indicate the iterative nature of the SEO process. The smaller loop occurs between the (re)assessment phase and the maintenance phase, and the larger loop occurs between the (re)assessment phase and the research phase. Moving forward, let's explore each of these phases.

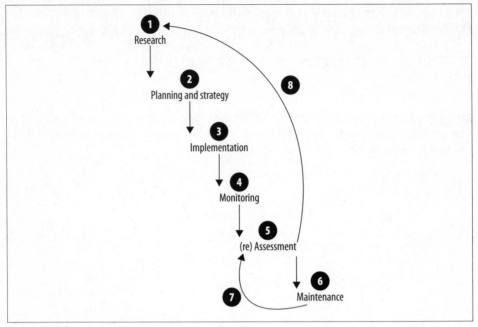

Figure 1-5. SEO process phases

The Research Phase

The research phase is the first phase of the SEO process. It usually consists of several different types of research, including business research, competitor analysis, current state assessment, and keyword research.

Business research

Before doing anything else, learn about your business in relation to its online presence. In this phase, you need to answer lots of questions, and most of them may be specific to your business. What does your company have that the competition does not? What is your selling point?

Many other questions and topics need to be asked and explored, and much of this may be outlined in your standard business and/or marketing plans as well as in your (website) business requirements. When it comes to your online marketing, ask yourself: how much do you understand about SEO and PPC? Are you looking to target certain demographics or geographical locations? What are your general and specific expectations? How do you measure success? What do you perceive as failure? What is your budget? Do you have resources available to handle SEO and/or SEM? Who is the owner (driver) of your SEO efforts? What does the project schedule look like? Are there specific timelines?

The more you know about the business, the better. The clearer the picture you have at the start, the more focused your efforts will be. Find answers to all of your questions early.

Competitor analysis

Once you know what the business is like and what the expectations are, it is time to see what others are doing. How can you base your SEO if you are not aware of the playing field? Rest assured that your site will be looked at, crawled, and scrutinized by your competitors or their SEO consultants!

Learn about all the players in your business area. Understand where they are now and how they got there. Find out who is linking to them. Explore how much content their site contains.

See how many pages they have indexed in Google and other search engines. Estimate their website traffic and investigate what keywords they are targeting. In general, the more you know about your competitors, the better. This book talks about a number of tools you can use to analyze your site and your competitors' sites.

Current state assessment

So, you are tasked with increasing the visibility of an existing site. Now you must dig deep into the site, dissecting it from all angles. In SEO vocabulary, this is labeled as the *site clinic*. This research process is very similar to competitor analysis, only this time your focus is solely on the site you are assigned to work with.

First things first: you check the current site rankings (if any). Next, you start examining the internal (on-page and on-site) factors, including site age, `<title>` tags, `<meta>` tags, internal linking structures, content duplication, search engine traps, and so forth. In parallel, you also look at the external factors. How many backlinks does this site have? Who is linking to this site?

From there, you inquire about current technology being used, current practices, the availability of any in-house technical expertise, web server logs, web analytics, and so on. Knowing the current website size and the current website performance can also help. Resource availability and budget need to be defined.

Keyword research

Conversion rate can mean several different things (depending on the site context). For some sites, conversion rate can be the number of visitors that bought a particular product. For other sites, it can mean the number of visitors that registered on the site. Conversion implies a specific gained value. In PPC, if the conversion rate is too low, the gained value may be less than the invested value, defeating the purpose of the PPC campaign.

Keyword research is the activity of identifying and targeting specific keywords with the goal of creating relevant search engine referrals. For existing sites, keyword research identifies keywords that are already "working" (i.e., keywords that convert) and tries to find new ones that can assist in attaining additional quality traffic.

Keyword research does not apply only to on-page textual elements. It also applies to domain name selection, inbound links, link composition, directory listings, and many other elements. The basic question is always: what keywords do I target? The answer is not always the same. Do you target the most popular (broad) keywords? Or do you target the niche (narrow) keywords?

Output of the research phase

After all of the research is done, it is helpful to produce a document (the SEO research artifact) summarizing the findings of the research phase. This document should contain all of your findings, including the business research, competitor analysis, current state assessment, and keyword research.

The Planning and Strategy Phase

The planning and strategy phase answers some fundamental questions based on the output of the research phase. You need to iron out several strategies in this phase, including those for handling content, link building, social media, and SEM, as well as technical strategies. All of these strategies can be rolled up into a single artifact: the SEO plan.

Content strategy

Your content strategy needs to address all aspects of content: creation, modification, dissemination, and archival. It also needs to address the area of content presentation: how will this content be presented to end users? Your content strategy also needs to answer many additional questions, such as whether the site will include blogs, press releases, testimonials, syndication, media files, and similar items. Also consider which content needs to be crawled (and indexed) and which does not need to be in the search engine index.

Link-building strategy

One of the pillars of SEO, a link-building strategy is crucial. Whether you are going after (paid or free) directory submissions, social media sites, social bookmarking, blog comments, direct solicitation, news syndication, or press releases, you must have solid inbound links. Content with no links can go only so far. Good content can foster natural link acquisitions. However, you cannot rely only on content.

Social media strategy

Engaging your clients on social media sites can be helpful and rewarding if done properly. You can consider this strategy as an important extension of the overall link-building strategy. The phenomenon of Twitter, Facebook, and LinkedIn, among others, is changing the landscape of link acquisitions.

Search engine targeting strategy

A search engine targeting strategy can mean several things. First, what search engines will you be targeting? This includes targeting regional as well as major search engines. There are search engines besides Google, Yahoo!, and Bing. If you are concerned about your presence overseas, there are many other search engines you need to worry about.

Big search engines also operate on several different search engine verticals. Do not confuse search engine verticals with vertical search engines (which specialize in specific areas or data). The reference is to the Blended Search results shown on Google, Yahoo!, and Bing. These are additional avenues that you may want to explore.

SEM strategy

Using PPC in parallel with SEO can be helpful. The benefits are multifold, especially if the site in question is brand new. PPC can provide accurate forecasts for targeted keywords. For example, within the Google AdWords platform you can target the same keywords in your ads that you are currently targeting on specific pages. You can then accurately forecast how your pages will convert for the same keywords once you start getting the equivalent SEO traffic.

Technical strategy

Developing a sound technical strategy involves many technical considerations. For starters, you should think about URL rewriting, avoiding content duplication (canonicalization), error messaging, and linking structures. After the basic SEO technical elements, think about some of the other elements.

For instance, what tools and platforms are required to build the site? Will you be developing custom software? In the case of custom software development, understanding the underlying software architecture is important. Even more important is for the custom software to make architectural provisions to allow for proper SEO.

You need to ask many other questions as well. What browsers will need to be supported? Do any hosting considerations need to be taken into account? Information on DNS, file space, traffic bandwidth, backups, CPU utilization, and so on can be helpful in painting an accurate technical picture. Make sure you understand the acceptable performance baselines, the scheduled maintenance times, and the change request methodology (if any).

Website performance is important. It is essential for large sites with many thousands of pages. In general, slow sites waste everyone's time and tend to be a big distraction to your web visitors. Also, web crawlers may not crawl all of the pages in a big site (if it is very slow).

Your technical strategy also needs to include provisions for monitoring, reporting, and analyzing SEO progress. Web server log analysis and web analytics are part of SEO monitoring. Analyzing web traffic is at the core of SEO activities. Converting traffic is what matters. Ranking high with no conversions is a wasted effort.

Output of the planning and strategy phase

The output of the planning and strategy phase is the SEO plan. The SEO plan contains information on internal and external proposed optimizations. This includes on-page and off-page optimizations as derived from particular strategies. The SEO plan is really a proposal and a call to action to address pertinent SEO requirements.

The SEO plan is also a road map. It documents the steps and activities that are required to get better rankings for a particular site. It also documents steps and procedures that will need to be followed for the addition or modification of any new content, after the SEO plan is implemented. The SEO plan should be revised every few months, as search engines and your rankings never stand still.

The Implementation Phase

After the SEO plan is approved, the implementation phase can start. The SEO implementation phase is where all the planning and strategy come into effect. This phase comprises two broad areas of work effort: internal and external optimizations. Table 1-3 lists some of the activities in each area. Note that the creation of compelling content is implied.

Table 1-3. Implementation phase activities

Internal optimization		External optimization
On-page optimization	**On-site optimization**	Authoritative backlinks
Title tag	Domain name selection	Social media
Meta description	Website (re)design	Link solicitation
Keyword density	Web server (re)configuration	Directory submissions
Keyword proximity	Geotargeting	Blog submissions
Keyword prominence	URL canonicalization	Forum submissions
Long-tail keywords	Linking architecture	Article writing
Short-tail keywords	Performance enhancements	Press releases
Anchor text	*robots.txt* file	Syndication
And more...	And more...	And more...

Internal optimization

Internal optimization refers to on-page and on-site activities. On-page activities include keyword optimizations of `<title>` tags, description meta tags, page copy, and link anchor text.

On-site optimization refers to holistic sitewide activities. Domain selection (in the case of new sites), website design or redesign, web server configuration, and sitewide performance tuning are all part of on-site optimization activities. For more detailed coverage of internal optimization, refer to Chapter 4.

External optimization

External optimization is just as important as internal optimization. The major goal of all external optimization activities centers on link building. It is all about your site's visibility. Each link referral can be viewed as a vote for your site. The more quality links you have, the more popular your site will be. For more detailed coverage of external optimization, refer to Chapter 5.

Output of the implementation phase

The implementation phase can vary drastically in size and complexity depending on the project. It does not have to be done all at once, and it usually never is. Introducing too many variables can get confusing when tracking SEO progress.

The output of the implementation phase can be several artifacts detailing any new technical knowledge gained, problems encountered, and lessons learned. Furthermore, any deviations from the original SEO plan should be documented with appropriate rationale noted (and any future actions that would need to be performed). Procedures and processes for adding new content or making website changes (e.g., backups, maintenance, and deployment) should also be formalized. Sticking to the SEO plan is a must. Introducing deviations could be counterproductive and could hinder (or confuse) the benefits of other work.

The Monitoring Phase

The monitoring phase comprises just that: monitoring. You need to monitor several things, including web spider activities, referral sites, search engine rankings, website traffic, conversions, hacker intrusions, and more. All of these activities are related and are highly dependent on the analysis of your web server logs. Chapter 6 explores several web stats monitoring tools, including Webalizer, AWStats, and WebLog Expert. Consult Chapter 7 for additional information on the subject.

Web spider activity

You've just done a lot of work on your site (in the implementation phase). No spider activity could signal problems. Watch spidering activities closely.

Website referrals

Knowing website referrals can help you identify which link-building strategies are working. It is all about time. There is no point wasting additional time in specific link-building avenues if they are not producing any referral hits.

Search engine rankings

The search engine page rankings are important. Without good rankings, you will not get any traffic. With no traffic, you will not get any conversions. Don't get too obsessed! Initially, your page rankings could be in a state of flux. Focus on your most important pages.

Website traffic

Although website traffic is different from converting traffic, it is still an indicator of your relative site visibility. An increase in visitor traffic is always good news (unless your site is having performance problems). Examining your web server logs can help you spot particular trends. You may even get some surprises in terms of which pages are getting hits.

Conversions

Ultimately, it is the conversions that matter. If you are selling products or services, you want to know how many people that came from search engines bought the product or service. More specifically, you may want to know the entry pages that contributed to these conversions. Depending on your organization and your level of expertise, this could be a challenge if you are employing SEO and SEM at the same time. Knowing how to differentiate SEO from SEM conversions is essential. Utilizing Google Analytics can help you achieve these goals.

Output of the monitoring phase

The output of the monitoring phase is sets of data, typically organized in monthly report summaries. This usually includes data from web stats tools and web analytics tools. This output serves as the input to the (re)assessment phase.

The Assessment Phase

The assessment phase uses the output of the monitoring phase as well as a series of checklists (on which to base the assessment). This phase is also referred to as the checkpoint phase. SEO checkpoints can be defined on a monthly, quarterly, semiannual, or yearly basis. At the very least, quarterly assessments are required.

The point of the assessment phase is to see what is and isn't working according to the SEO plan. The assessment phase can uncover many problems. Referring back to Figure 1-5, minor problems would be handled in the maintenance phase. Major problems might need a different approach, including getting a second SEO opinion or going back to the research phase.

Output of the assessment phase

The output of the assessment phase is the recommendation artifact. At times, this could be a call to action for further research or a call to action for further minor tweaks.

The Maintenance Phase

Once the major SEO work is done in the implementation phase, the focus will be on website maintenance. The maintenance phase takes care of problems (minor and major) found in the (re)assessment phase. In many ways, the maintenance phase is similar to the implementation phase.

Output of the maintenance phase

The output of the maintenance phase is a confirmation of all the SEO work performed, in addition to any problems encountered and any lessons learned.

SEO Alternatives

The Internet is not just about search engines. If your objective is solely to reach your desired level of traffic, there are many ways to "skin the cat." SEO alternatives (or complements) can be divided into two broad categories: online and offline. Online alternatives come in the form of paid ads, while offline alternatives are used in the traditional marketing sense.

Paid Ads (or Links)

Paid links can be highly targeted and produce excellent-quality traffic to your site—often outperforming search engine traffic. If your paid link traffic conversion rate is producing a profit, there is no reason to stop utilizing paid links.

The essence of organic SEO is in natural link acquisitions. Paid links are typically considered noise factors in search engine algorithms. Google is most vocal about paid links. This wasn't always the case, but Google is now looking at paid links carefully. If you use paid links, Google wants to ensure that it doesn't follow these paid links when spidering.

It's your responsibility to make sure paid links have the `nofollow` link attribute. If they don't, your site may be penalized. We will discuss paid links and the `nofollow` attribute in more detail throughout this book.

Traditional Marketing

Many books cover the topic of traditional marketing, so that is not the focus of this book. Nonetheless, you should be aware of any other promotions that your company is doing. Your URL should appear on all of the company's advertising; otherwise, it's a waste.

Summary

The value of using SEO is clear. Studies have shown that organic search results are more highly trusted than PPC (SEM) advertising. SEO is about having the right knowledge, applying proven techniques, experimenting with new ones, and letting the search engine do the rest. Naturally, the prerequisite to all of that is to have engaging content and a quality product (or service). Stay away from:

- Making changes to emulate the competition without knowing why the change was made
- Applying every SEO rule in the book (overdoing it)
- Not trying different keywords, and instead stopping at only one or a few
- Making frequent SEO-related changes without realizing the effects of previous changes

The SEO work for each website is different. What is similar, though, is the actual SEO process. You still have to go through the same exercise, regardless of whether you are working on a new site or an existing one.

The SEO process is always in motion. Along its path, several artifacts are produced to foster better tracking and management of overall SEO efforts. When done properly, working through the SEO process phases will take time.

Once the major SEO efforts are complete (in the implementation phase), SEO becomes more of an operational activity as opposed to a full-blown project. With the SEO fundamentals in place, your website will be on the right path toward increased search engine visibility.

## CHAPTER 2

Search Engine Primer

It is vital for you to understand—even if at only a basic level—how search engines work, as they are not all created equal, nor do they produce identical search engine results pages (SERPs). Website owners need to carefully examine which search engines they want to target. The current leader in the search engine marketplace is, of course, Google.

When performing SEO, it is important to target specific search engines. You cannot possibly target every search engine that exists. If you are in the Western parts of the world, your choices boil down to Google, Yahoo!, and Bing. According to comScore's June 2009 press release for U.S. searches (*http://bit.ly/sLQfX*):

> Google Sites led the U.S. core search market in June with 65.0 percent of the searches conducted, followed by Yahoo! Sites (19.6 percent), and Microsoft Sites (8.4 percent). Ask Network captured 3.9 percent of the search market, followed by AOL LLC with 3.1 percent.

Google is even more dominant in Europe, with approximately 80% of search engine market share. However, in Asia the situation is a bit different. comScore's press release for the Asia–Pacific region for July 2008 states the following (*http://bit.ly/16bz9j*):

> "Although Google leads the Asia–Pacific search market, powerhouse Chinese search engine Baidu.com follows closely on its heels with only a 6-percent difference separating the two," said Will Hodgman, comScore executive vice president for the Asia–Pacific region. "It will be interesting to watch Google and Baidu compete for the top spot in the region and the loyalty of the growing Asian population."

According to comScore, in the Asia–Pacific region Google is running neck-and-neck with Baidu. It will be interesting to watch how this situation develops in the coming months and years, as currently Baidu is eating away at Google's market share.

Another regional search engine powerhouse is Yandex, which owns more than 60% of Russia's search engine market share. Although it is hard to dispute Google's world dominance in terms of world searches, take these numbers with a grain of salt, as some search engines may be inflating their numbers.

Search Engines That Matter Today: Google

If you focus your design on Google's webmaster guidelines, chances are your website will also do well across all of the other (important) search engines. Google's rise from its humble beginnings to what it is today is nothing short of phenomenal.

Google was created by Larry Page and Sergey Brin at Stanford University. In many ways, Google was similar to most of the other major search engines, but its interface did not look like much, consisting of a simple form and search button. This simplicity, so different from portal-like search engine sites, was a welcome relief for many.

Over the years, Google evolved into the multiproduct company it is today, providing many other applications including Google Earth, Google Moon, Google Products, AdWords, Google Android (operating system), Google Toolbar, Google Chrome (web browser), and Google Analytics, a very comprehensive web analytics tool for webmasters. In 2008, the company even launched its own standards-compliant browser, Chrome, into what some feel was an already saturated market.

Designing your website around Google makes sense. The Google search network (search properties powered by Google's search algorithms) has 65% of the market share, according to comScore's June 2009 report (*http://bit.ly/MZN9C*).

Google's home page has not changed much over the years. Its default search interface mode is Web, and you can change this to Images, Maps, Shopping, or Gmail, among others. What have changed greatly are Google's results pages, mostly with the addition of ads and supplementary search results.

In the years ahead, Google will be hard to beat, as it is many steps ahead of its competition. Google is using many of its own or acquired tools and services to retain its grip on the search engine market.

Granted, Google's competitors are watching it. It is also clear that Google is not standing still in its pursuit to maintain and increase its search engine market share dominance. This is evident in its acquisition of YouTube.com and others.

According to comScore's press release for July 2008, YouTube drew 5 billion online video views in the United States:

> In July, Google Sites once again ranked as the top U.S. video property with more than 5 billion videos viewed (representing a 44 percent share of the online video market), with YouTube.com accounting for more than 98 percent of all videos viewed at the property. Fox Interactive Media ranked second with 446 million videos (3.9 percent), followed by Microsoft Sites with 282 million (2.5 percent) and Yahoo! Sites with 269 million (2.4 percent). Hulu ranked eighth with 119 million videos, representing 1 percent of all videos viewed.

In late 2006, Google made a deal with MySpace to provide search and ad services to MySpace users. Currently, with more than 100 million users and still growing, MySpace is one of the two biggest social networking websites.

Some additional notable Google offerings include:

- Google Book Search (*http://www.google.com/books?hl=en*)
- Google Desktop (*http://desktop.google.com/*)
- Google Finance (*http://finance.google.com/*)
- Google Scholar (*http://scholar.google.com/*)
- Google Talk (*http://www.google.com/talk/*)
- Google Groups (*http://groups.google.com/*)
- Google Webmaster Central (*http://www.google.com/webmasters/*)

To see even more Google products and services, visit *http://www.google.com/options/* and *http://en.wikipedia.org/wiki/List_of_Google_products*.

Yahoo!

Founded by Jerry Yang and David Filo, Yahoo! emerged in the clumsy form of *http://akebono.stanford.edu/yahoo* (this URL no longer exists, but you can read about Yahoo!'s history in more detail at *http://docs.yahoo.com/info/misc/history.html*). For the longest time, Yahoo! leveraged the search services of other companies. This included its acquisition of Inktomi technology. This changed in 2004, when it dropped Google as its search provider in favor of using its own acquired technology.

Yahoo! was Google's biggest rival for many years. What sets Yahoo! apart from Google is its interface. When you go to the Yahoo! website (*http://www.yahoo.com*), you actually see a web portal with all kinds of information. Many people see this design as cluttered, with too much competing superfluous information. Once you get to Yahoo!'s search results pages, things start to look similar to Google and Bing.

In 2008, Microsoft made a failed attempt to buy Yahoo!, which responded by forming an advertising relationship with Google. That changed in July 2009, when Yahoo! reached an agreement with Microsoft to use Bing as its search engine provider while focusing more heavily on the content delivery and advertising business.

As of this writing, Yahoo! is still using its own technology to provide its search results. It will take some time before Microsoft and Yahoo! are able to merge their systems. Today, Yahoo!'s main attraction is in its textual and video news aggregations, sports scores, and email services. Yahoo! is a strong brand, and the Yahoo! Directory continues to be one of the most popular paid web directories on the Internet.

Its search home page, *http://search.yahoo.com*, shows top link tabs that are similar to Google's and Bing's. Web is the default search mode; additional tabs include Images, Video, Local, Shopping, and More.

Popular tools owned by Yahoo! include:

- Finance Portal (*http://finance.yahoo.com/*)
- Yahoo! Messenger (*http://messenger.yahoo.com/*)
- Yahoo! Maps (*http://maps.yahoo.com/*)
- Yahoo! Weather (*http://weather.yahoo.com/*)
- APT from Yahoo! Advertising Platform (*http://publisher.yahoo.com/*)
- Yahoo! Groups (*http://groups.yahoo.com/*)
- Yahoo! Directory (*http://dir.yahoo.com/*)

Bing

Microsoft Bing is the successor to Microsoft Live Search, which failed to gain substantial market traction. Bing is also struggling to cut into Google's market share, but it has made some inroads thus far. Moreover, with Microsoft's 10-year agreement with Yahoo!, Bing will see a boost in its search user base by absorbing Yahoo!'s search traffic.

It may be a long time before the majority of people switch to Bing, if they ever do. The fact is that for many people, the word *Google* is synonymous with the term *search engine*. *Google* is even commonly used as a verb, as in "I'll Google it."

At the time of this writing, Microsoft is investing heavily in marketing Bing, spending tens of millions of dollars on Bing campaigns. Over the next few years, the general anticipation is that Microsoft will battle it out with Google for the top spot in the search engine market space. Microsoft did this with Netscape in the browser wars; there is no reason to believe it will not attempt to do the same thing with Google.

The Bing search interface is similar to any other search engine. Bing inherited the same (top) tabs from its predecessor, including Web, Images, Videos, News, Maps, and More.

Where it differs is in its search results. Figure 2-1 shows the Bing interface. The left side of Bing's search results page is called the Explorer pane. Within the Explorer pane, you are presented with results categories (quick tabs) if your particular search query has related search categories.

To the right of the Explorer pane are the actual search results, which are now more centered on the page when compared to Google's search results. Every search result is also accompanied by a Quick Preview pane. Bing will select additional text from the URL to show in this pane. The intent is to help searchers see more information about the destination URL before they click on the search result.

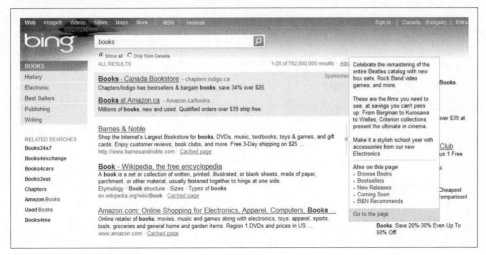

Figure 2-1. Microsoft Bing

Types of Search Engines and Web Directories

Many search engines exist on the Internet. How do you make sense out of all the of-ferings? The following subsections go into detail regarding several different types and groups of search engines, including primary, secondary, regional, topical, web spider (based), meta, and hybrid search engines.

First-Tier Search Engines

Google, Yahoo!, and Bing are considered first-tier, or primary, search engines, as they own most of the search engine market share in the Western parts of the world. These search engines usually scour the entire Web, and in the process create very large index databases.

For all intents and purposes (and if you reside in the Western world), primary search engines are the only ones you should really care about, as most of your visitors will have come from these search engine sources.

Second-Tier Search Engines

Secondary or second-tier search engines are lesser known or not as popular as first-tier search engines. They may provide value similar to that of the most popular search engines, but they simply cannot compete with them, or they may be new. You will obviously *not* be spending much of your time optimizing your sites for these types of search engines.

With Google, Yahoo!, and Microsoft holding most of the search market share, there is very little incentive to optimize for any other search engine. The ROI is just not there to warrant the additional work.

Regional Search Engines

Although Google may be the top dog in North America and Europe, it is not necessarily so in other parts of the world. The extent of your involvement with regional search engines will depend entirely on your target audience. For a list of regional or country-specific search engines, visit the following URLs:

- *http://www.philb.com/countryse.htm*
- *http://www.searchenginecolossus.com/*

Topical (Vertical) Search Engines

Topical search engines are focused on a specific topic. Topical search engines are also referred to as specialty search engines. Topics can be anything, including art, business, academia, literature, people, medicine, music, science, and sports, among others. Here are some of the most popular topical search engines on the Internet today:

- *http://www.yellow.com*
- *http://www.britannica.com*
- *http://www.artnet.com*
- *http://www.worldexecutive.com*
- *http://kids.yahoo.com*

Visit *http://bit.ly/19yvsU* for more examples of topical search engines.

Web Spider–Based Search Engines

Web spider–based search engines employ an automated program, the web spider, to create their index databases. In addition to Google, Yahoo!, and Microsoft, this class of search engine includes:

- Cuil (*http://www.cuil.com*)
- Exalead (*http://www.exalead.com*)
- Gigablast (*http://www.gigablast.com*)
- Teoma/Ask (*http://www.ask.com*)
- Walhello (*http://www.walhello.com*)

Hybrid Search Engines

Some search engines today contain their own web directories. The basic idea of hybrid search engines is the unification of a variety of results, including organic spidered results, directory results, news results, and product results.

Google has adopted this blended (SERP) model, calling it Universal Search. Yahoo! does the same thing once you get to its search results page. The premise of Blended Search results is that the multiple types of results complement each other, and ultimately provide the web visitor with more complete, relevant search results. This is illustrated in Figure 2-2.

Figure 2-2. Google Blended Results

In Figure 2-2, you can see how the Google SERP looks for the keyword *clothes*. On the righthand side of the screen you can see the Sponsored Links section. Similarly, at the top of the screen are shopping results, and just below those are organic results from website owners who have done their SEO homework.

If you do some further research on popular search terms, you will realize that extremely popular keywords usually produce SERPs with only the big players, such as Amazon, Wikipedia, and YouTube, showing up on the top of the first page of Google and others.

Meta Search Engines

If you search for an identical term on various spider-based search engines, chances are you will get different search engine results. The basic premise of meta search engines is to aggregate these search results from many different crawler-based search engines, thereby improving the quality of the search results.

The other benefit is that web users need to visit only one meta search engine instead of multiple spider-based search engines. Meta search engines (theoretically) will save you time in getting to the search engine results you need.

As shown in Figure 2-3, Dogpile.com compiles its results from several sources, including Google, Bing, Ask.com, and LookSmart. One thing to note about meta search engines is that aside from caching frequently used queries for performance purposes, they usually do not hold an index database of their own.

Dogpile.com is not the only meta search engine. There are many others, including Vivisimo.com, Kartoo.com, and Mamma.com.

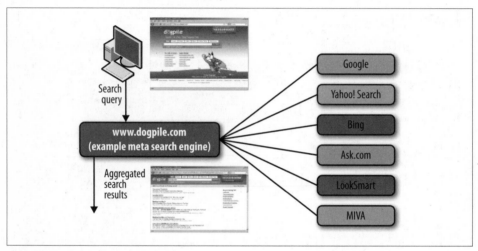

Figure 2-3. Meta search engine: Dogpile.com

Web Directories

Web directories are not search engines in the typical sense; they are collections of links that have been organized by humans. The advantage of web directories over typical search engines is that all the links are (usually) reviewed by human editors for quality, relevance, and suitability before being posted online. Make no mistake: some web directories are completely automated. You should avoid these types of directories.

The most famous web directory, Open Directory Project (*http://www.dmoz.org*), boasts 4,576,062 URLs in its listings at the time of this writing. Most web directories, including Dmoz.org, can also be searched.

Not all web directories are free. Some require yearly or one-time listing fees. One such directory is Yahoo! (*http://dir.yahoo.com*). Currently, you must pay a $299 yearly fee to be listed on Yahoo!.

Here is a list of additional web directories:

- Business Search Engine and Business Directory (*http://www.business.com*)
- Clush (*http://www.clush.com*)
- Family Friendly Sites (*http://www.familyfriendlysites.com*)
- JoeAnt (*http://www.joeant.com*)
- Links2go (*http://www.links2go.com*)
- The Librarians' Internet Index (*http://www.lii.org*)
- STPT (*http://www.stpt.com*)
- Best of the Web (*http://www.botw.org*)

For the longest time, Google stated that it would view listings on web directories as a good thing. Many directories lost their ability to pass on link juice in Google's crackdown on paid (automated garbage) directories.

Google rewards human-edited directories, although it does not want to see paid directories that are auto-generated with no human editing. Before you decide to put a link on a web directory, ensure that the benefit will be there. See Chapter 12 for more details.

Search Engine Anatomy

When I talk about important search engines, I am really talking about the "big three": Google, Bing, and Yahoo! Search. At the time of this writing, all of these search engines are using their own search technologies.

Web spider–based search engines usually comprise three key components: the so-called web spider, a search or query interface, and underlying indexing software (an algorithm) that determines rankings for particular search keywords or phrases.

Spiders, Robots, Bots, and Crawlers

The terms *spider*, *robot*, *bot*, and *crawler* represent the same thing: automated programs designed to traverse the Internet with the goal of providing to their respective search engine the ability to index as many websites, and their associated web documents, as possible.

Not all spiders are "good." Rogue web spiders come and go as they please, and can scrape your content from areas you want to block. Good, obedient spiders conform to Robots Exclusion Protocol (REP), which we will discuss in Chapter 9.

Web spiders in general, just like regular users, can be tracked in your web server logs or your web analytics software. For more information on web server logs, see Chapters 6 and 7.

Web spiders crawl not only web pages, but also many other files, including *robots.txt*, *sitemap.xml*, and so forth. There are many web spiders. For a list of known web spiders, see *http://www.user-agents.org/*.

These spiders visit websites randomly. Depending on the freshness and size of your website's content, these visits can be seldom or very frequent. Also, web spiders don't visit a site only once. After they crawl a website for the first time, web spiders will continue visiting the site to detect any content changes, additions, or modifications.

Googlebot is Google's web spider. Googlebot signatures (or traces) can originate from a number of different IPs. You can obtain web spider IPs by visiting *http://www.iplists .com/*.

A typical Googlebot request looks similar to the following HTTP header fragment:

```
GET / HTTP/1.1
Host: www.yourdomain.com
Connection: Keep-alive
Accept: */*
From: googlebot(at)googlebot.com
User-Agent: Mozilla/5.0 (compatible; Googlebot/2.1;
+http://www.google.com/bot.html)
Accept-Encoding: gzip,deflate
```

In this example, Googlebot has made a request for the index or root document of the *www.yourdomain.com* domain. Googlebot supports web server compression. Web server compression allows for faster file transmissions and should be used whenever possible.

Yahoo!'s web crawler is called Slurp, and the Bing spider is called MSNBot; they both exhibit similar behavior. Your job is to make their lives easier by feeding them properly optimized web content and ensuring that they can find everything you need them to find.

Web spider technology is not perfect. Sometimes web spiders will not be able to see the entirety of your website (referred to as a *search engine trap*). Other times you may want to prohibit them from crawling certain parts of your website, which you can do in your *robots.txt* file and via REP.

With the introduction of different (document type) indexing capabilities, Google and others are now using specialized spiders to handle media, syndication, and other content types.

You may want to block the indexing of your images and media files. Many times, malicious web users or even bloggers can create direct HTML references to your media files, thereby wasting your website's bandwidth and perhaps adversely affecting your website's performance.

In the beginning, search engines could handle only a limited range of indexing possibilities. This is no longer the case. Web spiders have evolved to such an extent that they can index many different document types. Web pages or HTML pages are only one subset of web documents. Table 2-1 lists the file indexing capabilities of Googlebot.

Table 2-1. Googlebot file types

File type(s)	Description
PDF	Adobe Portable Document Format
PS	Adobe PostScript
RSS, ATOM	Syndication feeds
DWF	Autodesk Design Web Format
KML, KMZ	Google Earth
WK1, WK2, WK3, WK4, WK5, WKI, WKS, WKU	Lotus 1-2-3
LWP	Lotus WordPro
MW	MacWrite
XLS	Microsoft Excel
PPT	Microsoft PowerPoint
DOC	Microsoft Word
WKS, WPS, WDB	Microsoft Works
WRI	Microsoft Write
ODT	Open Document Format
RTF	Rich Text Format
SWF	Shockwave Flash
ANS, TXT	Text files
WML, WAP	Wireless Markup Language

JSP, ASP, and PHP files are indexed in the same way as any HTML document. Usually, the process of indexing non-HTML documents is to extract all text prior to indexing.

Search engine web page viewer

Have you ever wondered how your web pages look to search engines? If you strip out all of the HTML, JavaScript, and CSS fragments on a web page, you will get the bare text. This is pretty much what a typical search engine would do before indexing your web pages. You can find the spider viewer script in Appendix A.

That code listing contains two distinct fragments. The top part of the code is mostly HTML. The bottom part of the code is mostly PHP. Once rendered in the web browser, the PHP code will show a small text field where you can enter a particular URL.

A few seconds after this form is submitted, you should see the "spider" view of your URL. Figure 2-4 shows the output of running this PHP script on the O'Reilly website (*http://oreilly.com/*).

Figure 2-4. Search engine view of http://oreilly.com/

This script can be useful for all websites, especially those that use a lot of graphics and media files. It should give you some insight as to what the search engine crawlers will see.

You can also use text browsers. One such tool, SEO Text Browser, is available at *http://www.domaintools.com*. You can navigate websites using text links as in the early web browsers.

The Search (or Query) Interface

The search or query interface is your door to the SERPs. Each search engine may have a slightly different interface. Nonetheless, each one will present you with the search form and a SERP with relevant links.

If the search term is popular, chances are you will see a lot of ads posted alongside or even mixed in with the organic search results. Each search engine uses different search ranking algorithms. Accordingly, the search results on one search engine will likely be different from the search results on another search engine, even for identical keywords.

For example, searching for *summer clothes* on Google and Bing produces the results pages shown in Figure 2-5.

Search engines are not perfect, and sometimes you will get spam result links that are completely irrelevant to what you are looking for. At those times, it might take some "keyword massaging" to get to the relevant links.

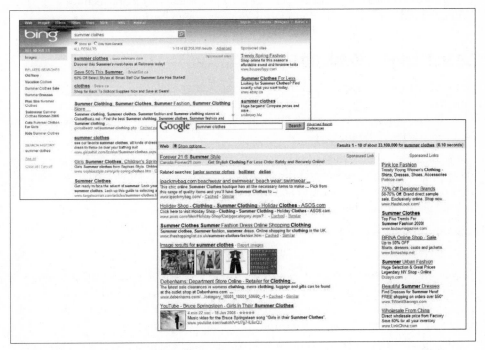

Figure 2-5. Bing and Google SERP comparison

Search Engine Indexing

Google and others are indexing more pages than ever. Many of the modern search engines now boast upward of a few billion indexed documents. Here is how Wikipedia describes the process of search engine indexing (*http://bit.ly/2jsIOL*):

> Search engine indexing collects, parses, and stores data to facilitate fast and accurate information retrieval. Index design incorporates interdisciplinary concepts from linguistics, cognitive psychology, mathematics, informatics, physics and computer science. An alternate name for the process in the context of search engines designed to find web pages on the Internet is Web indexing.

Although web spiders do their best to obtain as many documents as possible for search engines to index, not all documents get indexed. Search engine indexing is closely tied to the associated search engine algorithms. The search engine indexing formula is a highly secretive and intriguing concept to most SEO enthusiasts.

Search engine indexing is not an entirely automated process. Websites that are considered to be practicing various unethical (spamming) techniques are often manually removed and banned. On the other end of the spectrum, certain websites may receive a ranking boost based on their ownership or brand.

Although Google and others will continue to provide guidelines and tutorials on how to optimize websites, they will never share their proprietary indexing technologies. This is understandable, as it is the foundation of their search business.

Search Engine Rankings

Search engine rankings are determined by search engine algorithms. When search engine algorithms change, search engine rankings change. It is a well-known fact that Google and others are continually modifying their secretive search engine algorithms and thus their SERP rankings.

Some of these modifications have been so profound that listings of many websites disappeared from the SERPs literally overnight. Keeping track of web page or site rankings is one of the most common activities of any SEO practitioner. The driving force behind algorithm changes is almost always the following:

- Improvements in search results quality
- Penalization of signature search engine spam activities

Search engine algorithms are based on a system of positive and negative weights or ranking factors as designed by the search engine's engineers or architects. One of Google's search engine algorithms is called PageRank. You can view Google PageRank by installing the Google Toolbar. To quote Wikipedia (*http://bit.ly/JXh9W*):

> PageRank is a link analysis algorithm that assigns a numerical weighting to each element of a hyperlinked set of documents, such as the World Wide Web, with the purpose of "measuring" its relative importance within the set. The algorithm may be applied to any collection of entities with reciprocal quotations and references. The numerical weight that it assigns to any given element E is also called the PageRank of E and denoted by PR(E).

The PageRank (or PR) is Google's measurement of how important or popular a particular web page is, on a scale of 1 to 10, with 10 implying the most importance or highest popularity. You can also think of the PR value as an aggregate vote of all pages linking to a particular page.

You can visualize PageRank by looking at Figure 2-6, which illustrates the basic concept of PageRank. The figure is based on a slideshow created by Google search quality engineer Matt Cutts, which you can find at *http://bit.ly/13a6qu*. The numbers used in the diagram are for illustrative purposes only.

Examining Figure 2-6, you can observe how the PageRank flows from page to page. If you look at the top-left page, you can see that it has a score of 100. This page has several inbound links, all of which contribute to this score.

This same page has two outbound links. The two recipient pages split the link juice value, each receiving 50 points. The top-right page also contains two outbound links, each carrying a value of 26.5 to their destination page. Note that this page also received 3 points from the lower-left page.

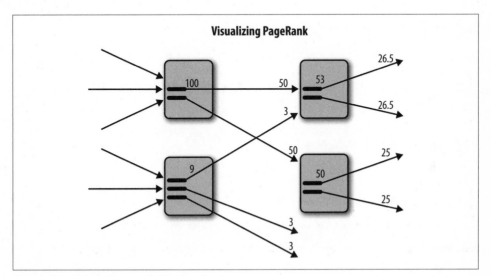

Figure 2-6. Visualizing Google PageRank

There are two key factors behind the inner workings of PageRank: the number of inbound links and the quality of those links. This means you should not obsess over getting the highest number of inbound links. Instead, focus on the quality of the inbound links. If you have the most interesting content, links will come—naturally.

Summary

Monitoring search engine market share news can be helpful in pursuing sound SEO choices. Although new search engines will continue to crop up from time to time, SEO activities need only focus on a select few primary search engines: Google, Bing, and Yahoo!. If your site needs to rank well in the Asia–Pacific region, you may also want to consider a regional search engine such as Baidu or Yandex.

After examining the big players, you learned about the different types of search engines, including first tier, second tier, regional, topical (vertical), web spider (based), meta, and hybrid search engines.

We also talked about the different web directories before turning our attention to search engine anatomy. In that section, we explored different web spiders, the search engine query interface, and search engine algorithms. We also created a spider viewer script. At the end of this chapter, we covered Google's PageRank in more detail.

## CHAPTER 3

Website Essentials

Keyword-rich domain names are an important ranking factor, especially for small sites that are just starting out. Website owners should take advantage of owning multiple domains. Choosing domain names includes more than just deciding among *.com*, *.net*, and *.org*. Owning multiple domain names is the norm today to protect and enhance your brand.

This chapter starts by exploring the various domain name extensions. We'll cover generic top-level domains (gTLDs) and country code top-level domains (ccTLDs) in detail. In the process we'll discuss the entire domain governance model.

If you are looking for a single-word English domain, you are likely to be disappointed unless you are willing to spend money to buy a domain from a domain seller. Single-word domain names can sell for millions of dollars. If you are like most of us, you will start to explore two- and three-word combinations as your potential domain names. If you are creative, you might go for a nonsensical domain name. If you are still struggling, at some point you might want to use a domain name broker to get you a domain that you like. Finally, you can also buy domain name misspellings to capture any lost traffic.

After you have secured your domain, you can start to think about your hosting requirements. Many different hosting options are available. You should consider them in parallel to your software platform selection. Your web application is either designed in-house or is a third-party tool. If you are creating an in-house application, be sure to include on-page and on-site SEO as part of your design.

Creating custom software makes sense if you cannot find anything to satisfy your business requirements. With so many available third-party free and paid tools, chances are something already exists that can fulfill your requirements.

Before we close this chapter, we will cover the important topics of website usability and website accessibility.

Domain Name Options

Although *.com* is by far the most popular website extension, business owners should consider buying other extensions, including applicable gTLDs and ccTLDs, to protect their brand and to safeguard their investment against the competition.

Domain Name Namespaces

Understanding the domain name governance model can be helpful in understanding the various domain extensions. The system of domain names is governed by the Internet Corporation for Assigned Names and Numbers, or ICANN (*http://www.icann.org*).

When I talk about domain name governance, I am really talking about specific domain name extensions identifying the class of a particular domain. Figure 3-1 illustrates the current governance model for gTLDs and ccTLDs. Domain registrars are companies that are accredited by ICANN or the national ccTLD authority for providing domain names.

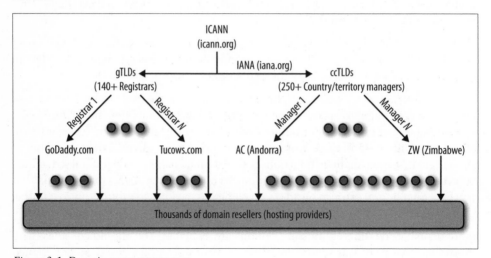

Figure 3-1. Domain name governance

Not everyone can be an ICANN registrar. For an accredited list of ICANN registrars, visit *http://www.icann.org/en/registrars/accredited-list.html*. For ccTLD details, consult with the Internet Assigned Numbers Authority, or IANA (*http://www.iana.org*).

Generic top-level domains

Domain names ending in *.com*, *.net*, or *.org* are part of the gTLD class. Table 3-1 provides a full list of gTLDs along with their descriptions.

TLDs can be further classified as either sponsored TLDs or TLDs that do not have a sponsor(s). TLDs that do not have a sponsor operate under policies defined by ICANN.

TLDs with a sponsor are typically governed by the sponsor. For more information, visit *http://www.icann.org/en/tlds/*.

Table 3-1. Generic top-level domains

gTLD	Description
.com	Utilized by all entities, as its rules of ownership are now unrestricted. The most popular and one of the oldest TLDs, .com was intended for commercial use only.
.net	Intended for computers running at network providers. Today it is used in an unrestricted fashion, and many times becomes the second-choice TLD if .com is not available.
.org	Intended for nonprofit organizations. Used by commercial and noncommercial sites.
.edu	Used almost exclusively by post-secondary institutions in the United States.
.gov	Used by federal, state, and local government departments within the United States.
.int	Used only by international (treaty-based) organizations.
.mil	Used by the U.S. Department of Defense.
.biz	Intended for commercial business entities. Was created to allow for an additional domain name pool due to the saturated .com namespace.
.info	Intended for informational sites (unrestricted TLDs).
.name	Intended for personal use only.
.pro	Intended for professionals in various professions, including doctors and lawyers.

Among these extensions, you will almost always use *.com*, *.net*, and/or *.org*. Simply put, these are the most popular (and most memorable) domain name extensions, and most people are aware of them.

For the sake of completeness, I should also mention sponsored gTLDs. Sponsored gTLDs include *.aero* (aviation industry), *.coop* (co-operatives such as credit unions), *.museum* (museums), *.cat* (Catalan community), *.jobs* (employment sites), *.tel* (Internet telephony applications), and *.travel* (travel industry). To see examples of these types of domains, you can use the Google `site:` command. Here are a few:

```
1 site:.aero
2 Newark Foods site:.coop
3 royal penguin australia site:.museum
4 china site:.tel
5 site:.jobs
6 "Costa Rica" site:.travel
```

The first and fifth examples return the approximate number of indexed documents for the specified domain extension. This will give you an idea of the size of these namespaces: as of this writing, Google indexed about 500,000 *.aero* results and only about 82,000 *.tel* results. By comparison, Google had more than 20 billion *.com* results in its index. This should speak volumes about the popularity of these TLDs. The other four examples included keywords that returned results within the particular TLD namespace. Refer to Table 3-2 for the full list of domain extensions and their associated Google index size.

Table 3-2. Domain extensions and Google document index

Extension	Index size
.com	20,400,000,000
.org	2,290,000,000
.net	2,110,000,000
.edu	248,000,000
.gov	232,000,000
.info	227,000,000
.biz	74,300,000
.cat	35,800,000
.int	8,230,000
.mil	8,130,000
.name	7,000,000
.travel	6,310,000
.coop	646,000
.aero	646,000
.pro	600,000
.museum	480,000
.tel	248,000
.jobs	117,000

Note that the Google index values are only approximations.

Country code top-level domains

For a list of country-specific registrars, visit *http://www.iana.org/domains/root/db/*. Note that IANA is also managed by ICANN.

Country-specific and external territory domain extensions fall into the ccTLD class. All ccTLDs are two characters in length and are managed by a designated trustee or manager approved by IANA.

Country code second-level domains

Many countries also use country code second-level domains (ccSLDs) to simulate gTLD segregation. For example, *.co.uk*, *.com.ba*, and *.co.il* represent the *.com* (commercial) equivalents for the United Kingdom, Bosnia, and Israel, respectively. Similarly, *.org.au*, *.org.in*, and *.org.cn* represent the *.org* equivalents for Australia, India, and

China, respectively. Each country may have additional second-level domains. Consult with the specific country registrar for more details.

Buying Domain Names

Now that you have a better understanding of domain name extensions, we can shift gears to buying domains. In the early days of the Internet, domain name selection was fairly easy. Nowadays, it can be a challenge to find the right domain name.

When buying domain names, you should consider several factors, including the domain name size (in characters), the domain registration period (in years), keyword-rich domain names, and nonsensical domain names.

Domain name size

Short domain names are easier to remember. Longer domain names can be more specific (or relevant when appearing in search results). Multiword search queries matching longer domain names could bring in highly targeted traffic and thus result in higher conversions. Shorter domain names (consisting of a single English vocabulary word) tend to attract more broad (untargeted) traffic.

There is no perfect size when it comes to domain names. It's a trade-off between how easy the name is to remember and its relevancy to the search results and to your business name. You can augment this gap by buying multiple domain names that satisfy several requirements, with one domain being the primary and others either employing 301 redirects or serving other brand-enhancing purposes.

Keyword-rich domain names

Most domains purchased today are either two- or three-word combinations. Try to come up with easy-to-remember word combinations. Think of all the words and phrases that can describe your site or operations. You can also use the keyword research tools that we will discuss in Chapter 11 to help you along the way. Table 3-3 lists some of the popular domain name suggestion tools.

Table 3-3. Domain name suggestion tools

URL	Description
DomainsBot (*http://www.domainsbot.com*)	Provides advanced (semantic) domain name lookup tools
DomainTools (*http://www.domaintools.com*)	Allows you to enter an existing domain name or a phrase and then shows you a list of 20 domain name suggestions and their availability for *.com*, *.net*, *.org*, *.info*, *.biz*, and *.us* extensions
BUST A NAME (*http://www.bustaname.com*)	Lets you add words in one pane, and then produces combinations of domain name suggestions

URL	Description
Nameboy	Allows for hyphen and rhyme options
(http://nameboy.com)	
MakeWords	Generates multilingual domain names
(http://makewords.com)	

Many hosting providers offer their own domain name suggestion tools. Try a few until you find the ones that create names to your liking.

Nonsensical domain names

Sometimes you just have to be creative. A simple way to create nonsensical names is to combine parts of two or more words into a new word. Perform an inventory of the most important keywords relevant to your site and then try to combine some words or their parts. You may also want to use online generators to help you along the way. Table 3-4 contains links to some of the online word generators.

Table 3-4. Nonsense word generators

URL	Details
Word Generator	Generates 50 words on each page refresh
(http://www.kessels.com/WordGenerator/)	
Web 2.0 Domain Name Generator	Generates 15 words after you click the Submit button
(http://www.hackslash.net/?page_id=48)	
SoyBomb	Generates 50 words on each page refresh
(http://www.soybomb.com/tricks/words/)	

Figure 3-2 illustrates a screen refresh of the Soybomb.com nonsense word generator. Simply press the F5 key or the "Click here to generate a new list" link to obtain more variations.

Domain registration period

Domain age is a ranking factor. If you are in a serious business (or any other entity), always buy domains with more than a one-year registration period. It is believed that domain names with multiyear registration periods are looked at more favorably by search engines than their single-year counterparts.

Tapping into expired domain names

When domain names within the gTLD namespace reach their domain expiry date, they enter a so-called expired (or grace) period that lasts for 40 days (if the domain owner

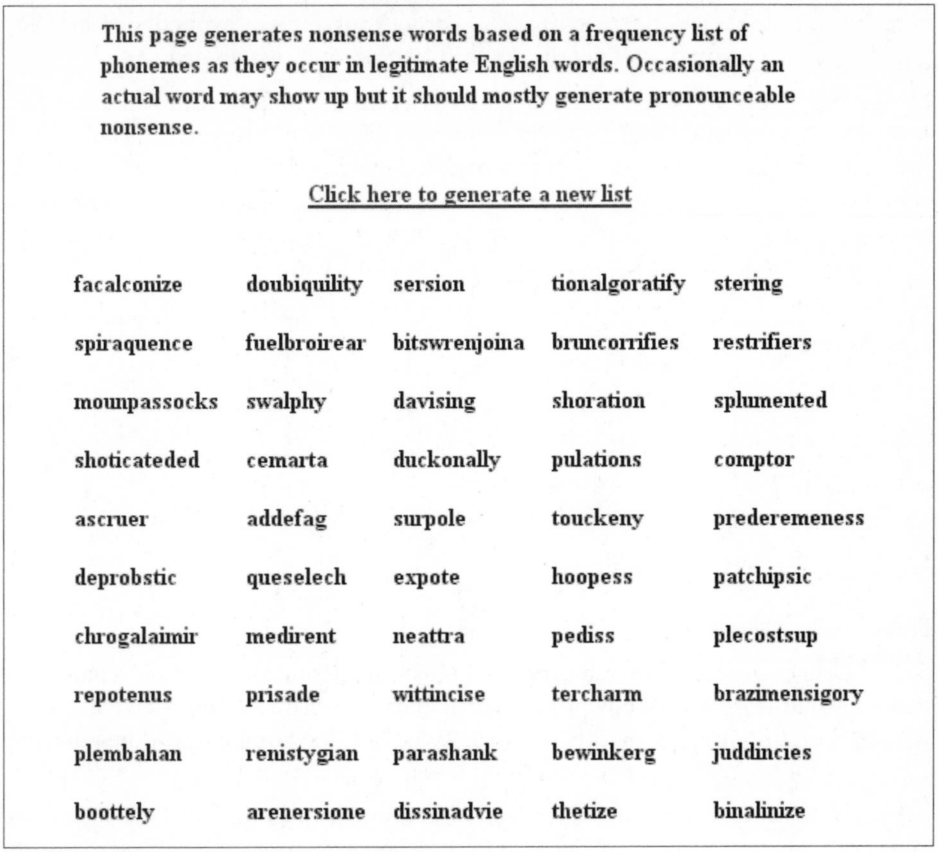

This page generates nonsense words based on a frequency list of phonemes as they occur in legitimate English words. Occasionally an actual word may show up but it should mostly generate pronounceable nonsense.

Click here to generate a new list

facalconize	doubiquility	sersion	tionalgoratify	stering
spiraquence	fuelbroirear	bitswrenjoina	bruncorrifies	restrifiers
moumpassocks	swalphy	davising	shoration	splumented
shoticateded	cemarta	duckonally	pulations	comptor
ascruer	addefag	surpole	touckeny	prederemeness
deprobstic	queselech	expote	hoopess	patchipsic
chrogalaimir	medirent	neattra	pediss	plecostsup
repotenus	prisade	wittincise	tercharm	brazimensigory
plembahan	renistygian	parashank	bewinkerg	juddincies
boottely	arenersione	dissinadvie	thetize	binalinize

Figure 3-2. Soybomb.com nonsense word generator

does not renew the domain before the expiry date). Typically at this point all of the domain services are halted.

If the domain owner chooses to renew the domain during the 40-day grace period, she typically pays the standard domain fee. If the domain is not renewed within the 40-day period, the domain enters a domain redemption cycle that lasts for another 30 days. A domain in this cycle takes a lot more work to renew. Fees for renewing a domain in this cycle are usually higher than typical renewal fees.

Finally, if the domain has not been renewed during the domain redemption period, the domain is deleted from the domain registry within the next five days. The exact time within this five-day period is not known. So, in total it takes 70 to 75 days after the official domain expiry date before a domain is released and is once again available to the public.

Although you could certainly sit and wait until a domain is finally available, that may not be your best option. Many other people could be doing the same thing. The wise approach is to use a provider (agent) to back-order your desired (expired) domain. You pay the fee, and if you do not get the domain, your money is refunded.

Not all back-order agents provide the same service levels. Some are known to be better than others. Some also employ bidding if more than one of their clients is bidding on the same domain. Some back-order brokers include Pool.com, GoDaddy.com, eNom.com, SnapNames.com, Moniker.com, and Sedo.com. For best results, you may want to use multiple agents to increase your chances of securing a particular domain. Stick to the reputable domain back-order agents already mentioned.

For lists of deleted or expired domains, you may want to visit the following URLs:

- *http://www.freshdrop.net*
- *http://www.justdropped.com*
- *http://www.deleteddomains.com*
- *http://www.domainbroadcasting.com*
- *http://www.namecaptor.com*
- *http://www.domainannounce.com*

Buying existing domains

Selling domain names is a big business. Many domain name owners are selling their domain names. Generic (one-word) domain names can sell for as high as several million dollars. For instance, as of this writing, Toys "R" Us bought the domain name Toys.com for $5.1 million, and TravelZoo bought Fly.com for $1.76 million.

There are many domain brokers. Some of the popular ones include GoDaddy.com, Sedo.com, Afternic.com, SnapNames.com, and DotPound.com. If you need to use domain name brokers, stick to the reputable ones.

Utilizing the unsolicited approach

You may know of an active domain that you really like. You might want to contact the website (domain) owner directly. To do that you need to find out who owns the domain. You can use one of the many online Whois providers to get this information.

Some of the better online Whois sites include *http://whois.domaintools.com*, *http://www .internic.net/whois.html*, *http://www.networksolutions.com/whois/index.jsp*, and *http:// who.is*. Using these sites is easy. Simply enter the domain name you are interested in and click the Submit button. After a few seconds, you should see a results page similar to the following fragment:

```
Registrant:
    Some Company, Inc.
    28 Oak Road North
    San Jose, California 95488
    United States
```

```
Domain Name: SOMECOOLDOMAINIWANT.COM
   Created on: 16-May-09
   Expires on: 16-May-10
   Last Updated on: 11-May-09

Administrative Contact:
   Contact, Admin  dac@somecooldomainiwant.com
   Some Company, Inc.
   28 Oak Road North
   San Jose, California 95488
   United States
   7058288000      Fax --

Technical Contact:
   Contact, Tech  tdc@somecooldomainiwant.com
   Some Company, Inc.
   28 Oak Road North
   San Jose, California 95488
   United States
   7058288000      Fax --

Domain servers in listed order:
   NS1.SOMECOOLDOMAINIWANT.COM
   NS2.SOMECOOLDOMAINIWANT.COM
```

In some cases, you will see at least one email address that you can use to contact the owner. If there is no email address, you may want to call the owner directly. Before making the contact, make sure you know your budget and try to be honest with your intentions. Sometimes it helps to use a personal email address or to simply not discuss any company details. If you appear to be part of a big company, the price might skyrocket before you know it. Be prepared for rejections, so target several domains in your approach.

 Some domain owners choose to make their registration (contact information) private. In those cases, first check to see whether there is any contact information on their website. If you still cannot find the contact information, try using a broker service as we already discussed.

Domain name resellers

There are thousands of domain resellers. When buying domain names, you should separate it from the process of buying a hosting service. There are several reasons for this suggested decoupling.

Smaller hosting providers will often charge more for the domain name than you really need to pay. Tying your domain name to a hosting provider often comes with a lot of red tape if you choose to move to another hosting provider, making it a lengthy process.

A more elegant solution is to use a service offered by the likes of GoDaddy.com, Namecheap.com, and eNom.com. Doing so allows you to quickly switch hosting providers by simply changing your DNS settings.

Many vendors provide discounts on domain purchases. Typically, you are asked to enter a discount code. Be sure to search for discount codes on Google (e.g., *godaddy promo codes*). Many vendors also provide bulk purchase discounts.

This is especially useful when buying domain variations such as domain name misspellings. Spammers and legitimate site owners use domain name misspellings to capitalize on popular site traffic. Google has bought domains such as Gppgle.com, Foofle.com, and Goolge.com, as they are all popular "google" misspellings.

Parking domains

Domain parking is a term used when buying new domains. Typically, your domain is "parked" as soon as you buy it! Your host typically puts up its (shameless) advertisement page and your page is parked. Sometimes you are allowed to enter your custom DNS server information whereby you can point your domain to your actual content.

Transferring domains

Domain transfer is the process of moving your domain from one vendor to another. Domain transfers can take several days and require the domain owner to go through the approval process of transferring your domain. The act of domain transfer automatically renews the domain for an additional year. The fees applied to domain transfers should be standard domain renewal fees and should not be considered penalties.

Renewing domains

Be sure to keep your domain registration information up-to-date. Pay special attention if you are switching to another email address, as you could miss your domain renewal notices (they are sent as reminders several times before your domain name reaches the expiry and redemption periods).

Domain renewal is a straightforward process. You pick the desired renewal period and pay the fee, and you are set for that many years. Each vendor has its own interface. Some vendors have automated billing options (by default), which will charge your credit card when a certain date is reached. This varies from vendor to vendor, so make sure to read the fine print. Typically, your domain may be set to renew on a yearly basis.

Hosting Options

Hosting is important to SEO for many reasons. Some search engines, including Google, pay attention to your site's IPs. If you are targeting the Australian market, your site had better be hosted in Australia. If your primary audience is in Australia and you are hosting your site in Los Angeles, your users in Australia will experience long network latency (slower site response times).

Depending on your selected hosting options, you can be severely limited in what you can do with your site, or you can have absolute freedom. You should consider having access to URL rewriting (*.htaccess* or *httpd.conf* configuration files), web server logs, and so on.

Website hosting comes in all sorts of flavors. In essence, you get what you pay for. So, depending on your budget and your specific technical and business requirements, you could be using managed hosting, comanaged hosting, collocation hosting, internal hosting, shared hosting, or free hosting.

Choosing Platforms

Before going into each available hosting option, it is important to choose your operating system, web and application server, database, and development platforms. These are the basic requirements of all dynamic websites. Without further ado, let's examine the various platforms.

Operating systems

There are two main camps when it comes to hosting technologies: Linux and Microsoft Windows. Technically speaking, it is possible to design sites on either platform with the same functionality. It all depends on your comfort level, available expertise, and budget.

At the operating system level, Windows and Linux platforms are quite different. The biggest difference (as it relates to SEO) is the file conventions used on both platforms. Windows filenames are case-insensitive, whereas Linux filenames are case-sensitive.

For example, on a Windows-based system you cannot have the files *a.html* and *A.html* residing in the same directory, as they are considered to be the same files. On Linux you can have *a.html*, *A.html*, *a.Html*, and *a.HTML* all residing in the same folder as different files.

Web and application servers

The two most popular web servers are Apache and Microsoft's Internet Information Server (IIS). To run PHP, Perl/CGI, or Python on an Apache web server, you must ensure that the appropriate modules are configured within the Apache configuration file, *httpd.conf*. After you do this, you are ready to code your application. One notable difference is with the Sun Java platform, which requires the use of an application server.

By application servers I am referring to the Java technology realm and the likes of Tomcat, Jetty, JBoss, WebSphere, and WebLogic. Evidently, Apache can act as both a web server and an application server. Java-based application servers are typically used in conjunction with an Apache web server. In this context, Apache's role is to serve static content while the application server's role is to serve dynamic content.

IIS is the biggest Apache competitor. According to a recent Netcraft survey (*http://bit.ly/4ej1fB*), Apache holds 46% of the server market share when compared to Microsoft, which holds 29%.

IIS naturally favors Microsoft development platforms such as ASP.NET and C#. If you have to run PHP, Perl/CGI, or Python on IIS, you will need to install and configure the corresponding Windows executables.

Selecting database servers

Database offerings for both platforms are quite similar. The most popular open source database in the world, MySQL (*http://www.mysql.com*), is available on many different platforms, including Windows and Linux. Oracle, IBM DB2, and Microsoft SQL Server are some of the more expensive offerings. SQL Server runs only on Windows Server, whereas Oracle and DB2 can run on several platforms.

You can choose your database platform independent of other architectural elements due to easy operability with different development platforms. In other words, PHP, CGI, Java Platform Enterprise Edition (Java EE), and Python applications can communicate with all of the popular databases currently available on the market.

Selecting the development platform

When it comes to choosing a development platform, you should consider the comfort level of the organization and the internal expertise. Most dynamic sites on the Internet are created in PHP. According to Zend.com, maker of PHP, there are more than five million PHP developers in the world (*http://www.zend.com/en/company/management/*). If you are a small business, an individual, or a small entity on a budget, it makes sense to use PHP. You can hire PHP developers reasonably quickly, and you can be sure that if at some point you require additional PHP development, the resources will be there. What makes PHP really appealing is that it is the most common programming language found on shared hosting providers.

Another popular language, ASP.NET, is Microsoft's answer to PHP. Microsoft's SharePoint platform is a hot technology across the corporate world. SharePoint is based on IIS and ASP.NET. ASP.NET is easier to learn than C#.

Hosting Types

Not all hosting types are created equal. If you are just starting a site, you may be able to get by with a shared host. As your site grows, so will your technical requirements to support the accompanying influx of new visitors. Leave room for eventual hosting upgrades should your site make significant gains in popularity.

Slow website performance can affect how much of your site gets crawled. It can also affect the search engine index freshness of your pages. The following subsections discuss some of the most popular hosting options, including free, shared, collocation, comanaged, managed, and internal hosting.

Free hosting

Many free hosts are available on the Internet. Some come with banner ads plastered over your site, while others are genuinely free, with no ads forced on your site. At the time of this writing, I can find hundreds of free hosting providers, including 000space.com, 123bemyhost.com, AgilityHoster.com, FreeBeeHosting.com, OxyHost.com, and Angelfire.lycos.com.

The problems with free hosts are multifold. First, there is usually some sort of catch to make you upgrade to paid (shared) hosting. The catch comes in the form of a limitation, such as insufficient space, limited website bandwidth, an insufficient number of email accounts, or insufficient database support. You are typically limited to a single domain or a subdomain, and sometimes you are prohibited from placing ads. If you must use free hosts, read the fine print and try several vendors to see what fits your requirements.

From an SEO perspective, you should avoid free hosts. Tens of thousands of sites might be sitting on the same physical server while being served from the same IP (which is the case to a lesser extent with shared hosting). All it takes is for one of the sites to be a source of spam (web, email, etc.) for the whole IP to get banned. Make no mistake: Google and others do index sites sitting on free hosts. At the time of this writing, I am easily able to identify many sites with a decent Google PageRank hosted on free servers.

Shared hosting

Shared hosting is also known as virtual hosting. Shared hosting (just like free hosting) uses virtual IPs to host multiple domains on the same web server. Some shared hosting providers will offer a dedicated IP as part of a package or as a paid add-on. This option should be on your list of add-ons from an SEO perspective.

Shared hosting is a benefit for new sites on a budget. Typically, you can get an account set up for a few dollars per month. Recently, many shared hosting providers began including unlimited space, unlimited MySQL databases, unlimited bandwidth, unlimited emails, and hosting of unlimited domains in their package price. Many good shared hosting providers are available. Some of the more popular providers are Host Monster.com, Lunarpages.com, BlueHost.com, JustHost.com, Webhostingpad.com, and GoDaddy.com.

Shared hosting comes in many variations. The vast majority of shared hosting providers offer the PHP/CGI/MySQL platform. This is followed closely by Windows-based shared hosting with ASP.NET. Next in line is Java/Tomcat hosting, which is typically the most expensive of the three combinations.

In addition to these benefits, shared hosting comes with several drawbacks. For instance, one site could leach all of your CPU cycles, making the response times of all other sites unacceptable. Good hosts have checks in place to handle this situation. This usually involves shutting down the culprit site. Now, if *your* site is the culprit, you are typically asked to clean up your site while access to your site is completely blocked. This is not a good situation, as your site will show a message from your hosting provider asking you to contact them to clean the offending script. Do you want web spiders crawling this page?

Running your site in the same IP neighborhood as another spam site could be harmful, and not just from a search engine perspective. Diligent hosting providers regularly scan their clients' sites for copyright violations and spam.

Dedicated server hosting

Dedicated server hosting is the next level in hosting. It is ideal for small businesses. There are numerous benefits to dedicated server hosting. You get a server all to yourself in addition to a much better service-level agreement (SLA). Many providers are available, including Theplanet.com, Rackspace.com, and Hostway.com.

Dedicated servers come preconfigured with all sorts of features on Linux or Windows. These include remote reboots, redundant power and network availability, and phone support, among other features. You can also use multiple IP addresses on the same box if you want to host multiple domains with their own separate IPs.

Collocation hosting

Collocation hosting involves placing your server hardware within your provider's data room. This arrangement is useful if you want to enjoy the benefits of your provider's Internet network backbone while still being able to manage your box in any way you like.

You can assign permissions to specific individuals within your organization to have physical access to your servers to perform administration and related support activities. Another benefit of collocation is power redundancy, which you would rarely have at your small-business office.

Collocation makes sense when you have nonstandard applications requiring fast Internet connections that only you know how to manage. For collocation hosting, use local providers in your area. The last thing you need is to drive two hours when your server goes down.

Comanaged and managed hosting

Large organizations typically seek comanaged and managed hosting arrangements. In managed hosting, the provider assumes most of the hosting responsibility. The onus is mostly (if not entirely) on the provider to ensure that everything is running smoothly at all times, as per the SLA. Comanaged hosting is a bit different. In this scenario, the provider typically takes care of the network infrastructure, hardware, and operating system (patching) while the client manages the applications. As you may imagine, managed hosting is more expensive than comanaged hosting.

Internal hosting

With internal hosting, your internal staff is responsible for most of the technical troubleshooting. Big companies typically have data rooms and multiple infrastructure and development teams managing all layers of their underlying IT architecture. Smaller companies typically lease DSL or fiber lines. Internal hosting is usually employed for systems that carry sensitive information, such as databases and filesystems.

Many small and large organizations employ virtual private servers (VPSs). The concept stems from mainframe computers in which one physical piece of hardware is logically partitioned to provide completely separate (virtual) servers. Each virtual server can run its own separate operating system that can be rebooted without affecting other virtual servers.

Custom Site Design or Third-Party Software

Sooner or later, you must decide what software your site will be running. Before taking the plunge into custom design and coding, it makes sense to evaluate what's available in terms of third-party software. Many quality open source software packages are worth exploring.

The following subsection discusses things you should consider when employing a custom design, followed by a section detailing some of the popular free and paid software packages available today.

Employing Custom Development

Software takes time to design, develop, and properly test. It may be your best option if nothing on the market fits your online software requirements. Taking the route of custom development has its advantages and disadvantages.

Benefits of custom development

In this context, when I talk about custom software I am talking about the design and architecture of dynamic sites or web applications. Developing a custom solution allows you to produce a web application exactly to your specifications. If designed properly, custom web applications provide an extra level of security against hackers who typically prey on popular software. In this sense, being unique is an advantage.

From an SEO perspective, custom application development could be advantageous— if you consider SEO when you start designing your software and architecture. In this case, you have full control over the application architecture and can make the provisions necessary to support various on-page and on-site SEO methodologies.

Disadvantages of custom development

Custom development takes time. Depending on the complexity of your software design and architecture, it could take a toll on your budget. Although this may be suitable for medium-size or large companies, it is hardly the case for small businesses, especially if the business is not technology-related. You will also need to maintain this custom code. You will want to ensure that the expertise will be there throughout the application life cycle to handle any support issues or bugs. You may also need to enhance the application from time to time.

Site page layouts

Keep the page layout consistent throughout the site. Figure 3-3 shows three sample site page layouts. A site page layout is important. When search engines read your HTML, they do so in a serial fashion. Depending on your page layout, menus, ads, and other irrelevant content is frequently placed near the top of the HTML file (within the <body> tags).

Content found near the top of the HTML file is perceived as more relevant. Having unrelated content in this location can introduce noise that might affect search engine indexing. You can use CSS to get around this problem.

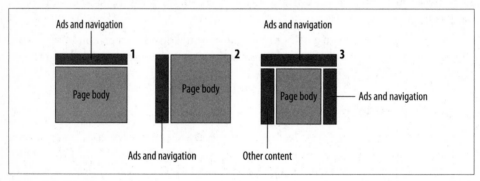

Figure 3-3. Sample page layouts

SEO-friendly site layout. Let's suppose your site has the layout shown in example 1 in Figure 3-3. That layout contains two general areas. The top area contains the main site navigation as well as the top banner ad. The lower area contains all of the content. To place the content near the top of the HTML file, you could use the following CSS fragment:

```
#navigation {
position: absolute;
top: 10px;
```

```
left: 50%;
width: 800px;
margin-left: -400px;
text-align: left;
}

#content {
position: absolute;
top: 150px;
left: 50%;
width: 800px;
margin-left: -400px;
text-align: left;
}

body {
    text-align: center;
    min-width: 600px;
}
```

The first chunk of CSS code is used for the navigation fragment, and the second is used for the content fragment. The last chunk is an Internet Explorer hack used for centering both fragments. The key part of this code is the absolute positioning of each DIV. The navigation portion is rendered at the top of the screen, while physically being placed below the main content. Here is how the skeleton HTML code (within the <body> tags) would look:

```
<body>
<div id="content"><!-- SEO optimized content text goes here.--></div>
<div id="navigation"><!-- navigational elements, ads go here--></div>
</body>
```

It is as simple and elegant as that! Figure 3-4 shows one example of using this particular layout. See Appendix A for the full source code of all three layouts shown in Figure 3-3.

Figure 3-4. Sample CSS layout

Building a dynamic site skeleton

Most dynamic sites in existence today use some sort of website template. Using website templates is a sound strategy as long as you can ensure that every page has a unique HTML `<title>` and `<meta>` description tag. Using the CSS technique we already discussed along with PHP `includes`, you can easily create a simple yet robust site structure. The following template fragment is a sample skeleton you could use (as your *index.php* file) to start building your own site structure:

```php
<?php
session_start();
include ('configuration.php'); // include configuration variables
include ('common.php'); // include common methods and/or variables
?>
<html>
<head>
    <?php generateCustomTitle(); ?>
    <?php generateCustomMeta(); ?>
    <!-- include any external template JavaScript Files -->
    <!-- include any external template CSS Files -->
</head>
<body>
<div class="maincontent">
<?php showMainBodyContent(); ?>
</div>

<div id="breadcrumbs">
<b>Current Location:</b> <?php showBreadCrumbs(); ?>
</div>

<div id="navigation">
  <?php showTopMenu(); ?>
  <?php showSearchform(); ?><br>
  <?php generateBannerAd(); ?>
</div>

<div id="leftcolumn">
<?php showCurrentUserstatus(); ?><br>
<?php showGoogleAdSense(10); ?>
</div>

<div id="rightcolumn">
<?php showLatestArticleIntros(5); ?><br>
<?php showNewComments(10); ?>
</div>

<!-- Analytics Code or other tracking Code -->
</body>
</html>
```

The preceding PHP code fragment should be easy to digest. The `session_start()` method creates a new session (or resumes the existing session) as passed by the HTTP request. The next two PHP `includes` include other (library) PHP files that would comprise all of the methods and variables your template needs.

The next set of PHP calls are specific to the creation of the custom HTML `<title>` and `<meta>` description tags. Just below the `<meta>` section you should place all of your external JavaScript and CSS files. These files could be required by the common template elements or other files required for the page to work.

Within the HTML `<body>` tags, we see several `DIV`s comprising the main layout elements. Each `DIV` contains call(s) to the specific PHP method(s) to render the dynamic content. Notice the placement of the breadcrumbs and the navigation `DIV`s. They are roughly in the middle of this layout. Using the CSS technique we already discussed, you can create a layout similar to example 3 in Figure 3-3. In addition, you can apply the same concepts to other web programming languages. Remember, this is *not* about PHP versus Python versus Rails versus Java. The same concepts apply to all.

Dealing with dynamic links

Dynamic sites can confuse search engines. Search engines like to see static-looking links. To accomplish this, you can use the old technique of URL rewriting. URL rewriting goes back to the Apache web server and the mod_rewrite module. For example, let's suppose you have a URL as in the following fragment:

```
http://www.mydomain.com/product?id=25&desc=basketball&cat=apparel&
```

In this example there are three variables. We can make this link look more static by using the URL rewriting rule in the *.htaccess* file as follows:

```
Options +FollowSymLinks
RewriteEngine on

RewriteRule product-id-(.*)-desc-(.*)-cat-(.*)\.html
            product.?id=$1&desc=$2&cat=$3
```

The resulting URL would look like this:

```
http://www.mydomain.com/product-id-25-desc-basketball-cat-apparel.html
```

Let's examine what happened to the original URL. For clarity, let's look at the two URLs together:

```
http://www.mydomain.com/product?id=25&desc=basketball&cat=apparel&
http://www.mydomain.com/product-id-25-desc-basketball-cat-apparel.html
```

Now, look back at the rewrite rule. The asterisk (*) in the rewrite rule signifies zero or more characters. The period (.) matches any single character. You can think of `$1`, `$2`, and `$3` as placeholders. If you want to learn more about URL rewriting on an Apache web server, you can visit the online guides located at the following URLs:

- *http://httpd.apache.org/docs/1.3/misc/rewriteguide.html*
- *http://httpd.apache.org/docs/2.0/misc/rewriteguide.html*
- *http://www.sitepoint.com/article/guide-url-rewriting/*

You can also rewrite URLs on IIS. Many plug-in filters are available for this. According to Microsoft (*http://bit.ly/ATAQa*):

> URL rewriting can be implemented either with ISAPI filters at the IIS Web server level, or with either HTTP modules or HTTP handlers at the ASP.NET level.

Some third-party (IIS) URL rewriting tools include:

- ISAPI_Rewrite (*http://www.isapirewrite.com/*)
- URL Rewrite Module (*http://learn.iis.net/page.aspx/460/using-url-rewrite-module/*)
- PageXchanger (*http://port80software.com/products/pagexchanger/*)

Utilizing Free or Paid Software

Thousands of free and paid software tools are available. Just because a particular tool is free does not mean it is of low quality. To use a web server parallel, the Apache web server is free but many mission-critical websites use it. You should choose your tool based on your business and technical requirements. In this book, we will be focusing on SEO-friendly tools.

Advantages of using third-party software

Utilizing third-party software allows you to focus more on your business requirements. Depending on your situation, chances are someone has already created something to fulfill your basic requirements. Using third-party applications will save you time. Time is critical, as it can make a big difference if you want to launch your idea today instead of six months from now. Your competitors are not standing still.

Disadvantages of using third-party software

Open source software isn't more prone to bugs than anything else. Paid software does come with someone to call (if you like waiting on hold) and someone to sue (which, as you know, can be very important). On the other hand, open source software frequently has active user mailing lists.

Regardless of whether the software is free or paid, the more popular it is the more prone to hacker attacks it will be. Sometimes using relatively unknown software may minimize this risk. Whatever the case, make sure you always apply regular software patches as they become available.

Free software

Most dynamic websites today are running some sort of content management system (CMS). The open source community has a lot to offer when it comes to CMSs. Many CMSs have various plug-ins or modules that allow you to run just about any type of site with decent on-page SEO support. The ultimate site for CMS comparison and research is *http://cmsmatrix.org*. Table 3-5 lists some of the most popular open source software available today.

Table 3-5. Open source software

Software	Details
b2evolution (*http://b2evolution.net*)	Full-featured weblog tool. PHP- and MySQL-based with extended file and photo-management features.
CMS Made Simple (*http://cmsmadesimple.org*)	One of the simplest CMSs out there. Can set up a site in minutes. More than 300 modules. PHP/MySQL based.
Django (*http://www.djangoproject.com*)	Python-based open source (model-view-controller) web application framework supporting PostgreSQL, MySQL, SQLite, and Microsoft SQL databases. Allows rapid application development.
Drupal (*http://drupal.org*)	Powerful, modular CMS running on Apache/IIS as well as MySQL and PostgreSQL.
e107 (*http://e107.org*)	Another PHP/MySQL CMS, with more than 250 plug-ins. Actively developed.
eZ Publish (*http://ez.no*)	An open source CMS, providing web content management solutions for intranets, e-commerce, and digital media publishing. Based on PHP and MySQL (or PostgreSQL).
Joomla! (*http://www.joomla.org*)	One of the most popular CMSs. PHP- and MySQL-based, boasting 4,400+ extensions.
Mambo (*http://mamboserver.com*)	Another popular PHP/MySQL CMS, with more than 100 extensions.
MediaWiki (*http://www.mediawiki.org*)	A free software wiki package (originally for use on Wikipedia). Based on PHP and MySQL (or PostgreSQL). Good for very large sites.
WordPress (*http://wordpress.org/*)	By far the most popular blogging software. Based on PHP and MySQL. Numerous extensions.
osCommerce (*http://www.oscommerce.com/*)	The most popular e-commerce (storefront) free software. Based on PHP and MySQL.
XOOPS (*http://www.xoops.org/*)	One of the most popular CMSs based on PHP and MySQL. Many module extensions.

Other popular CMS platforms include MODx, PHP-Nuke, phpWebSite, Plone, SPIP, TikiWiki, and Typo3. Also, many extensions or modules are specifically designed to enhance the SEO part of a particular platform.

Paid software

Many paid CMSs are available for you to use to start your website. To find what you are looking for, you can visit sites such as the following:

- *http://www.hotscripts.com*
- *http://www.tucows.com*
- *http://softpedia.com*
- *http://www.brothersoft.com*
- *http://snapfiles.com*
- *http://download.com*
- *http://www.shareware.com*

Some of the most popular enterprise-level commercial CMS solutions include RedDot (*http://websolutions.opentext.com*), Microsoft SharePoint (*http://sharepoint.microsoft.com/Pages/Default.aspx*), Interwoven (*http://interwoven.com*), Tridion (*http://tridion.com*), Day (*http://www.day.com*), and Sitecore (*http://sitecore.net*). These solutions are expensive and typically cost in the tens of thousands of dollars (or more) depending on your requirements.

No system will ever be perfect. Paid software is not exempt from this rule; it will also have some bugs. You will need to fully understand your platform to achieve the best SEO results. At times, you will need to perform small or big SEO-type hacks—if you're striving for perfection.

Website Usability

SEO and website usability are inseparable on many levels. For any website to gain net traction, it will need to adhere to some basic usability standards. To quote Wikipedia (*http://bit.ly/2uxuUO*):

> Web usability is an approach to make web sites easy to use for an end-user, without requiring her (or him) to undergo any specialized training. The user should be able to intuitively relate the actions he needs to perform on the web page, with other interactions he sees in the general domain of life e.g. press of a button leads to some action.

According to a Google Knol article (*http://bit.ly/mq20r*), good website usability leads to improved search rankings. Several books have been written about website usability. Every website owner should read at least one of them. Some titles include *Usability for the Web: Designing Web Sites That Work* by Tom Brinck et al. (Morgan Kaufmann), *Don't Make Me Think: A Common Sense Approach to Web Usability* by Steve Krug (New Riders Press), and *Handbook of Usability Testing: How to Plan, Design, and Conduct Effective Tests* by Jeffrey Rubin (Wiley). In this section, we will cover some of the important elements of website usability.

General Considerations

Strive to provide unique content. Make every page relevant to your business goals or your website's value proposition. Your home page should contain the most important links to your site. Provide help pages, FAQ pages, Sitemaps, and contact forms. Ensure that your users can get to their information quickly. Provide ways to get feedback regarding any issues or problems with your site. Let users know when they are leaving your site (if it is not obvious by clicking on an external link), as well as when they are browsing your site over HTTPS (SSL).

Linking Considerations

Concentrate on making easy, clear-cut, and logical interfaces with a focus on getting to the right information quickly. Link anchor text should be of reasonable size and should be similar to, or the same as, the destination page's HTML title tag text (if it exists).

Minimize the number of clicks to get to any page, especially those of higher importance. All pages should have common navigation elements that are strategically placed in a consistent fashion. One navigation example is the use of breadcrumbs. According to Wikipedia (*http://en.wikipedia.org/wiki/Breadcrumb_(navigation)*):

> Breadcrumbs or breadcrumb trail is a navigation aid used in user interfaces. It gives users a way to keep track of their location within programs or documents. The term comes from the trail of breadcrumbs left by Hansel and Gretel in the popular fairytale.

Breadcrumbs are used to tell users where they are within a site. You can also think of breadcrumbs as analogous to the directory location on a filesystem. Breadcrumbs are typically located at the top of every page, just below the banner ads or navigational elements. The following fragment is an example breadcrumb in HTML:

```
Location: <a href="index.html">Home</a> &gt;
<a href="services.html">Services</a> &gt;
<a href="hosting.html">Hosting</a>
```

Every page should link to your home page. This is especially helpful for 404 (Page Not Found) and 500 (Server Error) error pages. These pages should provide for graceful site reentry.

Use simple textual links with relevant keyword-rich anchor text. If you're using images as links, provide the link ALT text alternative for all semantically related images. Your website or company logo should be present on every page, and when clicked it should bring the user to your site's home page.

Know Your Demographics

Sites designed for an older audience are not the same as those designed for teenagers. It's not only about age. *Demographic* is a term used in marketing to describe age, sex, marital status, religious orientation, family size, education, geographic location, occupation, and many other segmentation metrics. There are many uses of demographics data.

Google AdWords, Facebook Ads, and Yahoo! Search Marketing provide demographics options for specific targeting of their respective paid ads. Similarly, your website will be targeting a specific population. Know your target audience, as this can be helpful when it comes to making website usability decisions such as font sizes, dynamic menus, and the like.

Ensure Web Browser Compatibility

Design sites to ensure cross-browser compatibility. According to MediaPost.com, Internet Explorer currently has 66.10% of the browser market, followed by Firefox with 22.48% and Safari at 8.21%. The top three browsers cumulatively hold more than 96% of browser market share.

Although these numbers may not correlate to your website stats, you should consider them as a general guideline in terms of your web browser support. Use online tools such as Browsershots (*http://browsershots.org*), BrowserCam (*http://www.browsercam .com*), and Litmus (*http://litmusapp.com*) to see how your web pages look in different web browsers.

Test your website at different screen resolutions. Ideally, they should all render gracefully, regardless of the resolution. If your site is specifically designed for certain resolutions, make this explicit. You can test your site against different screen resolutions by visiting *http://www.yournew.com/resolution_test.cfm*.

Be mindful of various web standards. Use HTML validators to ensure the greatest compatibility. Most web browsers support various versions of HTML or associated web-related protocols. Invalid HTML could lead to strange indexing problems with unexpected search result fragments.

Do not mess with standard browser operations such as disabling the browser's back button, disabling the right mouse click, obfuscating link colors, using custom (or changing the standard behavior of) browser scroll bars, or restricting manual font size changes.

Create Simple Page Layouts

Avoid horizontal scrolling. Break up big pages into smaller pages. Keep page layout as simple and intuitive as possible. Minimize animations, cascading menus, and other dynamic content.

Avoid overcrowding pages with elements such as images, widgets, and videos. Make each page intuitive enough so that you can easily identify its purpose. This is what simple page layouts help to do.

Place important information at the top of your pages. Long pages that require vertical scrolling may never be read fully. In those cases, you can use HTML anchors for faster scrolling.

Use Intelligent Page Formatting

Try using smaller paragraphs with mixed-case text. Use boldface, italics, uppercase, and different text color variations for emphasis. Employ browser-safe fonts such as Times New Roman, Georgia (serif font), Arial, Helvetica, or Verdana (sans serif font).

Strategically employ bulleted lists, headings, and subheadings for clarity and information organization. Using these options is helpful from an SEO perspective. Furthermore, employ sufficient alignments, whitespace, and text padding for additional clarity and web page look and feel.

Be mindful of web-safe colors. Use high-contrast color schemes for clarity and ease of reading. Be consistent with colors. Don't use too many colors. Try to stay away from image backgrounds.

Create Smart HTML Forms

Create forms that retain form data if a user returns to the same form page. This is especially important with search forms, which should be visible on all your pages. If your HTML forms contain drop-down lists for countries, regions, and cities, you can use a geo-IP database to provide for intelligent drop-down lists that will allow for faster navigation.

Your HTML forms should support submissions by either clicking on the Submit button or pressing the Enter key. They should also support the Tab key when moving from one form element to the next. Make your forms intuitive by clearly labeling the required fields.

Optimize Your Site for Speed

Nobody has unlimited patience these days. Not everyone has high-speed Internet. Stay away from (Flash) splash screens. Compress your media files for faster page loading. Use media files only when you need to. Also make sure to describe your graphics, videos, and sound files. For sound and video content, provide text transcripts. Make use of thumbnails for large images. Use web server compression for your HTML web server transmissions to speed up transmission for all your clients, including search engine web spiders.

Test Your Interface Design for Usability

Before endorsing a specific design, create several alternatives. You can conduct surveys and usability tests with specific demographics. By utilizing the results of these surveys and tests, you can make educated selections, thereby minimizing the potential risk of turning off your existing clients.

You can also use the pilot approach. If you have an existing site, you can select a pool of individuals to test your new designs before making everyone else switch to the new design. This method should provide you with the ability to make corrections along the way, while fine-tuning your design choices.

Website Accessibility

Ideally, websites should be designed with everyone in mind. This includes people with various disabilities. For example, U.S. government sites must comply with the Section 508 Federal Accessibility Standards (*http://www.section508.gov*), which make specific provisions addressing the needs of people with disabilities.

Website accessibility concerns several broad areas that web designers need to consider. These include provisions for creating alternatives or text equivalents for nontext web elements, provisions for creating specific alternatives to script-generated content, and provisions specifically related to choosing colors that can be differentiated.

These are just some website accessibility considerations. For more information, read *Web Accessibility: Web Standards and Regulatory Compliance* by Jim Thatcher et al. (friends of ED). You can also visit *http://www.w3.org/WAI/*, which is the website of the Web Accessibility Initiative (WAI). There you can find WAI's Authoring Tool Accessibility Guidelines (ATAG) 2.0.

Summary

Choosing a good domain name is beneficial. Domain names can appear in many places, including your emails, business cards, company letterhead, company newsletters, press releases, and various other marketing materials. A great domain name is a catalyst for reduced marketing costs. A domain name that is easy to remember will also give you additional benefits, as it will be easy for people to propagate the name by word of mouth.

After picking your domain name, consider the various parts of your software platform. Decide on specific web and application servers, database servers, and your development platform. Think about the hosting options that would be suitable for your technical requirements. Many different hosting options are available, including free, shared, dedicated server, collocation, comanaged, managed, and internal hosting.

Consider the type of web application you want to run. You can create a custom site design or you can utilize a third-party platform. Use intelligent (common) site page layouts and a basic site skeleton.

Third-party platforms are available in two flavors: free and paid. Although free software implies lower cost of ownership, this is not always the case if you consider some of the drawbacks, such as the time required to fix bugs. Nonetheless, there are proven, industry-grade free software platforms that small and big businesses are using today.

Keep things simple. Adhere to the basic elements of website usability. Consider website accessibility. All of these options can influence the various aspects of your SEO work.

## CHAPTER 4

Internal Ranking Factors

Internal ranking factors are things you control directly (as part of your site) that can affect your rank in the SERPs. There are two types of internal ranking factors: on-page ranking factors (things you can do in a particular web page, such as providing appropriate keywords) and on-site ranking factors (things you can do to your website as a whole).

How can you take into consideration hundreds of different ranking factors? You can't. The key is to home in on 20 or so of the most important known factors—those that have stood the test of time and produced results consistently. Knowing what to optimize can make SEO a lot easier. Instead of listening to Internet hype, website owners should rely on provable facts.

This chapter sets the stage for what is to come in Chapter 13. Its ultimate goal is to take out the guesswork and really focus on what makes search engines tick, as well as to identify the key internal ranking factors you should consider when optimizing your site. I wrote a Perl script that speaks directly to these factors by performing detailed statistical analysis. This tool or one of its variants should be a component in your SEO toolkit. The idea is to analytically prove what works for different search engines.

The last section of this chapter, "Putting It All Together" on page 80, contains the information you need to run a script that creates a comprehensive HTML ranking report. We show pertinent excerpts from this report throughout the chapter, so please refer to the script listing for further clarification if necessary. Further study of the script is recommended.

Analyzing SERPs

The abundance of myths, speculations, and theories in the SEO community makes it hard to focus on what's really relevant when it comes to ranking in the SERPs. To quantify the importance of different ranking factors, my Perl script analyzes and proves some of the theories. The *rankingfactors.pl* script appears in full in Appendix A.

The basic idea is to analyze the top results from the top search engines. Given a search term, the script collects the results from the major search engines, downloads those pages, and analyzes them to see why they got the rankings they did. The rest of our discussion in this chapter depends pretty heavily on the use of this script. Also note that we already discussed some of these ranking factors in some detail in previous chapters.

On-Page Ranking Factors

Many on-page ranking factors are related to the use of keywords. We'll cover those first, and then we'll cover some other factors that are not directly related to keywords.

Keywords in the <title> Tag

Your page titles will show up in the SERPs, so make them concise and relevant. The World Wide Web Consortium (W3C) provides the following recommendations for HTML titles (*http://bit.ly/4dyALc*):

> Authors should use the TITLE element to identify the contents of a document. Since users often consult documents out of context, authors should provide context-rich titles. Thus, instead of a title such as "Introduction", which doesn't provide much contextual background, authors should supply a title such as "Introduction to Medieval Bee-Keeping" instead.

One of the most critical on-page factors, the `<title>` tag is not to be dismissed. Search engines tend to use the `<title>` tag text as search results titles. All pages should have unique page titles. All page titles should be crafted wisely, using the most important keywords found in the page copy.

The page title should contain specific keyword phrases to describe the page. Using a company name in the page title by itself can prove ineffective if it is not accompanied by additional text that briefly describes the product, service, or topic being discussed.

Titles in search results

Titles in search results have a maximum length. A long title will not hurt your site, but it may not appear in its entirety in the search results. If you have to use longer page titles, from a usability perspective ensure that the part of the title that could show up in search results contains relevant keywords. The last thing you want is for your keywords to get cut off in the search results. Don't be afraid to change your HTML page titles. Here are some good examples that are concise and to the point:

```
<title>Unity St. Pizza - Best Pizza in Boston - 1-800-242-0242 -
Order Online</title>

<title>Java Tutorial - Programming - TechnologyFirmABC.com </title>
```

In the case of known brand names such as O'Reilly, HTML titles may not be as big a concern due to the probable bias by some search engines, such as Google.

The next set of examples shows poorer-quality page titles:

```
<title>http://bestbostonpizza.com</titles>

<title>Best Pizza in Town, Town's best pizza, Excellent Pizza</title>

<title>
The purpose of this article is not to debate the right or wrong of
third parties utilizing search engine records to probe into the
activities of others. There are those in the United States and other
countries that believe that giving up privacy for the purpose of
prosecuting a handful of crimes is not justified. Then there are
those who gladly hand over privacy for a perceived sense of security.
</title>

<title>Make Money! Make Money Now! Great way to Make Money! </title>
```

In the first example, the fictional website is using its URL as the page title. Although the actual URL contains keywords, it is not very helpful in terms of telling searchers what the page is really about.

The second example seems to be alternating between different keywords that mean the same thing. This could be interpreted as search engine spam. It does not read well to web visitors.

The third example is a really long page title. The first part of the text contains many stop words. Most of this text is unlikely to show up in search results.

The last sample title uses many poison words that could flag this page as suspicious.

Finally, the following titles are the worst kind:

```
<title></title>
<title>Default Title</title>
<title>Document 1</title>
<html><body>...</body></html>
```

Pages using no titles or default titles as generated by various HTML programs are useless and can be detrimental to your site's visibility.

Title keywords in the page copy

Titles need to be relevant to the page copy. You need to ensure that most, if not all, of the words found in the `<title>` tag can also be found in the page itself. Of course, some pages will be exempt from this rule, but this should be the goal for any page. Figure 4-1 shows the script output for the keyword *o'reilly book*.

#	URL	Google Title	Page Title	Keyword(s) found in Title? [Y|N]	Title Keywords In Page Copy [%]
0	http://oreilly.com/	O'Reilly Media - Spreading the knowledge of technology innovat	O'Reilly Media - Spreading the knowledge of technology innovators	Y	62.5
1	http://oreilly.com/store /complete.html	O'Reilly Media -- Bookstore: Complete L	O'Reilly Media -- Bookstore: Complete List	Y	80.0
2	http://my.safaribooksonline.com/	Safari Books Online - Home P	Safari Books Online - Home Page	Y	100.0
3	http://ug.oreilly.com /bookreviews.html	O'Reilly User Group Program: Book Revi	O'Reilly User Group Program: Book Reviews	Y	100.0
4	http://online-books.oreilly.com/	online-book..oreilly.com -- Welcome to the O'Reilly Online Bo	online-book..oreilly.com -- Welcome to the O'Reilly Online Books	Y	90.0
5	http://docstore.mik.ua/oreilly/	O'Reilly's CD booksh	O'Reilly's CD bookshelf	Y	100.0
6	http://caml.inria.fr/pub/docs /oreilly-book/	Developing applications with Objective C	Developing applications with Objective Caml	N	100.0

Figure 4-1. Title metrics

The column labeled "Google Title" in Figure 4-1 represents the title found in Google's SERPs, and the column labeled "Page Title" represents the actual page title found in the HTML. The "Keyword(s) found in Title? [Y|N]" column states whether the keyword is found in the HTML title. The column labeled "Title Keywords in Page Copy [%]" lists the percentage of words found in the page title that are also found in the page copy.

Keywords in the Page URL

Keywords in a page URL are useful—and not just for SEO. Many of the newer CMSs, blog sites, and news sites allow for URL rewriting techniques to make their URLs stand out by using keywords in the URLs. The keywords I am referring to here are those found after the base domain name. Figure 4-2 shows an example.

Amazon.com: **Blue Suede Shoes**: Barbara Bach, Eric Clapton, George ...
Amazon.com: **Blue Suede Shoes**: Barbara Bach, Eric Clapton, George Harrison, Olivia
Harrison, Carl Perkins, Ringo Starr, Tom Gutteridge: Movies & TV.
www.amazon.com/**Blue-Suede-Shoes**-Barbara-Bach/dp/B000FTJ700 - 269k -
Cached - Similar pages

Figure 4-2. Example Google search result

Figure 4-2 shows a search result for the keyword *blue suede shoes*. From a usability perspective, Google also highlights in bold the words matching the search query keywords, which makes this result stand out further.

Optimizing URLs can sometimes make them very long and hard to remember. This drawback is offset by the benefit of their perceived relevance when displayed in search results.

Keywords in the Page Copy

When I talk about keywords in the page copy, I mean the number of times a particular keyword or keywords occur in the body of a document. Before optimizing your keywords, do the necessary research and figure out what people are searching for in the particular topic you are writing about.

Use tools such as Google AdWords to obtain keyword suggestions as well as to check what your competitors are using. You may want to target no more than two or three keywords per page.

High keyword densities may be viewed with more suspicion. Typically, keyword densities range between 0.2% and 4%. This does not mean your site will be penalized if your keyword density is 10%, nor does it mean your page will not rank if your keyword density is less than 0.2%.

Figure 4-3 shows the keyword density for the top search results on Google for the keyword *o'reilly book*.

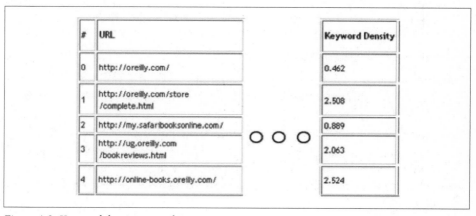

Figure 4-3. Keyword density example

Keywords in the <meta> Description Tag

The text in the <meta> description tag is not visible on the page itself, but is often displayed in search results. This should be enough of an imperative to fully optimize this tag. Here is the format of a <meta> description tag:

```
<meta name="description" content="Optimized Description with Important
Keywords. This text can be a short paragraph. Use important page copy
keywords in this description.">
```

Here are some examples of good <meta> description tags:

```
<meta name="description" content="Learn how to develop web applications
with ASP. Learn ASP programming quickly with our three-
part tutorial." />
```

```
<meta name="description" content="CompanyXYZSEO.com are experts in
Organic SEO.  Performance-based guarantee with low cost SEO entry
packages for small businesses and the enterprise. Based out of San
Franciso, CA." />
```

```
<meta name="description" content="O'Reilly Media spreads the knowledge
of technology innovators through its books, online services, magazines,
and conferences. Since 1978, O'Reilly has been a chronicler and
catalyst of leading-edge development, homing in on the technology
trends that really matter and spurring their adoption by amplifying
'faint signals' from the alpha geeks who are creating the future.
An active participant in the technology community, the company has a
long history of advocacy, meme-making, and evangelism." />
```

The first two examples are straight-to-the-point, one- or two-line descriptions. The third (long) example is from O'Reilly's main website. Notice the highlighted sentence. This is the part that Google is using in its SERP, while the rest is ignored.

Here are some examples of bad <meta> description tags:

```
<meta name="description" content="seo,organic seo, seo consultant,
small business seo, small business search engine optimization
consultant, small business search engine optimization" />
```

```
<html><body>...</body></html>
```

The first example employs confusing keywords and <meta> description tags. This sort of description was meant for search engines only, not human visitors. The second example illustrates the lost opportunity of not including any <meta> description tags.

Unless you are an established brand, make sure to include <meta> description tags for all pages. Don't get lazy and reuse the same text for every page. Every page needs to have its own unique <meta> description tag. Figure 4-4 shows the report segment pertinent to <meta> description tags. Search keywords tend to be found in <meta> description tags.

#	URL	META Description Exact Match	META Description Partial Match
0	http://oreilly.com/	N	Y
1	http://oreilly.com/store/complete.html	Y	Y
2	http://my.safaribooksonline.com/	N	N
3	http://ug.oreilly.com/bookreviews.html	N	Y
4	http://online-books.oreilly.com/	N	N

Figure 4-4. Meta description example

Search engine alternative to <meta> description tags

There is one "curveball" when it comes to <meta> description tags: search engines will sometimes opt to ignore them in favor of the description used at Dmoz.org or in the Yahoo! Directory (if you have a listing there).

To help webmasters control this scenario, new meta tag variations were created to force search engines to use the <meta> description tag instead of the description found in the directory listings. Here are examples that detail ways to block either Dmoz.org or Yahoo! Directory descriptions:

```
<!-- Tells Yahoo! to not use Yahoo! Directory description -->
<meta name="robots" content="noydir" />

<!-- Tells search engines to not use ODP description -->
<meta name="robots" content="noodp" />

<!-- Tells search engines to not use either of the two directories -->
<meta name="robots" content="noodp,noydir" />
```

If you wish to target only specific spiders, you can do the following:

```
<meta name="googlebot" content="noodp">
<!-- Note: Only Yahoo! uses Yahoo! Directory -->
<meta name="slurp" CONTENT="noydir">
<meta name="msnbot" CONTENT="noodp">
```

Keywords in the Heading Tags

Make proper use of your H1 heading tags. Webmasters have used multiple H1 tags in the belief that search engines give those tags priority. The problem with this and similar techniques is that search engines are not stupid and will adapt very quickly to counterattack less scrupulous techniques such as this. Use H1 tags where and when they are appropriate.

The final HTML report, as produced by the script, contains two columns: "Header Tags" and "Header Tag Keywords." The first column uses the following format:

```
Format: [H1]|[H2]|[H3]|[H4]|[H5]|[H6]

Example: 1|40|100|0|0|0|
```

The preceding example is of a page using a single H1 tag, 40 H2 tags, and 100 H3 tags. The second column uses the following format:

```
Format: [Y|N]|[Y|N]|[Y|N]|[Y|N]|[Y|N]|[Y|N]|

Example: Y|Y|Y|N|N|N
```

This example signifies the existence of keywords in H1, H2, and H3 tags.

Keyword Proximity

Keyword proximity refers to how close two or more keywords are to each other in page copy. Whenever possible, avoid using *stop words* to break up your important keywords. Here is an example:

```
We sell green iPods at a discounted rate.
We sell discounted iPods in various colors including white, green and
blue.
```

In this case, the keyword *green iPods* have better keyword proximity in sentence one than they do in sentence two. In terms of keyword proximity, you must consider all text—whether it is part of the page copy, `<title>` tag, or `<meta>` tags—if you want to be included in search results. Here is an example of how this information would be rendered in the final HTML report:

```
14|17|21|154|157|161|212|223|236|244|247|655|658|662|1078|1081|1085|
1107|1150|1151|1183|1188|1377|1506|1712|1721|1726|
```

This list represents sample output of the (relative) keyword locations within a given page.

Keyword Prominence

Keyword prominence refers to relative keyword positions with respect to the start of the HTML page. Common agreement within the SEO community is that the earlier your keywords are found within the physical HTML file, the better.

The keyword prominence factor increases in importance as the document size increases. If your page is very large, ensure that your most important keywords are close to the beginning of the page.

Of course, your keywords should also appear throughout the page. It is not uncommon for Google and other search engines to pick up a phrase in the middle of your document and then place it within your search result. Keyword prominence is usually easy to achieve with semantic HTML pages. Minimize the use of inline JavaScript and CSS, and keep those in separate documents.

Aside from page copy, keyword prominence is also applicable to your `<title>` and `<meta>` tags, as your keywords should appear in these tags, as we already discussed. Here is some sample output that I obtained after running my script for one of the page copies and for the keyword *o'reilly book*:

```
***************************0*1********************
*****1********************************************
**************************************************
*********************************0*1**************
*************************************1*************
**************************************************
**************************************************
**************************************************
```

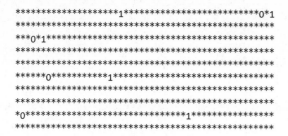

In this case, 0 signifies the relative position of the keyword *o'reilly* and 1 signifies the relative position of the keyword *book*.

All other words are signified by the star (*) character. For single keywords, you would see only 0s. For multiword phrases, you would see 0, 1, 2, and so forth. In other words, 0 is the first keyword, 1 is the second keyword, and so on.

With this mapping, it is easy to see where your keywords are in the context of the whole page. Note that the keyword map shown does not represent the actual web page layout as seen in a web browser. It is only a serial representation of words found in each page.

Keywords in the Link Anchor Text

The link anchor text is all about keyword relevance. In general, all links should contain relevant keywords in the link anchor text. Here is the basic format:

```
<a href="some-link-with-keywords.html">Anchor Text with Keywords</a>
```

Here are some real examples:

```
<a href="perl-cookbook.html">The Perl Cookbook is a comprehensive
collection of problems, solutions, and practical examples for anyone
programming in Perl.</a>

<a href="sharp-aquos-tvs.asp">AQUOS LCD TV at TorontoSharpDeals.com
</a>

<a href="valentine-gifts.pl">Valentine's Day Gifts & Ideas</a>
```

Search engines are keeping a close eye on link anchor text, thanks in part to so-called Google bombing. *Google bombing* is a technique people use to fool Google, by employing deceptive anchor text that is not necessarily related to the destination URL. Although Google has changed its algorithm to try to remove Google bombs, some people still succeed in creating them.

Link anchor text is important. This can become quite obvious in your web server logs when you compare search engine queries to your link anchor text. In many cases, the search engine queries and your link anchor text will be identical, or at least a very close match.

Link anchor text can be especially important with your inbound links. If you can control the anchor text of your inbound links, think carefully about what the anchor text should be. For best results, try to use a keyword suggestion tool such as the Google AdWords Keyword Tool (*https://adwords.google.com/select/KeywordToolExternal*) as well as any proven (converting) keywords.

For example, let's say you are a small online shop selling crystal jewelry. If you run a query for *crystal jewelry* in the AdWords Keyword Tool, you'll get the results shown in Figure 4-5. Leverage these suggestions, if you can, when performing your link-building work.

The point is to try to use many different variations of anchor text, not just one. Search engines may get suspicious if your site starts to attain too many inbound links with the same anchor text too fast. It is best to have as many variations as possible, as this way your site will be getting hits for many different combinations of keywords.

Also note that you should be creating your link anchor text for your visitors, not just for the search engines; that is, your links should look natural, with no excessive keyword stuffing. Make sure you use the most popular anchor text phrases (on the most popular authoritative sites), as those inbound links will hold the greatest value.

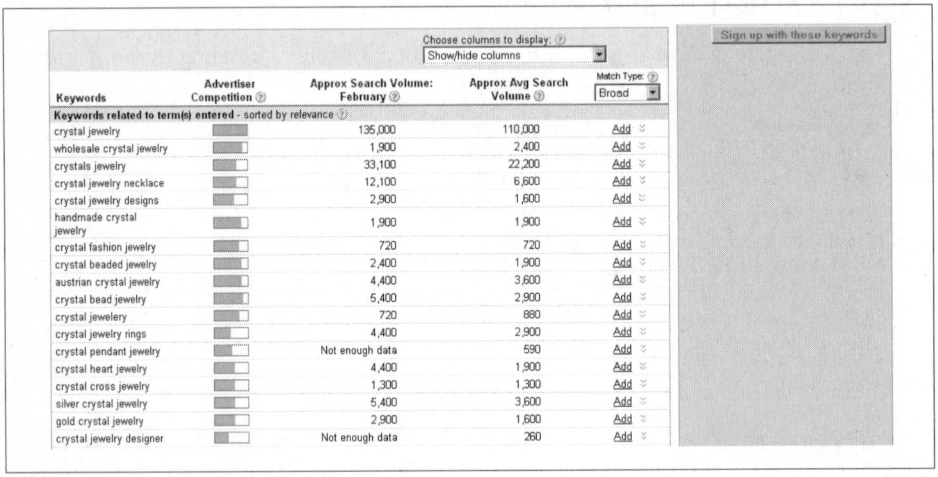

Keywords	Advertiser Competition	Approx Search Volume: February	Approx Avg Search Volume	
Keywords related to term(s) entered - sorted by relevance				
crystal jewelry		135,000	110,000	Add
wholesale crystal jewelry		1,900	2,400	Add
crystals jewelry		33,100	22,200	Add
crystal jewelry necklace		12,100	6,600	Add
crystal jewelry designs		2,900	1,600	Add
handmade crystal jewelry		1,900	1,900	Add
crystal fashion jewelry		720	720	Add
crystal beaded jewelry		2,400	1,900	Add
austrian crystal jewelry		4,400	3,600	Add
crystal bead jewelry		5,400	2,900	Add
crystal jewelery		720	880	Add
crystal jewelry rings		4,400	2,900	Add
crystal pendant jewelry		Not enough data	590	Add
crystal heart jewelry		4,400	1,900	Add
crystal cross jewelry		1,300	1,300	Add
silver crystal jewelry		5,400	3,600	Add
gold crystal jewelry		2,900	1,600	Add
crystal jewelry designer		Not enough data	260	Add

Figure 4-5. Google AdWords Keyword Tool

Handle internal links in similar ways. Proper keyword selection for anchor text is important. Avoid using "Click here," "Next page," and "Read more" as your anchor text. Use semantically related anchor text instead.

Quality Outbound Links

Staying on focus is the underlying idea behind having quality outbound links. It is about what your web visitors want. Can you provide them with great content on your site plus any relevant links where they can find related information?

Keywords in outbound links

Using keywords in outbound links is a good idea. Figure 4-6 shows the part of the final HTML report that is pertinent to keywords found in outbound links. In this example, we see the top results from Google.

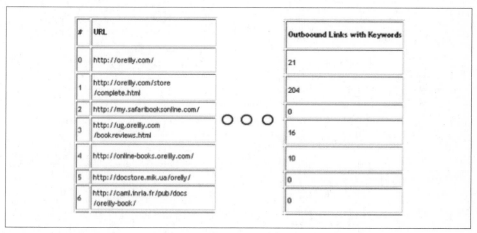

Figure 4-6. Outbound links with keywords

Web Page Age

For certain websites and topics, pages gain greater trust with age. This is different from the freshness boost for pages found in forums, message boards, news portals, and so forth. Note that not all web pages will return the "last modified" date. This could be an indication that the page is not to be cached. Figure 4-7 shows the "Page Age" section of our final report.

Web Page Size

There is no right or wrong answer when it comes to the perfect page size, as it obviously depends largely on what the page is about. However, your HTML should strive to be within reasonable size limits and should not contain erroneous information. To get a rough idea of the page size variable, we can use our script. Figure 4-8 shows the output section related to the page size for the keyword *o'reilly book*.

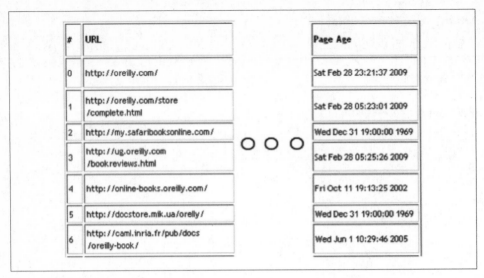

Figure 4-7. Page age example

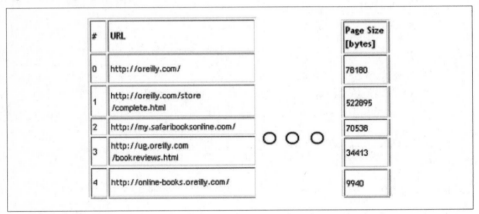

Figure 4-8. Page size

Calculating the optimum number of words per page

The physical web page file size can differ greatly from your page copy text. Although there are no magic numbers or rules, a general guideline is to have at least 200 words per page. Figure 4-9 illustrates this concept for the keyword *o'reilly book*.

On-Site Ranking Factors

So far, we have discussed ranking factors pertinent to each web page. In this section, we will cover factors that are applicable to the entire website. This includes domain

---

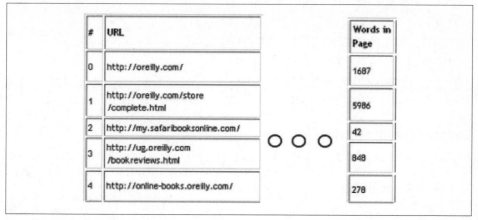

Figure 4-9. Words per page

name keywords, the size (or quantity) of content, linking considerations, and the freshness of pages.

Domain Name Keywords

If your domain name contains an exact (or partial) match to a search query, chances are it will show up on the first page of the SERPs—at least on Google. Google gives keyword matching domains preferential treatment.

The exception to this rule is for competitive keywords. However, the chances of acquiring a popular keyword domain are minimal, as most, if not all, dictionary words are taken, in addition to the most popular two- or three-keyword phrase combinations. This has led to the recent popularity of *nonsense words* as business names.

For niche keywords, you already won half the battle when you purchased your domain name. Add an index page with related keywords, and you'll be on the first page of Google's search results in a relatively short period of time.

You can use the following sample formats when creating your domain name:

```
http://www.keyword1-keyword2.com
http://www.keyword1keyword2keyword3.com
http://www.keyword.com
http://www.keyword.somedomain.com
http://keyword.basename.com
```

Note that the guidelines for subdomains are the same as for domains. The benefits of subdomains are multifold, but subdomains can also be viewed as search engine spam if you create too many of them. With subdomains, you can pick any name you like, as you are in control of the domain record. Table 4-1 summarizes a few other scenarios and the expected outcomes if you were to run the Perl script for certain keywords.

Table 4-1. Keywords in domain name examples

Keyword(s)	URL	Expected result
new york times	http://www.nyt.com	No match
o'reilly book	http://www.oreilly.com	Partial match
pragmatic programmers	http://www.pragprog.com	No match
Etech	http://www.etech.ohio.gov	Full and partial matches

Exact keyword matching

Exact keyword matching refers to keywords (as entered on Google) that are found in domain names. If a particular keyword or all keywords are found in a domain name, you can think of this scenario as an exact match.

Partial keyword matching

Aside from exact matching, there could be a partial match for multiword search phrases. Figure 4-10 showcases the power of having keywords as part of a domain name. This output was generated when we ran the script for the keyword *o'reilly book*.

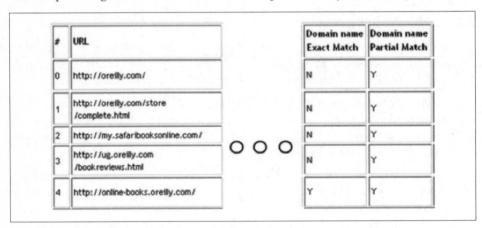

Figure 4-10. Domain keyword matching

Size or Quantity of Content

When I talk about content size, I mean the amount of indexed documents on a particular site. Therefore, content size applies not only to your sites, but also to your competitors' sites.

Estimating size of content

Although you could certainly write a web spider to crawl all of the URLs on the Web, there is an easier way to estimate content size. Popular search engines show this information in their search results. To get the approximate size of a site, you can utilize Google's `site:` command (see Figure 4-11).

Figure 4-11. Estimating the size of a site

Figure 4-11 shows the approximate size of the O'Reilly website, which comprises 374,000 indexed documents at the time of this writing. You could also retrieve this data by using web scraping techniques. Looking at the HTML source of Google's search results, you need to home in on a specific part of the HTML, as highlighted in Figure 4-12.

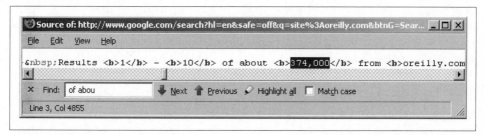

Figure 4-12. Scraping Google SERPs

After running the script, it should be fairly obvious that big (good-quality) sites get better rankings—most of the time. The size of a site implies its authority. The bigger the site, the greater the site owner's perceived authority. Of course, all of this depends on the quality of the content.

Figure 4-13 shows sample output of the final HTML report generated for the keyword *o'reilly book*.

Linking Considerations

The following subsections discuss things to consider when linking, including the internal link structure, pagination problems, distributed link popularity, and URL canonicalization.

Internal link architecture

Website linking architecture is important when it comes to SEO, especially when your site has many pages or is continuously growing. To create a sound linking structure for

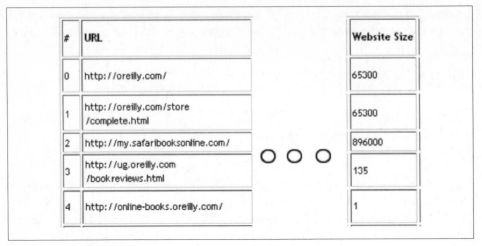

#	URL	Website Size
0	http://oreilly.com/	65300
1	http://oreilly.com/store/complete.html	65300
2	http://my.safaribooksonline.com/	896000
3	http://ug.oreilly.com/bookreviews.html	135
4	http://online-books.oreilly.com/	1

Figure 4-13. Website size

your site, you will likely need to partition your site into distinct subsections (or categories), forming a uniform (inverted) treelike structure. Sometimes creating subdomains can help in this regard. Other times, using XML Sitemaps can help showcase your most important links.

Pagination problems

Bringing inner pages to the forefront is a challenge for many webmasters. Community sites, blogs, forums, message boards, and other types of sites suffer from this "inner page invisibility" syndrome. If it takes more than four clicks to get to a page, it is safe to say that this page may not see the light of day in the SERPs. There are solutions to pagination issues. These include pagination software reengineering, the use of Sitemaps, and the use of the `nofollow` link attribute.

 Search engines don't treat all sites in the same way. If yours is an important authority website or the site for a big respected brand, search engines will bend the rules and index your site more than they usually would, in that they will dig deeper into your sublevels—whereas if you were the owner of a new site, you would be lucky if the search engines dug down four levels when indexing your site.

Distributed internal link popularity

A true testament of a site's performance can be viewed in terms of its distributed internal link popularity. Does your link juice dissipate quickly as soon as you leave your home page? If that's the case, you have work to do. Sometimes you may have search engine traps that you are not aware of, and hence Google cannot see some of your pages. Check for these situations by browsing your website with a text browser or by using Google Webmaster Tools.

Strive to create multiple inner hotspots with gradual PageRank dissipation. Ideally, having an inner page with the same or even higher link juice as the site's home page is desirable. One way to accomplish this is to have referral sites linking to your inner pages, and not just to your home page.

Figure 4-14 illustrates a website with three main links from its home page. The first link is just as popular as the home page, and the second link is even more popular. The third link, to Page C, has rapidly diminishing PageRank. Two clicks away from the home page, the PageRank value has gone down to zero.

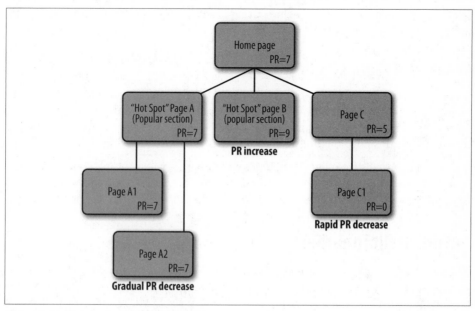

Figure 4-14. Varying internal link popularity

URL canonicalization

The subject of URL canonicalization comes up when dealing with content duplication. The word *canonicalization* comes from computer science, and Wikipedia defines it as "a process for converting data that has more than one possible representation into a 'standard' canonical representation" (*http://bit.ly/z92Dw*).

In terms of SEO, this has to do with how search engines interpret the same content referenced by different link variations. For example, the following links could all point to the same physical page but be interpreted as different by the search engines:

```
http://somedomain.com
http://somedomain.com/
http://somedomain.com/index.asp
http://www.somedomain.com
http://www.somedomain.com/index.html
```

```
http://www.somedomain.com/Index.html
http://www.somedomain.com/default.asp
```

Technically speaking, it is possible to serve different content for each of these URLs. So, what is the real problem of having different ways to get to the same content? It boils down to interpretation. Google and others may split your link juice across all of the different variations of URLs, hence affecting your PageRank. There are many ways to deal with canonical links.

The basic idea is to stick with one URL format throughout your website. One way to do this is to explicitly tell Google what your canonical or preferred link is via Google Webmaster Tools. Other ways include using permanent 301 redirects, custom coding, and the canonical link element in the HTML header.

Freshness of Pages

Depending on the site, your ratio of new to old pages could play a role in how search engines rank your site (or it could have no impact at all). For a news or portal site, a large ratio of new to old pages is beneficial. For sites that sell products or services that never change, this ratio might be much smaller.

For news portals, the frequency of updates will be higher when compared to other sites. Sites with fresh news tend to get a temporary ranking boost. This boost typically reaches its peek before slowly descending to few or no referrals for a particular news article.

Putting It All Together

Throughout this chapter, we referred to the HTML report produced by the *ranking-factors.pl* script, which you can find in Appendix A. We'll finish the chapter by discussing how to run this script, and showing the final HTML report. We'll also talk about the program directory structure that is required to support script execution.

Running the Script

The following fragment illustrates typical script execution:

```
>perl rankingfactors.pl 100 seo
Starting..
..cleanup done
..getting SERPs
..got the SERPs
..got the real titles
..finished partial title comparisons
..finished keyword title comparisons
..finished title page copy comparisons
..finished domain name exact keyword analysis
..finished domain name partial keyword analysis
..finished description META analysis
..finished header tags analysis
```

```
..finished keyword proximity analysis
..finished outbound links analysis
..finished outbound link PR analysis
..finished average page size analysis
..finished optimum number of words analysis
..finished website size analysis
```

In this example, we would be producing a report based on the keyword *seo*. We are also telling it to use the top 100 SERPs when doing the analysis. Note that you can choose between 10 and 100 top SERPs for analysis. Depending on your selection, script execution time will vary.

Program directory structure

Ensure that your file and directory structure is as follows:

```
\serptemp
\report
rankingfactors.pl
```

Final HTML Report

To see the final report, go to the *report* folder and open the *index.html* file. Your report should resemble Figure 4-15.

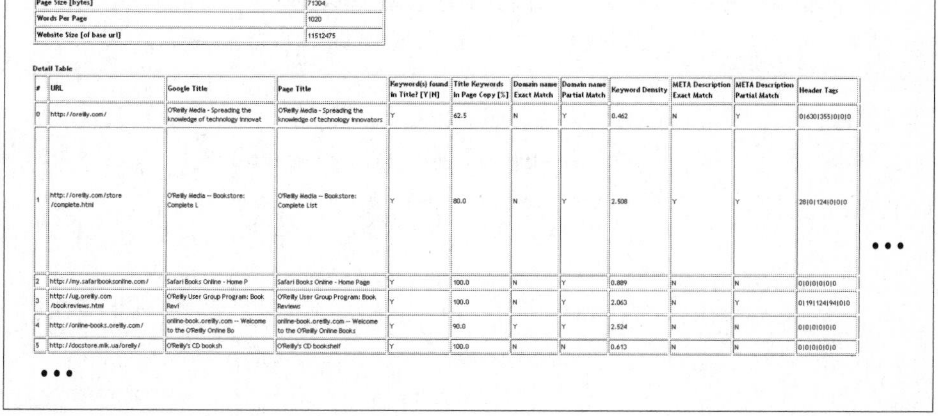

Figure 4-15. Internal ranking factors: Report summary screen

The final report contains two tables. The top table is a summary table showing several averages, including "% Title Match," "% Keyword Domain Exact Match," "% Keyword Domain Partial Match," "% Keyword Density," "Page Size [bytes]," "Words Per Page," and "Website Size [of base url]." Immediately below the summary table is the detail table. This table is rather large and usually requires horizontal and vertical scrolling.

Report metrics summary

Table 4-2 summarizes all of the key metrics shown in the final HTML report.

Table 4-2. Report metrics summary

Column	Description
#	Signifies the relative rank
[Google | Bing] Title	Shows the title found in a particular SERP
Page Title	Represents the actual HTML title found on the destination result
Keyword(s) Found in Title? [Y|N]	Signifies the existence of keyword(s) in the HTML `<title>` tag
Title Keywords in Page Copy [%]	Represents the percentage of `<title>` tag keywords found in the page copy
Domain Name Exact Match	Signifies the existence of *all* keywords in the domain name
Domain Name Partial Match	Means that some or all keywords are found in the domain name
Keyword Density	Represents the percentage of keywords in relation to all text on the page
META Description Exact Match	Signifies the existence of all keywords in the HTML `<meta>` description tag
META Description Partial Match	Signifies the existence of some or all keywords in the HTML `<meta>` description tag
Header Tags	Shows the usage of heading tags (from `<h1>` to `<h6>`)
Header Tag Keywords	Indicates the existence of keyword(s) in heading tags; related to the "Header Tags" column
Keyword Positions in Page	Shows the relative keyword position in a given HTML page
Keyword Prominence Map	Displays a link to the specific keyword map in each row
Outbound Links with Keywords	Displays a number of outbound links with keyword(s)
Outbound Link PRs	Shows the Google PageRank value for the root domain for each outbound link
Page Size [bytes]	Shows the given link page size in bytes
Words in Page	Displays the number of words found in a given page
Website Size	Shows the value found on Google for each of the resulting URLs
Page Age	Shows the page age if returned by the web host of the given URL

Summary

With so many variables used in search engine rankings, optimizing for the most important ranking factors is paramount. Nobody has time to optimize for everything.

This chapter covered internal ranking factors. Internal ranking factors are divided into two broad categories: on-page and on-site ranking factors.

On-page ranking factors are pertinent to each page. Many on-page ranking factors are related to keywords. This includes keywords in the title tags, the page URL, the `<meta>` description tags, and the HTML heading tags. Other on-page factors include the keyword proximity (and prominence), the link anchor keywords, the quality of outbound links, the page age, and the page size.

On-site ranking factors affect the entire site. These factors include the domain name keywords, the size or quantity of content, the linking architecture, and the page freshness.

We examined all of these factors in detail using a custom Perl script to help you in your SEO efforts.

## CHAPTER 5

External Ranking Factors

In Chapter 4 we covered internal ranking factors, which are elements over which you have absolute control, such as adding appropriate keywords on your pages and using a consistent linking site structure to ensure easy navigation. In this chapter we will cover external ranking factors, which are factors that do not depend entirely on you and, in some cases, in which you have no say at all.

When I talk about external ranking factors, I am talking about many different things, including the number of external inbound links, user behavior patterns, website performance, website age, and so forth.

There are many different external ranking factors. Each factor will be in its own context with its own set of rules. In cases where you can sway these factors in your favor, you want to take full advantage by being proactive.

I will reference several scripts in this chapter, including the *mymonitor.pl* script, which appears in its entirety in Appendix A. By the end of this chapter, you will have an overall picture of the most important external ranking factors.

External Links

External links are also known as backlinks, inbound links, and referral links. According to Wikipedia (*http://bit.ly/yhhEp*), backlinks are defined as follows:

> Backlinks (or back-links (UK)) are incoming links to a website or web page. In the search engine optimization (SEO) world, the number of backlinks is one indication of the popularity or importance of that website or page (though other measures, such as PageRank, are likely to be more important). Outside of SEO, the backlinks of a webpage may be of significant personal, cultural or semantic interest: they indicate who is paying attention to that page.

Know Your Referrers

As your website gains in popularity, managing external inbound links will become a necessity. It is important to know who is linking to your site, especially if you are in an industry where reputation is paramount. Although you can certainly create a rigorous "terms of service" page—accessible via a link in the page footer of all pages—not all webmasters will abide by these rules.

To see who is linking to your site, you can use Google's `link:` command:

```
link:yourdomain.com
```

The effectiveness of this command has decreased somewhat over the years as Google's algorithm has changed. Recently, Google added similar, albeit limited, functionality in its Webmaster Tools that allows website owners to see their website's backlinks. Although this can be very useful information, it does not say much about your competitors' backlinks.

Utilizing Yahoo! Site Explorer

To augment Google's `link:` command, you can utilize Yahoo!'s Site Explorer tool (*http://siteexplorer.search.yahoo.com/*), which can provide similar functionality. Although it is still possible to write a scraper script to pick up Yahoo!'s results, being able to get a clean text file may be more than sufficient for smaller sites.

With Yahoo! Site Explorer, you can export the first 1,000 backlinks to a file in Tab Separated Value (TSV) format just by clicking on the TSV link, as shown in Figure 5-1.

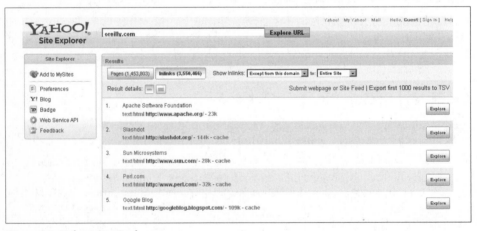

Figure 5-1. Yahoo! Site Explorer

After downloading the TSV file, you can parse the 1,000 links to see the link anchor text in each destination page. You can also sign up with Yahoo! to get its API to extract the same data.

Parsing the TSV file. Before you parse the TSV file, you need to understand its format. The following fragment shows the first four lines of the TSV file downloaded in Figure 5-1:

```
List of inlinks to the site oreilly.com
TITLE                        URL                      SIZE    FORMAT
Apache Software Foundation    http://www.apache.org/   22809   text/html
Slashdot                      http://slashdot.org/     144476  text/html
...
```

The preceding code contains four fields: `Title`, `URL`, `Size`, and `Format`. The one we are really interested in is the `URL` field. We can scrape each URL while recording the link anchor text. This is exactly what the *inlinksAnalysis.pl* Perl script does. Please refer to Appendix A for more details.

Running the script is straightforward:

```
perl inlinksAnalysis.pl oreilly.com_inlinks.txt oreilly.com
```

The first parameter represents the name of the file saved from Yahoo! Site Explorer, and the second parameter reflects the name of the domain we are analyzing. Running the script for the Oreilly.com domain produces a text report that, at the time of this writing, appears as follows:

```
http://radar.oreilly.com/, 260, "O'Reilly Radar"
http://www.oreilly.com/, 108, "O'Reilly Media"
http://www.oreilly.com, 105, "Oreilly Logo"
http://oreilly.com/, 103, "O'Reilly Media"
http://jobs.oreilly.com/, 69, "Jobs"
http://press.oreilly.com/, 68, "Press Room"
http://en.oreilly.com/webexny2008/public/content/home, 66, "Web 2.0 Expo"
http://toc.oreilly.com/, 66, "Tools of Change for Publishing"
http://academic.oreilly.com/, 66, "Academic Solutions"
http://oreilly.com/feeds/, 66, "RSS Feeds"
http://oreilly.com/contact.html, 66, "Contacts"
http://oreilly.com/terms/, 66, "Terms of Service"
http://oreilly.com/oreilly/author/intro.csp, 66, "Writing for O'Reilly"
http://digitalmedia.oreilly.com/, 65, "Digital Media"
http://ignite.oreilly.com/, 64, "Ignite"
. . .
```

The report is sorted in descending order and is truncated to the first 20 lines of output. The most popular URLs appear at the top of the report. In this example, *http://radar .oreilly.com* was the most popular link from the 1,000 referring URLs.

Companies such as O'Reilly Media can take full advantage of having so many highly popular websites. This is especially the case in promoting new products or services on new domains or subdomains, as O'Reilly is now in full control of providing self-serving external links to its new websites.

Links from highly popular sites such as Wikipedia.org, Oreilly.com, and NYTimes.com are an indication of trust from those sites to the sites receiving the vote. Search engines are increasingly relying heavily on trust, as evidenced by their search results' bias.

You can find backlinks in other ways as well. Google's `link:` command and Yahoo!'s Site Explorer are just two quick ways.

Quantity and Quality of External Links

Having more external inbound links is something to be desired. If these links can be quality links with a lot of link juice, that's even better. For best results, try to acquire inbound links from sites or pages with high PageRank values. As a rule of thumb, backlinks with a minimum PageRank value of 4 yield the best results.

As long as those links are not from link farms or other link schemes, you should be in good shape. The more backlinks you acquire from high-PageRank sites, the better.

Backlinks say a lot about a website's popularity. You can think of backlinks as votes for your link or URL. This is what search engines consider in their rankings as well. The benefit is multifold, as you will be receiving traffic from your backlinks as well as from the search engines.

Speed of backlink accumulation

How fast are you accumulating backlinks? This can become a negative ranking factor if your site is found to be using an unethical linking scheme.

If all your backlinks are using the same anchor text, search engines may view this as suspicious activity, which might trigger a manual inspection by the search engines and a delisting of your site. Let's say your site had 20 backlinks yesterday, and today you suddenly have more than 100,000. Wouldn't that look suspicious?

Topical link relevance

It is important for backlinks to contain relevant anchor text. Here are some examples of good and bad anchor text:

```
<!--Good-->
<a target=_new href="http://yoursite.com/basketball>Learn about
Basketball</a>
<a target=_new href="http://yoursite.com/basketball>Talk about
Basketball at www.yoursite.com</a>

<--Bad-->
<a target=_new href="http://yoursite.com/basketball">Click Here</a>
<a target=_new href="http://yoursite.com/basketball">
http://yoursite.com</a>
<a target=_new href="http://yoursite.com/basketball">more..</a>
<a href="http://yoursite.com/basketball"><img
src="http://www.somesite.net/pic1.jpg"></a>
```

The good examples use relevant text in the links. The bad examples, although they use the same destination URL, do not use relevant text. Ideally, the referring sites should also be talking about the same subject matter. At the very least, the referring page should be on the same topic.

Backlinks from expert sites and the Hilltop Algorithm

For good or bad, search engines have given certain websites a biased advantage over all other sites for most of the popular keywords. The basis of this practice stems from a popular ranking algorithm developed at the University of Toronto, called the Hilltop Algorithm.

The creators of the Hilltop Algorithm define it as follows (*http://ftp.cs.toronto.edu/pub/ reports/csrg/405/hilltop.html*):

> ...a novel ranking scheme for broad queries that places the most authoritative pages on the query topic at the top of the ranking. Our algorithm operates on a special index of "expert documents." These are a subset of the pages on the WWW identified as directories of links to non-affiliated sources on specific topics. Results are ranked based on the match between the query and relevant descriptive text for hyperlinks on expert pages pointing to a given result page.

At the time of this writing, in a search for the keyword *hilltop algorithm*, Google's search results look like Figure 5-2.

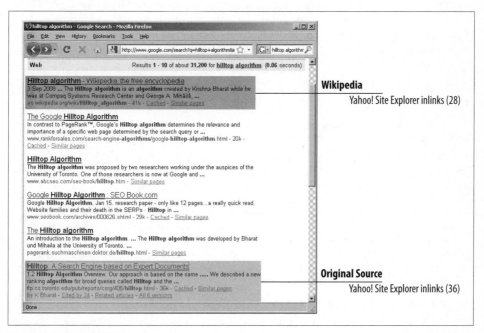

Figure 5-2. Biased SERP

In this example, the Wikipedia search result came in ahead on Google, as it did on Yahoo! and Bing. Now, if we open the Wikipedia result, we don't really see much except for the definition. So a single-paragraph page with a ton of useless Wikipedia links gets a PageRank value of 5 and the first spot on Google. Meanwhile, all other search results on the first page contain much more information on the given keywords.

Google at least showed one page from the University of Toronto in its top 10 results—unlike Yahoo! and Bing. This is because the Wikipedia page contains the exact same link from the University of Toronto!

This should speak volumes about the importance of backlinks from expert sites. The pattern of Wikipedia importance is repeated countless times, so get a link on Wikipedia if you can!

Backlinks from .edu and .gov domains

When Matt Cutts (Google search quality engineer) was asked about the extra ranking boost from inbound links originating from *.edu* and *.gov* TLDs, he responded as follows (*http://bit.ly/Oh9aA*):

> This is a common misconception—you don't get any PageRank boost from having an .edu link or .gov link automatically.

Although Google denies that *.edu* and *.gov* links get a PageRank boost, you can easily construe that the domain extension does matter in some sense. When Google flat out denies something, it is almost always because it is not true. But when Google is cagey about something, you need to beware. Most people believe that *.edu* and *.gov* links are more valuable than others because those sites typically have strong PageRank and therefore more link juice. It is doubtful that Google actually gives these sites greater weight simply because of the TLD extension. When your site has a link from an *.edu* or *.gov* link, it says a great deal about the site's trust and authority.

It is very hard to get an *.edu* or *.gov* domain. Only one registrar today has permission to grant *.edu* domains: EDUCAUSE, a nonprofit organization that won the right to be the sole registrar of all *.edu* domains in 2001. Not everyone can get an *.edu* domain, and *.edu* domains are not transferable. Eligibility requirements are very strict (*http://net.educause.edu/edudomain/*):

> Eligibility for a .edu domain name is limited to U.S. postsecondary institutions that are institutionally accredited, i.e., the entire institution and not just particular programs, by agencies on the U.S. Department of Education's list of Nationally Recognized Accrediting Agencies. These include both "Regional Institutional Accrediting Agencies" and "National Institutional and Specialized Accrediting Bodies" recognized by the U.S. Department of Education.

The situation is similar for *.gov* TLDs; these domains can be registered only at *http://www.dotgov.gov* (see *http://bit.ly/1givpb*):

> To maintain domain name integrity, eligibility is limited to qualified government organizations and programs. Having a managed domain name such as .gov assures your customers that they are accessing an official government site.

Attaining links from TLDs such as *.edu* and *.gov* is valuable provided that the referring page is on the same topic as the recipient page. Historically, very little spam has originated from these domains. The added value of these links is that they tend to change very little over time, and age is an important off-page ranking factor, as we'll discuss later in this chapter.

In some countries, there are strict regulations in terms of domain name assignments for ccTLDs. Country-specific TLDs, especially expansive TLDs, are believed to carry more clout, as spammy sites are usually those of cheap TLDs such as *.com* or *.info*.

Other places where domain extensions matter are in localized searches. The benefit of country-specific TLDs can also be augmented by ensuring that web servers hosting the domain are using IPs from the same region. If the question is whether to pursue getting some inbound links from these foreign TLDs, the answer is almost always yes.

Backlinks from directories

Traditionally, specialized web directories carried more authority than regular sites. Google and others have relied on directories not just in terms of ranking factors, but also in using directory descriptions as their own descriptions in search results. Directories are considered similar to other "expert" sites such as Wikipedia.

Be careful which directory you choose to use for your site, as not all are created equal. Check the PageRank of each directory to determine whether it is worth having your listing there. The higher the PageRank is, the better. Also ensure that these directories are passing link juice.

Age of backlinks

The age of the backlinks conveys a message of trust, and therefore a perceived link quality. A new backlink on a page that is constantly changing is not as beneficial as an old backlink on the same page.

In some cases, new backlinks exhibit a state of "purgatory" before they attain trust. In other words, the real benefit of new backlinks takes time to propagate. You have to start somewhere, so build your links for their future benefits.

Relative page position

Backlinks found closer to the top of an HTML page are perceived as being more important than those found farther down the page.

This makes sense from a website usability perspective as well. Links found on long scrolling pages are much more likely to do better if they are found at the top of the page.

Be careful with this, though. With some simple CSS, links rendered at the top of a page in a typical web browser can easily be placed at the bottom of the actual (physical) HTML file.

Spilling PageRank effect

Your backlinks may not be the only backlinks on a particular referring site. The greater the number of other links found on the same page, the less of a benefit you will incur. The incoming PageRank is split among all other outbound links found on that page.

Relative popularity among peer sites

If your site is one of many on the same subject, its relative popularity among all the other peer sites comes into play. Even if you feel your content or product is better than your competition, your rankings may be suffering due to a lack of relative popularity.

Broken Outbound Links

Although site updates and migrations are part of your website life cycle, broken links can be a significant cause of lost visitors, especially if your site is not being updated on a regular basis. How you handle broken links, or 404 errors, is important both from the human visitor's perspective and from the web spider's perspective.

In this section, we will focus on outbound links. We view broken links as an external factor because some or all of the broken links on a page worked at some point.

Broken links can say a lot about someone's website. Many broken links on a site could be interpreted in the wrong way. Search engines could perceive the website as having been abandoned, and will remove it from their indexes. Two scenarios can cause broken links: old link references and invalid link references.

Old link references occur when sites linking to your site have not updated their links. This can happen if you decide to change your website's pages without informing your referral sites. This will, of course, produce 404 errors to anyone clicking on these referral links. This situation will look bad on your website and on the referrer sites, since they have not updated their links.

Erroneous link references refer to sloppy coding, such as when your links are pointing to misspelled documents which do not exist. For all intents and purposes, pages resulting in server errors can also be interpreted as broken links as they are not the intended result.

Handling Broken Links

There really is no excuse for having broken links on your website. Many tools are available for checking your site for broken links. One such tool, *linkchecker.pl*, is available in Appendix A.

Running linkchecker.pl

You can run *linkchecker.pl* with the following code:

```
> perl linkchecker.pl http://www.somedomain.com > somedomain.csv
```

Depending on the size of the site, it can take anywhere from a few seconds to several hours to check the site for broken links. If you have a really large site, you may want to partition this activity into several smaller checks. After the script is finished, you can open the report file in Excel. Figure 5-3 shows sample output.

Level	Parent Page or Location	Unique URL	Link Type	Title	Status Codes
1	http://www.seowarrior.net	http://www.seowarrior.net/	relative	Home	200
1	http://www.seowarrior.net	http://www.seowarrior.net/contact/	relative	Contact	200
1	http://www.seowarrior.net	http://www.seowarrior.net/sitemap/	relative	Sitemap	200
1	http://www.seowarrior.net	http://www.seowarrior.net/archive/	absolute internal	Archive	200
1	http://www.seowarrior.net	http://www.seowarrior.net/register/	absolute internal	Register	200
1	http://www.seowarrior.net	http://www.seowarrior.net/search-engine/internet-search-engines-an	absolute internal	Internet Search Engines and the Privacy of their Users	200
1	http://www.seowarrior.net	http://www.seowarrior.net/search-engine/how-the-search-engine-is-e	absolute internal	How the Search Engine Is Embraced By the Pop Culture	200
1	http://www.seowarrior.net	http://www.seowarrior.net/ppc/google-adwords-how-they-work-and-h	absolute internal	Google Adwords: How They Work and How Do You Use The	200
1	http://www.seowarrior.net	http://www.seowarrior.net/search-engine/a-general-look-at-using-inte	absolute internal	A General Look at Using Internet Search Engines	200
1	http://www.seowarrior.net	http://www.seowarrior.net/search-engine/protecting-children-from-un	absolute internal	Protecting Children from Undesired Search Engine Results	200
1	http://www.seowarrior.net	http://www.seowarrior.net/login/	absolute internal	Login	200
1	http://www.seowarrior.net	http://www.seowarrior.net/pagerank/understanding-pagerank/	absolute internal	Understanding PageRank	200
1	http://www.seowarrior.net	http://www.seowarrior.net/seo-tips/adding-urls-to-search-engines-is-	absolute internal	Adding URLs to Search Engines Is Not Necessary	200
1	http://www.seowarrior.net	http://www.seowarrior.net/seo-tips/quick-tips-on-search-engine-optir	absolute internal	Quick Tips on Search Engine Optimization	200
1	http://www.seowarrior.net	http://www.seowarrior.net/seo-tips/internet-search-engine-page-subr	absolute internal	Internet Search Engine Page Submissions	200

Figure 5-3. Link checker report

The spreadsheet in Figure 5-3 shows the following columns:

- "Level" (represents a depth from 1 to 4)
- "Parent Page or Location" (represents the parent HTML page)
- "Unique URL" (URL not found on parent levels)
- "Link Type" (can be inbound, outbound, absolute, or relative)
- "Title" (text used in the title tag)
- "Status Codes" (HTTP status codes)

Simply inspect the spreadsheet for 404 status codes to find your broken links, whether they happen to be internal or external. You may also want to inspect 500 status codes, as they indicate server errors.

User Behavior Patterns

Once they are perfected, user behavior patterns may be the greatest ranking method for all of the major search engines. Google is clearly the front-runner in this arena, as it has already unleashed a powerful array of tools for formulating, disseminating, and analyzing user patterns.

Although user behavior patterns can be a great help to search engines, they do come at a price: privacy. Everything you do can be used by search engines in user behavior analysis. For instance, Google is pushing the envelope to such an extent that it claims it can provide personalized search results.

In the opinion of some, personalized results can never truly be provided, as too many unknown variables are at stake. Theoretically speaking, for personalized search to really function, Google or others would have to store a separate, unique searchable index for every single person using their service. That's about 8 billion indexes. Even Google cannot handle this sort of storage.

But there is another side to this argument: Google does not need everyone to use Google Analytics, Webmaster Central, and the Google Toolbar to get a fairly accurate assessment of a particular website or of the search patterns of the masses.

Analyzing the Search Engine Query Interface

In this section, we will take on the role of a search engine and examine what we can learn about behavior patterns.

First point of contact: the search form

We can learn a lot about a visitor as soon as he arrives on our home page. First, we know his IP address. Using his IP address we can pinpoint his geographic location. Based on his geographic location, we can create a customized index based on the patterns of previous visitors from the same geographic location.

We can also record cases in which another link referred the visitor to our home page. Depending on his Internet service provider and his assigned IP range, we can be so precise that we can pinpoint his city or town location!

In addition to IP and referrer values, we can also learn a great deal of additional information, including browser version, associated (installed) browser software, operating system version, current screen resolution, whether the visitor's browser cookies are enabled, the speed of his Internet connection, and more. That's a lot of information already, and the visitor has not even clicked on the Search button!

Interactions with SERPs

Once the visitor clicks on the Search button, things start to get more interesting. First, the visitor is telling the search engine what he is looking for. The search engine responds with a results page based on the current index for the specific region the visitor is coming from. Between the time that the results page shows up and the time the visitor clicks on a specific search result, many things can be recorded, including:

- The time it took to click on the first result (not necessarily the first SERP result)
- The time it took to click on other results (if any)
- Whether the visitor clicked on subsequent SERPs
- Which result in the SERPs the visitor clicked on first, second, and so on
- The time between clicks on several results
- The CTR for a specific result

As you can see, we can learn many things from a single visitor. But the picture becomes much clearer when we combine these stats with those from thousands or even millions of other visitors. With more data available, it becomes easier to spot patterns. Just using a small sample of visitor data is often enough to approximate which links are popular and which are not so useful.

For example, say that for a particular keyword, most visitors clicked on the third result, immediately followed by the sixth result. This could indicate that the third result did not contain good or sufficient information for this keyword, as visitors kept coming back to inspect the sixth result. It could also say that other results shown on the SERPs were not enticing enough for visitors to click on.

As another example, say that visitors clicked on the first result and then came back 10 minutes later to click on the fourth result. This could signify that visitors liked the information in the first result but chose to research further by clicking on the fourth result.

Now let's consider CTR, which is the number of times a specific result is clicked on in relation to the total number of times it is shown. A high CTR is something all webmasters want for their URLs. A low CTR could signal to search engines that the result is not interesting or relevant.

Search engines can also gather information on multiple search queries, especially if they were all performed through the same browser window in the same session. These sorts of search queries can indicate keyword correlation. Although such information is already empowering search engines, it is not perfect. There are ways to make it better or more accurate.

Google Analytics

With the pretext of aiding webmasters, Google can now collect data from websites just like web server logs can. Although the Analytics platform certainly provides many helpful tools, some webmasters choose to stay away from it due to data privacy concerns.

Anytime a Google Analytics tracking code is inserted into a page of a website, Google records who is visiting the site. With this sort of information, Google Analytics *could* be used to do all sorts of things, including being used as a critical part of the overall Google ranking algorithm. Only Google knows whether this *does* occur.

It is also easy to see why every search engine would want to know these sorts of stats. We will discuss the Google Analytics platform in more detail in Chapter 7. Alternatives to Google Analytics include Webtrends Analytics (*http://www.webtrends.com*) and SiteCatalyst (*http://www.omniture.com*).

Google Toolbar

Microsoft's CEO, Steve Ballmer, was recently quoted as saying the following (*http://bit .ly/1a0HQU*):

> Why is that (Google) toolbar there? Do you think it is there to help you? No. It is there to report data about everything you do on your PC.

Google has acknowledged that when the advanced toolbar features are turned on, every visit to every page is sent to Google, which then sends the PageRank value back to the toolbar.

This sort of information can have profound benefits for Google. First, it can help Google learn various user patterns. In addition, it can help Google learn about so-called personalized searches. Finally, Internet Explorer preinstalled with the Google Toolbar can help improve Google's ranking algorithms.

It's easy to verify that the Google Toolbar does send statistics to Google. The following is sample output from the Windows `netstat` command when browsing a typical site:

```
Proto  Local Address        Foreign Address            State
TCP    seowarrior:2071      gw-in-f100.google.com:http  ESTABLISHED
TCP    seowarrior:2072      qb-in-f104.google.com:http  ESTABLISHED
TCP    seowarrior:2073      qb-in-f147.google.com:http  ESTABLISHED
TCP    seowarrior:2074      qb-in-f100.google.com:http  ESTABLISHED
TCP    seowarrior:4916      qb-in-f104.google.com:http  CLOSE_WAIT
```

Examining the TCP packets when browsing *http://www.google.com* in Internet Explorer reveals the following information:

```
//Request to Google
GET /search?client=navclient-auto&iqrn=ql7B&orig=OBKqM&ie=UTF-8&
oe=UTF-8&features=Rank:&q=info:http%3a%2f%2fwww.google.com%2f&
googleip=O;72.14.205.103;78&ch=78804486762 HTTP/1.1
User-Agent: Mozilla/4.0 (compatible; GoogleToolbar 5.0.2124.4372;
Windows XP 5.1; MSIE 7.0.5730.13)
Host: toolbarqueries.google.com
Connection: Keep-Alive
Cache-Control: no-cache
Cookie: PREF=ID=54ac8de29fa2745f:TB=5:LD=en:CR=2:TM=1234724889:
LM=1234753499:S=AgFeyxE1VD2Rr5iO;
NID=20=GoJF_PXD5UZ_I5wdy6Lz4kMcwo9DsywL5Y4rrrE46cNTWpvVdt7ePFkHNe2t
5qIG8CPJrZfkqOdvKvGgVC1rOOrnOWhtNhe8PR7YpKjMQonnuAtYrIvEbSl-gPgqBSFw

//First Google Response
HTTP/1.1 200 OK
Cache-Control: private, max-age=0
Date: Tue, 24 Feb 2009 08:38:19 GMT
Expires: -1
Content-Type: text/html; charset=UTF-8
Server: gws
Transfer-Encoding: chunked
```

```
//Second Google Response
c
Rank_1:2:10
0
```

The Google Toolbar initiates the request to *toolbarqueries.google.com*, which then sends a couple of packet replies. The first one simply sends the HTTP header information, and the second one contains the PageRank part that is consumed by the Google Toolbar.

In this case, the last three lines are part of a separate TCP packet, which is Google's response indicating the PageRank value of 10 for *http://www.google.com*; and so on for any other links you enter in your web browser running the Google Toolbar.

User Behavior Lessons

It is inevitable that search engines will continue to evolve. User behavior patterns are becoming a powerful ally to search engines. With these advances, the importance of relevant content increases exponentially.

Without relevant content, it is too easy for search engines to weed out unpopular or useless sites. If they cannot do this algorithmically, they can certainly fill the void with more precise user behavior data obtained from their external tools and platforms.

Website Performance and Website Age

We will close this chapter with a discussion of two other important external ranking factors: website performance and website age.

Website Performance

There is an unwritten law on the Internet that states that every page must load within the first four seconds; otherwise, people will start to get impatient and leave before the page loads. You must take this into consideration. It is important not only from a usability perspective, but also from the sense that web spiders will learn of your website performance.

Monitoring website performance

If you are on a dedicated server, you may already have access to website monitoring tools and insight into your website performance. If your website is on a shared host, chances are that all the websites sharing that host are competing for a slice of the available CPU pie.

Every serious website owner needs to proactively monitor his website's performance, as poor performance can have adverse web crawling and indexing effects. You can monitor a website with a relatively simple Perl script. One such script is *mymonitor.pl*, which you can find in Appendix A. Running the script is as simple as:

```
perl mymonitor.pl http://www.somedomain.net/somelink.html
```

The script records the elapsed time it takes to download the supplied URL while writing to several text files. Each line of these text files is formatted in the following way:

```
mm-dd-yyyy hh:mm:ss;10;15;20;[actual elapsed time]
```

Example text file content looks like this:

```
12-6-2009 6:0:4;10;15;20;3.25447
12-6-2009 6:5:3;10;15;20;1.654549
12-6-2009 6:10:2;10;15;20;1.765499
12-6-2009 6:15:9;10;15;20;8.2816
```

Numbers 10, 15, and 20 represent markers in seconds for easier viewing on a chart. Several free graphics packages are available on the market. Plotting our data with amCharts' (*http://amcharts.com/*) charting Flash demo version software yields a graph similar to Figure 5-4.

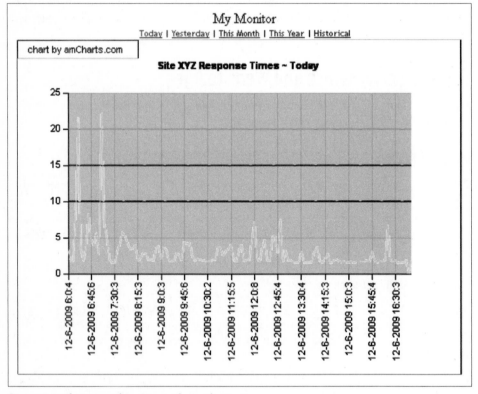

Figure 5-4. Plotting performance with amCharts.com

Figure 5-4 illustrates degraded performance from about 6:00 a.m. to 7:30 a.m. Knowing such information is valuable, as it can provide clues for further analysis. The last thing left to do is to automate the process of running the script. If you are on a Linux system, you can simply set up a crontab job. To run the script every five minutes, you could set up your crontab as follows:

```
#Run test every 5 minutes

*/5 6-22 * * * perl mymonitor.pl http://www.domain.net/link1.html
```

The preceding crontab entry would run every five minutes between 7:00 a.m. and 11:00 p.m. every day. This is only one link, and nobody is preventing you from setting up several links to track. Also note that you could use the Windows Task Scheduler to set up the script-running schedule.

Website Age

New websites tend to exhibit more ranking fluctuations than their older counterparts. The *Google Dance* refers to the index update of the Google search engine. It can affect any domain at any time. Today, Google index updates occur more frequently than they have in the past. It is relatively easy to check website age by simply using online Whois tools.

Domain registration years

A longer registration period suggests a serious domain owner, whereas short registrations such as single-year registrations could be interpreted as suspicious. This is of no surprise, as most search engine spam tends to come from short-lived domains.

Expired domains

Google recently confirmed that expired domains, when renewed, are essentially treated as new domains. In other words, if an expired domain had a high PageRank, that PageRank will be wasted if the domain is allowed to expire before someone else buys it.

Plan for long-term benefits

Domains that have existed for a long time carry an age trust factor. New pages added to these domains tend to get higher rankings more quickly. As we discussed, older domains convey authority and are given much more leeway than newer ones. If your domain is new and relevant, focus on the daily activities of your business while building compelling and relevant content—and plan for the long term.

Summary

In this chapter, we covered the most important external ranking factors. Be proactive and check your outbound links. Beware of user patterns becoming increasingly prevalent as key ranking factors. Create enticing content and stay away from spammy shortcuts. And always make sure you check your website performance regularly.

## CHAPTER 6

Web Stats Monitoring

Analyzing your website stats is at the core of your SEO work. Although Google Analytics, which we will cover in Chapter 7, may be an appealing choice for online marketers, it is based on JavaScript, which means that only web pages are tracked when using the out-of-the-box configuration. Any clients with disabled JavaScript will also be missed, as will any pages with the missing Google Analytics code.

As such, more often than not marketing departments will need to ask their IT folks to produce web stats reports based on web server logs because they cannot get the information they need from Google Analytics.

This chapter opens with a discussion of web server logs, with a focus on the NCSA log formats. Next, we'll turn our attention to three popular web stats tools: the relatively inexpensive WebLog Expert, as well as two free tools, AWStats and Webalizer.

Web Server Logs and Formats

Each time visitors come to your website, the web server hosting your files records this activity. A *web hit* is a single file request from your website. Typically, when you browse to a web page, chances are you will see text, graphics, animations, and/or videos as part of the page.

It is likely that most of the nontext elements are stored in separate files. Although all you did was type a single URL, the web browser has placed multiple requests to create or render the page. In doing so, it has effectively created multiple web hits on your behalf.

Each website hit is recorded on its own line within a logfile. So, if you have 1 million hits for a particular day, your logfile will be 1 million lines long. Along with your regular visitors, you will also have visits by search engine spiders, including those operated by Google, Microsoft, and Yahoo!. The more popular your website is, the bigger your web server logfiles will be.

If you are hosting your website on a shared hosting provider, some sort of web stats or analytics tool is usually included in your hosting package. If you are hosting your website on a dedicated server, chances are you are in a managed or comanaged hosting contract. Usually these sorts of arrangements provide for some sort of website monitoring service.

In any case, you have plenty of options in terms of available software. This chapter discusses two of the most popular web stats packages commonly available through most of the current shared hosting providers. We will also look at one commercial offering.

Granted, web server logfiles are not meant to be read by people, and they are quite "ugly" to look at. Logfiles provide raw data, specifically formatted to be processed by various web stats programs. They are all helpful in spotting web user and web spider usage patterns.

Generally speaking, web server log formats can be configured on each web server platform to record more or less information in relation to each web hit. NCSA is one of the most popular formats, as it is used by the Apache web server and most of the shared hosting providers. It comes in several formats, including NCSA Common and NCSA Combined.

NCSA Common Format

The NCSA Common logfile format is a text-based format that is ASCII standards compliant. It is employed in web servers as well as in FTP, SMTP, and NNTP servers. The NCSA Common log format is the simplest and is defined as follows:

    [hostip] [rfc931] [username] [date:time] [request] [code] [bytesize]

Table 6-1 shows a parameter summary of the NCSA Common logfile format.

Table 6-1. NCSA Common format

Parameter	Details
hostip	Numerical IP address of the requesting host/computer
rfc931	ID used to identify the client initiating the request; - is used if none is specified
username	Username used by the client to communicate; - is used if none is specified
date:time	Date string [dd/Mmm/yyyy:hh:mm:ss +-hhmm] in GMT
request	Request string containing HTTP method, request, and protocol version
code	HTTP status code indicating various scenarios including success, failure, redirect, moved permanently, etc.
bytesize	Total size of the HTTP transfer in bytes

The following code fragment shows example logfile entries:

```
99.23.161.18 - johndoe [10/Oct/2008:21:15:05 +0600]
"GET /index.cgi HTTP/1.0" 200 588
99.23.161.18 - johndoe [10/Oct/2008:21:15:05 +0600]
"GET /style.css HTTP/1.0" 200 5382
99.23.161.18 - johndoe [10/Oct/2008:21:15:06 +0600]
"GET /mainscript.js HTTP/1.0" 200 7245
99.23.161.18 - johndoe [10/Oct/2008:21:15:06 +0600]
"GET / HTTP/1.0" 200 5382
99.23.161.18 - johndoe [10/Oct/2008:21:15:07 +0600]
"GET /games.jpg HTTP/1.0" 200 15022
```

Obviously, none of this is memorable, and to the average eye it is nonsensical. Not to worry; you will almost always want to process this with a web stats program.

NCSA Combined Format

The NCSA Combined format is a more useful format, as it records more information. It is defined as follows:

```
[hostip] [remote] [username] [date:time] [request] [code] [bytesize]
[referrer] [useragent] [cookies]
```

There are three extra fields in the NCSA Combined format, as shown in Table 6-2.

Table 6-2. Additional fields in NCSA Combined format

Parameter	Detail
referrer	URL that pointed to this web page (element)
useragent	A string representing the name of the client (Firefox, Internet Explorer, Chrome, Googlebot, etc.) used to request this page (element)
cookies	A string representation of name/value pairs of clients' cookies

Although the referrer and useragent fields are optional, there is no reason not to use these fields in your website's server logfiles. Example logfile entries would look similar to the following web log fragment:

```
99.23.161.18  - johndoe [10/Oct/2008:21:15:07 +0600]  "GET /index.html
HTTP/1.0" 200 2225 "http://www.somesite.com" "Mozilla/4.0 (compatible;
MSIE 7.0; Windows NT 5.1; .NET CLR 1.0.3705; .NET CLR 1.1.4322; Media
Center PC 4.0; .NET CLR 2.0.50727; .NET CLR 3.0.04506.30)"
"prefcolor=blue;prefsong=28"
```

Without going into great detail, it is worth mentioning that there is a third NCSA format: NCSA Separate. The basic idea is that the NCSA Separate log format uses three separate logfiles, comprising access logfiles, referral logfiles, and agent logfiles.

In addition to these NCSA log formats, the IIS web server and others use additional log formats. These include W3C, WAS, and custom log formats. For more information on these formats, consult your specific platform documentation.

NCSA Combined Format in Apache

The default Apache installs may generate three logfiles, namely the Access Log, Agent Log, and Referrer Log. The most popular of the formats is NCSA Combined. Setting up NCSA Combined logging is relatively straightforward in the Apache web server. In your Apache *http.conf* file, make sure to enable or add these two lines:

```
LogFormat "%h %l %u %t \"%r\" %>s %b \"%{Referer}i\" \"%{User-Agent}i\"
 \"%{cookie}i\"" combined
CustomLog /logs/access_log combined
```

If there are other definitions of `LogFormat`, you may want to disable them.

Converting IIS W3C to NCSA Combined

If you are running your site on IIS and you need to convert your log format to NCSA Combined, it is best to use W3C logging in IIS and then use a converter tool to get the NCSA Combined equivalent. One such tool is the Rebex Internet Log Converter (rconvlog), which you can find at *http://www.rebex.net/rconvlog/default.aspx*.

You may also achieve the same thing by writing a custom converter script. One such approach is discussed in detail at *http://bit.ly/vrPZk*. This may not be necessary, as most of the newer web stats tools support the W3C log format and many others.

Spotting a Web Spider in Web Logs

How do you know when a web spider has crawled your website? All web spiders, including Google's Googlebot, leave plenty of information behind so that you know they were there and, more importantly, what they crawled. Here are some typical web spider trails in web server logs:

```
74.6.22.170 - - [31/Oct/2008:03:23:36 -0600] "GET
/robots.txt HTTP/1.0" 200 680 "-" "Mozilla/5.0 (compatible; Yahoo!
Slurp; http://help.yahoo.com/help/us/ysearch/slurp)"

66.249.73.47 - - [31/Oct/2008:04:46:15 -0600] "GET /robots.txt
HTTP/1.1" 200 718 "-" "Googlebot-Image/1.0"

66.249.73.47 - - [31/Oct/2008:08:48:49 -0600] "GET
/modules/myalbum/photo.php?lid=28&cid=3 HTTP/1.1" 200 6562 "-"
"Mozilla/5.0 (compatible; Googlebot/2.1;
+http://www.google.com/bot.html)"
```

In the preceding log fragment, you can see three frequent web spider signatures. The first one is that of the Yahoo! web spider, Slurp. The second and third signatures are those of the Google image spider (Googlebot-Image) and the main Google crawler (Googlebot).

There are many different spiders, not just those from Google and Yahoo!. Web spiders, just like regular web users, do leave trails in web server logs. OK, you've had enough of cryptic logfiles; it is time to examine the tools that process these logfiles.

Popular Web Stats Tools

Many different free and paid web stats tools are available. Table 6-3 shows some of the best known web stats tools, along with their pros and cons.

Table 6-3. Popular web stats tools

Tool	Pros	Cons
Webtrends (*http://www.webtrends.com*) Price: $10,000+	• Powerful analytics package • Offers everything other tools offer, and more	• Expensive • Difficult for novice users
Analog (*http://www.analog.cx*) Price: Free	• Solid offering • Popular	• Everything shown on a single HTML file
WebLog Expert (*http://www.weblogexpert.com*) Price: $74.95–$124.95	• Elegant interface and graphics • Different report styles (*.html*, *.pdf*, etc.) • Relatively inexpensive	• Does not have features of high-end tools
AWStats (*http://awstats.sourceforge.net*) Price: Free	• Professional-looking interface • Popular • Written in Perl	• Could have some additional graphs found in paid tools
Webalizer (*http://www.webalizer.com*) Price: Free	• Fast, written in C • Simple interface • Straight-to-the-point approach	• Takes some time to get used to stacked metric diagrams • Could have some additional graphs found in AWStats

Webalizer and AWStats are readily available on a plethora of shared hosting providers, whereas WebLog Expert is the notable inexpensive alternative to Webtrends and other commercial offerings.

You can use any web stats package as long as it can give you the information you need to do your SEO. At a minimum, you need to be able to get the following types of metrics to have a good picture of how your website is doing:

- Number of visitors
- Unique visitors
- Number of hits
- Number of page views

- Referrers
- Search engine hits
- Searches/keywords
- Spider hits

It should be easy to apply the information I'll provide in this chapter to any web stats package you use. The principles are much the same.

Using WebLog Expert

The following subsections discuss some of the most important web stats metrics, with example screenshots taken from the WebLog Export application. I use the terms *metric* and *statistic* interchangeably, as I am referring to the same thing. Note that I will present equivalent information and graphs in AWStats and Webalizer later in this chapter.

Number of Visitors

This statistic shows the total number of visitors you have for a given day. Figure 6-1 shows a sample graph.

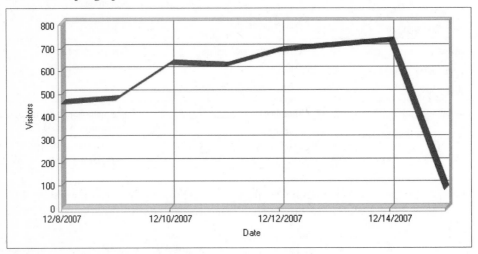

Figure 6-1. Web statistics: Daily visitors

These visitor numbers are the sum total of all visitors, including web spiders.

Unique Versus Total Visitors

There is a big difference between the total number of visitors and the unique visitors to a site. The "total visitors" metric does not discriminate against multiple visits by the same visitor. The "unique visitors" metric, on the other hand, tries to calculate exactly what it implies: unique visitors. Most web stats packages calculate this by calculating the total number of unique IPs. If you are not familiar with IP addresses, you can think of them as the unique address of every computer on the Internet.

Although the "unique visitors" metric is useful, it is not entirely accurate. Large organizations or even home and small office networks share the same IP address most of the time. In other words, if an organization has 1,000 people all hitting the same website, the web stats will show this as only a single unique visitor.

Number of Hits

This statistic shows the total number of hits you received in a given day. Figure 6-2 shows a sample graph. Depending on the design of your website, this number could be quite misleading. If your web pages contain a lot of images and other nontext elements, this number would not mean much.

If your website is mostly textual, however, the number would have a better meaning. Try not to take your web stats at face value. Think of what these metrics could mean in relation to your website.

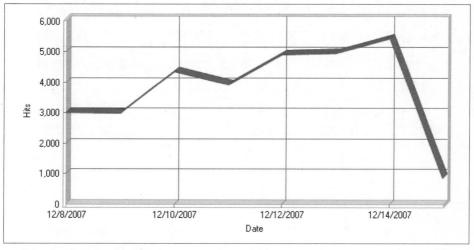

Figure 6-2. Web statistics: Daily hits

Number of Page Views

The number of page views represents the number of times a particular HTML file was viewed. A single page can consist of multiple externally loaded parts, including images, JavaScript code, stylesheets, and so forth. This metric ignores all of these parts, as it counts only the actual HTML page hits. Figure 6-3 shows a Summary table that WebLog Expert generates to give you an idea of the total number of page views per day.

When I talk about HTML pages, I also mean ASP, PHP, CGI, ColdFusion, JSP, and other formats.

If your website is using Ajax or a similar technology to load multiple HTML fragments seemingly into a single page, the daily page views number will be skewed. Understanding your Ajax-based website will allow you to make some approximations if necessary.

Summary	
Hits	
Total Hits	30,474
Average Hits per Day	3,809
Average Hits per Visitor	6.93
Cached Requests	3,979
Failed Requests	233
Page Views	
Total Page Views	5,296
Average Page Views per Day	662
Average Page Views per Visitor	1.20
Visitors	
Total Visitors	4,396
Average Visitors per Day	549
Total Unique IPs	3,038
Bandwidth	
Total Bandwidth	567.48 MB
Average Bandwidth per Day	70.94 MB
Average Bandwidth per Hit	19.07 KB
Average Bandwidth per Visitor	132.19 KB

Figure 6-3. Web statistics: Page views

Referrers

This statistic shows which websites are "referring" to yours, via a link to one of your pages. A link from a popular website can generate tons of traffic. Figure 6-4 shows a sample graph taken from WebLog Expert.

An increased number of unique referrers usually means your website is gaining in popularity. This is desirable, as now you are getting not only search engine referrals, but also referrals from different websites. This can also happen when you open a new search engine marketing channel (such as Google content ads), and does not necessarily mean increased organic link exposure.

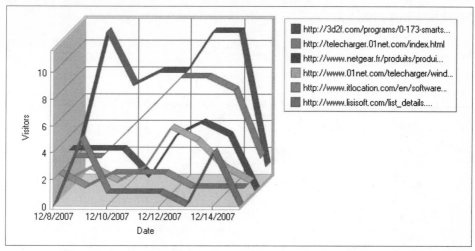

Figure 6-4. Web statistics: Daily referring sites

Search Engine (Referral) Hits

The website shown in Figure 6-5 is getting hits from Google, but hardly any from other search engines. This could be an indication that your site is optimized only for Google. This is not necessarily a bad thing, but you are likely missing out on some additional search engines.

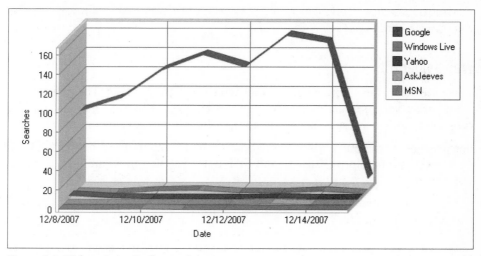

Figure 6-5. Web statistics: Daily search engines

Searches/Keywords

Each time search engines send you referrals, keywords are part of the HTTP headers that are stored in your web server logfiles. Figure 6-6 shows a graph of daily search phrases. This is one of the most important statistics in SEO.

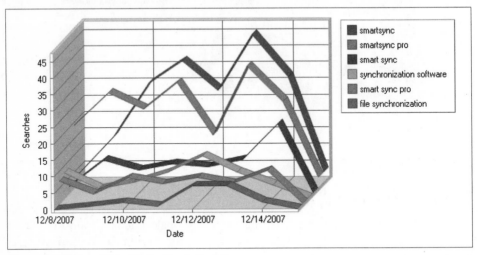

Figure 6-6. Web statistics: Daily search phrases

Viewing these stats will give you a good idea of how well optimized your website is for your targeted or desired keywords.

Web Spider Hits

These are the hits that automated search engine programs generate. The Internet has many web spiders serving their respective search engines in their ultimate goal of crawling countless websites. Being able to track their activities is important.

For the most part, you will only care about the most important web spiders of the bunch: Googlebot, Slurp (Yahoo!), and MSNBot. The chart in Figure 6-7 illustrates web spider hits.

For more information on WebLog Expert, you can download a trial version at *http://www.weblogexpert.com/*.

Using AWStats

Some people prefer using AWStats due to its fancy report format. I like AWStats since it shows some additional graphs when compared to Webalizer (which I cover later in this chapter). Figure 6-8 shows a sample AWStats summary page. You are presented with a lot of information.

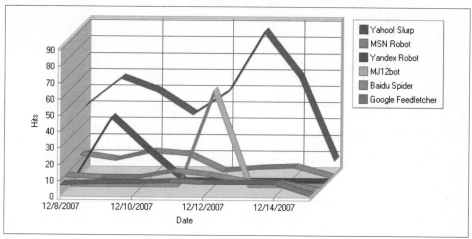

Figure 6-7. Web statistics: Spiders, bots, and crawlers

Notice that the current or selected month summary is presented at the top of the screen, whereas the 12-month summary is presented immediately below. If you see a lot of zeros across the whole month, this could mean a number of things, including:

- The website moved from another provider.
- The website is new.
- Web stats reporting functionality was just enabled.

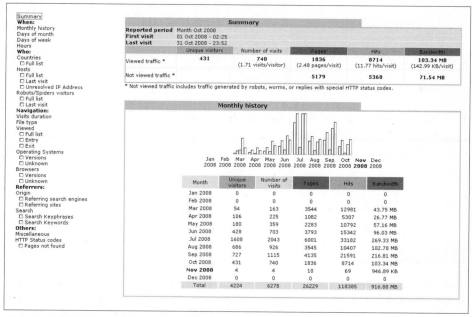

Figure 6-8. AWStats sample summary page

Also notice the key metrics, including unique visitors, number of visits, pages, hits, and bandwidth. Figure 6-9 shows the Robots section.

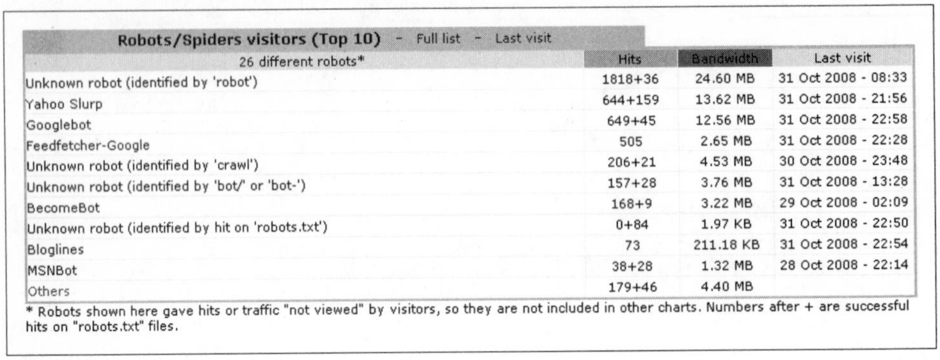

Robots/Spiders visitors (Top 10) – Full list – Last visit			
26 different robots*	Hits	Bandwidth	Last visit
Unknown robot (identified by 'robot')	1818+36	24.60 MB	31 Oct 2008 - 08:33
Yahoo Slurp	644+159	13.62 MB	31 Oct 2008 - 21:56
Googlebot	649+45	12.56 MB	31 Oct 2008 - 22:58
Feedfetcher-Google	505	2.65 MB	31 Oct 2008 - 22:28
Unknown robot (identified by 'crawl')	206+21	4.53 MB	30 Oct 2008 - 23:48
Unknown robot (identified by 'bot/' or 'bot-')	157+28	3.76 MB	31 Oct 2008 - 13:28
BecomeBot	168+9	3.22 MB	29 Oct 2008 - 02:09
Unknown robot (identified by hit on 'robots.txt')	0+84	1.97 KB	31 Oct 2008 - 22:50
Bloglines	73	211.18 KB	31 Oct 2008 - 22:54
MSNBot	38+28	1.32 MB	28 Oct 2008 - 22:14
Others	179+46	4.40 MB	

* Robots shown here gave hits or traffic "not viewed" by visitors, so they are not included in other charts. Numbers after + are successful hits on "robots.txt" files.

Figure 6-9. AWStats: Robot/spider visitors

Figure 6-10 shows the top search keyword phrases and keywords.

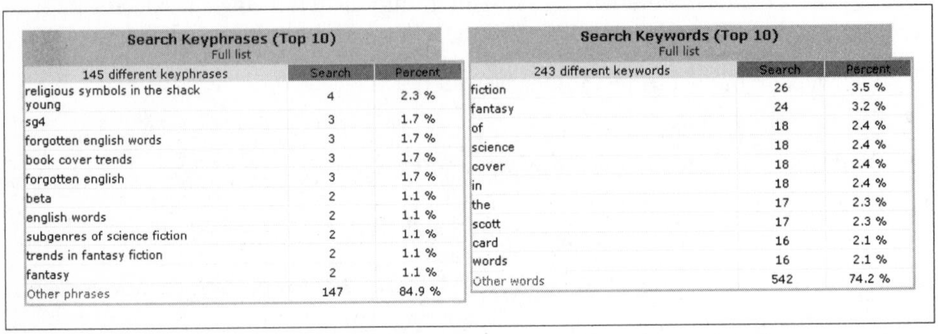

Search Keyphrases (Top 10) Full list				Search Keywords (Top 10) Full list		
145 different keyphrases	Search	Percent		243 different keywords	Search	Percent
religious symbols in the shack	4	2.3 %		fiction	26	3.5 %
young	3	1.7 %		fantasy	24	3.2 %
sg4	3	1.7 %		of	18	2.4 %
forgotten english words	3	1.7 %		science	18	2.4 %
book cover trends	3	1.7 %		cover	18	2.4 %
forgotten english	3	1.7 %		in	18	2.4 %
beta	2	1.1 %		the	17	2.3 %
english words	2	1.1 %		scott	17	2.3 %
subgenres of science fiction	2	1.1 %		card	16	2.1 %
trends in fantasy fiction	2	1.1 %		words	16	2.1 %
fantasy	2	1.1 %		Other words	542	74.2 %
Other phrases	147	84.9 %				

Figure 6-10. AWStats: Search keyword phrases/keywords

To see a breakdown of search queries for each search engine, click on the "Referring search engines" link on the left navigation pane. Your screen should look similar to Figure 6-11.

Using Webalizer

Some shared hosting providers allow for web log downloading (typically via FTP). This is to allow people to process their logs on their PCs. This is probably a good idea, as most providers tend to keep only the last month of web server logs.

If you are on a shared host, you can usually find Webalizer through a web page interface called CPANEL. Depending on your hosting provider, you may see slightly different screens. At first, CPANEL can look a bit daunting, with so many different icons to choose from.

Links from an Internet Search Engine				
9 different referring search engines	Pages	Percent	Hits	Percent
Google	146	78.9 %	146	77.2 %
Unknown search engines	18	9.7 %	19	10 %
Ask Jeeves	6	3.2 %	6	3.1 %
AOL	4	2.1 %	4	2.1 %
Google (Images)	4	2.1 %	6	3.1 %
Yahoo	4	2.1 %	4	2.1 %
Mamma	1	0.5 %	1	0.5 %
MSN	1	0.5 %	2	1 %
Dogpile	1	0.5 %	1	0.5 %

Figure 6-11. AWStats: Search engine hits breakdown

To make it even more confusing, you may need to enable your web stats packages to start getting the reports. If this is the case, you will not be able to see the reports for some time, usually a day or so. Come back in a couple of days to see some early graphs. Your screen (summary page) will look similar to Figure 6-12.

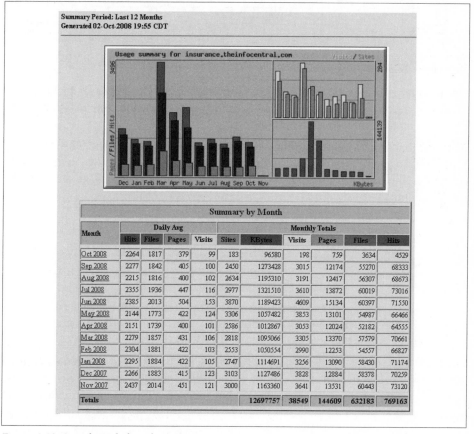

Summary Period: Last 12 Months
Generated 02-Oct-2008 19:55 CDT

Usage summary for insurance.theinfocentral.com

Month	Daily Avg				Monthly Totals					
	Hits	Files	Pages	Visits	Sites	KBytes	Visits	Pages	Files	Hits
Oct 2008	2264	1817	379	99	183	96580	198	759	3634	4529
Sep 2008	2277	1842	405	100	2450	1273428	3015	12174	55270	68333
Aug 2008	2215	1816	400	102	2634	1195310	3191	12417	56307	68673
Jul 2008	2355	1936	447	116	2977	1321510	3610	13872	60019	73016
Jun 2008	2385	2013	504	153	3870	1189423	4609	15134	60397	71550
May 2008	2144	1773	422	124	3306	1057482	3853	13101	54987	66466
Apr 2008	2151	1739	400	101	2586	1012867	3053	12024	52182	64555
Mar 2008	2279	1857	431	106	2818	1095066	3305	13370	57579	70661
Feb 2008	2304	1881	422	103	2553	1050554	2990	12253	54557	66827
Jan 2008	2295	1884	422	105	2747	1114691	3256	13090	58430	71174
Dec 2007	2266	1883	415	123	3103	1127486	3828	12884	58378	70259
Nov 2007	2437	2014	451	121	3000	1163360	3641	13531	60443	73120
Totals						12697757	38549	144609	632183	769163

Figure 6-12. Sample Webalizer home page

Top 44 of 113 Total Referrers		
#	Hits	Referrer
1	1848 48.06%	- (Direct Request)
2	234 6.09%	http://cursinginheels.blogspot.com/
3	40 1.04%	Google
4	4 0.10%	http://search.live.com/results.aspx
5	3 0.08%	http://cursinginheels.blogspot.com/2008/05/boy.html
6	3 0.08%	http://search.aol.ca/aol/search
7	2 0.05%	AOL
8	2 0.05%	MSN
9	2 0.05%	http://cursinginheels.blogspot.com/2008/08/tell-me-what-to-do.html
10	2 0.05%	http://cursinginheels.blogspot.com/2008/10/ah-nostalgia.html
11	2 0.05%	http://cursinginheels.blogspot.com/2008/10/sticking-to-daily-prophet.html
12	2 0.05%	http://cursinginheels.blogspot.com/search
13	2 0.05%	http://image.youdao.com/imagesa
14	2 0.05%	http://search.live.com/images/results.aspx
15	1 0.03%	Yahoo!

Figure 6-13. Webalizer: Referrers section

On the summary page you can see important metrics such as daily average hits, daily average visits, monthly average hits, and monthly average visits. Note that page views are represented in the "Pages" column.

Also note that unique IPs or unique visitor numbers are displayed in the "Sites" column. This should make sense to you since the number of total visits, as shown in the "Visits" column, is almost always greater than the number of unique visitors, as shown in the "Sites" column.

There are three more metrics we need to go over:

- Referrers
- Searches/keywords
- Spider hits

The initial (or index) summary page provides a summary view for the past 12 months of your website's activity. To see more details of a particular month, you would simply click on that month.

Once you are in the monthly summary page, click on the "Referrers" top menu link to see your website's referrers. Some of the referrer links may be from your own website. Ignore them, as they do not provide much value. Figure 6-13 shows an example referrers section.

Referrers can be websites that have direct links to your website (or other minor search engines), or they can be part of a search engine marketing content network. Click on the "Search" top menu link to see all the keywords. These keywords are the sum aggregation of all keywords for your entire website. Figure 6-14 shows the search section.

Top 10 of 91 Total Search Strings		
#	Hits	Search String
1	67	35.83%	webalizer
2	11	5.88%	borg
3	5	2.67%	borg collective
4	4	2.14%	the borg
5	4	2.14%	web log analysis
6	3	1.60%	user-agent statistics
7	2	1.07%	free web statistics software
8	2	1.07%	internet usage statistics
9	2	1.07%	log analysis
10	2	1.07%	log files
View All Search Strings		

Figure 6-14. Webalizer: Search

Finally, to see the spider hits, click on the "Agent" top menu link to examine stats on web spider activity. *User agent* (or just *agent*) represents a type of web user. There are basically two types: human users and automated web spiders. This summary table shows all kinds of agent signatures.

You will get to see not just web spider signatures, but also web browser signatures in addition to any other signatures possibly generated by some custom automated scripts. See Figure 6-15 for more details.

Some people like using Webalizer because it's a great tool for viewing web stats quickly. Others prefer using AWStats due to its fancy report format. Although the type of information AWStats displays is similar to the type of information Webalizer displays, for some statistics the reporting values might vary between Webalizer and AWStats due to the way they process logs. To choose the one that's right for you, review both types of reports. One report may be clearer or easier to understand for a specific web metric. You may also have an aesthetic preference. The key is to find something that works for you and meets your needs and comfort level.

#	Hits		User Agent
		Top 30 of 53 Total User Agents	
1	1465	38.10%	Mozilla/5.0
2	1465	38.10%	Netscape 6 compatible
3	654	17.01%	MSIE 7.0
4	449	11.68%	MSIE 6.0
5	188	4.89%	Yahoo! Slurp
6	181	4.71%	ichiro/3.0 (http://help.goo.ne.jp/door/crawler.html)
7	138	3.59%	Feedfetcher-Google; (+http://www.google.com/feedfetcher.html;
8	126	3.28%	Googlebot/2.1
9	71	1.85%	BecomeBot/3.0
10	64	1.66%	ScoutJet
11	61	1.59%	MJ12bot/v1.2
12	55	1.43%	Bloglines/3.1 (http://www.bloglines.com; 1 subscriber)
13	40	1.04%	MSIE 5.5
14	36	0.94%	Opera
15	34	0.88%	ConveraCrawler/0.9e (+http://ews.converasearch.com/crawl.htm)
16	34	0.88%	MSIE 8.0
17	33	0.86%	Netscape 4 (or compatible)
18	32	0.83%	Mozilla/4.0 (compatible;)
19	30	0.78%	Ask Jeeves/Teoma
20	27	0.70%	MLBot (www.metadatalabs.com/mlbot)
21	26	0.68%	Opera/9.6
22	22	0.57%	Googlebot-Image/1.0
23	22	0.57%	Yanga WorldSearch Bot v1.1/beta (http://www.yanga.co.uk/)
24	18	0.47%	msnbot-media/1.1 (+http://search.msn.com/msnbot.htm)
25	8	0.21%	Opera"
26	7	0.18%	R6_FeedFetcher(www.radian6.com/crawler)
27	7	0.18%	Windows-RSS-Platform/1.0 (MSIE 7.0; Windows NT 6.0)
28	6	0.16%	Snapbot/1.0 (Snap Shots, +http://www.snap.com)
29	6	0.16%	Yahoo! Slurp/3.0
30	5	0.13%	Java/1.6.0-oem

Figure 6-15. Webalizer: Agents section

Tying Searches to Individual Web Pages

Knowing what search phrases visitors typed to drive traffic to your website is essential. It's even more important to tie the search phrases back to the actual web pages. Some of the available web stats tools on shared hosting providers do not show this sort of relationship.

You can tie searches to individual web pages with a simple Perl script: *searchPhraseReportGoogle.pl*, which appears in full in Appendix A. This script can handle multiple logfiles. To run the script, type in the following:

```
perl searchPhraseReportGoogle.pl logfile1.log logfile2.log
```

The assumption is that the logfiles are stored in the NCSA Combined format. After you run the command, a file called *keywordsummary.html* is generated. If you open the file in a web browser, it should render similarly to Figure 6-16.

Google Summary

Resource/URL	Keyword	Count
/	fantasy fiction	203
/	english words	149
/	forgotten	70
/	book cover trends	48
/	subgeres of science fiction	30
/	science fiction	26
/	trends in	19
/	fantasy	14

Figure 6-16. Keyword summary page for Google

As you can see in Figure 6-16, you can clearly see which page or file got the most hits for a particular keyword. The forward slash (/) indicates the default page for this domain. You should have no doubts about where the hits are going and for what keywords.

You can modify the preceding Perl script to do the same thing for Bing searches. The modified version, *searchPhraseReportBing.pl*, is also available in Appendix A. To run it, execute the following command:

```
perl searchPhraseReportBing.pl logfile1.log logfile2.log
```

Simply list filenames separated by a space.

Web Spider Patterns

Web spiders evolve and change just as your websites evolve and change. The more you give the more you get. The "give" comes in the form of content. The "get" comes in the form of search engine referrals for your keyword-optimized web pages.

Web spiders start with a "feeling out" process. They come once in a while to say "hello" until they get a better idea about your site. Once they get a good sense of your website, they come back with a fury if your website offers them food in the way of good content.

Depending on the type of website you are running, spider visits can be less or more frequent. If you are constantly providing new content, spiders will follow you every step of the way. If your website's content does not change much, spiders will still visit your site, albeit less frequently.

User Patterns

There are several key user pattern concepts to take note of, including user entry pages, user exit pages, and user click paths. User patterns say a lot about many things regarding your website. They say a lot about SEO, but also about your website's usability, psychology, and impressions. Take a look at the sample website structure shown in Figure 6-17. You could have visitors landing on just about any page within your website.

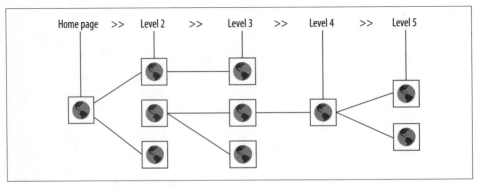

Figure 6-17. Sample website structure

If you're using Webalizer, you can see where your web visitors are entering your website by clicking on the "Entry" link. Your screen will look similar to Figure 6-18.

		Top 20 of 135 Total Entry Pages		
#	Hits		Visits		URL

#	Hits		Visits		URL
1	434	11.29%	426	44.70%	/feed/atom/
2	104	2.70%	81	8.50%	/feed
3	93	2.42%	70	7.35%	/feed/
4	76	1.98%	62	6.51%	/
5	30	0.78%	23	2.41%	/2008/06/27/science-fiction-and-fantasy-defining-genres-and-subgenres/
6	26	0.68%	20	2.10%	/2008/07/29/
7	22	0.57%	13	1.36%	/2008/07/30/can-you-manufacture-a-bestselling-novel/
8	21	0.55%	13	1.36%	/2008/09/19/book-cover-trends-in-fantasy-and-science-fiction-part-2/
9	18	0.47%	9	0.94%	/2008/05/30/
10	17	0.44%	9	0.94%	/2008/09/14/book-cover-trends-in-fantasy-and-science-fiction-part-1/
11	21	0.55%	7	0.73%	/wp-login.php
12	10	0.26%	6	0.63%	/category/forgotten-english-word-of-the-day/

Figure 6-18. Webalizer: Entry pages

Now, what if you want to know where your web visitors exited? Figure 6-19 shows the exit pages.

#	Hits		Visits		URL
	Top 20 of 134 Total Exit Pages				
1	434	11.29%	426	44.61%	/feed/atom/
2	93	2.42%	82	8.59%	/feed/
3	104	2.70%	80	8.38%	/feed
4	76	1.98%	63	6.60%	/
5	26	0.68%	18	1.88%	/2008/07/29/
6	30	0.78%	14	1.47%	/2008/06/27/science-fiction-and-fantasy-defining-genres-and-subgenres/
7	21	0.55%	14	1.47%	/2008/09/19/book-cover-trends-in-fantasy-and-science-fiction-part-2/
8	22	0.57%	12	1.26%	/2008/07/30/can-you-manufacture-a-bestselling-novel/

Figure 6-19. Webalizer: Exit pages

Knowing how web users use your site is important. This is where the metric called *click path* (or *top path*) comes in. This feature is not available in Webalizer or AWStats (as of this writing). Figure 6-20 shows how this feature looks in WebLog Expert.

Lots of paths may be single web pages or web documents, as shown in Figure 6-20. In such cases, think of it as web users coming to a particular web page and then exiting your website without clicking on anything else.

Web stats tools, just like any other software, are prone to bugs. My advice is to use multiple web stats tools before drawing any conclusions. Don't accept anything at face value, but rather, question what you see if you think something does not make sense.

	Top Paths Through Site		
	Path	Visitors	% of Total
1	/	1,479	45.22%
2	/ -> /downloads/	246	7.52%
3	/downloads/	224	6.85%
4	/support/	187	5.72%
5	/smartsyncpro/	106	3.24%
6	/smartsyncpro/uninstall.php	101	3.09%
7	/support/key-request.html	72	2.20%
8	/ -> /smartsyncpro/how-to-backup.html	68	2.08%
9	/smartsyncpro/registration.html	64	1.96%
10	/smartsyncpro/whatsnew.html	31	0.95%
11	/smartsyncpro/lostkey.html	18	0.55%
12	/smartsyncpro/uninstall.php -> /smartsyncpro/uninstalled.php	17	0.52%
13	/smartsyncpro/testimonials.html	15	0.46%
14	/support/netgear.html	15	0.46%
15	/smartsync/screenshots.asp	14	0.43%
16	/ -> /downloads/	14	0.43%
17	/smartsync/	14	0.43%

Figure 6-20. WebLog Expert: Top Paths Through Site screen

Filtering Specific Data

Before we finish this chapter, it is important to put things in the right perspective. Web stats are a great tool for SEO. Although web stats can provide an abundance of information, not all of this information is useful. For most websites, knowing the number of web page views is much more useful than knowing or reporting on the number of website hits.

Types of Web Page Elements

The vast majority of web pages on the Internet comprise much more than just plain text. Table 6-4 lists some of the most common web page elements.

Table 6-4. Common web page elements

Element	Details
JavaScript	JavaScript files are stored in external *.js* files
Stylesheet	Stylesheet files are stored in external *.css* files
Images	Graphics files are stored in external files (e.g., *.gif*, *.png*, *.jpg*)
Flash	Flash files are stored in external *.swf* files
Java applet	Java applets are stored in external *.class* or *.jar* files
Sound/music	Music files are stored in external files including *.mp3* and *.mid*
Videos	Video files are stored in external files including *.asf* and *.avi*

Some web stats tools provide ways of focusing on only the information you are interested in, by way of *filters*. You can filter on many different things. For example, WebLog Expert has extensive filtering options, as shown in Figure 6-21.

Conversion tracking with web server logs

You can easily track conversions by using web server logs. A conversion is successful when a web user reaches his goal page. For example, suppose you are selling a product. At the end of every purchase the user is brought to a thank-you page (e.g., *thankyou.php*). You can use the filter shown in Figure 6-21 to track the number of times this file is accessed. Similarly, you can track the number of times a particular landing page is accessed to measure the relative conversion rate.

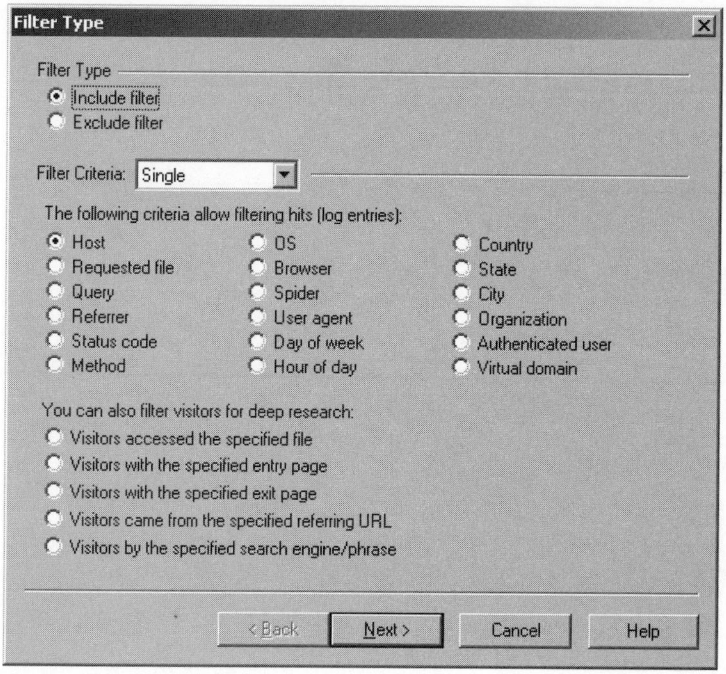

Figure 6-21. WebLog Expert: Filter Type screen

Summary

By now, you should have a better understanding of web stats as a tool for basic SEO monitoring. Many web stats tools are available, and although we covered only some of the most popular ones, do not be afraid to experiment with others until you find the one that meets your requirements. Fully understanding your web stats often requires use of multiple tools.

The free tools we covered are the standard tools in shared hosting environments. In the next chapter, we will examine Google Analytics and Webmaster Tools, and discuss more advanced features in SEO monitoring and troubleshooting.

## CHAPTER 7

Google Webmaster Tools and Google Analytics

This chapter is divided into two parts. First we'll cover Google Webmaster Tools. The Google Webmaster Tools platform gives webmasters an easy way to track their web page traffic, analyze their *robots.txt* file, add their Sitemap files, and so forth. It would be foolish not to utilize Webmaster Tools, as it is an indispensable resource for conducting SEO.

The second part of the chapter covers the Google Analytics platform. Google Analytics is the preferred marketing tool for viewing general web stats and, more importantly, conversions. Both of these are great tools, and best of all, they are free. Both of these tools should become part of your SEO toolkit.

Google Webmaster Tools

Google Webmaster Tools is a good resource for webmasters. With it you can easily spot all kinds of problems. The following subsections explore Google Webmaster Tools in detail.

Webmaster Tools Setup

Just as you do when using any other Google tool, you need to register for a Google account before you can use Google Webmaster Tools. If you already have a Google account, sign in at *http://google.com/webmasters/tools/*. Once you are signed in, you will want to add your site to Google Webmaster Tools. Before you can add your site, Google will ask you to prove that the site in question is truly yours. Figure 7-1 shows the two methods you can use to validate your site.

The default method is to use the HTML meta tag. The second way is to upload a text file with the exact (random) name as generated by Google.

Figure 7-1. Google Webmaster Tools site validation

Once you validate your site, you will be ready to use Webmaster Tools. Note that it will take some time for you to see any data. Just come back later.

Dashboard

Upon every logon to Webmaster Tools, you will see a list of your sites. Clicking on any of your sites brings you to the (summary) Dashboard page, as shown in Figure 7-2.

The Dashboard screen lists your top search queries, crawl errors, links to your site, and Sitemaps. You can use the navigation panel on the left side of the screen to view more details, as well as to use additional tools. We'll examine those in the following sections.

The "Site configuration" Section

Selecting the "Site configuration" menu option opens additional options, including Sitemaps, "Crawler access," Sitelinks, "Change of address," and Settings. We explore each in the following subsections.

Sitemaps

You use the Sitemaps option to submit new Sitemaps, see the status of existing Sitemaps, delete and resubmit Sitemaps, and export Sitemap-related data to an Excel spreadsheet. If your Sitemaps have any errors, you will see an indication of such under the Status field of your Sitemap listing. Figure 7-3 highlights the key parts of the Sitemaps interface.

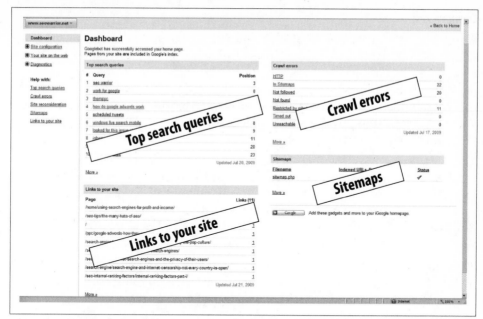

Figure 7-2. Google Webmaster Tools: Dashboard page

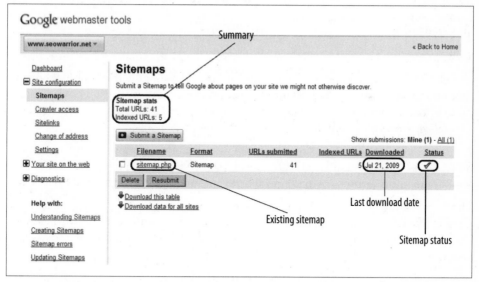

Figure 7-3. Google Webmaster Tools: Sitemaps interface

Crawler access

You use the "Crawler access" option to manage your *robots.txt* file. You can do many things while on the "Crawler access" page. Figure 7-4 shows the default "Crawler access" screen. At the top you are presented with three tabs. The "Test robots.txt" tab is the default tab and is used for testing the *robots.txt* file. Clicking on the "Generate robots.txt" tab presents you with another screen where you can interactively assemble your new *robots.txt* file, which you can upload to your server. The "Remove URL" tab brings you to a page where you can tell Google to remove specific URL(s).

You will spend most of your time in the default (*robots.txt* testing) tab. Just below the three tabs, you should see the current status of your existing (or missing) *robots.txt* file. Immediately below that you will find what you can think of as your *robots.txt* testing area. There are three major fields you can play with here. The first text area field downloads your existing website *robots.txt* file by default. You can change this to anything you want, as the field is fully editable.

The next text area field is where you can list your URLs. Your domain name in the URL must match your actual domain name for the domain session you are currently viewing within Webmaster Tools. Each URL should be listed on a separate line.

Google also allows you to test your URL and *robots.txt* combinations with several different spiders, including Googlebot-Mobile, Googlebot-Image, Mediapartners-Google, and AdsBot-Google.

Sitelinks

Google Sitelinks is a feature for enhancing relevant site listings with additional hotspot links found on a particular site. Sitelinks typically appear as the top result on the Google SERPs. If you own a new site, don't expect to get your Google site links right away. Figure 7-5 shows an example as taken from Webmaster Tools.

Every site should strive to get sitelinks, as they imply authority as well as web presence. Sitelinks also occupy additional search results screen real estate, the space that pushes your competitors farther down the results page—something to be desired.

Once you earn your sitelinks, you can remove any unwanted links that appear in the Google SERPs using the Sitelinks section of Webmaster Tools. According to Google, sitelinks are completely auto-generated. Visit *http://bit.ly/4EORUm* to read more about sitelinks.

Change of address

Google makes it easy when you have to move your site to another domain. Google states that doing this will help the company update its index faster and "smooth the transition for your users." Figure 7-6 shows a screenshot of the "Change of address" subsection.

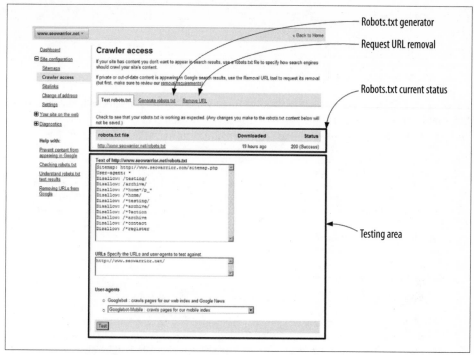

Figure 7-4. Google Webmaster Tools: Specifying crawler access

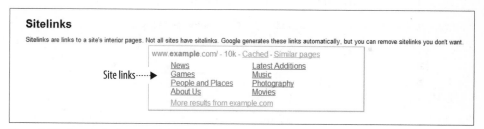

Figure 7-5. Google Webmaster Tools: Sitelinks

As you can see in Figure 7-6, Google provides you with step-by-step instructions for moving your site.

Settings

With the Settings option you can customize your geographic target, preferred domain, and desired crawl rate. Figure 7-7 shows a portion of this subsection.

If you wish, you can target users in a specific country by enabling the "Geographic target" checkbox. The default setting is Off. If you are worried about link canonicalization, you can tell Google about your preferred domain. Note that this is only one level of potential content duplication.

Change of address

If you're planning to move your site to a new domain, use the Change of Address tool to tell Google about your new URL. This will help us update our index faster and smooth the transition for your users.

For best results, follow these steps:

1. **Set up the new site**
   Review our guidelines for moving your site to a new domain. Set up your content on your new domain, then make sure all internal links point to the new domain.

2. **Redirect all traffic from the old site**
   Use a 301 redirect to permanently redirect the pages on your old site to your new site. This tells users and search engines that your site has permanently moved. Ask webmasters to update their links to point to your new domain and make sure incoming links to your old site are redirected correctly using the 301 redirects.

3. **Add your new site to Webmaster Tools**
   Make sure you have added and verified your new domain.

4. **Tell us the URL of your new domain**

   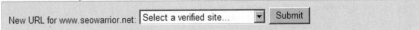

   New URL for www.seowarrior.net: [Select a verified site... ▼] [Submit]

   After submitting the change of address, check your Webmaster Tools data periodically to see if your new site has been crawled and indexed (if you have a Sitemap, one way to determine this is by checking Sitemap details for the new site to see how many of the pages have been crawled and indexed).

Figure 7-6. Google Webmaster Tools: Specifying a change of address

You can also set your own custom crawl rate. Google provides no guarantees when it will crawl your site. You are better off letting Google determine your site's crawl rate.

Settings

		Learn more
Geographic target	Target ☐ users in: [United States ▼]	
Preferred domain	○ Don't set a preferred domain ◉ Display URLs as **www.seowarrior.net** ○ Display URLs as **seowarrior.net**	Learn more
Crawl rate	◉ Let Google determine my crawl rate **(recommended)** ○ Set custom crawl rate	Learn more

Figure 7-7. Google Webmaster Tools: Settings options

The "Your site on the web" Section

The "Your site on the web" menu option contains several subsections, including "Top search queries," "Links to your site," Keywords, "Internal links," and "Subscriber stats."

Top search queries

By selecting the "Top search queries" option, you can see keyword queries where your site appeared on Google search results. Figure 7-8 illustrates the key parts of this page.

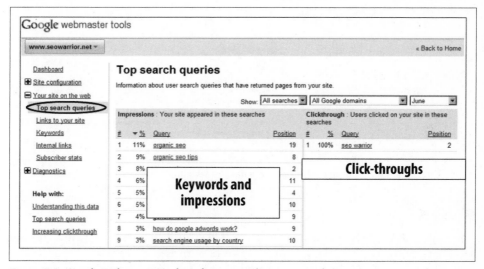

Figure 7-8. Google Webmaster Tools: Information about top search queries

The "%" column indicates the percentage of impressions of a particular keyword compared to all of your keywords. You also can see the actual rank or position of each keyword in the last column to the right.

On the righthand side of the screen is a section regarding your site's click-throughs. It shows all searchers' queries that made it to your site in a similar breakdown.

Links to your site

The "Links to your site" option is useful for current state backlink analysis. You can see who is linking to your internal pages, and enter your internal URLs to see whether they have earned any backlinks. You can also view the anchor text of your backlinks. Figure 7-9 shows parts of these screens to illustrate the concepts.

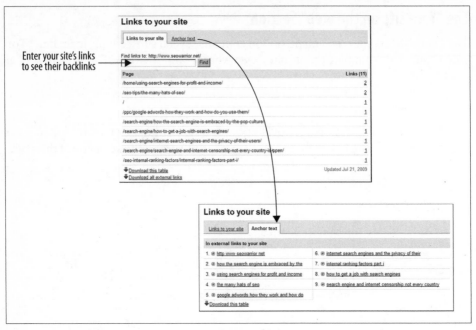

Figure 7-9. Google Webmaster Tools: Analyzing links to your site

Keywords

The Keywords page shows the most important keywords found on your site. You can see what keywords are working. You may also be surprised by some keywords. If you see irrelevant keywords, your site may have been hacked. If you do not see your targeted keywords, you may wish to check for any crawl errors in addition to checking whether your particular page was crawled.

Internal links

The "Internal links" page is similar to the "Links to your site" page. Here, you can search for internal links linking to other internal links. This is important, as it pertains to the flow of your link juice.

Subscriber stats

The "Subscriber stats" page shows your existing feed(s) and their Google subscribers; see Figure 7-10. You also have the option to add your feed as your Sitemap; as we will discuss in Chapter 10, it is best not to use this option.

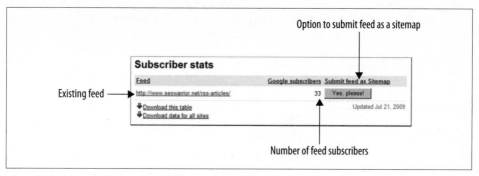

Figure 7-10. Google Webmaster Tools: Analyzing subscriber stats

The Diagnostics Section

The Diagnostics section consists of three parts: "Crawl errors," "Crawl stats," and "HTML suggestions." The following subsections discuss the details.

Crawl errors

The "Crawl errors" page shows you your site's crawling problems. There are three main tabs on this page: Web (which is the default), Mobile CHTML, and Mobile WML/XHTML. Figure 7-11 shows a portion of this page.

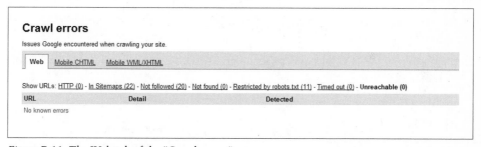

Figure 7-11. The Web tab of the "Crawl errors" page

Crawl errors come in all sorts of flavors. This option is particularly useful when tracking any broken links that Google bots are finding. The tool will also report pages that are restricted by your *robots.txt* file. In addition, you will see pages that time out or are unreachable.

Crawl stats

The "Crawl stats" page shows a breakdown of Googlebot activities. Figure 7-12 shows a portion of this page. The first graph shows the number of pages crawled per day over a period of time. The second graph shows the number of kilobytes downloaded per day, and the last graph shows the download speed during that period. Each graph is augmented with statistical data, including data highs, lows, and averages.

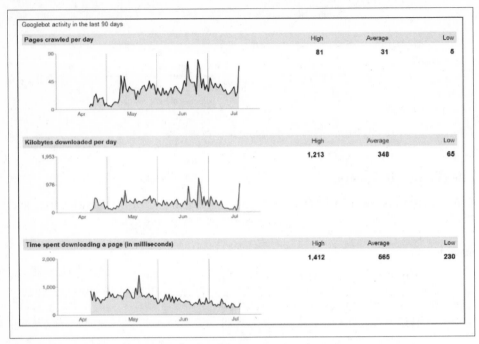

Figure 7-12. Google Webmaster Tools: Googlebot activity crawl stats

At the bottom of the "Crawl stats" page is a graph of your site's PageRank distribution (see Figure 7-13).

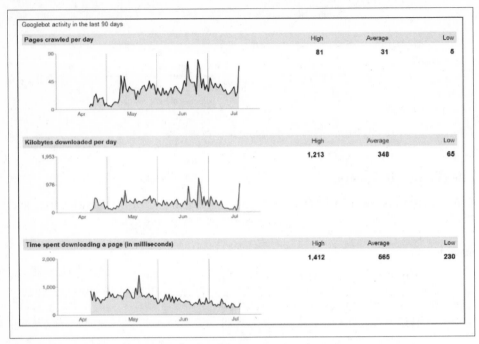

Figure 7-13. Google Webmaster Tools: Crawl stats PageRank distribution

HTML suggestions

Another gem of the Google Webmaster Tools platform is in the "HTML suggestions" page (see Figure 7-14).

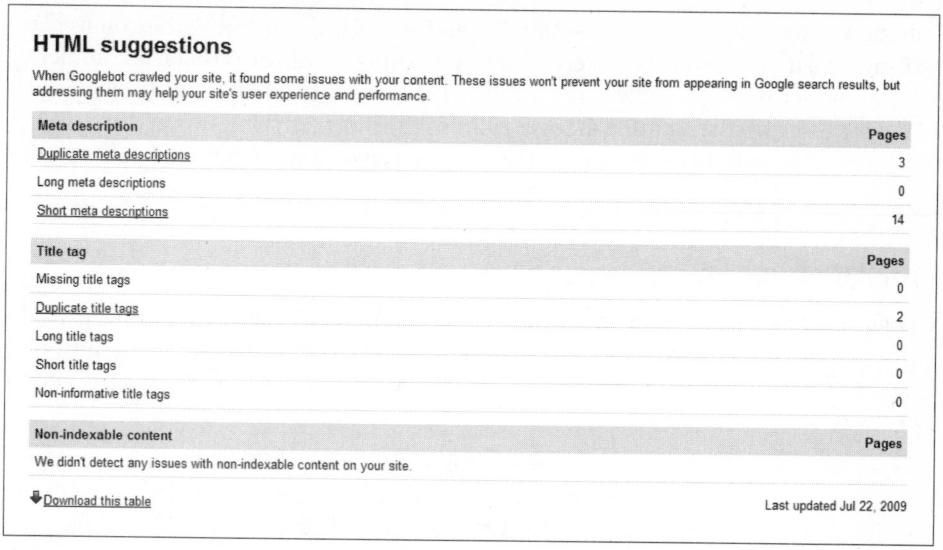

HTML suggestions

When Googlebot crawled your site, it found some issues with your content. These issues won't prevent your site from appearing in Google search results, but addressing them may help your site's user experience and performance.

Meta description	Pages
Duplicate meta descriptions	3
Long meta descriptions	0
Short meta descriptions	14

Title tag	Pages
Missing title tags	0
Duplicate title tags	2
Long title tags	0
Short title tags	0
Non-informative title tags	0

Non-indexable content	Pages

We didn't detect any issues with non-indexable content on your site.

⬇ Download this table

Last updated Jul 22, 2009

Figure 7-14. Google Webmaster Tools: HTML suggestions

On this page, Google will tell you what it thinks of your site's pages in terms of your meta descriptions, title tags, and nonindexable content. In each subsection, you will find tips regarding duplicate, short, and long meta descriptions; missing, duplicate, long, short, and uninformative title tags; and similar information.

Google Analytics

If you prefer a simple, online web analytics tool, Google Analytics may be just what you are looking for. If Google Webmaster Tools is for webmasters, Google Analytics is for marketers. For many marketers, Google Analytics seems to be the tool of choice for all web analytics needs.

Google Analytics has seen several upgrades and face-lifts over the past few years. Google didn't start with Google Analytics from scratch. In fact, it bought the idea from another company. According to Wikipedia (*http://en.wikipedia.org/wiki/Google_Analytics*):

> Google's service was developed from Urchin Software Corporation's analytics system, Urchin on Demand (Google acquired Urchin Software Corp. in April 2005). The system also brings ideas from Adaptive Path, whose product, Measure Map, was acquired and used in the redesign of Google Analytics in 2006. Google still sells the standalone installable Urchin software through a network of value-added resellers; In April 2008, Urchin 6 was released.

Google touts its Analytics platform as "enterprise-class features delivered on Google's world-class platform." One of the major benefits of Google Analytics is integration with Google's other landmark platforms, such as AdWords and AdSense.

Additional benefits include cross-channel and multimedia tracking, customized reporting, and data visualization. Perhaps its most enticing feature is that it is completely free. Without a doubt, Google Analytics is a solid offering that you should not overlook if you are OK with the fact that Google will (for the most part) know everything about your site. The following sections present a brief overview of the Google Analytics platform.

Installation and Setup

Google Analytics feeds off a small piece of JavaScript code that you need to place in every page that requires tracking. Before you can use Google Analytics, you must register for a Google account. You can sign up for an account by visiting *http://www.google .com/analytics/*.

The account signup process is relatively painless and takes about two minutes to complete. There are four screens in total. On the last screen, Google provides you with the JavaScript code you can place in your web pages. The code looks similar to the following fragment:

```
<script type="text/javascript">
var gaJsHost = (("https:" == document.location.protocol) ?
"https://ssl." : "http://www.");
document.write(unescape("%3Cscript src='" + gaJsHost +
"google-analytics.com/ga.js' type='text/javascript'%3E%3C/script%3E"));
</script>
<script type="text/javascript">
try {
var pageTracker = _gat._getTracker("UA-9899851-1");
pageTracker._trackPageview();
} catch(err) {}</script>
```

You are also given the option of using Google's legacy code, which lacks some of the features in the latest version. Google supports the old code, as many sites are still using it. Do not use both pieces of code, as this may produce inaccurate reported data.

With the Google tracking code in hand, the next thing to do is to place it within your HTML. Instead of placing this code into every single HTML file, factor it out into an external file that is called by your site template file (if you are using templates).

Should Google ever decide to change the code, you will need to modify only the single external file carrying the Google code. Google suggests that you place its code just before the closing </BODY> tag of your modified code. It will take some time before Google validates your code. You can check the status by logging in to your Google Analytics account. You will see a green checkmark once your account is validated.

Navigating Google Analytics

Google Analytics contains numerous features. To a novice user, it may be a bit daunting at first. Figure 7-15 shows the main navigation sections of the Google Analytics platform.

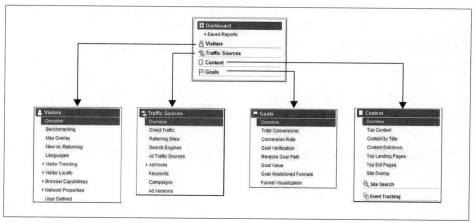

Figure 7-15. Google Analytics: Main navigation options

We will start our discussion of Google Analytics by looking at its Dashboard (home) page.

Dashboard

Assuming your account is up and running, the first thing you see when you log in to Google Analytics is the Dashboard page. Figure 7-16 shows a sample Google Analytics Dashboard page. The first part of the screen shows a visitor graph over time. The next section gives you a breakdown of your site's usage. This includes the number of unique visits, number of page views, average number of viewed pages per visit, average page bounce rate, average time visitors spent on the site, and percentage of new visitors.

Other sections included in the Dashboard page are labeled Visitors Overview, Map Overlay, Traffic Sources Overview, Content Overview, and Goals Overview. Note that you can customize your Dashboard page view as well.

By default, the Dashboard page shows data in relation to all visits; no other segmentation is applied. As the time of this writing, Google was introducing an Advanced Segment (beta) feature, which allows you to generate additional graphs and data segregated to each segment. You can use this option by clicking on the button next to the Advanced Segments label in the top-righthand corner of the Dashboard page.

You should be able to select among several different segments, including New Visitors, Returning Visitors, Paid Traffic, Non-paid Traffic, Search Traffic, Direct Traffic,

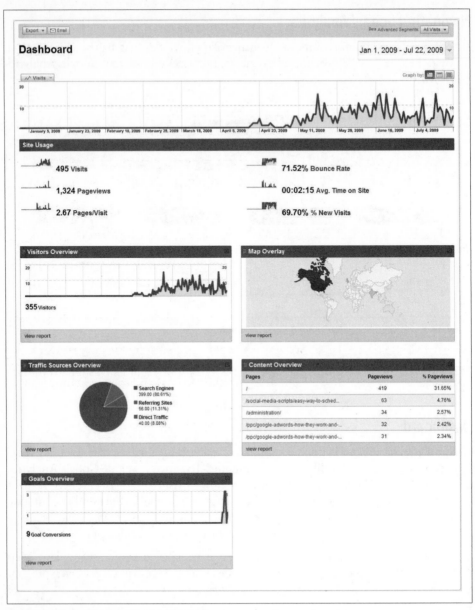

Figure 7-16. Google Analytics: Dashboard page

Referral Traffic, Visits with Conversions, Visits from iPhones, and Non-bounce Visits. Figure 7-17 illustrates some of the options as well as the graph that results when you select an additional segment.

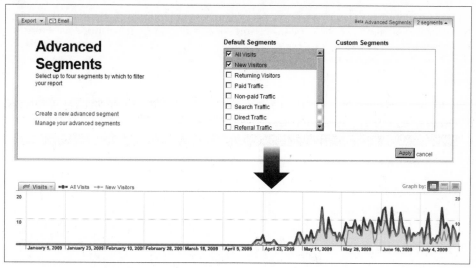

Figure 7-17. Google Analytics: Advanced segments

As you can see in Figure 7-17, once you introduce additional segments, the graph is redrawn in such a way that each segment is superimposed over the other segments. Also note that you can create custom segments by clicking on the "Create a new advanced segment" link shown on the lefthand side of the screen. Finally, when you add segments, all graphical and textual data is augmented with segment-specific details.

Visitors Overview page

When you click on the Visitors menu item, you will see a summary page that looks similar to Figure 7-18.

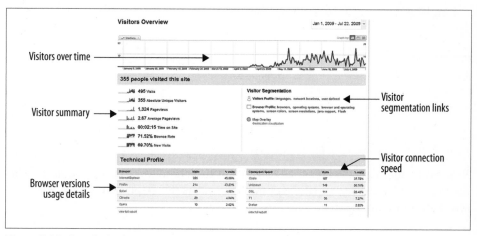

Figure 7-18. Google Analytics: Visitor overview

As shown in Figure 7-18, you can view a visitor time graph, visitor (metrics) summary, browser versions matrix, visitor connection speed summary, and visitor segmentation links.

Benchmarking

The Benchmarking page is particularly interesting. When you open it, you will see comparative graphical analyses of your site compared to other sites of similar size. Figure 7-19 shows one sample.

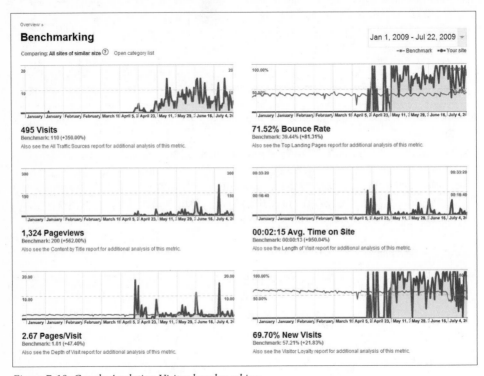

Figure 7-19. Google Analytics: Visitor benchmarking

As you can see from Figure 7-19, the metrics used when benchmarking include the number of visits, site bounce rate, number of page views, average time visitors spent on the site, number of pages viewed per visit, and percentage of new visitors. Benchmarking is available only if you agree to share your data with Google and make your data available to others as part of Google's combined vertical market data for your market. It typically takes two weeks for benchmarking data to appear after it has been enabled.

Map Overlay page

On the Map Overlay page, you can see a world map mashed up with your visitor stats. Just below the map you will see a list of countries and the corresponding number of visitors originating from a particular source country.

New versus returning visitors

The "New vs. returning" page shows a breakdown of new and old visitors. You can compare the two metrics by viewing the generated pie graph. We will discuss the topic of goals and conversions later. For now, know that if you have defined any goals, they will show up on this page, broken down by old and new visitors, under the "Goal conversion" tab.

Languages

The Languages page is similar in style to the preceding two pages. You get a table listing of languages sorted by popularity. As before, you can also see this sort of breakdown under the "Goal conversion" tab.

Visitor trending

The "Visitor trending" menu option opens another set of submenu options, including those for absolute unique visitors, page views, average page views, time visitors spent on the site, and bounce rate. All of these submenu items produce pages with historical (per-day) listings.

Visitor pages

The "Visitor loyalty" menu item opens with a secondary menu offering different options including visitor loyalty, visitor recency, length of visit, and depth of visit. The "Visitor loyalty" screen shows the number of repeat visits.

The "Visitor recency" page is concerned with previous visits and will tell you when the last visit occurred. The "Length of visit" page shows a breakdown of all visits based on length of time, and the "Depth of visit" page shows a similar breakdown per page view.

Browser capabilities

The "Browser capabilities" menu option opens a secondary menu that contains different options, including those for browsers, operating systems, screen colors, screen resolutions, Flash versions, and Java support.

Network properties

The "Network properties" menu option opens a secondary menu that contains different options, including those for network location, hostnames, and connection speeds.

Traffic Sources

The Traffic Sources section shows the various views pertinent to your website traffic. Figure 7-20 is a portion of the Traffic Sources Overview page.

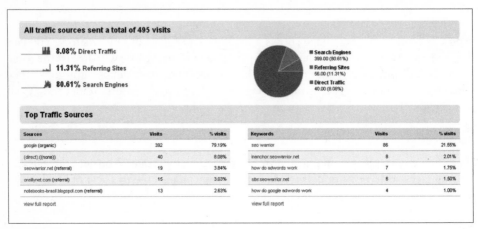

Figure 7-20. *Google Analytics: Traffic sources overview*

On this page, you can see a summary of your inbound traffic. This includes direct traffic, search engine traffic, and referring sites traffic. The top part of the page shows this type of information.

The bottom part of the page is divided into two tables. The table on the lower left shows a summary of your main sources of traffic. The table on the lower right shows the pertinent keywords bringing the traffic.

The submenu options under the Traffic Sources main menu item include pages that show segregated views of traffic. If you are using Google AdWords, you will see the options relevant to AdWords paid ad traffic. Other SEM networks can have tagging included in the destination URLs so that they also show up as paid ads in Google Analytics.

Content

In the Content section, page views are one of the important metrics. In the Overview page, you can see a summary similar to the one in Figure 7-21.

At the top-left corner, you can see several different summary metrics, including the number of page views, number of unique visitors, and percentage bounce rate. On the righthand side you can see several links in relation to navigation analysis, landing page optimization, and click patterns.

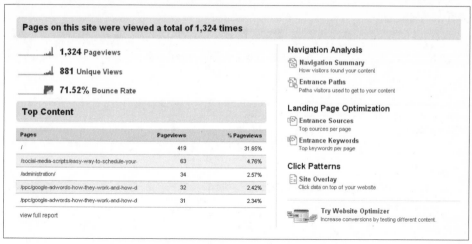

Figure 7-21. Google Analytics: Content overview

At the bottom-left corner you can see your top performing pages. You can see the relative URL path along with the number of page views and corresponding percentage page views.

The submenu options under the Content menu item include pages that show segregated views of your content. One of the most interesting options is the site overlay, which displays another browser window with your site shown as a mashup augmented by Google's statistical data. If you hover your mouse pointer over any of your internal links, you will see a tool tip showing statistical data regarding your visitors' clicks and goals.

Goals

Perhaps one of the most important features of Google Analytics, goal reports can help you keep track of your visitor conversions. Before you can view the goal reports (using the Goal submenu items), you will need to have some goals defined. The following subsection explains how you can create your goals.

Defining goals

To define your conversion goals, click on the Analytics Settings link on the top-left corner of the Google Analytics screen, and then click on the Edit button for the desired profile (site). You should see a screen similar to the portion shown in Figure 7-22.

You can define four different goals for each profile. In this case, you should click on the Edit link as shown in Figure 7-23. You should then see the screen in Figure 7-24, shown later in this chapter.

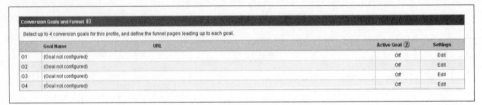

Figure 7-22. Google Analytics: Goal creation step 1

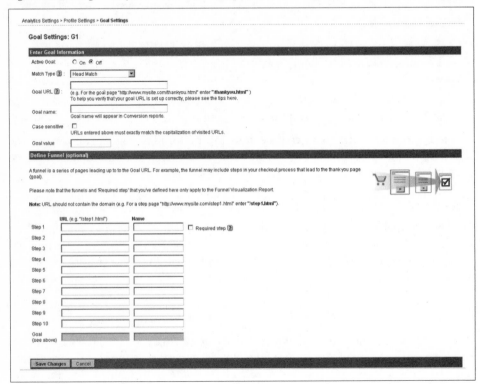

Figure 7-23. Google Analytics: Goal creation step 2

Filling out the top portion of the form is mandatory. Let's examine those details first. There are several key fields. The first field allows you to make the goal active or inactive. Since this is a new goal, select the On radio button.

The next field, Match Type, has three options: Exact Match, Head Match, and Regular Expression Match. Exact Match implies identical URLs of the target goal page and the one you specify in this form. Head Match implies a partial match (useful for dynamic URLs).

If the URL you specify in this form matches any part of a user's URL, the goal condition will have been met. The situation is similar with a regular expression match. If the expression matches the user's URL, you have your goal condition (conversion).

Regular Expression Match is the most powerful of the three match types. For more information, review the Google guide at *http://bit.ly/1QUZyZ*.

Moving down the form we get to the "Goal URL" field. In this field you enter the destination (conversion) URL based on the previous field (match type). For the simplest case, just add your goal (relative or absolute) link. Make sure your match type is set to Exact Match.

The next field is "Goal name." You can enter any name that makes sense for your particular goal. For example, if your goal is for people to sign up for your email newsletter, you can enter "Email Newsletter."

Moving farther down we get to the "Case sensitive" field. By default, the URL characters are case-insensitive. If you wish to change that, check this option to enable case sensitivity.

The last field, "Goal value," allows you to add a particular (e.g., monetary) value to the goal. If you are not sure what to add, you can just leave it at zero. How you define your conversion value depends entirely on your site. If you are selling an e-book product, for instance, you could put the e-book's price as your goal value.

Defining funnels

What is a funnel? A *funnel* is an ordered set of pages leading to a goal page. Let's suppose you are an online retailer and are selling different products. The following code fragment illustrates the typical order of operations on your site, starting from browsing for products:

```
/ProductCatalog.asp?prroductid=1234&  (Product Catalog Page)
/AddToCart.asp                        (Add to Cart Page)
/Checkout.asp                         (Checkout Page)
/Shipping.asp                         (Shipping Page)
/Billing.asp                          (Billing Page)
/ThankYouConfirmation.asp             (Purchase Order Goal)
```

You could use this exact sequence when creating your funnel. Once you set it up, you can view reports to see whether all people went from the first step to the last or whether some people changed their minds in the middle of your funnel sequence.

If some people changed their minds, you can then research why this could be the case. For example, some people may not like your shipping rates, whereas others may not like your billing options. Figure 7-24 illustrates how this would look in a complete form.

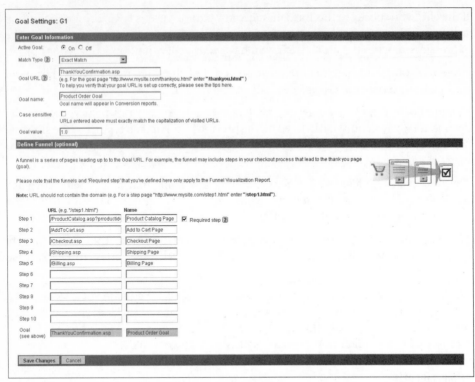

Figure 7-24. Google Analytics: Goal and funnel setup

Viewing goal stats

You can see all the things we discussed in the preceding subsections related to goals and funnels by using the submenu options under the Goal main menu item: namely, Total Conversion, Conversion Rate, Goal Abandoned Funnels, Goal Value, and Funnel Visualization. Note that the Goal Abandoned Funnels feature is being phased out.

Google Analytics Shortcomings

Although the Google Analytics platform continues to improve, it is still not perfect. Many times you need to use different workarounds to get what you want. The following subsections illustrate some of these shortcomings.

Based on JavaScript

Because it is based on JavaScript, Google Analytics is not 100% accurate. JavaScript resides in HTML pages. All of your other files, including image, video, and audio files, are not supported out of the box. You typically need to create some sort of workaround.

For more information on tracking your file downloads with Google Analytics, visit *http://www.google.com/support/googleanalytics/bin/answer.py?answer=55529*.

Furthermore, Google Analytics will not record any data on devices that do not support, or that disable, JavaScript. Many mobile devices fall into this category. Including Google Analytics code in every HTML file creates a bit of overhead. To speed up screen rendering, many mobile devices will ignore the JavaScript by intent or by user selection.

Metrics accuracy

No tool is perfect. Although Google Analytics provides lots of cool metrics, its accuracy is questionable at best. For example, how does Google calculate the average time a visitor spent on a site? Let's suppose there are only two pages on a website. The user arrives on the first page, reads the page, and then moves off to the second page. How does Google know whether the user read the second page? What if the user moved away from the computer, came back 30 minutes later, and then returned to the first page? You can see how this metric could be skewed, and this is only one scenario.

Now let's consider the bounce rate. Again, it sounds like a great metric, telling you the number of users who come to the first page of the website and then leave. But what if a user comes to a single-page site? The user goes to this site, reads the page copy, and leaves 10 minutes later. Does this indicate a user who did not find what he was looking for?

Although Google Analytics is great at many things it does, it is far from perfect. You can accomplish everything Google Analytics does and more with old-fashioned web server logs and a solid third-party analytics tool. Web server logs do not lie or report inaccurate data.

Google Analytics does have its benefits, as it is (almost) live and can be accessed from anywhere. With Google's integration of Analytics with its other flagship platforms, the reasons for joining Google Analytics are plentiful.

Summary

In this chapter, we covered two of the most important Google tools: Google Webmaster Tools and Google Analytics. You can leverage both when auditing sites. Marketers like using Google Analytics due to its conversion tracking and comprehensive reporting features. As a rule of thumb, it would be best to use at least two different tools of this type to make intelligent SEO decisions.

## CHAPTER 8

Search Engine Traps

Although search engine technology is getting better, it is still not good enough to index every bit of dynamic content. This is why it is always better to stick to basic text or HTML on your web pages—in theory. In practice, that is not always feasible. If you have to use dynamic content, yet need to ensure proper search engine crawling, you must be careful how you do it. This chapter goes over many search engine traps and how to deal with them in your code.

JavaScript Traps

JavaScript is a client-side scripting language that runs on web browsers. For the most part, you cannot see this code if you are just looking at a web page. You do get to see some of its effects when you see pop-up/pop-under windows, animations, and so forth.

JavaScript-Generated Content

You will want to put any content you want to index outside the JavaScript code. Here is some example code that shows dynamic text within JavaScript:

```
<HTML>
<head>

<title>Example of Dynamic Text</title>

<script type="text/javascript">
function defaultInfo1(){
    var infoText1="";
    document.getElementById('infoblock').innerHTML = infoText1;
}
function onMouseOverInfo1(){
        var infoText1="Product A description goes here.";
        document.getElementById('infoblock').innerHTML = infoText1;
}
function defaultInfo2(){
    var infoText2="";
```

```
        document.getElementById('infoblock').innerHTML = infoText2;
}
function onMouseOverInfo2(){
        var infoText2="Product B description goes here.";
        document.getElementById('infoblock').innerHTML = infoText2;
}
</script>
</head>

<body>
<img src="productA.jpg" onmouseover="onMouseOverInfo1()"
onmouseout="defaultInfo1();"/>

<img src="productB.jpg" onmouseover="onMouseOverInfo2()"
onmouseout="defaultInfo2();"/>

<br>
<br>

<div id="infoblock"></div>
</body>

</HTML>
```

If you examine the code, you will see that the text used for image mouseovers is buried
in the actual JavaScript code. Most search engines will ignore this. If you point your
mouse cursor over either image (`productA.jpg` or `productB.jpg` in the code), you can
see the dynamically generated text immediately below the image, as shown in Figure 8-1. In this example, the mouse was moved over the "Product A" image.

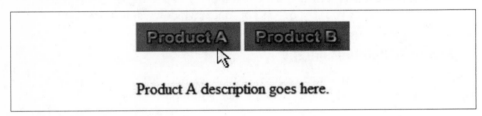

Figure 8-1. Dynamic text: OnMouseOver output

This example is frequently used in sites that want to show more information but in the
same screen real estate. Here is code that achieves the same effect, but in an SEO-
friendly way:

```
<HTML>
<head>
<title>Example of Dynamic Text</title>
<style>
div.infoblock1 {
  display:none;
}
div.infoblock2 {
  display:none;
```

```
    }
    </style>
    <script type="text/javascript">
    function defaultInfo1(){
        document.getElementById('infoblock').innerHTML = "";
    }
    function onMouseOverInfo1(){
            document.getElementById('infoblock').innerHTML =
     document.getElementById('infoblock1').innerHTML;
    }
    function defaultInfo2(){
        document.getElementById('infoblock').innerHTML = "";
    }
    function onMouseOverInfo2(){
            document.getElementById('infoblock').innerHTML =
     document.getElementById('infoblock2').innerHTML;
    }
    </script>
    </head>

    <body>

    <img src="productA.jpg" onmouseover="onMouseOverInfo1()"
     onmouseout="defaultInfo1();"/>
    <img src="productB.jpg" onmouseover="onMouseOverInfo2()"
     onmouseout="defaultInfo2();"/>

    <br>
    <br>

    <div id="infoblock"></div>

    <div id="infoblock1" class="infoblock1">Product A description goes
    here.</div>

    <div id="infoblock2" class="infoblock2">Product B description goes
    here.</div>

    </body>
    </HTML>
```

The output of this code is identical to that of the previous code. The only difference is that in this code you are placing all your text with the HTML instead of the JavaScript. Another option is to put your CSS into separate files and prohibit search engines from accessing the CSS files within your *robots.txt* file.

At the time of this writing, some rumors are circulating that Google does not index hidden (HTML) DIV tags. The premise is that search engine spammers are using these techniques to fool search engines. Although this may be true, many times this sort of functionality is necessary to present more information in the same screen real estate. When in doubt, simply ask yourself whether the method is deceptive or designed only for web crawlers. If the answer is no in both cases, you should be fine.

JavaScript Dynamic Links and Menus

Many sites use JavaScript to create links to other website pages. Here is some example code with different link types that you may want to avoid:

```html
<HTML>
<head>
<title>Link Examples ~ Things to stay away from</title>

<script type="text/javascript">
function gotoLocationX(){
    window.location.href='http://www.cnn.com';
}
function gotoLocationY(){
    window.location.href='http://www.yahoo.com';
}
function gotoLocationZ(){
    window.location.href='http://www.google.com';
}
</script>

</head>
<body>

Example 1:
<a href="#" onClick="javascript:window.location.href=
'http://www.cnn.com'">News on CNN</a>
<br><br>

Example 2:
<a href="#" onClick="javascript:gotoLocationY()">Yahoo Portal</a>
<br><br>

Example 3:
<form>
<input name="mybtn" value="Google Search Engine" type=button
onClick="window.location.href='http://www.google.com'">
</form>
<br><br>
</body>
</html>
```

When you open this code in your browser, you will see a screen similar to Figure 8-2.

This is not to say that you can never use dynamic links. You obviously can, but you need to think about tweaking your code to help web spiders see what they need to see. Looking back at the preceding example, instead of this:

```html
<a href="#" onClick="javascript:gotoLocationY()">Yahoo Portal</a>
```

use this:

```html
<a href="http://www.yahoo.com" onClick="javascript:gotoLocationY()">
Yahoo Portal</a>
```

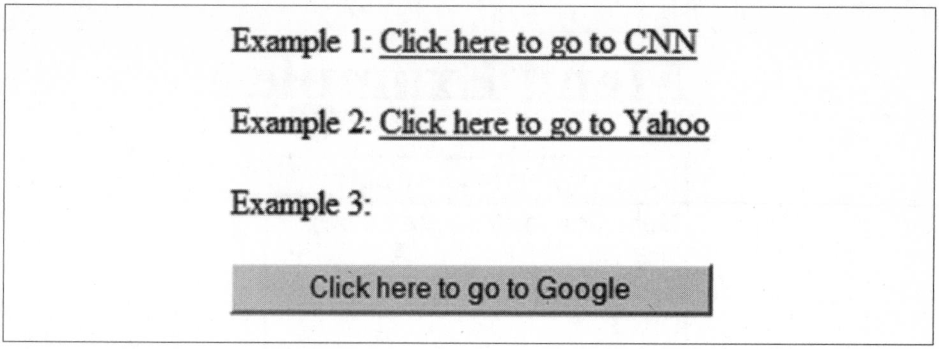

Example 1: <u>Click here to go to CNN</u>

Example 2: <u>Click here to go to Yahoo</u>

Example 3:

Click here to go to Google

Figure 8-2. Bad link examples output

Plenty of sites are using dynamic JavaScript menus. The following code fragment is one such variant:

```html
<html>
<head>
<script type="text/javascript">
function goTo( form ) {
    var optionIndex = form.menuOption.selectedIndex;
    if ( optionIndex == 0 ) {
        //do nothing
    } else {
        selectedURL = form.menuOption.options[ optionIndex ].value;
        window.location.assign( selectedURL );
    }
}
</script>
</head>
<body>
<h1>Menu Example</h1>
<form name="myform">
<select name="menuOption" size="1" onChange="goTo( this.form )">
  <option>Menu Options (choose below)</option>
  <option value="http://www.abcde.com/keyword1.html">Link 1</option>
  <option value="http://www.abcde.com/keyword2.html">Link 2</option>
  <option value="http://www.abcde.com/keyword3.html">Link 3</option>
  <option value="http://www.abcde.com/keyword4.html">Link 4</option>
  <option value="http://www.abcde.com/keyword5.html">Link 5</option>
</select>
</form>
</body>
</HTML>
```

This HTML code renders in your browser as shown in Figure 8-3. Note that the figure represents the state of the drop-down box upon clicking the down arrow button.

If you click on any of the choices shown in Figure 8-3, your browser opens the corresponding link. The basic problem with this approach is that we are using a nonstandard link to go to a particular page. This type of linking would present problems to web spiders, and hence would leave some of your links unspidered. There are even worse

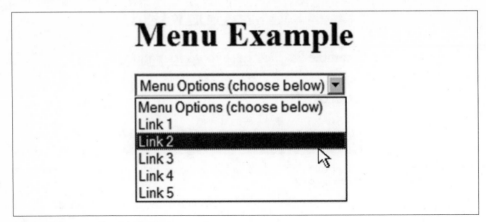

Figure 8-3. Example of bad menus, part 2

examples in which the actual links are stored in external JavaScript or HTML files. Stay away from these designs.

Many free menu scripts on the Internet are SEO-friendly. You can find several of them at *http://www.dynamicdrive.com* and similar websites. The basic idea behind SEO-friendly menus is that all links are placed with the proper link tags within `DIV`s in plain HTML. The "cool" effects are achieved with the clever use of CSS and JavaScript.

There are other ways to improve the readability of your links. If for some reason you cannot specify links within the link tags, you can use these methods:

- Create a Sitemap listing of your links. A Sitemap is a simple HTML page that contains links. If your Sitemap is too large, you can break it up. You may also create search engine–specific Sitemaps.

- List all your dynamic links within the `<noscript>` tags. This is legitimate, as you are trying to help the search engine see only identical links.

Ajax

Ajax is a technology based on JavaScript and XML, and stands for Asynchronous Java-Script and XML. It is used to change certain parts of a web page by reloading only related fragments instead of the full page.

The basic problem with Ajax is that web crawlers will not execute any JavaScript when they read an HTML file containing Ajax. Let's look at a typical Ajax implementation loading external file content:

```
<HTML>

<head>
<script type="text/javascript">
function externalFileImport(resourceOrFile, pageElementId) {
```

```
    var objInstance = (window.ActiveXObject) ? new ActiveXObject(
"Microsoft.XMLHTTP") : new XMLHttpRequest();
  if (objInstance) {
    objInstance.onreadystatechange = function() {
      if (objInstance.readyState == 4 && objInstance.status == 200) {
        pageElement = document.getElementById(pageElementId);
        pageElement.innerHTML = objInstance.responseText;
      }
    }
    objInstance.open("GET", resourceOrFile, true);
    objInstance.send(null);
  }
}
</script>
</head>

<body>

<div id="mycontent"></div>

<script type="text/javascript">
externalFileImport('header.html','mycontent');
</script>

</body>
</HTML>
```

If you examine the source code, you will notice that this HTML file does not have any content in itself. It tries to load *header.html*, an external HTML file, with a call to the externalFileImport JavaScript/Ajax function. The output of this HTML file looks like Figure 8-4.

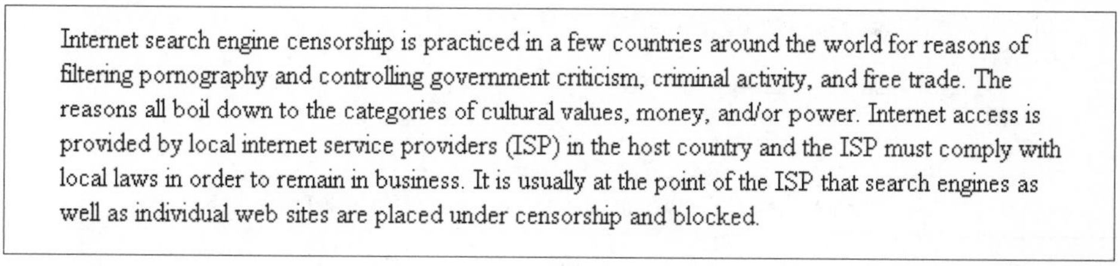

Internet search engine censorship is practiced in a few countries around the world for reasons of filtering pornography and controlling government criticism, criminal activity, and free trade. The reasons all boil down to the categories of cultural values, money, and/or power. Internet access is provided by local internet service providers (ISP) in the host country and the ISP must comply with local laws in order to remain in business. It is usually at the point of the ISP that search engines as well as individual web sites are placed under censorship and blocked.

Figure 8-4. Output of Ajax code

Now, this should give you a hint of the content within the *header.html* file. The content of *header.html* is plain text:

```
Internet search engine censorship is practiced in a few countries
around the world for reasons of filtering pornography and
controlling government criticism, criminal activity, and free trade.
The reasons all boil down to the categories of cultural values, money,
and/or power. Internet access is provided by local internet service
providers (ISP) in the host country and the ISP must comply with local
laws in order to remain in business. It is usually at the point of the
ISP that search engines as well as individual web sites are placed
under censorship and blocked.
```

Considering the fact that web spiders will never execute any JavaScript in the HTML code, this means the search engines will never index any content found in *header.html*.

We advise you to stay away from Ajax if you want to allow the search engines to properly index your website. Nonetheless, using Ajax is a very attractive way to improve the web user experience. However, be selective in terms of where you employ it.

Dynamic Widget Traps

Dynamic widget traps are Flash files, Java applets, and ActiveX controls. All of these technologies are similar in the sense that they provide features that are not usually available within JavaScript, CSS, or DHTML. Be careful when using widgets based on these platforms.

Using Flash

Flash specifically refers to advanced graphics or animations programmed in Action-Script for the Adobe Flash platform. Although Flash is almost always used for animations, sites without animation can be built in Flash, but doing so is a bad idea from an SEO point of view.

Whenever you see online video games with advanced graphics/animation, chances are they were done in Flash. Many web designers use Flash to create their sites. Flash is not a problem in general, but the same rules apply as with JavaScript. If the content you are presenting in Flash needs to be indexed, take it out of Flash. Here is a typical example of HTML source code with an embedded Flash application:

```
<HTML>
<HEAD>
    <TITLE>Flash Page Example</TITLE>
</HEAD>
<BODY>
<OBJECT classid='clsid:D27CDB6E-AE6D-11cf-96B8-444553540000' codebase
='http://download.macromedia.com/pub/shockwave/cabs/flash/swflash.cab
#version=5,0,0,0'
 WIDTH=100% HEIGHT=100% id=ShockwaveFlash1>
<PARAM NAME=movie VALUE='busi_01_01.swf'>
<PARAM NAME=menu VALUE=false>
<PARAM NAME=quality VALUE=high>
<PARAM NAME=scale VALUE=exactfit>
<PARAM NAME=bgcolor VALUE="#FFFFFF">

<EMBED src='flashappABC.swf'
        menu=false
        quality=high
        scale=exactfit
        bgcolor="#FFFFFF"
        WIDTH=100%
        HEIGHT=100%
        TYPE='application/x-shockwave-flash'
```

```
PLUGINSPAGE='http://www.macromedia.com/shockwave/download/index.cgi?
P1_Prod_Version=ShockwaveFlash'>
</EMBED>
</OBJECT>
</BODY>
</HTML>
```

The key item to note in the source code is the filename of the Flash application: *flashappABC.swf*. In most cases, everything this application needs, including graphics, text, and animations, is stored in this file or is loaded from other external files usually not usable by search engine spiders.

Google's support of Adobe Flash

In June 2008, Google announced the improved ability to index Flash files. You can confirm this on Adobe's website, which states, "Google has already begun to roll out Adobe Flash Player technology incorporated into its search engine." Other search engines are likely to follow. For more information, visit the following URLs:

- *http://googlewebmastercentral.blogspot.com/2008/06/improved-flash-indexing .html*
- *http://www.adobe.com/devnet/flashplayer/articles/swf_searchability.html*

If you are curious what Googlebot will index in your Flash *.swf* files, download the *swf2html* utility from the Adobe website.

Using Java Applets

Java applets are similar to Adobe Flash technology. Java applets have many practical purposes, including financial applications, games, and chat applications. Java applet technology is based on Java technology created by Sun Microsystems.

The same rules apply for Java applets as for Flash content. Any content you wish to be visible to search engines should stay out of Java applets. Here is how Java applets are embedded in HTML code:

```
<HTML>
<head>
<title>Sample Applet</title>
</head>
<body>
<H1> Sample Applet </H1><br>
You need a Java enabled browser to view these. <br>
<hr>
<applet code="ExampleApplication.class" width=700 height=400>Pheonix
 Applet</applet>
<hr>
</body>
</HTML>
```

As you can see, the HTML source code contains hardly any content. Everything the applet needs is embedded in the "class" file.

Using ActiveX Controls

ActiveX controls are similar to Java applets and Flash files. They typically run on the Internet Explorer browser and are web components based on Microsoft technology:

```
<HTML>

<head>
<title>Sample Active X Control</title>
</head>

<body>
<H1> Sample Active X Control </H1>
<br>
<hr>
<OBJECT ID="colorCtl" WIDTH=248 HEIGHT=192
    CLASSID="CLSID:FC25B790-85BE-12CF-2B21-665553560606">
    <PARAM NAME="paramA" VALUE="121">
    <PARAM NAME="paramB" VALUE="133">
    <PARAM NAME="paramC" VALUE="144>
    <PARAM NAME="paramD" VALUE="red">
    <PARAM NAME="paramE" VALUE="blue">
    <PARAM NAME="paramF" VALUE="green">
</OBJECT>
<hr>
</body>
</HTML>
```

The same rules apply to ActiveX controls as to Java applets and Flash files. If you need web spiders to index anything inside an ActiveX control, remove that content from the ActiveX control.

HTML Traps

There are several HTML-related traps. These include the use of frames, iframes, external DIVs, graphical text, large HTML files, and complex (or erroneous) HTML.

Using Frames

For better or for worse, HTML frames are still used on many websites today. The idea of HTML frames was to help in website navigation by separating distinct screen areas into more easily manageable units. Figure 8-5 shows a typical frame layout.

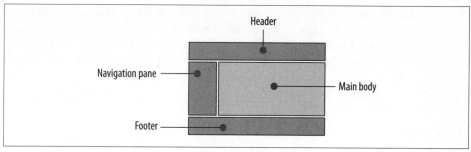

Figure 8-5. Sample frame structure

The following HTML code created the layout in Figure 8-5:

```
<HTML>
<head>
<title>Frame Example</title>
</head>
<noframes>
This website was designed with frames. Please use a browser that
supports frames.
</noframes>

<frameset rows="15%,70%,15%">
   <frame src=header.html">
   <frameset cols="20%,80%">
     <frame src="navigation.html">
     <frame src="mainbody.html">
   </frameset>
   <frame src="footer.html">
</frameset>
</HTML>
```

So, where is the problem? The biggest problem is that some search engines may not be able to crawl all of your pages. Some of these search engines might even choose to ignore anything within the `<frameset>` and `</frameset>` tags. To help the situation, you can add links to your main content between the `<noframes>` and `</noframes>` tags.

Now, let's say the search engine can index all your pages within your framed structure. There is still a problem: search engines will more than likely return your frame fragments instead of the frameset definition page. Do you want to show *navigation.html* or *footer.html* or even *mainbody.html* by itself or as part of the whole framed structure? In most cases, you probably want to avoid these scenarios. Although there are some clever JavaScript ways to address this problem, these workarounds are hardly a good solution.

The consensus these days is to stay away from frames for proper search engine indexing. Some people would disagree with that statement. Strictly from a design standpoint, frames can look clunky and outdated, but the bottom line is that all new web browsers and most search engines still support frames.

If you do use HTML frames, chances are Google will index your pages, but again, the users who get to your site from Google might arrive in a way that you did not intend (e.g., by seeing pages individually, even though you intended that they be shown in combination with other pages). I stay away from frames because most of the websites I design are dynamic, and this framing effect can be done easily in JSP, PHP, ASP, CGI, Python, or ColdFusion, thereby defeating the purpose of using HTML frames.

Using Iframes

Iframe stands for *inline frame*. Some people call iframes a poor man's frames. They have fewer features and are harder to set up, but are still used. Google and others can read iframe tags with no problems. They will also follow an iframe's page link (if present). The problem is that the iframe source URL is indexed separately. Here is an example page with an iframe using content from an outside file:

```
<HTML>
<head>
<title>Loading Content with IFRAME Example</title>
</head>

<body>
Lorem Ipsum 1 | Lorem Ipsum 1 | Lorem Ipsum 1 | Lorem Ipsum 1 |
Lorem Ipsum 1 | Lorem Ipsum 1 | Lorem Ipsum 1 | Lorem Ipsum 1 |
Lorem Ipsum 1 | Lorem Ipsum 1 | Lorem Ipsum 1 | Lorem Ipsum 1 |
Lorem Ipsum 1 | Lorem Ipsum 1 | Lorem Ipsum 1 | Lorem Ipsum 1 |
Lorem Ipsum 1 | Lorem Ipsum 1 | Lorem Ipsum 1 | Lorem Ipsum 1 |
Lorem Ipsum 1 | Lorem Ipsum 1 | Lorem Ipsum 1 | Lorem Ipsum 1 |
Lorem Ipsum 1 | Lorem Ipsum 1 | Lorem Ipsum 1 | Lorem Ipsum 1 |
Lorem Ipsum 1 | Lorem Ipsum 1 | Lorem Ipsum 1 | Lorem Ipsum 1 |
Lorem Ipsum 1 | Lorem Ipsum 1 <br><br>

<iframe src="externalIframeContent.html" scrolling="no"
id="externalContent"
name="externalContent" height="400" width="100%" frameborder="0" >
If you are seeing this text your browser does not support Iframes.
</iframe>
</body>
</HTML>
```

Here is the content of the *externalIframeContent.html* file:

```
Lorem Ipsum 2 | Lorem Ipsum 2 | Lorem Ipsum 2 | Lorem Ipsum 2 |
Lorem Ipsum 2 | Lorem Ipsum 2 | Lorem Ipsum 2 | Lorem Ipsum 2 |
Lorem Ipsum 2 | Lorem Ipsum 2 | Lorem Ipsum 2 | Lorem Ipsum 2 |
Lorem Ipsum 2 | Lorem Ipsum 2 | Lorem Ipsum 2 | Lorem Ipsum 2 |
Lorem Ipsum 2 | Lorem Ipsum 2 | Lorem Ipsum 2 | Lorem Ipsum 2 |
Lorem Ipsum 2 | Lorem Ipsum 2 | Lorem Ipsum 2 | Lorem Ipsum 2 |
Lorem Ipsum 2 | Lorem Ipsum 2 | Lorem Ipsum 2 | Lorem Ipsum 2 |
Lorem Ipsum 2 | Lorem Ipsum 2 | Lorem Ipsum 2 | Lorem Ipsum 2 |
Lorem Ipsum 2 | Lorem Ipsum 2 <br><br>
```

So, the overall output of the main HTML file that contains the iframe definition looks similar to Figure 8-6.

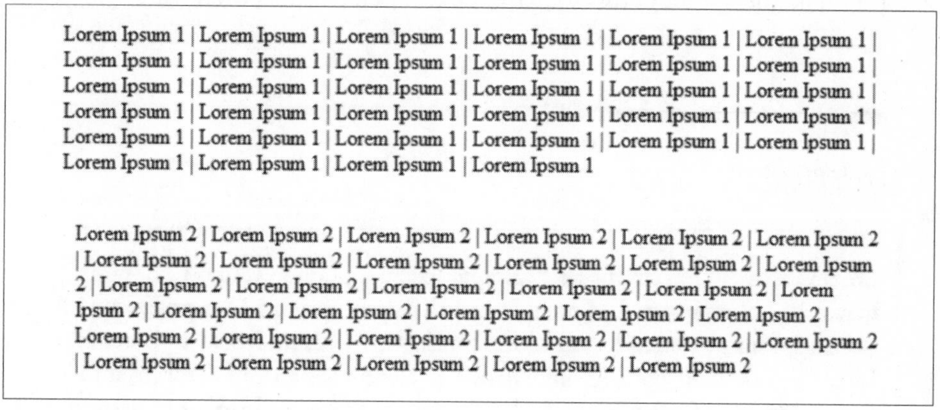

Lorem Ipsum 1 | Lorem Ipsum 1 | Lorem Ipsum 1 | Lorem Ipsum 1 | Lorem Ipsum 1 | Lorem Ipsum 1 | Lorem Ipsum 1 | Lorem Ipsum 1 | Lorem Ipsum 1 | Lorem Ipsum 1 | Lorem Ipsum 1 | Lorem Ipsum 1 | Lorem Ipsum 1 | Lorem Ipsum 1 | Lorem Ipsum 1 | Lorem Ipsum 1 | Lorem Ipsum 1 | Lorem Ipsum 1 | Lorem Ipsum 1 | Lorem Ipsum 1 | Lorem Ipsum 1 | Lorem Ipsum 1 | Lorem Ipsum 1 | Lorem Ipsum 1 | Lorem Ipsum 1 | Lorem Ipsum 1 | Lorem Ipsum 1 | Lorem Ipsum 1 | Lorem Ipsum 1 | Lorem Ipsum 1 | Lorem Ipsum 1 | Lorem Ipsum 1 | Lorem Ipsum 1 | Lorem Ipsum 1 | Lorem Ipsum 1 | Lorem Ipsum 1 | Lorem Ipsum 1 | Lorem Ipsum 1 | Lorem Ipsum 1 | Lorem Ipsum 1 | Lorem Ipsum 1 | Lorem Ipsum 1

Lorem Ipsum 2 | Lorem Ipsum 2 | Lorem Ipsum 2 | Lorem Ipsum 2 | Lorem Ipsum 2 | Lorem Ipsum 2 | Lorem Ipsum 2 | Lorem Ipsum 2 | Lorem Ipsum 2 | Lorem Ipsum 2 | Lorem Ipsum 2 | Lorem Ipsum 2 | Lorem Ipsum 2 | Lorem Ipsum 2 | Lorem Ipsum 2 | Lorem Ipsum 2 | Lorem Ipsum 2 | Lorem Ipsum 2 | Lorem Ipsum 2 | Lorem Ipsum 2 | Lorem Ipsum 2 | Lorem Ipsum 2 | Lorem Ipsum 2 | Lorem Ipsum 2 | Lorem Ipsum 2 | Lorem Ipsum 2 | Lorem Ipsum 2 | Lorem Ipsum 2 | Lorem Ipsum 2 | Lorem Ipsum 2 | Lorem Ipsum 2 | Lorem Ipsum 2 | Lorem Ipsum 2 | Lorem Ipsum 2

Figure 8-6. Iframe example

If the external content loaded by the iframe is important to your parent page, you may want to reconsider your design, as it will not be indexed as part of the parent page.

Iframes present an additional SEO problem if you are trying to use JavaScript to change the page's content dynamically. We already saw something similar with the use of Ajax. For completeness, here is sample HTML that shows this scenario with iframes:

```
<HTML>

<head>
<title>Dynamic External File Loading with an IFRAME</title>
</head>

<body>

Click on links to see different  files!
<br><br>

<a href="#" onclick="javascript:externalContent.document.location
 ='file1.html'">Link 1</a> |

<a href="#" onclick="javascript:externalContent.document.location
 ='file2.html'">Link 2</a>

<br><br>

<iframe name="externalContent" scrolling="No" width="500"
height="300" frameborder="Yes" >
</iframe>


</body>
</HTML>
```

The *file1.html* file contains a bunch of "Lorem Ipsum 1" text strings. Similarly, *file2.html* contains a bunch of "Lorem Ipsum 2" text strings. So, when you click on the "Link 1" link, the output of this source code would look similar to Figure 8-7.

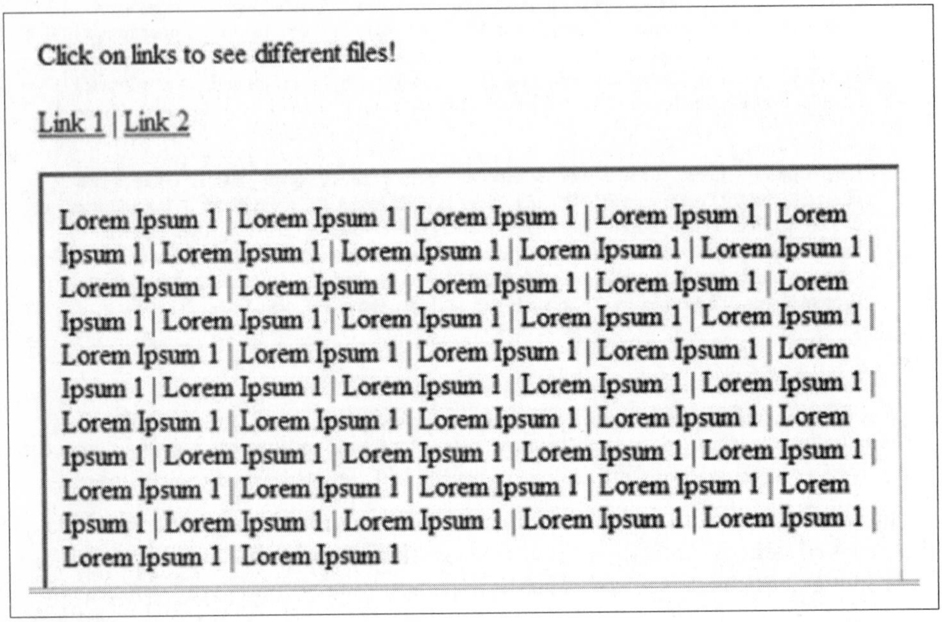

Click on links to see different files!

Link 1 | Link 2

Lorem Ipsum 1 | Lorem Ipsum 1 | Lorem Ipsum 1 | Lorem Ipsum 1 | Lorem Ipsum 1 | Lorem Ipsum 1 | Lorem Ipsum 1 | Lorem Ipsum 1 | Lorem Ipsum 1 | Lorem Ipsum 1 | Lorem Ipsum 1 | Lorem Ipsum 1 | Lorem Ipsum 1 | Lorem Ipsum 1 | Lorem Ipsum 1 | Lorem Ipsum 1 | Lorem Ipsum 1 | Lorem Ipsum 1 | Lorem Ipsum 1 | Lorem Ipsum 1 | Lorem Ipsum 1 | Lorem Ipsum 1 | Lorem Ipsum 1 | Lorem Ipsum 1 | Lorem Ipsum 1 | Lorem Ipsum 1 | Lorem Ipsum 1 | Lorem Ipsum 1 | Lorem Ipsum 1 | Lorem Ipsum 1 | Lorem Ipsum 1 | Lorem Ipsum 1 | Lorem Ipsum 1 | Lorem Ipsum 1 | Lorem Ipsum 1 | Lorem Ipsum 1 | Lorem Ipsum 1 | Lorem Ipsum 1 | Lorem Ipsum 1 | Lorem Ipsum 1 | Lorem Ipsum 1 | Lorem Ipsum 1 | Lorem Ipsum 1 | Lorem Ipsum 1 | Lorem Ipsum 1 | Lorem Ipsum 1 | Lorem Ipsum 1 | Lorem Ipsum 1

Figure 8-7. Iframe: Dynamic content example

The `frameborder` property was set to `yes` to give you a visual hint that whatever is within this border would not be considered part of this page in an SEO sense. It is also possible that search spiders will fail to pick up the two dynamic JavaScript links.

Using External DIVs

Similar types of scenarios can occur if you're loading external files into `DIV` tags. For the most part, using `DIV`s is not a problem. It is the more elegant approach when compared to HTML tables. The major advantage of `DIV`s is that you can show them in a completely different order compared to their source code order.

The problem comes when you are trying to change their content dynamically with the use of JavaScript. We already saw one example with Ajax loading the content of an external file into a `DIV`.

The same rule applies here as with JavaScript. Content that search engines need to index should not be generated by DHTML/JavaScript.

Using Graphical Text

Although there are legitimate uses for graphical text, some people make the mistake of unnecessarily using large amounts of text as images. Figure 8-8 shows an example.

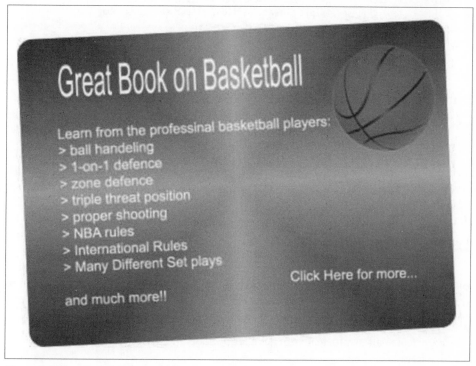

Figure 8-8. Text-in-image example

You could represent this advertisement in HTML as follows:

```
<HTML>
<head>
<title>Special Basketball Book</title>
</head>
<body>
<!-- some unrelated text here -->
<a href="somelink.html"><img src="images\bookimage.jpg"></a>
<!-- some unrelated text here -->
</body>
</HTML>
```

If you are a search engine, what would you think this page or image is about? You would have no clue! Try to think like a search engine; in other words, help the search engine do its job. Here is how the revised HTML code would look:

```
<HTML>
<head>
```

```
<title>Special Basketball Book</title>
</head>
<body>
<!-- some related text here -->
<a href="greatbookonbasketball.html"><img alt="Great book on
Basketball;Learn from basketball professionals ball handling, 1-on-1
defense, zone defense, triple threat position, proper shooting, nba
rules, international rules and much more"
src="images\books\GreatBookOnBasketBallByJohnSmith.jpg"></a>
<!-- some related text here -->
</body>
</HTML>
```

In this example, we optimized the code in three different ways:

- We optimized the actual relative link.
- We qualified the name of the image file.
- We added an ALT description of the image.

At first, this may seem like too much to do, but remember that once most pages are designed, they are rarely modified.

Extremely Large Pages

Sometimes if you're using lots of different third-party JavaScript code, or if you're using older versions of web design software such as Microsoft FrontPage, you may run into trouble with your page size. Here are some things you can do if you are using large HTML files:

- Externalize all or most of your JavaScript code and stylesheets (e.g., .css files) to separate files.
- Place most of the relevant content in the top portion of the HTML.
- Place most of the important links in the top portion of the HTML.

The following HTML code fragment shows these three guidelines in action:

```
<!-- first 100k start -->
<HTML>
<head>
<link rel="stylesheet" type="text/css" href="mystylesheet.css" />
<script src="myjavascript.js" type="text/javascript">
</script>
</head>
<body>
<!--
In this section place:
            > important keywords
            > important links
-->
<!-- first 100k end -->
<!-- rest of document -->
</HTML>
```

Complex HTML and Formatting Problems

You may experience complex HTML and formatting problems when JavaScript and HTML are tightly coupled and JavaScript is all over the HTML code. It is possible that some web spiders might get confused, especially if your HTML code is not well formatted. Here are some examples of how this situation can occur:

- No opening tag
- No closing tag
- Misspelled opening or closing tag
- JavaScript closing tag not found
- Incorrect tag nesting

You should always validate your pages before going live. Many free HTML validators are available on the Internet. One such validator is available at *http://validator.w3 .org/*. When you go to this website, you are presented with a simple form in which you are prompted to enter the URL of the web page you want to validate. A few seconds after you submit your page, you'll get the full report.

 A word of caution regarding HTML validations: you do not have to fix every error or warning you see in a validation report. Focus on the most important points I identified in this section. I use HTML validators in parallel with web spider viewers. Web spider viewers are SEO tools that transform your HTML pages into output resembling what most web spiders will see. This output is essentially clean text with no HTML tags or elements.

If you are new to HTML, you may want to use a user-friendly web page design tool to help you prototype your web pages. In most cases, these tools take care of HTML formatting so that you don't have to worry about HTML validation. One such tool is Adobe Dreamweaver (*http://www.adobe.com/products/dreamweaver/*).

Website Performance Traps

Website performance is important from two perspectives: the web spider's and the web user's. If your site has many thousands of pages, you will want to make sure your site response times are reasonable.

Very Slow Pages

Web spiders are busy creatures. If any of your dynamic pages are computationally intensive, the web spiders might give up waiting on your page to finish loading. In technical terms, this is called *timing out on a request*.

Dynamic pages aren't the only issue that will cause a web spider to give up. If your website is running on a server that is hosting many other sites, it may be slow to respond because of the overwhelming load caused by one of the other sites. As a result, your website might take many seconds to respond. Another problem could be with your web host if it experiences network latency due to limited bandwidth.

You can do some things to remedy these situations. The basic idea is to speed up page transitions to any web client, not just the web spider. Consider using the following:

- Web server compression
- Web page caching

Web server compression

The best way to understand web server compression is to think of sending ZIP files instead of uncompressed files from your web server to your web user. Sending less data over the network will minimize network latency and your web users will get the file faster.

The same thing applies to web spiders, as the major ones support HTTP 1.1. In fact, search engines would appreciate the fact that they will need to use a lot less network bandwidth to do the same work.

Web server compression is a technology used on the web server where you are hosting your pages. If you have full control of the web server, you can set up this compression to occur automatically for all websites or pages this server is hosting.

If you do not have this luxury, you can set this up in your code. To set up web server compression in PHP, you can use the following PHP code:

```
<?php
ob_start("ob_gzhandler");
?>
<HTML>
<body>
<p>This is the content of the compressed page.</p>
</body>
</HTML>
```

You can enable web server compression in your code in another way that is even easier than the approach we just discussed. You can use the *php.ini* file that usually sits in your root web folder. If it does not exist, you can create it. You can also place this file in your subfolders to override the root *php.ini* settings. Here is the required fragment:

```
zlib.output_compression=on
```

Note that web server compression may not be enabled on your web hosting provider. If it is, you should consider using it, as it does have a lot of benefits, including the following:

- It speeds up the loading of your pages on clients' PCs.
- It reduces the overall web traffic from your hosting provider to your web visitors.
- It is supported by virtually all newer web browsers.

 The only caveat for the use of web server compression is that some older browsers, including specific versions of Internet Explorer 6, have a bug in handling web server compression (which is a standard based on HTTP 1.1). The chances of someone coming to your site with these older browsers are pretty slim, though.

Web page caching

Many commercial and noncommercial products come with caching options. Inspect your applications and evaluate whether you need to use caching. If you are developing a new application or are using an existing application that does not have a caching capability, you can implement one yourself with very little programming.

There are many ways to accomplish web caching. In this subsection, I will explain how to implement one of the simplest web caching techniques. It involves obtaining a particular dynamic web page snapshot in time and then serving this static version to end users.

Furthermore, to ensure content freshness, there is usually a scheduled, automated task that repeats the process at defined intervals. The most popular use of web application caching is for news websites.

Making this work well requires knowing and using the so-called *welcome files* in the right order. You can think of welcome files as default web page files that will open if a web user requests a URL, only specifying a directory at the end of the URL. The web server then looks at the welcome file list to determine what to serve. Usually, on PHP hosts the first file to be served is *index.html* or *index.htm*. This is followed by *index.php*.

Here is the general procedure for adding a caching capability to any of your news websites. Let's suppose your home page is computationally intensive, with lots of page elements needing lots of time to generate their HTML fragments:

1. Issue a `wget -output-document=index.html` *http://www.abcde.com/index.php* command to grab a snapshot of your current page while storing the snapshot as *index.html*.
2. FTP the *index.html* file to your root web folder as *index.html*.
3. Do this over and over again by creating a scheduled task in your PC.

Figure 8-9 illustrates the information flow.

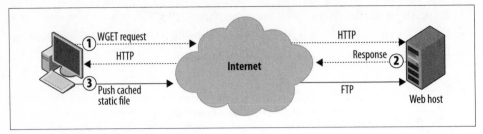

Figure 8-9. Caching content for performance

Use the setup I am describing here if you are using a shared host. You can also perform the scheduled task on the server end. Some shared hosting providers offer the so-called cron job interface using their CPANEL software.

Error Pages

If your website is using server-side scripting languages, chances are you have seen some error pages. In most cases, these error messages are very cryptic or technical and do not provide any help whatsoever. Imagine a web spider hitting a web page that is producing a cryptic error message. This is precisely what search engines will index: the actual error message instead of your desired content.

Different types of errors can occur. One of the most common is the 404 message, which says the page cannot be found. The next most common is the 500 message, which usually signifies a problem in your code. Another frequent message type is the 403 message, which occurs when someone tries to access a web page for which she does not have permission.

To help this situation, you can set up custom web pages to be shown when these errors occur. Although there are different ways to do this, I will mention the simplest one. This method uses the good old *.htaccess* file that usually resides in your web root folder.

With *.htaccess*, you can tell the server to display a special page to the user in case of an error. Ideally, this page should tell the user that something is wrong, downplay the fact that someone messed up (probably you as the webmaster!), and provide a set of links to the major sections of the site so that the user can at least look for what is missing.

Another use is to include a search form on the 404 page. In addition, you can tell the server to run a CGI script instead of simply displaying a static page. If you do this, you can tell the script to log the error for you, or the script can send you an email about the error.

If the file is not there, simply create one with a text editor and add these lines in the file while using your specific path on your server:

```
ErrorDocument 403 /some-relative-path/403.html
ErrorDocument 404 /some-relative-path/404.html
ErrorDocument 500 /some-relative-path/500.html
```

After your *.htaccess* file has been created or updated and placed in the web root of your server, carefully create the corresponding HTML files. In these files, you may want to provide ways for web users—or in our case, web spiders—to gracefully continue on their path, as opposed to seeing nothing to go to in the unhandled error page scenario. If you are familiar with server-side web programming languages, you can handle any sort of runtime errors with even finer-grained control.

Session IDs and URL Variables

Session IDs are legitimate ways to keep user sessions, as some web users have their browser cookies disabled. Many web applications use session IDs. These are unique identifiers that map each user's web session to the current application state. Even Google admits that session IDs are not a great idea. Lots of web users do not allow cookies on their web browsers. This scenario forces web applications to store the session IDs as part of the URLs.

Here are some examples of URLs with session IDs and/or other variables:

- *http://www.abcde.com/product.do?id=123&page=201&items=10&*
- *http://www.abcde.com/product.php?id=fji5t9io49fk3et3h4to489*
- *http://www.abcde.com/product.cgi?sid=485fjh4toi49f4t9iok3et3*
- *http://www.abcde.com/product.asp?sessionid=h49fk5et3489fji4t9io4to*

The basic problem with session IDs stems from the fact that the ID will always be different the next time the web spiders hit your website, thereby giving the impression of a different page (which could be considered as duplicate content).

To help search engine spiders, you can attempt to detect web spider signatures and disable the usage of session IDs in your URLs. Doing so may also get you into trouble, though, as you are now handling web spiders in a different fashion when compared to regular human visitors. This could be considered search engine cloaking.

The situation is a bit easier to handle when it comes to other URL parameters, as long as there are not too many of them. Many website owners deal with URL parameters by way of obfuscation. They use techniques of URL rewriting in tandem with the *.htaccess* file. The net effect is the seeming disappearance of the URL variables. The URL essentially looks static after applying the URL rewriting filter.

Consider the following link:

> *http://www.abcde.com/product.php?id=30*

What if you wanted to rewrite the preceding link to the following?

> *http://www.abcde.com/basketball-30.html*

You could accomplish that with the following snippet of code in the *.htaccess* file:

```
RewriteEngine on
RewriteRule ^basketball-([0-9]+)\.html$ product.php?id=$1
```

Keep in mind that the *.htaccess* file is a very powerful tool for all kinds of things. Be careful anytime you edit or create this file. If you edit this file, be sure to create a backup before making any changes. Do lots of testing before making a move!

Splash or Doorway Pages

Splash/doorway pages usually do not contain any content. To keep this in perspective, we will address legitimate uses of splash or doorway pages. Figure 8-10 illustrates the concept.

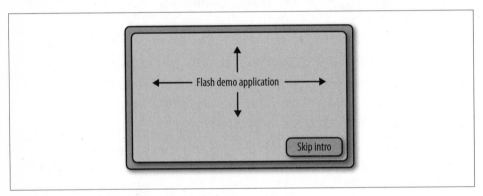

Figure 8-10. Sample Flash doorway or splash page

If all you had was a Flash file as shown in Figure 8-10, the web spider would be stuck and would not have anywhere to go. Ensure that the Skip Intro button is outside the Flash application and is part of your HTML text content. It is imperative that you provide additional links or information around your splash Flash application, such as a link to your Sitemap.

Robots.txt

Yes, that's right! If you are not very careful with the *robots.txt* file, you could be blocking web spiders from crawling content you do want to be indexed. Most reputable web spiders will obey your instructions within *robots.txt*. So, be very careful when you use and edit the *robots.txt* file. Also note that Google Webmaster Tools provides a *robots.txt* checker, so you can enter a URL and confirm whether a given URL will be crawled.

Summary

In this chapter, you saw lots of ways to confuse search engines. As a rule of thumb, anything that you want to be indexed for a particular keyword should be in HTML. It is as simple as that. Although Google and others are continuously improving their search engine technology, stick to the basics to be safe. You'll be surprised at what you can accomplish.

Summary

## CHAPTER 9

Robots Exclusion Protocol

The story of Robots Exclusion Protocol (REP) begins with the introduction of the *robots.txt* protocol in 1993. This is thanks in part to a Perl web crawler hogging network bandwidth of a site whose owner would become the eventual *robots.txt* creator (*http://bit.ly/bRB3H*).

In 1994, REP was formalized by the consensus of a "majority of robot authors" (*http://robotstxt.org/orig.html*). Originally, REP was only meant to allow for resource exclusion. This has changed over time to include directives for inclusion.

When we talk about REP today, we are talking about several things: *robots.txt*, XML Sitemaps, `robots` meta tags, X-Robot-Tag(s), and the `nofollow` link attribute. Understanding REP is important, as it is used for various SEO tasks. Content duplication, hiding unwanted documents from search results, strategic distribution of link juice, and document (search engine) index removal are just some of the things REP can assist with.

Adoption of REP is nonbinding, and it is not necessarily adopted by all search engines. However, the big three search engines (Yahoo!, Google, and Bing) have adopted a strategy of working together in supporting REP in almost a uniform way, while also working together to introduce new REP standards. The goal of these efforts is to provide consistent crawler behavior for the benefit of all webmasters.

This chapter covers REP in detail. Topics include *robots.txt* and its associated directives, HTML meta directives, the *.htaccess* file for simple access control, and the HTTP Header X-Robot-Tag(s). We will also discuss ways for dealing with rogue spiders.

Understanding REP

Before we dig deeper into REP, it is important to reiterate the key differences between indexing and crawling (also known as *spidering*). There is no guarantee if a document is crawled that it will also be indexed.

Crawling Versus Indexing

Crawling is the automated, systematic process of web document retrieval initiated by a web spider. The precursor to indexing, crawling has no say in how pages are ranked. Ideally, all crawling activities should be governed by the agreed-upon standards of REP.

Indexing is the algorithmic process of analyzing and storing the crawled information in an index. Each search engine index is created with a set of rules, ranking factors, or weights governing the page rank for a particular keyword.

Why Prohibit Crawling or Indexing?

You may want to prohibit crawling or indexing for many reasons. Sometimes this is done on just a few pages or documents within certain portions of a site, and other times it is done across the entire site. Here are some typical scenarios.

New sites

Say you've just purchased your domain name. Unless you already changed the default DNS server assignments, chances are that when you type in your domain name, you get to a domain parking page served by your domain registrar. It can be somewhat annoying to see the domain registrar's advertisements plastered all over your domain while passing (at least temporarily) your domain's link juice (if any) to its sites.

Most people in this situation will put up an "Under Construction" page or something similar. If that is the case, you really do not want search engines to index this page. So, in your *index.html* (or equivalent) file, add the following `robots` meta tag:

```
<meta name="robots" content="noindex">
```

The suggested practice is to have a "Coming Soon" page outlining what your site will be all about. This will at least give your visitors some ideas about what to expect from your site in the near future. If for some reason you want to block crawling of your entire site, you can simply create a *robots.txt* file in the root web folder:

```
User-agent: *
Disallow: /
```

The star character (*) implies all web spiders. The trailing slash character (/) signifies everything after the base URL or domain name, including the default document (such as *index.html*).

Content duplication

Content duplication is a common issue in SEO. When your site is serving the same content via different link combinations, it can end up splitting your link juice across the different link permutations for the page.

The *robots.txt* file can be helpful in blocking the crawling of duplicated content, as we will discuss in some examples later in this chapter. We will discuss content duplication in detail in Chapter 14.

REP and document security

Hiding specific pages or files from the SERPs can be helpful. When it comes to documents that should be accessed by only authenticated clients, REP falls short in providing that sort of functionality. Using some sort of authentication system is required. One such system is the *.htaccess* (Basic authentication) method.

Protecting directories with .htaccess. Implementing *.htaccess* protection is relatively straightforward—if you are running your site on an Apache web server on a Linux-flavored OS. Let's look at an example. Suppose we have a directory structure as follows:

```
.\public_html\
.\public_html\images\
.\public_html\blog\
.\public_html\private\
```

We are interested in using Basic HTTP authentication for the *private* subdirectory. Using Basic HTTP authentication requires the creation of two text files, namely *.htaccess* and *.htpasswd*. Here is how the *.htaccess* file might look:

```
AuthType Basic
AuthName "Restricted Area"
AuthUserFile "/home/nonpublicfolder/.passwd"
require valid-user
```

AuthType corresponds to the authentication type, which in our case is Basic HTTP authentication. AuthName corresponds to a string used in the authentication screen after the "The site says:" part, as shown in Figure 9-1. AuthUserFile corresponds to the location of the password file.

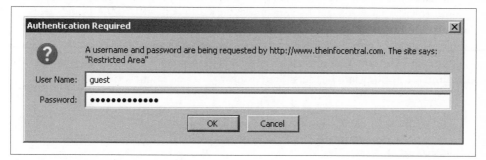

Figure 9-1. Basic HTTP authentication

The *.passwd* file might look as follows:

```
guest:uQbLtt/C1yQXY
john:11Ji97iyY2Zyc
jane:daV/8w4ZiSEf.
mike:DkSWPG/1SuYa6
tom:yruheluOelUrg
```

The *.passwd* file is a colon-separated combination of username and password strings. Each user account is described in a separate line. The passwords are encrypted. You can obtain the encrypted values in several ways. Typically, you would use the following shell command:

```
htpasswd -c .htpasswd guest
```

Upon executing this command, you are asked to enter the password for user *guest*. Finally, the *.htpasswd* text file is created. On subsequent additions of users, simply omit the `-c` command-line argument to append another user to the existing *.htpasswd* file. You can also create encrypted passwords by using the online service available at the Dynamic Drive website (*http://tools.dynamicdrive.com/password/*).

Website maintenance

All sites need to perform maintenance at some point. During that time, Googlebot and others might try to crawl your site. This begs the question: should something be done to present spiders with a meaningful message as opposed to a generic maintenance page? The last thing we want is for search engines to index our maintenance page.

The most appropriate response is to issue the HTTP 503 header. The HTTP 503 response code signifies service unavailability. According to the W3C, the HTTP 503 code is defined as follows (*http://www.w3.org/Protocols/rfc2616/rfc2616-sec10.html*):

> The server is currently unable to handle the request due to a temporary overloading or maintenance of the server. The implication is that this is a temporary condition which will be alleviated after some delay. If known, the length of the delay MAY be indicated in a Retry-After header. If no Retry-After is given, the client SHOULD handle the response as it would for a 500 response.

Handling this scenario is easy with some PHP code. Using the PHP header method, we can write the appropriate headers. Here is how the code might look:

```php
<?php
ob_start();
header('HTTP/1.1 503 Service Temporarily Unavailable');
header('Status: 503 Service Temporarily Unavailable');
header('Retry-After: 7200');
?><html>
<head>
<title>503 Service Temporarily Unavailable</title>
</head>

<body>
<strong>Service Temporarily Unavailable</strong><br><br>
```

```
We are currently performing system upgrades. Website is not available
until 5am. <br>Please try again later and we apologize for any
inconvenience.
<!--file:maintenance.php-->
</body>
</html>
```

The sample code accomplishes two things: it communicates the service outage to the user while also letting spiders know they should not crawl the site during this time. Please note that for this solution to fully work you would also need to write a rewrite rule that would be used to forward all domain requests to this page. You can do this with a simple *.htaccess* file, which you should place in the root folder of your website. Here is how the file might look:

```
Options +FollowSymlinks

RewriteEngine on
RewriteCond %{REQUEST_URI} !/maintenance.php$
RewriteCond %{REMOTE_HOST} !^57\.168\.228\.28

RewriteRule $ /maintenance.php [R=302,L]
```

The *.htaccess* file also allows you as the administrator to browse the site from your hypothetical IP address (57.168.228.28) during the upgrade. Once the upgrade is complete, the maintenance *.htaccess* file should be renamed (or removed) while restoring the original *.htaccess* file (if any).

Anyone hitting the site during the maintenance period would see the following HTTP headers, as produced by running the *maintenance.php* script:

```
GET /private/test.php HTTP/1.1
Host: www.seowarrior.net
User-Agent: Mozilla/5.0 (Windows; U; Windows NT 5.1; en-US; rv:1.9.0.7)
Gecko/2009021910 Firefox/3.0.7
Accept: text/html,application/xhtml+xml,application/xml;q=0.9,*/*;q=0.8
Accept-Language: en-us,en;q=0.5
Accept-Encoding: gzip,deflate
Accept-Charset: ISO-8859-1,utf-8;q=0.7,*;q=0.7
Keep-Alive: 300
Connection: keep-alive
Cookie: PHPSESSID=308252d57a74d86d36a7fde552ff2a7f

HTTP/1.x 503 Service Temporarily Unavailable
Date: Sun, 22 Mar 2009 02:49:30 GMT
Server: Apache/1.3.41 (Unix) Sun-ONE-ASP/4.0.3 Resin/3.1.6
mod_fastcgi/2.4.6 mod_log_bytes/1.2 mod_bwlimited/1.4
mod_auth_passthrough/1.8 FrontPage/5.0.2.2635 mod_ssl/2.8.31
OpenSSL/0.9.7a
Retry-After: 7200
X-Powered-By: PHP/5.2.6
Connection: close
Transfer-Encoding: chunked
Content-Type: text/html
```

The boldface strings are the string values we specified in the PHP file. The first string represents the HTTP status code (503). The second string is the Retry-After segment representing a note to the web crawler to try crawling the site again in two hours (7,200 seconds).

Saving website bandwidth

Although website bandwidth is relatively inexpensive today when compared to the early days of the mainstream Internet, it still adds up in terms of cost. This is especially the case with large websites. If you are hosting lots of media content, including images, audio, and video, you may want to prohibit crawlers from accessing this content. In many cases, you may also want to prohibit crawlers from indexing your CSS, JavaScript, and other types of files.

Before implementing any crawler blocking, first check with your web logs for web spider activities to see where your site is taking hits. Keep in mind that anything you block from crawling will potentially take away some traffic. For example, all the big search engines provide specialized search for images. Sometimes people can learn about your site when only searching for images.

Preventing website performance hits

Certain web pages may be hogging your website's CPU cycles. Taking additional hits on these pages during peak utilization hours can further degrade your site's performance, which your visitors will surely notice.

Sometimes you have no choice but to ensure that crawlers can see these pages. You can utilize several different performance optimizations. These include the use of web page caching, web server compression, content compression (images, video, etc.), and many others techniques. Sometimes you have no other choice but to limit crawling activities by preventing crawl access to CPU-intensive pages.

More on robots.txt

Using *robots.txt* is the original way to tell crawlers what not to crawl. This method is particularly helpful when you do not want search engines to crawl certain portions or all portions of your website. Maybe your website is not ready to be browsed by the general public, or you simply have materials that are not appropriate for inclusion in the SERPs.

When you think of *robots.txt*, it needs to be in the context of crawling and never in terms of indexing. Think of crawling as rules for document access on your website. The use of the *robots.txt* standard is almost always applied at the sitewide level, whereas the use of the robots HTML meta tag is limited to the page level or lower. It is possible to use *robots.txt* for individual files, but you should avoid this practice due to its associated additional maintenance overhead.

All web spiders do not interpret or support the *robots.txt* file in entirely the same way. Although the big three search engines have started to collaborate on the *robots.txt* standard, they still deviate in terms of how they support *robots.txt*.

Is *robots.txt* an absolute requirement for every website? In short, no; but the use of *robots.txt* is highly encouraged, as it can play a vital role in SEO issues such as content duplication.

Creation of robots.txt

Creating *robots.txt* is straightforward and can be done in any simple text editor. Once you've created the file, you should give it read permissions so that it is visible to the outside world. On an Apache web server, you can do this by executing the following command:

```
chmod 644 robots.txt
```

Validation of robots.txt

All *robots.txt* files need to be verified for syntax and functional validity. This is very important for large or complex *robots.txt* files because it takes only a little mistake to affect an entire site.

Many free validators are available on the Web. One such tool is available in the Google Webmaster Tools platform. Microsoft also provides a *robots.txt* validator service (*http: //www.bing.com/webmaster/*). For best results, verify your *robots.txt* files on both platforms.

Google's *robots.txt* analysis tool is particularly useful, as you can verify specific URLs against your current *robots.txt* file to see whether they would be crawled. This can be helpful when troubleshooting current problems or when identifying potential problems.

Placement of robots.txt

The *robots.txt* file must reside in the root folder of your website. This is the agreed standard and there are no exceptions to this rule. A site can have only one *robots.txt* file.

Important Crawlers

Not all crawlers are created equal. Some crawlers crawl your web pages, whereas others crawl your images, news feeds, sound files, video files, and so forth. Table 9-1 summarizes the most popular web crawlers.

Table 9-1. Important crawlers

Google:	
Crawler	**Description**
Googlebot	Crawls web pages (it's the most important of the bunch)
Googlebot-Mobile	Crawls pages specifically designed for mobile devices
Googlebot-Image	Crawls images for inclusion in image search results
Mediapartners-Google	Crawls AdSense content
AdsBot-Google	Crawls AdWords landing pages to measure their quality
Yahoo!:	
Crawler	**Description**
Slurp	Crawls web pages
Yahoo-MMAudVid	Crawls video files
Yahoo-MMCrawler	Crawls images
Bing:	
Crawler	**Description**
MSNBot	Crawls web pages
MSNBot-Media	Crawls media files
MSNBot-News	Crawls news feeds

Thousands of crawlers are operating on the Internet. It would make no sense to pay attention to all of them. Depending on your site's content and the region you are targeting, you may need to pay more attention to other crawlers. Refer to the robots database located at *http://www.robotstxt.org/db.html* for more information on many other web crawlers.

Understanding the robots.txt Format

The *robots.txt* file is composed of a set of directives preceded by specific user-agent heading lines signifying the start of directives for a particular crawler. The following is an example *robots.txt* file that instructs three different crawlers:

```
1 User-agent: *
2 Disallow: /
3 Allow: /blog/
4 Allow: /news/
5 Allow: /private
6
7 User-agent: msnbot
8 Disallow:
9
10 User-agent: googlebot
11 Disallow: /cgi-bin/
```

The first five lines of this example are the instructions for the catchall web crawler. There is a single `Disallow` directive and three `Allow` directives. The remaining lines are specific instructions for Google and Bing crawlers.

If Yahoo!'s Slurp paid a visit to this site, it would honor the first five lines of *robots.txt*—as it does not have its own custom entry within this *robots.txt* file. This example has several interesting scenarios. For instance, what would Slurp do if it had the following URLs to process?

- *http://mydomain.com/blog*
- *http://mydomain.com/blog/*

Which URL would it crawl? The answer would be the second URL, as it fully matches the `Allow` directive on line 3 of the preceding code. The trailing slash signifies a directory, whereas the absence of the trailing slash signifies a file. In this example, it is quite possible that the web server would return the same page.

Similarly, what would happen if Slurp had the following URL references?

- *http://mydomain.com/privatejet.html*
- *http://mydomain.com/private/abcd.html*

Slurp would crawl both of these URLs, as they both match the `Allow` pattern on line 5. Line 5 is also the longest directive. The longest directive always takes precedence!

Robots.txt Directives

The following subsections talk about the various supported *robots.txt* directives.

The Allow directive

The `Allow` directive tells web crawlers that the specified resources can be crawled. When multiple directives are applicable to the same URL, the longest expression takes precedence. Suppose we had a *robots.txt* file as follows:

```
1 User-agent: *
2 Disallow: /private/
3 Allow: /private/abc/
```

We have one `Disallow` directive for the *private* directory. In addition, we have one `Allow` directive for the *abc* subdirectory. Googlebot comes along and has to decide which URL references it needs to crawl:

- *http://www.seowarrior.net/private/abc/*
- *http://www.seowarrior.net/private/abc*
- *http://www.seowarrior.net/private/abc/pv*
- *http://www.seowarrior.net/private*

The answer is that Googlebot needs to crawl all but the second URL, since the longest directive it matches is the `Disallow` directive on line 2 of the preceding code. The first URL is a perfect match of the `Allow` directive. The third URL also matches the `Allow` directive. Finally, the last URL is allowed, since it does not match the `Disallow` directive.

When in doubt, always ask the following question: what is the longest directive that can be applied to a given URL? As a rule of thumb, if no directive can be applied to a given URL, the URL would be allowed.

Let's examine another example. What happens if you have an empty `Allow` directive? Here is the code fragment:

```
User-agent: *
Allow:
```

The simple answer is that nothing happens. It makes no sense to place `Allow` directives when there is not a single `Disallow` directive. In this case, all documents would be allowed for crawling.

The Disallow directive

The `Disallow` directive was the original directive created. It signified the webmaster's desire to prohibit web crawler(s) from crawling specified directories or files. Many sites choose to use this directive only. Its basic format is:

```
Disallow: /directory/
Disallow: /file.ext
```

For the sake of completeness, let's see what happens if we have an empty `Disallow` directive. Consider the following code fragment:

```
User-agent: *
Disallow:
```

In this case, all documents would be allowed for crawling. This seems counterintuitive. But let's think for a moment. Yes, the `Disallow` directive is used, but it does not have any arguments. Since we did not specify any file (or directory) to disallow, everything would be allowed. Let's look at another example:

```
User-agent: *
Disallow: /
```

In this case, everything would be disallowed for crawling. The forward slash (`Disallow`) argument signifies the web root of your site. What a difference a single character makes! Note that both `Allow` and `Disallow` can employ wildcard characters.

The wildcard directives

Two wildcards are used in *robots.txt*: $ and *. Both have functionality similar to how they're used in Perl regular expression matching. You use the dollar sign wildcard ($) when you need to match everything from the end of the URL. You use the star wildcard character (*) to match zero or more characters in a sequence. Let's look at some examples in the following fragment:

```
1 User-agent: *
2 Disallow: *.gif$
3
4 User-Agent: Googlebot-Image
5 Disallow: *.jpg$
6
7 User-Agent: googlebot
8 Disallow: /*sessionid
```

The catchall block (the first two lines) prohibits all obeying spiders from crawling all GIF images. The second block tells Google's image crawler not to crawl any JPG files. The last block speaks to Googlebot. In this case, Googlebot should not crawl any URLs that contain the `sessionid` string. As an example, suppose we have Googlebot and Googlebot-Image crawlers deciding what to do with the following link references:

- *http://mydomain.com/images/header.jpg*
- *http://mydomain.com/product?id=1234&sessionid=h7h1g29k83xh&*
- *http://mydomain.com/images/header.gif*

The net result would be that the Google-Image crawler would not crawl *header.jpg* while crawling *header.gif*. The GIF image would be crawled because the Google-Image crawler ignores the catchall crawler segment when it finds the Google-Image segment. Furthermore, Googlebot would not crawl the second URL, which contains a match for the `Disallow` directive on line 8.

The Sitemap location directive

The big three search engines collaborated on the introduction of the `Sitemap` directive. Here is an excerpt from Yahoo! Search Blog (*http://bit.ly/1FOCMp*):

> All search crawlers recognize robots.txt, so it seemed like a good idea to use that mechanism to allow webmasters to share their Sitemaps. You agreed and encouraged us to allow robots.txt discovery of Sitemaps on our suggestion board. We took the idea to Google and Microsoft and are happy to announce today that you can now find your sitemaps in a uniform way across all participating engines.

The `Sitemap` location directive simply tells the crawler where your Sitemap can be found. Here is an example of the *robots.txt* file utilizing the `Sitemap` directive:

```
Sitemap: http://mydomain.com/sitemap.xml

User-Agent: *
Disallow:
```

The location of the `Sitemap` directive is not mandated. It can be anywhere within the *robots.txt* file. For full coverage of the Sitemaps protocol, see Chapter 10.

The Crawl-delay directive

Only Yahoo! and Bing use the `Crawl-delay` directive. They use it to tell Slurp and MSNBot crawlers how frequently they should check new content. Here is an example:

```
Sitemap: /sitemap.xml

User-agent: *
Disallow: /private/

User-agent: Slurp
Disallow:
Crawl-delay: 0.5

User-agent: MSNBot
Disallow:
Crawl-delay: 15
```

In this example, we have three crawler blocks in addition to the `Sitemap` directive placed at the beginning of *robots.txt*. The first crawler block is of no interest to us, as it is the catchall crawler. The second block tells the Slurp crawler to use a `Crawl-delay` value of 0.5. The last block instructs the MSNBot crawler to use a `Crawl-delay` of 15.

The values of the `Crawl-delay` directive have different meanings to Slurp and MSNBot. For MSNBot, it represents the number of seconds between each crawl. The current allowed range is between one and 600 seconds.

Slurp interprets the `Crawl-delay` directive a bit differently. Here is what Yahoo! says (*http://help.yahoo.com/l/us/yahoo/search/webcrawler/slurp-03.html*):

> Setting the "delay value" in robots.txt to a high value, for example 5 or 10, sets a greater delay for Yahoo! web crawlers accessing your server. Yahoo! suggests that you start with small values (0.5–1), and increase the "delay value" only as needed for an acceptable and comfortable crawling rate for your server. Larger "delay values" add more latency between successive crawling and results in decreasing the optimum Yahoo! web search results of your web server.

Although Google does not support the `Crawl-delay` directive via *robots.txt*, it does have its own alternative. Under the Settings section of Google Webmaster Tools, you can set up the specific crawl rate for your site, as shown in Figure 9-2.

You do not have to set up Google's crawl rate unless you are experiencing performance degradations attributed to crawler activities. The same is true of the `Crawl-delay` directive.

Case Sensitivity

Apache and IIS web servers handle filenames and URLs in different ways. Apache is case-sensitive, which can be attributed to its Unix roots. IIS is case-insensitive. This could have implications when it comes to content duplication issues and link canonicalization.

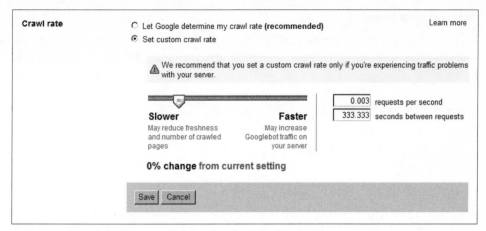

Figure 9-2. Setting the site's crawl rate in Google Webmaster Tools

The *robots.txt* file is case-sensitive. If you are running your website on an IIS platform, you will need to pay close attention to your file and directory naming conventions. This is especially the case if you have various (but really the same) link references to the same content. Let's consider an example. The following fragment shows an arbitrary *robots.txt* file:

```
User-Agent: *
Disallow: /Shop*/*sessionid
```

In this example, we are dealing with a catchall crawler block. There is a single `Disallow` directive with two wildcards. All URLs found that match the given string regular expression should be blocked from crawling.

Now, suppose that crawlers have the following link references to process:

- *http://mydomain.com/Shop-computers/item-1234/sessionid-3487563847/*
- *http://mydomain.com/shop-printers/item-8254/sessionid-3487563847/*

Based on the `Disallow` directive and the fact that *robots.txt* files are case-sensitive, only the first link would be blocked (not crawled).

Common robots.txt Configurations

You can view many examples of common *robots.txt* configurations on the Web just by issuing the `filetype:txt robots.txt` command in Google. The following subsections discuss some typical uses of *robots.txt*. We'll discuss how to block crawling images, allow crawls by Google and Yahoo! only, block crawls of Microsoft Office documents, and block crawls by the Internet Archive.

Disallowing image crawling

You can disallow image crawling in a few ways. These include prohibiting specific image crawlers, prohibiting specific image folders, and prohibiting specific file extensions.

Let's suppose we want to prohibit all image crawling for the most popular search engines. We also want to accomplish this on the sitewide level. The following fragment shows how we can do this:

```
User-agent: Yahoo-MMCrawler
Disallow: /

User-agent: msnbot-media
Disallow: /

User-Agent: Googlebot-Image
Disallow: /
```

In this example, all other crawlers would be able to crawl your images. In some situations you might not care about other crawlers. You can extend this example by explicitly using folder names.

You should always store your images in centralized directories to allow for easy maintenance, and to make it easier to block crawlers. The following fragment speaks to the major crawlers in addition to any other crawlers obeying REP:

```
User-agent: Yahoo-MMCrawler
Disallow: /images/
Allow: /images/public/

User-agent: msnbot-media
Disallow: /images/
Allow: /images/public/

User-Agent: Googlebot-Image
Disallow: /images/
Allow: /images/public/

User-Agent: *
Disallow: /images/
```

In this example, we are blocking all crawlers from crawling all images in the *images* folder, with one exception. Google, Yahoo!, and Bing are allowed to crawl any images that contain */images/public/* in their URL path.

The easiest way to block all images is by using *robots.txt* wildcards. Suppose you are using only three image types: GIF, PNG, and JPG. To block crawling of these types of images, you would simply use the following code:

```
User-agent: *
Disallow: /*.gif$
Disallow: /*.jpg$
Disallow:/*.png$
```

Allowing Google and Yahoo!, but rejecting all others

If your target audience is in North America or Europe, you may want to target only Google and Yahoo!. The following fragment shows how to implement this sort of setup:

```
User-agent: slurp
Disallow:

User-agent: googlebot
Disallow:

User-agent: *
Disallow: /
```

Blocking Office documents

You already saw examples of blocking specific image file types. Nothing is restricting you from blocking the crawling of many other file types. For example, to restrict access to Microsoft Office files, simply use the following fragment:

```
User-agent: *
Disallow: /*.doc$
Disallow: /*.xls$
Disallow: /*.ppt$
Disallow: /*.mpp
Disallow: /*.mdb$
```

Blocking Internet Archiver

Did you know that the Internet Archive website (*http://www.archive.org*) contains billions of web pages from the mid-1990s onward? For archiving purposes, the Internet Archiver makes use of its crawler, which is called `ia_archiver`. Most website owners are not even aware of this. Sometimes this is something you may not wish to allow. To block your site from being archived, use the following fragment:

```
User-agent: ia_archiver
Disallow: /
```

Summary of the robots.txt Directive

It took many years before major search engines started to endorse a common approach in supporting REP consistently. Webmasters and content publishers do appreciate this "coming together" of the big three search engines, as they can now develop sites more easily by having a nearly identical set of rules when it comes to REP. Table 9-2 provides a summary of all of the *robots.txt* directives.

Table 9-2. REP directives summary

Directive (support)	Description
Allow	Instructs crawlers to crawl a specific page (or resource).
	Example:
	`Allow: /cgi-bin/report.cgi`
	This code instructs crawlers to crawl the *report.cgi* file.
Disallow	Instructs crawlers *not* to crawl all or parts of your site. The only exception to the rule is the *robots.txt* file.
	Example:
	`Disallow: /cgi-bin/`
	This code prohibits crawlers from crawling your *cgi-bin* folder.
Sitemap	Instructs crawlers where to find your Sitemap file.
	Example:
	`Sitemap: http://domain.com/sitemap.xml`
	Hint: use absolute paths for cross search engine compatibility. Multiple `Sitemap` directives are allowed.
$ wildcard	Instructs crawlers to match everything starting from the end of the URL.
	Example:
	`Disallow: /*.pdf$`
	This code prohibits crawlers from crawling PDF files.
* wildcard	Instructs crawlers to match zero or more characters.
	Example:
	`Disallow: /search?*`
	All URLs matching the portion of the string preceding the wildcard character will be crawled.
Crawl-delay	Directive specific to MSNBot and Slurp specifying a search engine–specific delay.
	Example:
	`Crawl-delay: 5`
	Google does not support this directive.

Robots Meta Directives

The robots meta directives were introduced a few years after *robots.txt*. Operating on a page (or document) level only, they provide indexing instructions to the obeying search engines. There are two types of meta directives: those that are part of the HTML page, and those that the web server sends as HTTP headers.

HTML Meta Directives

HTML meta directives are found in the actual HTML page. According to the W3C (*http://www.w3.org/TR/REC-html40/appendix/notes.html#h-B.4.1.2*):

> The META element allows HTML authors to tell visiting robots whether a document may be indexed, or used to harvest more links. No server administrator action is required.

You place these directives within the HTML `<head>` tag. The big three search engines support several common directives, as listed in Table 9-3.

Table 9-3. HTML meta directives

Directive	Description
Noindex	Instructs search engines *not* to index this page.
	Example:
	`<meta name="robots" content="noindex" />`
Nofollow	Instructs search engines *not* to follow or drain any link juice for any outbound links.
	Example for all spiders:
	`<meta name="robots" content="nofollow" />`
Nosnippet	Instructs search engines *not* to show any search results for this page.
	Example:
	`<meta name="robots" content="nosnippet" />`
Noarchive	Instructs search engines *not* to show a cache link for this page.
	Example:
	`<meta name="robots" content="noarchive" />`
Noodp	Instructs search engines *not* to use Open Directory Project descriptions in the SERPs.
	Example:
	`<meta name="robots" content="noodp" />`
Follow	Default implied directive that says "follow" all outbound links.
	Example:
	`<meta name="robots" content="follow" />`
Index	Default implied directive that says "index" this page.
	Example:
	`<meta name="robots" content="index" />`

Mixing HTML meta directives

It is perfectly acceptable to combine HTML meta directives into a single meta tag. For example, you may want to `noindex` and `nofollow` a particular page. You would simply list both directives, separated by a comma, as in the following example:

```
<meta name="robots" content="noindex,nofollow" />
```

Let's say you have a page that is not your canonical (preferred) page, but is being linked to by some highly trusted site. In this case, you may want to do the following:

```
<meta name="robots" content="noindex,follow" />
```

In this example, crawlers can follow any outbound links away from this page, as you might feel that some of these links are your canonical links (such as your home page).

Targeting HTML meta tags

You can define HTML meta tags to target specific spiders. For example, to instruct Googlebot and Slurp *not* to index a particular page, you could write:

```
<meta name="googlebot" content="noindex" />
<meta name="slurp" content="noindex" />
```

Yahoo!-specific directives

Yahoo! uses a couple of extra directives, namely `noydir` and `robots-nocontent`. The first directive is used to instruct Yahoo! *not* to use Yahoo! directory descriptions for its search engine results pertaining to this page. Here is the basic format:

```
<meta name="robots" content="noydir" />
```

The second directive, `robots-nocontent`, operates on other HTML tags. It is *not* to be used with meta tags. Utilizing this tag allows you to prevent certain portions of your page, such as navigational menus, from being considered by Yahoo!'s indexing algorithms. The net effect of this method is increased page copy relevance (higher keyword density). Here are some examples:

```
<div class="robots-nocontent"><!--menu html--></div>

<span class="robots-nocontent"><!--footer html--></span>

<p class="robots-nocontent"><!-- ads html--></p>
```

These examples should be self-explanatory. Marking text that is unrelated to the basic theme or topic of this page would be advantageous. Note that there are other ways of doing the same thing for all search engines.

One such way is by loading ads in iframes. The actual ads would be stored in external files loaded by iframes at page load time. Crawlers typically ignore iframes. You could also use Ajax to achieve the same effect.

Google-specific directives

There are three Google-specific directives: `unavailable_after`, `noimageindex`, and `notranslate`. The first directive, `unavailable_after`, instructs Google to remove the page from its index after the date and time expiry. Here is an example:

```
<meta name="googlebot" content="unavailable_after: 12-Sep-2009
12:00:00 PST">
```

In this example, Googlebot is instructed to remove the page from its index after September 12, 2009, 12:00:00 Pacific Standard Time. The second directive, `noimageindex`, instructs Google not to show the page as a referring page for any images that show up on Google image SERPs. Here is the format:

```
<meta name="googlebot" content="noimageindex">
```

The third directive, `notranslate`, instructs Google not to translate the page or specific page elements. It has two formats. The following fragment illustrates the meta format:

```
<meta name="google" value="notranslate">
```

Sometimes it is useful to translate only certain parts of a page. The way to accomplish that is by identifying page elements that are not to be translated. The following fragment illustrates how you can do this:

```
<span class="notranslate">Company Name, Location</span>
<p class="notranslate">Brand X Slogan</p>
```

HTTP Header Directives

We need HTTP header directives because not all web documents are HTML pages. Search engines index a wide variety of our documents, including PDF files and Microsoft Office files. Each page directive has its own HTTP header equivalent.

For example, let's say your site has Microsoft Word files that you do not wish to index, cache, or use for search result descriptions. If you are using an Apache web server, you could add the following line to your *.htaccess* files:

```
<FilesMatch "\.doc$">
Header set X-Robots-Tag "noindex, noarchive, nosnippet"
</Files>
```

In this example, the three directives will be added to the HTTP header created by the Apache web server. Webmasters who prefer to do this in code can use built-in PHP functions.

The nofollow Link Attribute

A discussion of REP would not be complete without the inclusion of the `nofollow` link attribute. This attribute was introduced to discourage comment spammers from adding their links. The basic idea is that links marked with the `nofollow` attribute will not pass any link juice to the spammer sites. The format of these links is as follows:

```
<a href="http://www.spamsite.com/" rel="nofollow">some nonesensical
text</a>
```

In this case, the hypothetical website *http://www.spamsite.com* would not receive any link juice from the referring page. Spammers will continue to attack sites. In most cases they are easily detected. Here are some example posts:

```
Please visit my great <a href="http://www.spamsite.com/"
rel="nofollow">Viagra Site</a> for great discounts.

<a href="http://www.spamsite2.com/" rel="nofollow">Free Porn Site</a>

<a href="http://www.spamsite3.com/" rel="nofollow">I was reading
through your site and I must say it is great! Good Job.</a>
```

We discuss `nofollow` link attributes in several other parts of this book.

Dealing with Rogue Spiders

Not all crawlers will obey REP. Some rogue spiders will go to great lengths to pose as one of the big spiders. To deal with this sort of situation, we can utilize the fact that major search engines support reverse DNS crawler authentication.

Reverse DNS Crawler Authentication

Setup of reverse DNS crawler authentication is straightforward. Yahoo! discusses how to do it on its blogging site (*http://bit.ly/2elndm*):

1. For each page view request, check the user-agent and IP address. All requests from Yahoo! Search utilize a user-agent starting with 'Yahoo! Slurp.'

2. For each request from 'Yahoo! Slurp' user-agent, you can start with the IP address (i.e. 74.6.67.218) and use reverse DNS lookup to find out the registered name of the machine.

3. Once you have the host name (in this case, *lj612134.crawl.yahoo.net*), you can then check if it really is coming from Yahoo! Search. The name of all Yahoo! Search crawlers will end with '*crawl.yahoo.net*,' so if the name doesn't end with this, you know it's not really our crawler.

4. Finally, you need to verify the name is accurate. In order to do this, you can use Forward DNS to see the IP address associated with the host name. This should match the IP address you used in Step 2. If it doesn't, it means the name was fake.

As you can see, it is relatively easy to check for rogue spiders by using the reverse DNS approach. Here is the Yahoo! approach translated to PHP code:

```
<?php
$ua = $_SERVER['HTTP_USER_AGENT'];
$httpRC403 = "HTTP/1.0 403 Forbidden";
$slurp = 'slurp';
if(stristr($ua, $slurp)){
    $ip = $_SERVER['REMOTE_ADDR'];
    $host = gethostbyaddr($ip);
    $slurpDomain = '\.crawl\.yahoo\.net';
    if(!preg_match("/$slurpDomain$/", $host) ) {
```

```
        header("$httpRC403");
        exit;
    } else {
        $realIP = gethostbyname($host);
        if($realIP != $ip){
            header("$httpRC403");
            exit;
        }
    }
}
?>
```

You could extend this script to include other bots. Including this file in all of your PHP files is straightforward with the PHP `include` command:

```
<?php include("checkcrawler.php"); ?>
```

Most CMSs, blogs, and forums are based on modern application frameworks. It is likely that you would have to include this file in only one template file that would be rendered in every page.

Summary

A full understanding of Robots Exclusion Protocol is crucial. Note that REP is not fully supported in the same way by every search engine. The good news is that the most popular search engines are now working together to offer more uniform REP support. The benefits of this are obvious in terms of the work required to address the needs of different search engines.

Using *robots.txt* to block crawlers from specific site areas is an important tactic in SEO. In most cases, you should use *robots.txt* at the directory (site) level. With the introduction of wildcards, you can handle common SEO problems such as content duplication with relative ease. Although the use of the `Sitemap` directive is a welcome addition to *robots.txt*, Google is still encouraging webmasters to add their Sitemaps manually by using the Google Webmaster Tools platform.

Using HTML meta tags and their HTTP header equivalents is a way to specify indexing directives on the page level for HTML and non-HTML file resources. These types of directives are harder to maintain and you should use them only where required.

Not all web spiders honor REP. At times, it might be necessary to block their attempts to crawl your site. You can do this in many different ways, including via coding, server-side configuration, firewalls, and intrusion detection devices.

## CHAPTER 10

Sitemaps

The concept of website Sitemaps is not new. In the early days of the Internet, having a Sitemap was as important as it is today, but in those days, Sitemaps were primarily intended for human visitors; that they also were helping search engine crawlers was just a side benefit. HTML Sitemaps are the organized collection of site links and their associated descriptions. Use of HTML Sitemaps was and still is one of the "nuts and bolts" of SEO, and they are still the most popular Sitemap type.

Over the years, search engines realized the benefit of Sitemaps. Google jumped on this concept in 2005 with the creation of its own Google Sitemap Protocol. Shortly after, Yahoo!, Microsoft, Ask, and IBM jumped on the bandwagon. During 2006, Google Sitemaps Protocol was renamed XML Sitemap Protocol, to acknowledge its "universal" acceptance. The work of these joint efforts is now under the auspices of Sitemaps.org.

The premise of using XML Sitemap Protocol was that it would help search engines index content faster while providing ways to improve their existing crawling algorithms. Using XML Sitemap Protocol does not guarantee anything in terms of better page rankings. Furthermore, use of XML Sitemap Protocol is not mandatory for all sites. In other words, a website will not be penalized if it is not using XML Sitemaps.

This chapter covers several different Sitemap types, including plain-text URL listings, HTML, XML, RSS/Atom, video, and mobile Sitemaps. Not all search engines treat Sitemaps the same, nor do they provide the same Sitemap services.

Understanding Sitemaps

Sitemaps are divided into two broad categories: those created for human users and those specifically created for search engine crawlers. Ultimately, both of these categories are equally important.

Why Use Sitemaps?

It is important to use Sitemaps because they help your visitors quickly get to the information they need, and they help web spiders find your site's links.

There is no universal Sitemap rule that you can apply to every site. Understanding different Sitemap options should help you identify the right type for each situation. The following subsections discuss some of the reasons for using Sitemaps.

Crawl augmentation

Although web spiders are continuously improving, they are far from perfect. Search engines have no problems admitting this. Here is what Google says about crawl augmentation (*http://bit.ly/1RJSxz*):

> Submitting a Sitemap helps you make sure Google knows about the URLs on your site. It can be especially helpful if your content is not easily discoverable by our crawler (such as pages accessible only through a form). It is not, however, a guarantee that those URLs will be crawled or indexed. We use information from Sitemaps to augment our usual crawl and discovery processes.

Poor linking site structure

Not all sites are created equal. Sites with poor linking structures tend to index poorly. Orphan pages, deep links, and search engine traps are culprits of poor site indexing. The use of Sitemaps can alleviate these situations, at least temporarily, to give you enough time to fix the root of the problem.

Crawling frequency

One of the biggest benefits of using Sitemaps is in timely crawls or recrawls of your site (or just specific pages). XML Sitemap documents let you tell crawlers how often they should read each page.

Sites using Sitemaps tend to be crawled faster on Yahoo! and Google. It takes Google and Yahoo! minutes to respond to Sitemap submissions or resubmissions. This can be very helpful for news sites, e-commerce sites, blogs, and any other sites that are constantly updating or adding new content.

Content ownership

Many malicious web scraper sites are lurking around the Internet. Having search engines index your content as soon as it is posted can be an important way to ensure that search engines are aware of the original content owner. In this way, a copycat site does not get the credit for your content. Granted, it is still possible for search engines to confuse the origins of a content source.

Page priority

As you will see later in this chapter, XML Sitemap Protocol allows webmasters to assign a specific priority value for each URL in the XML Sitemap file. Giving search engines suggestions about the importance of each page is empowering—depending on how each search engine treats this value.

Large sites

Using Sitemaps for large sites is important. Sites carrying tens of thousands (or millions) of pages typically suffer in indexing due to deep linking problems. Sites with this many documents use multiple Sitemaps to break up the different categories of content.

History of changes

If all your links are contained in your Sitemaps, this could be a way to provide a history of your site's links. This is the case if your site is storing your Sitemaps in the code versioning control. This information can help you analyze changes in page rankings, the size of indexed documents, and more.

HTML Sitemaps

Creating HTML Sitemaps can be straightforward for small sites. You can build HTML Sitemaps using a simple text editor such as Notepad. For larger sites, it may make more sense to use automated tools that will help you gather all your links. Google suggests the following (*http://bit.ly/OyVXj*):

> Offer a site map to your users with links that point to the important parts of your site. If the site map is larger than 100 or so links, you may want to break the site map into separate pages.

HTML Sitemap Generators

If your site has hundreds or thousands of links, Sitemap generation tools will help you to create multipage Sitemaps. Some of the tools available for this on the Internet include:

- XML Sitemap Generator (*http://www.xml-sitemaps.com/*)
- AutoMapIt (*http://www.automapit.com*)
- Site Map Pro (*http://www.sitemappro.com*)

Most Internet websites are small. Typically, a small business website would have only a few links, and all the pages would have links to each other. Having a Sitemap in those cases is still valuable, as most sites on the Internet are not designed by professionals, nor do they knowingly employ SEO.

When creating your HTML Sitemap, you should describe all of the links. A link with no description (using its own URL value as the link anchor text) provides very little value. Just placing the URLs without providing any context is plain lazy.

You can automate HTML Sitemap creation for large sites, as long as all your web pages are using unique <title> tags. One such GNU General Public License (GPL) tool that can utilize <title> tags in place of link anchor text is Daniel Naber's *tree.pl* script, which you can download from his website (*http://www.danielnaber.de/tree/*).

Creating a custom HTML Sitemap generator

It doesn't take much effort to create your own custom generator. You could start with the following Perl code fragment:

```
use HTML::TagParser;

@files=`find . /home/site -type f -name "*.html"`;
$baseurl='http://www.somedomain.com/';

foreach $file (@files) {
 if($file =~ /^\//) {
   $filetmp = `cat $file`;
   $html = HTML::TagParser->new( "$filetmp" );
   $elem = $html->getElementsByTagName( "title" );

   print "<a href='" . $baseurl . getFileName($file)."'>" .
         $elem->innerText() . "</a><br>\n";
 }
}

sub getFileName {
   $takeout='/home/site/public_html/';
   $name=shift;

   @nametmp = split(/$takeout/, $name);

   $name = $nametmp[1];
   $name =~ s/^\s+//;
   $name =~ s/\s+$//;
   return $name;
}
```

This code fragment utilizes three system commands:

- The find and grep commands to obtain a list of files to process
- The cat command to slurp the contents of each file into a single variable

Let's suppose your directory and file structure are as follows:

```
$ ls -laR
.:
drwxrwxrwx+ 3 john None    0 Dec 27 14:53 public_html
-rw-r--r--  1 john None  635 Dec 27 15:42 sitemap.pl
./public_html:
```

```
-rwxrwxrwx  1 john None 85 Dec 27 15:27 page1.html
-rwxrwxrwx  1 john None 78 Dec 27 14:39 page2.html
-rwxrwxrwx  1 john None 76 Dec 27 14:39 page3.html
-rwxrwxrwx  1 john None 75 Dec 27 14:40 page4.html
drwxrwxrwx+ 2 john None  0 Dec 27 14:54 sectionX
./public_html/sectionX:
-rwxrwxrwx  1 john None 77 Dec 27 14:44 page5.html
```

Running the script would produce the following:

```
$ perl sitemap.pl
<a href='http://www.somedomain.com/page1.html'>Company Home Page</a>
<br><a href='http://www.somedomain.com/page2.html'>Contact Us</a><br>
<a href='http://www.somedomain.com/page3.html'>Services</a><br>
<a href='http://www.somedomain.com/page4.html'>Sitemap</a><br>
<a href='http://www.somedomain.com/sectionX/page5.html'>Service X</a>
<br>
```

You could pipe this output to an HTML file that you could then reorganize in your HTML editor to create the final *sitemap.html* file. Note that the name of the HTML Sitemap file is arbitrary and that this code will work on sites that do not require URL rewriting. To handle sites with enabled URL rewriting, you need to take another approach that involves the use of the HTTP protocol and the design of a web spider script.

XML Sitemaps

Although XML Sitemaps are written only for web spiders, they are easy to create. They are collections of links with their respective (optional) attributes formatted according to the XML schema (*http://www.sitemaps.org/schemas/sitemap/0.9*).

At the time of this writing, XML Sitemap Protocol is at version 0.9 (as signified by its schema version). You must save each XML Sitemap file using the UTF-8 encoding format. Other rules apply as well. If you are familiar with XML, these rules should be easy to understand.

XML Sitemap Format

Each link in an XML Sitemap can have up to four attributes. The first attribute, `loc`, is the URL location and is mandatory. The rest of the attributes are optional and include `lastmod`, `changefreq`, and `priority`. Here is an example Sitemap file with a single link:

```
<?xml version='1.0' encoding='UTF-8'?>
<urlset xmlns="http://www.sitemaps.org/schemas/sitemap/0.9"
        xmlns:xsi="http://www.w3.org/2001/XMLSchema-instance"
        xsi:schemaLocation="http://www.sitemaps.org/schemas/sitemap/0.9
        http://www.sitemaps.org/schemas/sitemap/0.9/sitemap.xsd">

    <url>
        <loc>http://mydomain.com/</loc>
        <lastmod>2010-01-01</lastmod>
```

```
    <changefreq>weekly</changefreq>
    <priority>0.5</priority>
</url>

</urlset>
```

In this example, we can see the XML file header which describes the rules that this XML document is bound to. Note that the XML header would need to change only if you wanted to support the upgraded schema.

The next (bolded) section represents a single URL entry enclosed by <url> tags. Within this block we see all of the possible attributes. Each attribute is bound by specific rules. The following subsections go into more details regarding each attribute.

Understanding <loc>

The loc attribute tag represents the actual URL or link value. Several rules govern the use of loc. According to Sitemaps.org (*http://www.sitemaps.org/protocol.php*):

> ...as with all XML files, any data values (including URLs) must use entity escape codes...all URLs (including the URL of your Sitemap) must be URL-escaped and encoded for readability by the web server on which they are located.... Please check to make sure that your URLs follow the RFC-3986 standard for URIs, the RFC-3987 standard for IRIs, and the XML standard.

All url tag values must use entity escape codes for certain characters. Table 10-1 provides a summary of entity escape codes.

Table 10-1. XML Sitemaps: Entity escape codes

Character	Escape code
Ampersand (&)	&amp;
Double quote (")	&quot;
Single quote (')	&apos;
Greater than sign (>)	&gt;
Less than sign (<)	&lt;

Most popular blog and CMS products on the market have already updated their code bases to support automated creation of XML Sitemaps. Here is an example of a URL that would need to be rewritten:

http://www.mydomain.com/store?prodid=10&

The properly escaped version would be:

```
<loc>http://www.mydomain.com/store?prodid=10&amp;</loc>
```

Note that the http part is mandatory. Also note that the URL should not be longer than 2,048 characters, as this is a known URL length limit for some of the server platforms.

Understanding <lastmod>

As its name implies, the `lastmod` attribute tag represents the time and date when a particular link was last modified. This is an optional attribute but a very powerful one, as you can use it as a signal to the incoming search engine crawlers that this document or page may need to be crawled again.

The `lastmod` attribute tag has two data value formats. You can use the short form without the time part and the long form with the full date and time. Furthermore, the `lastmod` attribute tag needs to be in the W3C datetime format, as described at *http://www.w3.org/TR/NOTE-datetime*. The following fragment is an example of both formats:

```
...
    <lastmod>2010-01-01</lastmod>
...
    <lastmod>2010-01-01T09:00:15-05:00</lastmod>
...
```

The first example indicates a last modification date of January 1, 2010. The second example indicates the same date as well as a time of 9:15 a.m. (U.S. Eastern Standard Time).

Understanding <changefreq>

The `changefreq` attribute represents a hint as to how often a particular link might change. It does not have to be 100% accurate; search engines will not penalize you if the `changefreq` attribute is not accurate. The `changefreq` attribute is an optional attribute tag with a range of values, including:

```
...
    <changefreq>always</changefreq>
...
    <changefreq>hourly</changefreq>
...
    <changefreq>daily</changefreq>
...
    <changefreq>weekly</changefreq>
...
    <changefreq>monthly</changefreq>
...
    <changefreq>yearly</changefreq>
...
    <changefreq>never</changefreq>
...
```

According to Sitemaps.org, you should use the **always** value when a particular page changes on every access, and you should use the **never** value for archived pages. Note that web spiders could recrawl all your URLs in your Sitemap at any time, regardless of the `changefreq` settings.

Understanding <priority>

The `priority` attribute tag is perhaps the most important of all the optional link attributes. Its values range from 0.0 to 1.0. The median or default value for any page is signified by a value of 0.5.

The higher the `priority` value, the higher the likelihood of that page being crawled. Using a `priority` value of `1.0` for all URLs is counterproductive and does not influence ranking or crawling benefits. The `priority` value is only a strong suggestion. It does not have any correlation with the corresponding page rank.

XML Sitemap Example

Now that you understand the basic syntax of XML Sitemaps, let's look at a small example with multiple links:

```
<?xml version='1.0' encoding='UTF-8'?>
<urlset xmlns="http://www.sitemaps.org/schemas/sitemap/0.9"
        xmlns:xsi="http://www.w3.org/2001/XMLSchema-instance"
        xsi:schemaLocation="http://www.sitemaps.org/schemas/sitemap/0.9
        http://www.sitemaps.org/schemas/sitemap/0.9/sitemap.xsd">
    <url>
        <loc>http://www.mydomain.com/</loc>
    </url>
    <url>
        <loc>http://www.mydomain.com/shop.do?item=74&amp;</loc>
        <priority>0.5</priority>
    </url>
    <url>
        <loc>http://www.mydomain.com/services.html</loc>
        <lastmod>2010-11-23</lastmod>
    </url>
    <url>
        <loc>http://mydomain.com/dailyonsaleproducts.html</loc>
        <changefreq>daily</changefreq>
        <priority>1.0</priority>
    </url>
    <url>
        <loc>http://mydomain.com/aboutus.html</loc>
        <lastmod>2009-01-01</lastmod>
        <changefreq>monthly</changefreq>
        <priority>0.6</priority>
    </url>
    ...
</urlset>
```

The first URL is that of the main home page. In this part, we are using only the `<loc>` tag and no optional tags. The second URL is an example of the online store product page with the escaped ampersand character. The priority of this page is set to normal (0.5).

The third URL is for a page called *dailyonsaleproducts.html*. As the filename suggests, this URL is using the `daily` indicator for its `<changefreq>` tag. In addition, the priority is set to 1.0 to indicate the highest importance.

The last example is that of the *aboutus.html* page. All optional tags are used to indicate the last date of modification, the monthly change frequency, and a slightly higher page priority.

Why Use XML Sitemaps?

You should use XML Sitemaps to promote faster crawling and indexing of your site. Doing a bit of math along with making some assumptions can help us see the bigger picture. Let's suppose we have three websites, each with a different number of pages or documents:

Site A
> 100 pages, 1 second average per-page crawler retrieval time

Site B
> 10,000 pages, 1.2 seconds average per-page crawler retrieval time

Site C
> 1 million pages, 1.5 seconds average per-page crawler retrieval time

Now suppose you changed one of the pages on all three sites. Here is the worst-case scenario (modified page crawled last) of retrieving this page by a web crawler:

Site A
> 100 pages × 1 second = 100 seconds (1.67 minutes)

Site B
> 10,000 pages × 1.2 seconds = 12,000 seconds (3.3 hours)

Site C
> 1 million pages × 1.5 seconds = 1.5 million seconds (17.4 days)

When you consider that web crawlers typically do not crawl entire sites all in one shot, it could take a lot longer before the modified page is crawled. This example clearly shows that big sites are prime candidates for using XML Sitemaps.

XML Sitemap Auto-Discovery

As we discussed in Chapter 9, XML Sitemaps are now discovered within *robots.txt*. You can have multiple XML Sitemap files defined. The relative order of appearance does not matter. The following is an example of a *robots.txt* file utilizing two XML Sitemaps:

```
1 Sitemap: http://www.mydomain.com/sitemap1.xml
2
3 User-agent: *
4 Disallow: /cgi-bin/
```

```
   5
   6 Sitemap: http://www.mydomain.com/sitemap2.xml
   7
   8 User-agent: Googlebot-Image
   9 Disallow: /images/
```

In this example, we have two Sitemap declarations alongside other *robots.txt* entries. They are shown on lines 1 and 6. They would be crawled by all search engine crawlers supporting REP.

Multiple XML Sitemaps

Let's suppose you have a large site composed of several key hotspots with the following URL structure:

```
http://www.mydomain.com/presidentsblog/
http://www.mydomain.com/products/
http://www.mydomain.com/services/
http://www.mydomain.com/news/
http://www.mydomain.com/pressreleases/
http://www.mydomain.com/support/
http://www.mydomain.com/downloads/
```

Instead of combining all these Sitemaps into one big Sitemap, XML Sitemap Protocol allows us to deal with this situation more elegantly with the use of the XML Sitemap Index file. Using our current example, we would have the following Sitemap files:

```
http://www.mydomain.com/presidentsblog/sitemap.xml
http://www.mydomain.com/products/sitemap.xml
http://www.mydomain.com/services/sitemap.xml
http://www.mydomain.com/news/sitemap.xml
http://www.mydomain.com/pressreleases/sitemap.xml
http://www.mydomain.com/support/sitemap.xml
http://www.mydomain.com/downloads/sitemap.xml
```

Creating the XML Sitemap Index file is similar to creating XML Sitemap files. Here is an XML Sitemap Index file that we could use to represent XML Sitemap files:

```xml
<?xml version='1.0' encoding='UTF-8'?>
<sitemapindex xmlns="http://www.sitemaps.org/schemas/sitemap/0.9"
    xmlns:xsi="http://www.w3.org/2001/XMLSchema-instance"
    xsi:schemaLocation="http://www.sitemaps.org/schemas/sitemap/0.9
    http://www.sitemaps.org/schemas/sitemap/0.9/siteindex.xsd">
    <sitemap>
        <loc>http://www.mydomain.com/presidentsblog/sitemap.xml</loc>
        <lastmod>2010-01-01T09:00:15-05:00</lastmod>
    </sitemap>
    <sitemap>
        <loc>http://www.mydomain.com/products/sitemap.xml</loc>
        <lastmod>2010-01-01</lastmod>
    </sitemap>
    <sitemap>
        <loc>http://www.mydomain.com/services/sitemap.xml</loc>
        <lastmod>2010-01-01</lastmod>
```

```
    </sitemap>
    <sitemap>
        <loc>http://www.mydomain.com/news/sitemap.xml</loc>
        <lastmod>2010-01-01</lastmod>
    </sitemap>
    <sitemap>
        <loc>http://www.mydomain.com/pressreleases/sitemap.xml</loc>
    </sitemap>
    <sitemap>
        <loc>http://www.mydomain.com/support/sitemap.xml</loc>
    </sitemap>
    <sitemap>
        <loc>http://www.mydomain.com/downloads/sitemap.xml</loc>
    </sitemap>
</sitemapindex>
```

XML Sitemap Index files have the single optional tag, `<lastmod>`. The `<lastmod>` tag tells the crawler the date when a particular Sitemap was modified. XML Sitemap Index files have similar rules to XML Sitemap files. For more information on XML Sitemap Index files, visit *http://www.sitemaps.org/*.

Sitemap Location and Naming

XML Sitemaps can refer only to files in the folder in which they are placed, or files located in any child folders of that folder. For example, a Sitemap corresponding to a URL location of *http://www.mydomain.com/sales/sitemap.xml* can refer only to URLs starting with *http://www.mydomain.com/sales/*.

You are also allowed to host Sitemaps on different domains. For this to work, you need to prove the ownership of the domain hosting the Sitemap. For example, let's say DomainA.com hosts a Sitemap for DomainB.com. The location of the Sitemap is *http://domainA.com/sitemapDomainB.xml*. All that is required is for DomainB.com to place this URL anywhere within its *robots.txt* file, using the `Sitemap` directive.

Although your XML Sitemap can have arbitrary names, the recommended name is *sitemap.xml*. Many people choose to name their XML Sitemaps another name. This is to prevent rogue site scrapers from easily obtaining most, if not all, of the URLs for the site.

XML Sitemap Limitations

The use of XML Sitemaps has some limitations. For instance, an XML Sitemap file can have no more than 50,000 links. In this case, creating multiple Sitemaps is useful. You may also want to create an XML Sitemap Index file to indicate all of your XML Sitemaps. The XML Sitemap Index file can contain up to 1,000 XML Sitemaps. If you do the math, that is a maximum of 50 million URLs. Recently, Bing introduced enhanced support for large Sitemaps. See *http://bit.ly/K99mQ* for more information.

In addition to the URL limitation, each XML Sitemap should be less than 10 MB in size. Sometimes the Sitemap size limit will be reached before the URL limit. If that is the case, you can compress the XML Sitemap by using gzip. Here is an example of using compressed XML Sitemaps within the XML Sitemap Index file:

```
<?xml version='1.0' encoding='UTF-8'?>
    <sitemapindex xmlns="http://www.sitemaps.org/schemas/sitemap/0.9"
    xmlns:xsi="http://www.w3.org/2001/XMLSchema-instance"
    xsi:schemaLocation="http://www.sitemaps.org/schemas/sitemap/0.9
    http://www.sitemaps.org/schemas/sitemap/0.9/siteindex.xsd">
    <sitemap>
       <loc>http://www.mydomain.com/sitemap1.xml.gz</loc>
    </sitemap>
...
    <sitemap>
       <loc>http://www.mydomain.com/sitemap1000.xml.gz</loc>
    </sitemap>
</sitemapindex>
```

You can also submit compressed XML Sitemaps (or XML Sitemap Index files) via *robots.txt*, using the `Sitemap` directive.

XML Sitemap Generators

Creating XML Sitemap generators is straightforward for sites with intelligent (basic) linking structures. If you are reasonably sure that a text browser can reach each page of your site, you can write a crawler script to go through your site to create the XML Sitemap.

If you do not have the time to create a script, many XML Sitemap generators (both free and paid) are available. Table 10-2 lists some of the available tools for creating XML Sitemaps.

Table 10-2. XML Sitemap generators

Tool	Description
SitemapDoc (*http://www.sitemapdoc.com/*)	Online tool: will create XML Sitemaps with up to 500 URLs; this is often sufficient for smaller sites
iGooMap (*http://www.pointworks.de/*)	Comprehensive XML Sitemap generator for the Mac platform
Google Sitemap Generator (*http://code.google.com/p/googlesitemapgenerator/*)	Google's own Python-based XML Sitemap generator
SiteMap Generator (*http://wonderwebware.com/sitemap-generator/*)	Freeware XML Sitemap generator for the Windows OS
Mapsbuilder (*http://www.mapsbuilder.com/*)	Win32 application for creating XML Sitemaps

The bigger your site is, the more it makes sense to use XML Sitemap generators. No auto-generated Sitemap is perfect. Manual intervention is almost always necessary—if you care about the little details. If your site has dynamic links or search engine traps, no automated tool will be able to create a full Sitemap using the HTTP protocol method.

XML Sitemap Validators

There is no point in hosting XML Sitemaps without knowing that they pass validation. Google provides an interface via Google Webmaster Tools to submit XML Sitemaps. Visit the following link when troubleshooting your XML Sitemap validation problems with Google Webmaster Tools:

http://www.google.com/support/webmasters/bin/answer.py?hl=en&answer=35738

Although Google's response is relatively quick, it is not quick enough if you want to see validation results immediately. In this case, you may want to use one of the online validators listed in Table 10-3.

Table 10-3. XML Sitemap validators

Validator	Description
Validome	Can validate XML Sitemaps as well as XML Sitemap Index files; free
(*http://www.validome.org/google/validate*)	
XML Sitemap Validator	Free online validation for XML Sitemaps
(*http://www.xml-sitemaps.com/validate-xml-sitemap.html*)	
Google Sitemap Checker	Another free online validator
(*http://www.webmasterwebtools.com/sitemap-validation/*)	

XML Sitemap Submissions

You can let search engines know of your XML Sitemaps in three ways. For instance, some search engines allow you to submit Sitemaps through their sites if you have an account with them (an example is Google). The second way is to use the ping method. The third way is to use *robots.txt* along with the embedded `Sitemap` directive (we discussed this in Chapter 9). When using the ping method, you can also submit your Sitemaps using your web browser.

Using Google Webmaster Tools to submit Sitemaps

Before you can submit your Sitemaps to Google, you need to register for a Google account. You can do this at *https://www.google.com/accounts/NewAccount*. To activate your account, you will need to respond to Google's confirmation email. Once you click on the confirmation link, your account should be ready. When you log in, you will be presented with a Dashboard page. Figure 10-1 shows the pertinent part of the Dashboard page.

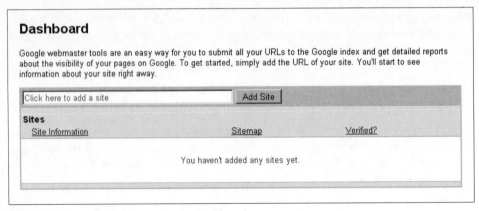

Figure 10-1. Google Webmaster Tools: Dashboard page

Next, you need to add your site's URL. After you do that, Google will ask you to verify the ownership of your site. Figure 10-2 shows the portion of the screen requesting your site's ownership verification.

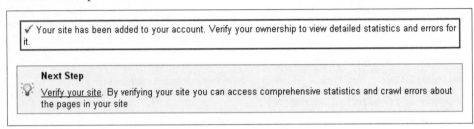

Figure 10-2. Google Webmaster Tools: Site ownership verification

As of this writing, Google allows for two types of verifications. The first method is by using the Google-generated HTML file (which you must place in your web root). The second method is by placing the Google-generated meta tag in your website's index file, such as *index.html*. Most people prefer using the first method.

Once your site verification is complete, you can click on the Sitemaps menu link to add your Sitemap(s) to Google. Figure 10-3 shows the Sitemaps section of Google Webmaster Tools.

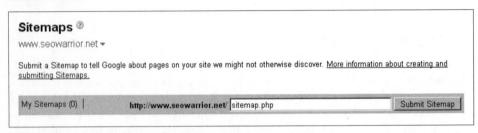

Figure 10-3. Google Webmaster Tools: Sitemaps section

Simply point Google to your Sitemap location and click the Submit Sitemap button. Figure 10-3 shows an example of adding a Sitemap called *sitemap.php* to the *http://www .seowarrior.net* domain. After you click on the Submit Sitemap button, Google provides a confirmation, as shown in Figure 10-4.

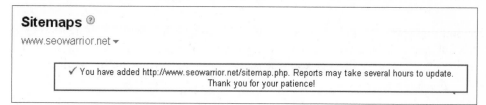

Sitemaps ⓘ

www.seowarrior.net ▼

✓ You have added http://www.seowarrior.net/sitemap.php. Reports may take several hours to update. Thank you for your patience!

Figure 10-4. Google Webmaster Tools: Add Sitemap confirmation

Typically, it takes only a few minutes for Google to crawl your Sitemap. Come back in about an hour and check your Sitemap status. If Google cannot process your Sitemap (for whatever reason), it will provide you with an indication of a faulty Sitemap. Figure 10-5 shows an example report indicating errors.

The Sitemap validation report in Figure 10-5 shows pertinent data, including the Sitemap type, its format, the time of the Sitemap submission, the time it was last downloaded, the Sitemap status (whether it is valid or not), the total number of URLs found, and the number of indexed URLs.

Property	Status
Sitemap type	Web
Format	Sitemap
Submitted	4 hours ago
Last downloaded by Google	4 hours ago
Status	ERRORS
Total URLs in Sitemap	0
Indexed URLs in Sitemap ⓘ	–

Figure 10-5. Google Webmaster Tools: Sitemap validation report

Using the ping method to submit Sitemaps

Google, Yahoo!, and Ask already have a public HTTP ping interface for submitting Sitemaps. The following fragment shows how to submit the Sitemap found at *http:// www.mydomain.com* to all three search engines:

```
Google
http://www.google.com/webmasters/sitemaps/ping?sitemap=http://www.
mydomain.com/sitemap.xml
```

```
Yahoo!
http://search.yahooapis.com/SiteExplorerService/V1/ping?sitemap=
http://www.mydomain.com/sitemap.xml

Ask.com
http://submissions.ask.com/ping?sitemap=http%3A//www.mydomain.com/
sitemap.xml
```

Submitting your website's Sitemap is easy with your web browser. Simply browse to the full ping URL and you are done. After you enter this URL in your web browser's address bar, Google's success response is as follows (at the time of this writing):

```
Sitemap Notification Received

Your Sitemap has been successfully added to our list of Sitemaps to
crawl. If this is the first time you are notifying Google about this
Sitemap, please add it via http://www.google.com/webmasters/tools/ so
you can track its status. Please note that we do not add all submitted
URLs to our index, and we cannot make any predictions or guarantees
about when or if they will appear.
```

This is merely an acknowledgment that your submission was received. It does not indicate anything about the validity of the Sitemap. Note that in all three interfaces there is a `sitemap` URL parameter. You can also automate these submissions by writing a small script.

Automating ping submissions. Google makes a specific point of not sending more than a single ping per hour. You can automate these pings using a small PHP script, as shown in the following fragment:

```
<?
$ch = curl_init();
curl_setopt($ch, CURLOPT_URL,
'http://www.google.com/webmasters/sitemaps/ping?sitemap=
http://www.mydomain.com/sitemap.xml');
curl_setopt($ch, CURLOPT_HEADER, 1);
curl_setopt($ch, CURLOPT_RETURNTRANSFER, 1);
$response = curl_exec($ch);
curl_close($ch);
$logFile = "googleping.txt";
$fileHandle = fopen($logFile, 'a');
fwrite($fileHandle, $response);
?>
```

This PHP script would ping Google servers, letting them know of any changes to your Sitemap. Furthermore, the script appends the returned message (including the HTTP header) to a logfile (*googleping.txt*). This return data should look similar to the following fragment:

```
HTTP/1.1 200 OK
Content-Type: text/html; charset=UTF-8
Expires: Tue, 28 Apr 2009 04:21:06 GMT
Date: Tue, 28 Apr 2009 04:21:06 GMT
Cache-Control: private, max-age=0
X-Content-Type-Options: nosniff
```

```
Content-Length: 1274
Server: GFE/2.0

<html>
<meta http-equiv="content-type" content="text/html; charset=UTF-8">
<head>
<title>Google Webmaster Tools - Sitemap Notification Received</title>
<!-- some JavaScript code removed from this section for simplicity -->
</head>
<body><h2>Sitemap Notification Received</h2>
<br>
Your Sitemap has been successfully added to our list of Sitemaps to
crawl. If this is the first time you are notifying Google about this
Sitemap, please add it via
<a href="http://www.google.com/webmasters/tools/">
http://www.google.com/webmasters/tools/</a>  so you can track its
status. Please note that we do not add all submitted URLs to our index,
and we cannot make any predictions or guarantees about when or if
they will appear.
</body>
</html>
```

If you know how often your content is changing, you can also set up a crontab job (or a Windows scheduled task) to call your PHP script at known time intervals. You can further extend the script by sending email alerts when the HTTP response code is *not* 200, or by initiating ping retries for all other HTTP response codes.

Utilizing Other Sitemap Types

Many other Sitemap types exist. These include pure text, news, RSS (and Atom), mobile, and video Sitemaps. We cover all of these types in the following subsections.

Pure Text (URL Listing) Sitemaps

In this format, each URL is listed on a separate line, with up to 50,000 URLs in a single (UTF-8) text file. Here is an example:

```
http://www.mydomain.com/services.html
http://www.mydomain.com/products.html
...
http://www.mydomain.com/support/downloads.html
```

This approach is the simplest way to create Sitemaps, especially if you were not going to use any of the optional XML Sitemap attributes. For more information, refer to the Google Webmaster Tools website.

Yahoo! supports the same format. However, the name of the Sitemap file must be *urllist.txt* (or *urllist.txt.gz* if compressed). So, if you are using *robots.txt* as a way to let search engine crawlers know of your text file Sitemap, use this name for all search engines. Otherwise, you will have duplicate Sitemaps for non-Yahoo! search engines.

News Sitemaps

You should use news Sitemaps (another Google XML Sitemap extension) when describing news articles. Articles up to three days old should appear in news Sitemaps. Otherwise, they will be ignored. Here is one article example:

```
<?xml version="1.0" encoding="UTF-8"?>
<urlset xmlns="http://www.sitemaps.org/schemas/sitemap/0.9"
xmlns:news="http://www.google.com/schemas/sitemap-news/0.9">
    <url>
        <loc>http://mydomain.com/article012388.html</loc>
        <news:news>
          <news:publication_date>2009-01-01T06:06:36-05:00
          </news:publication_date>
          <news:keywords>New Year's Eve, New York, Los Angeles, Boston, US,
Europe, Asia, Africa, World</news:keywords>
        </news:news>
    </url>
</urlset>
```

Note the use of the `<news:keywords>` tag. This tag can be helpful if and when Google indexes this news article. Examples of news Sitemaps include:

- *http://www.cnn.com/sitemap_news.xml*
- *http://www.news.com.au/adelaidenow-sitemap.xml*
- *http://www.telegraph.co.uk/news/newsSitemap.xml*
- *http://www.nytimes.com/sitemap_news.xml.gz*

RSS and Atom Sitemaps

Google and Yahoo! support news feed formats including RSS 0.9, RSS 1.0, RSS 2.0, Atom 0.3, and Atom 1.0. Although RSS and Atom feeds are great channels of communication, they are not particularly useful as Sitemaps, as they usually contain only the last few articles from your site.

Mobile Sitemaps

Google supports mobile content including XHTML (WAP 2.0), WML (WAP 1.2), and cHTML (iMode) markup languages. Yahoo! offers a similar type of support for mobile devices. Creating mobile Sitemaps is similar to creating other XML Sitemaps. Here is an example:

```
<?xml version="1.0" encoding="UTF-8" ?>
<urlset xmlns="http://www.sitemaps.org/schemas/sitemap/0.9"
  xmlns:mobile="http://www.google.com/schemas/sitemap-mobile/1.0">
    <url>
        <loc>http://m.mydomain.com/story08245.html</loc>
        <mobile:mobile/>
    </url>
...
```

```
<url>
    <loc>http://m.mydomain.com/wml/games</loc>
    <lastmod>2010-01-01</lastmod>
    <mobile:mobile />
</url>
</urlset>
```

All URLs listed in a mobile Sitemap must be specifically designed for mobile devices in one of the acceptable formats. For more information about mobile Sitemaps, visit *http://bit.ly/2rBIHc*.

Video Sitemaps

Video Sitemaps are yet another extension of XML Sitemap Protocol. Video Sitemaps can be helpful if your videos show up in Google SERPs. The following fragment shows a basic video Sitemap with one example video:

```
<urlset xmlns="http://www.sitemaps.org/schemas/sitemap/0.9"
        xmlns:video="http://www.google.com/schemas/sitemap-video/1.1">
<url>
  <loc>http://mydomain.com/article23423.html</loc>
    <video:video>
      <video:content_loc>http://mydomain.com/videos/article23423.flv
      </video:content_loc>
    </video:video>
</url>
</urlset>
```

For simplicity reasons, just one video is listed with only the single optional tag of `<video:content_loc>`. You can use many other optional tags to further classify videos. For more information on all the optional video tags, visit *http://bit.ly/3QnO3j*.

Summary

Sitemaps come in many different forms. Often, using HTML Sitemaps with Sitemaps created around XML Sitemaps Protocol is the ideal choice. HTML Sitemaps address the specific needs of your website visitors, whereas XML Sitemaps talk directly to search engine spiders. XML Sitemaps offer benefits to webmasters as well as search engines. Webmasters enjoy faster site crawls while search engine spiders get to augment their natural crawls—often discovering new pages not discovered by conventional natural crawls. There are other mutual benefits, including the ability for search engines to provide fresh URLs faster in their search results.

Smaller sites with infrequent site updates can do fine with only HTML Sitemaps. Larger sites carrying thousands of pages will see great value in using XML Sitemap types. With the convergence of search engine support of XML Sitemap Protocol (as defined at Sitemaps.org), using XML Sitemaps makes sense as more and more search engines come on board.

Using mobile, video, and news Sitemaps provides additional opportunities for SEO practitioners to consider. With search engines continuously enhancing their search capabilities with mixed (media-enriched) results, search engines are sending a strong message to site owners to spice up their sites with rich media content.

## CHAPTER 11

Keyword Research

Although the old days of keyword stuffing are long gone, keywords and keyword research are essential to SEO. In a search engine context, keywords are the words or phrases someone types into the search engine search box to obtain relevant results. Search engines rely on keywords in their search engine ranking algorithms. Keywords indicate relevancy.

As you saw in Chapter 5, keywords are used just about everywhere. In terms of websites, keywords are words or phrases found in your web pages, site and page URLs, and so forth. Before you plow into the world of keyword research, you should have a clear strategy. Targeting one- or two-word keywords may not work as expected due to too much competition.

Picking the right combination of words is important. Search engines have begun to pay attention to page–copy word relationships. With that in mind, it is important to understand the topics of keyword stemming, keyword modifiers, and latent semantic indexing to make intelligent keyword decisions.

Keyword research activities are part of a multistep iterative process. This process usually starts with a keyword brainstorming session, closely followed by utilization of keyword research tools. Some tools are free and some are commercially available. In this chapter, we will examine several popular keyword tools, including the Google AdWords Keyword Tool, Yahoo! Search Marketing, and Microsoft adCenter Labs. No tool is perfect, so it is important for you to get familiar with several tools to make better keyword decisions. The choice between free and paid tools is yours to make, but many people have found the Google AdWords Keyword Tool to be sufficient for their needs.

Evaluating and prioritizing your keyword list is essential. Using keyword search volume numbers as well as their underlying competition numbers can be extremely helpful in keyword selection and prioritization. Before you invest time in using specific keywords, you may want to consider some testing to validate your research.

Keyword popularity is a moving target for many keywords. As they say, one day you are hot, the next day you are not! Some keywords are long lasting, and others are only short lived. Considering keyword trends should be part of your keyword strategy for creating predictable SEO results.

Keyword Strategy

Sound SEO calls for a sound keyword strategy. You need to know what keywords you should target. Creating new pages with arbitrary (untargeted) keywords in your page title, page copy, and so on will not work. You need to be cold and calculating.

Let's look at an example. Say you want to open an online business selling trading cards. You may be tempted to optimize your page copy for *cards* or *trading cards*. Performing a quick search on Google reveals that more than 440 million URLs are competing for the keyword *cards* and more than 33 million URLs are competing for the keyword *trading cards*. You can see this in Figure 11-1.

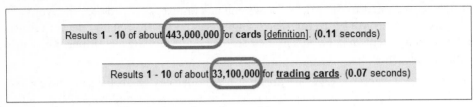

Figure 11-1. Google results: "cards" and "trading cards"

This is only one part of the story. Although the Google results suggest a heavy level of competition, they do not say anything about search volume. This is where you can use the Google AdWords Keyword Tool. Figure 11-2 shows the estimated search volume related to the terms *cards* and *trading cards*.

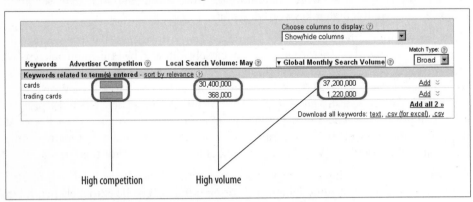

Figure 11-2. Google AdWords Keyword Tool: Volume and search estimates

From a strategic perspective, having a high volume of searches is obviously a good thing. But in this case, both sets of keywords are targeted by the competition. In other words, we need to find keywords with less competition to increase our chances of success.

Long Tail Keywords

You can go after two different types of keywords: broad and narrow. Broad keywords are extremely competitive. Narrow keywords are typically attributed to much lower levels of competition.

You may be able to rank for broad keywords. However, ranking high on the first page of Google is very hard to do and requires a lot of effort. As we discussed earlier in this book, the first page of SERPs for a broad keyword search is typically littered with mixed, biased results. Showing up on the third or eleventh SERP is not going to cut it.

Long tail keywords explained

Chris Anderson coined the term *the long tail* in 2004. Long tail keywords represent the narrow keyword spectrum. Long tail keywords are multiword keywords that are highly specific and narrow in focus. Although long tail keywords do not enjoy the same volume of search traffic as broad keywords, they do enjoy other benefits, such as higher conversion rates and lower competition.

The higher conversion rate is only natural, as in this case web searchers are using several words to express their full intent. This implies that web searchers are using actionable (purpose-driven) keywords and are ready to act on finding satisfactory information on your page.

If your page contains identical search keywords, ideally in the same order, and if you are specifically targeting these keywords, chances are good that your page rank will be higher, as will your conversions.

Lower competition levels mean your site or page will have a higher chance of standing above the smaller crowd. Figure 11-3 illustrates what is meant by long tail keywords.

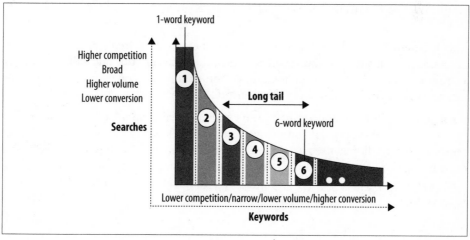

Figure 11-3. Long tail keywords

Implementing a long tail strategy does not mean you should build 10-word keywords. There is a delicate balance between the volume of searches and the number of words in your keywords.

Going back to our example of a trading card business, we could use the AdWords Keyword Tool to get some long tail keyword suggestions. Figure 11-4 shows a portion of a screenshot indicating search volumes of suggested keywords that are related to the keyword *trading cards*.

As you can see in Figure 11-4, not all keywords have the highest competition (as indicated by the solid green rectangle). Also note that for some suggested keywords, Google does not have sufficient data to show in terms of number of searches. All keyword suggestion tools have questionable accuracy, at best. This is much the case for low-volume keywords as well.

For best results, use at least two (and ideally several) tools. Later in this chapter, we will examine additional ways to figure out your keyword competition.

trading cards		368,000	1,220,000	Add ⌄
ccg trading cards		Not enough data	368,000	Add ⌄
trading card		450,000	368,000	Add ⌄
pokemon trading cards		18,100	246,000	Add ⌄
magic trading cards		1,900	165,000	Add ⌄
star trading cards		8,100	22,200	Add ⌄
artist trading cards		12,100	14,800	Add ⌄
star wars trading cards		3,600	14,800	Add ⌄
webkinz trading cards		Not enough data	14,800	Add ⌄
marvel trading cards		8,100	12,100	Add ⌄
basketball trading cards		6,600	22,200	Add ⌄
rare trading cards		1,000	5,400	Add ⌄
trading card guide		6,600	5,400	Add ⌄
trading cards value		8,100	5,400	Add ⌄
baseball trading card		8,100	4,400	Add ⌄
magic the gathering trading cards		720	4,400	Add ⌄
price trading cards		6,600	4,400	Add ⌄

Figure 11-4. Google AdWords Keyword Tool: Suggested keywords

The question you may be asking at this point is: how many search referrals per month do I need? If your site is new, you will not know the answer to this question. The better question to ask is: how many converting visitors do I need? You should not settle for just any visitor. You want visitors that convert.

So, if you require 1,000 converting visitors with a conversion rate of 10%, this means you require 10,000 visitors. If your conversation rate is lower, you can do the math and see the kind of traffic you need. Compare these requirements with the anticipated traffic of your targeted keywords. Ultimately, your conversion rate is a true indication of the quality of your landing pages, the choice of your keywords, and the quality of your site's content.

Keywords and Language

A keyword can be any word, found anywhere on your site! This includes nouns, verbs, and adjectives. A keyword can also be a collection of words or a phrase. When creating your keywords, you can use keyword modifiers to create different keyword combinations.

The Importance of Word Stemming

Word stemming refers to the concept of various word derivations from their basic (root) stems. This concept is important, as using it can help in perceived page relevance. Using multiple-word variations can assist you in attaining additional targeted traffic. To quote Wikipedia (*http://en.wikipedia.org/wiki/Stemming*):

> Stemming is the process for reducing inflected (or sometimes derived) words to their stem, base or root form—generally a written word form. The stem need not be identical to the morphological root of the word; it is usually sufficient that related words map to the same stem, even if this stem is not in itself a valid root. The algorithm has been a long-standing problem in computer science; the first paper on the subject was published in 1968. The process of stemming, often called conflation, is useful in search engines for query expansion or indexing and other natural language processing problems.

Let's look at an example of keyword stemming. When searching for the four-word phrase *social network automate tweet*, I got the SERP fragment shown in Figure 11-5. If you look closely, it should be clear how Google relates the word stem and its derivative.

Google sees the connection between the search term *network* and the word *networking*, as indicated by the boldface words in the SERP result. Google highlights the plural of *tweet* (my search term) as *Tweets*. The search term *automate* is associated with the highlighted result *automation*. Finally, Google offers the search suggestion of the term *automatic*.

This example should speak volumes about keyword stemming. Even if your keyword is not an exact match, if it contains either the stem or its grammatical derivative, Google will rank your pages, as they will be perceived as relevant. If your keyword is an exact match, this will typically translate to enhanced page rankings.

Figure 11-6 shows the same article when searching for *schedule your tweets*. This particular keyword is an exact match of the article. You can see how the page rank improved over the previous example (the four-term keyword).

So, what is the point of keyword stemming? When you write your page copy, be very descriptive while using word variations (singular, plural, various tenses, etc.), and write more descriptive page copy than your competitors.

Figure 11-5. Importance of keyword stemming

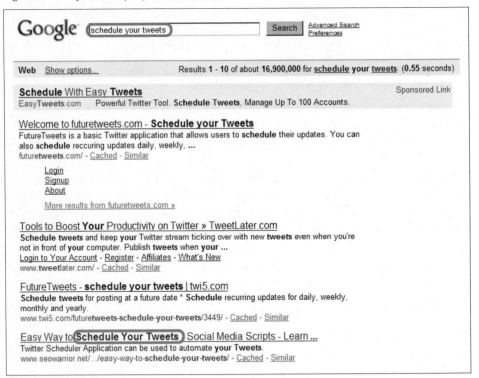

Figure 11-6. Exact match

Keyword Modifiers

Keyword modifiers are words that are used adjacent to your core (root) keywords. Keyword modifiers can help strengthen your long tail keyword strategy. The easiest way to find appropriate keyword modifiers is to start with your basic root words.

Types of modifiers

There are many types of modifiers. Figure 11-7 shows generic and money modifiers. *Generic modifiers* can be used on any site. These modifiers are usually part of popular search queries. *Money modifiers* are typically used to catch searches with buying intentions. You can create further subcategories or classifications of modifiers based on the modifiers shown in Figure 11-7.

POPULAR MODIFERS

GENERIC MODIFIERS				"MONEY" MODIFIERS		
NOUNS	**ADJECTIVES**	**VERBS**		auction	discount	review
archive	adequate	achieve		bargain	features	sale
art	amazing	acquire		best	fee	second hand
audio	astonishing	amaze		buy	foreclosure	sell
blog	astounding	astonish		buying	gift	shopping
business	basic	bewilder		cheap	holiday	specials
community	best	buy		cheapest	lease	store
company	better	catch		classified	limited time	used
design	cool	contact		clearance	options	inexpansive
event	enhanced	develop		closeout	price	expansive
feed	extravagant	discover		compare	property	value
freeware	fabulous	download		comparison	purchase	lowest
fun	fantastic	extend		coupon	rate	brand name
industry	formal	find		coupon	retail	authentic
internet	incredible	get		shipping	free	product
marketing	informal	grow		online service	estimate	quote
movie	large	listen		rfp	rfi	
mp3	luxurious	locate				
news	mind-blowing	obtain				
organization	miraculous	manage				
photo	outstanding	overwhelm		Note: each niche will have its own specific modifiers		
photo	premium	produce				
problem	pure	progress		Note: Don't forget to use keyword stemming		

Figure 11-7. Popular generic and money keyword modifiers

Niche modifiers

Niche modifiers are modifiers that are specific to a particular industry. Let's suppose your client owns a small car dealership of new and used cars, and you are in the process of creating a site for this client. When doing your keyword research, you can start by using several root keywords, such as *car dealership* and *car dealer*. Your basic root words in this case would be *car* and *dealer*.

As part of your keyword research, you should go through the client's car inventory to determine which cars are selling best. You may also want to determine which options are the most popular.

You can summarize the information you collect in a spreadsheet, as shown in Figure 11-8.

Keyword Permutation Matrix

Root	Variations	Related	Geo	\multicolumn{10}{c}{Specific (Characteristic) Terms}									
				style	color	year	make	model	version	type	class	warranty	extras	condition
car	cars	automobile	street	award winning	beige	1999	bmw	Civic	ex	gas	compact	basic	air freshener	new
truck	trucks	auto	town	consumer choice	black	2000	chevrolet	Accord	lx	hybrid	convertible	corrosion	anti rust coating	old
van	vans	move	county	economical	blue	2001	chevy	CR-V	coupe	hydrogen	economy	drivetrain	brake light	used
suv	suvs	dealer	province	fast	brown	2002	chrysler	Element			full-size	kms	bumper protector	rusted
jeep	jeeps	dealership	location	fuel economy	green	2003	dodge	Fit			intermeddiate	labor	custom	mint
brand name	autos	parts		low mileage	red	2004	ford	Insight			luxury	parts	extra horn	
company name	automobiles	automotive		luxury	silver	2005	gmc	Odyssey			mini	powertrain	floor maps	
dealer	vehicles	finance		small	white	2006	honda	Pilot			minivan	rust	fog lights	
shop	dealers	leasing		sporty	yellow	2007	jaguar	Ridgeline			premium	year	front crash guard	
	deals	renting		top of class		2008	mercedes	Clarity			sport utility	years	gps	
		lease		top rated		2009	nissan				sports car		halogen bulbs	
		renting				2010	porsche				standard		lcd tv	
		tuning					saturn						luggage carrier	
		loan					toyota						mp3 player	
		sale					volvo						neon headlights	
		moving											radar detectors	
		speeding											reading light	
		vehicle											rear view mirror	
													remote locking	
													reverse musical horn	
													seat covers	
													security system	
													steering cover	
	Note: This is only a small sample.												tissue box	
													window films	

Figure 11-8. Car dealership keyword permutation matrix

Starting from your root words, you can come up with different term variations and related words (using word stemming, synonyms, etc.). For our car dealer, it is important that the dealer's geographical information is indexed in the search engines, as its core target audience is its immediate neighborhood.

The next thing you may want to do is to create an inventory of all the cars and associated parts the dealer is selling. In addition, you may want to create several subcategories under which to list all of these characteristics. These may include the car style, color, year, make, version, type, warranty, extras, and condition.

Keyword combinations

As shown in Figure 11-8, you can come up with many different keyword variations. Simply scan the spreadsheet from one side to the other and back, and choose terms from different columns. Create a list of these keyword permutations and add them to your draft keyword list. You may also want to create a small script to create the different keyword permutations for you.

Latent Semantic Indexing (LSI)

Analyzing page copy for keyword density provides a statistical breakdown of the use of each keyword. In the past, search engines used keyword density as one of the most important ranking factors. Although keyword density still plays a role, another keyword relationship technique is coming to the forefront.

Page and site theme

Search engines have started to look at general page and site themes, which are the semantic relationships found on pages throughout a site.

Let's suppose you are running a sports website, and you are writing an article on the Los Angeles Lakers. The keywords found in this article should be highly predictable. You are likely to talk about specific players, coaches, draft picks, game schedules, the club's history, the NBA league, and club owners. This should make sense, as all of these things are highly relevant to your overall site theme.

The concept of a page theme is not new, having been developed at Bell Laboratories in 1988. According to Wikipedia (*http://bit.ly/Bic75*):

> Latent Semantic Indexing (LSI) is an indexing and retrieval method that uses a mathematical technique called Singular Value Decomposition (SVD) to identify patterns in the relationships between the terms and concepts contained in an unstructured collection of text. LSI is based on the principle that words that are used in the same contexts tend to have similar meanings. A key feature of LSI is its ability to extract the conceptual content of a body of text by establishing associations between those terms that occur in similar contexts.

LSI is also known as Latent Semantic Analysis (LSA). The same article goes on to say that:

> LSI overcomes two of the most severe constraints of Boolean keyword queries: multiple words that have similar meanings (synonymy) and words that have more than one meaning (polysemy). Synonymy and polysemy are often the cause of mismatches in the vocabulary used by the authors of documents and the users of information retrieval systems. As a result, Boolean keyword queries often return irrelevant results and miss information that is relevant.

It is easy to see why LSI is becoming a powerful ally to search engines. LSI can help improve the quality of search results. So, what's the takeaway with LSI? Simply put, create quality pages, and ensure that you create page copy using your main keywords as well as many related keywords. So, if you are writing copy about cat food, for instance, don't include information on buying electronics unless you are talking about cat tag IDs.

Keyword Research Process

You need to ask several basic questions when conducting sound keyword research. For instance, what would someone type to get to your site? What keywords are associated with your line of business? What would you type to find products, services, and information you are trying to sell? Before you can answer these questions, you must understand your niche or business. The more you know about the business, the more targeted your keyword research will be. Scan through your existing site. If your site is new, use your existing business products, services, and publications for keyword ideas. Find out about your competitors. Learn what keywords they are using. See Chapter 13 for more details.

Establish a Current Baseline

Leverage your web server logfiles to see what keywords are already working for you. Compile a list of current search engine referrals in a spreadsheet such as the one shown in Figure 11-9. You can download the template at *http://book.seowarrior.net*.

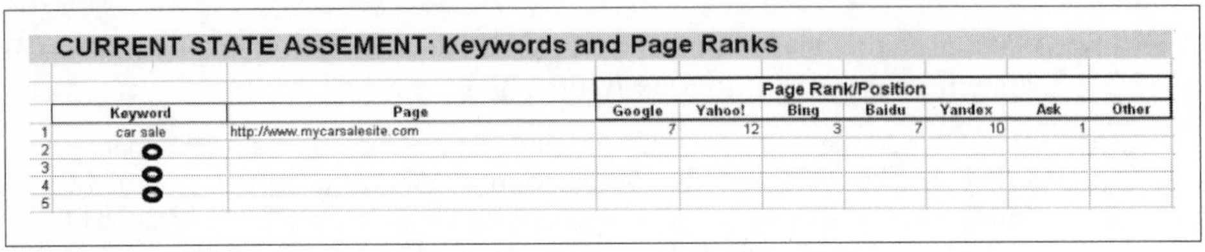

CURRENT STATE ASSEMENT: Keywords and Page Ranks

	Keyword	Page	Page Rank/Position						
			Google	Yahoo!	Bing	Baidu	Yandex	Ask	Other
1	car sale	http://www.mycarsalesite.com	7	12	3	7	10	1	
2									
3									
4									
5									

Figure 11-9. Current state assessment: Keywords and page ranks

To compile this information you can use several sources, including your web server logfiles, Google Webmaster Tools, and Google Analytics. The most definitive source will always be your web server logfiles. Figure 11-10 shows how this data looks in Google Webmaster Tools.

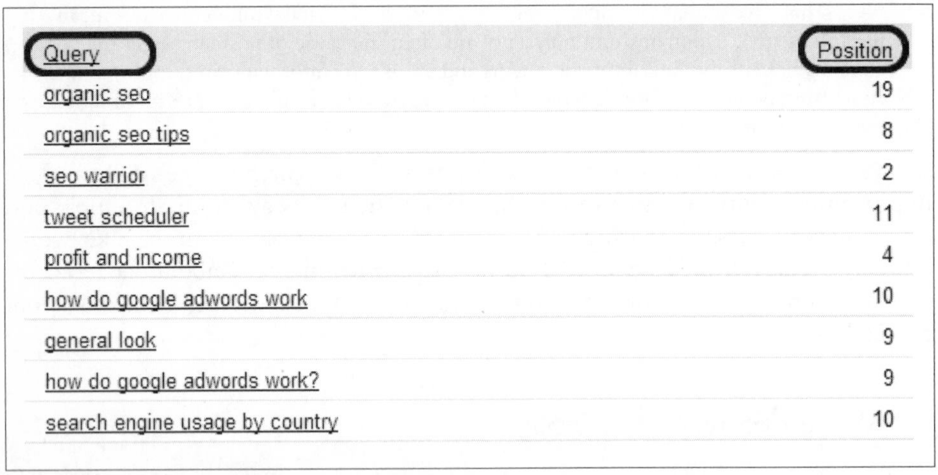

Query	Position
organic seo	19
organic seo tips	8
seo warrior	2
tweet scheduler	11
profit and income	4
how do google adwords work	10
general look	9
how do google adwords work?	9
search engine usage by country	10

Figure 11-10. Google Webmaster Tools: Keyword positions

To find your keyword rankings on other search engines, you can write a script such as the one we will discuss in Chapter 13. You can also use online ranking aggregator services such as those at *http://www.url.com/* and *http://jux2.com/*.

When you have to check many keywords across multiple search engines, it makes sense to automate this task. If you prefer to use graphical tools, you can try those from

UPposition (*http://www.upposition.com/*), Web CEO Ltd. (*http://webceo.com/*), and Caphyon (*http://www.advancedwebranking.com/*). Assessing your current rankings is essential for tracking your progress as you modify and grow your site.

Compile a Draft List of Keywords You Wish to Target

If you own an existing site, the keyword process can be a bit simpler. You already know a lot if you have an existing website. You can leverage the existing keywords that you rank for by introducing new keyword variations to catch additional traffic. If you are a new site, this part of the process is lengthier. Let's assume you are starting a new site.

Keyword brainstorming

For this exercise, let's imagine we are creating a resume submission service website. Users come to your site, upload their resumes, pay the submission fee, and their resumes get sent to thousands of recruiters. Your target audience is North America and the United Kingdom.

Forget all the tools for a moment. The first thing you want to do is brainstorm your keywords. You want to put down everything you think is related to your business. At this point, you may have a list such as that shown in the following fragment:

```
resume submission service
online resume submission service
submit resume to head hunters
automated resume submission
submit resume to recruiters
```

At the most basic level, you ought to know your audience. Employ words or phrases that your audience would use to get to your site.

Make use of localized terms. People in different countries speak different versions of the same language. Since your site will also be targeting UK searchers, consider Scottish, UK English, and Welsh terminology. With that in mind, you might add the following keywords for your UK audience:

```
curriculum vitae submission
submit your cv
automated cv submission
submit cv to job agents
```

Language is not just different between countries. Languages spoken in different parts of the same country can be significantly different as well, so you will need to keep this in mind.

You can also add geographical keyword modifiers if you want to target keyword queries that include names of cities, towns, and so forth. Some people prefer domestic products and services. Make your sites look (or be perceived as) local. For example, you could add the following:

```
resume submission service ontario
cv blaster london uk
resume blaster canada
```

Utilize keyword stemming

Look closely at all of the keywords we have thus far. Some terms are singular, some are plural, and most are in the present tense. Create some additional combinations based on the keyword stemming we discussed earlier. For example:

```
submitting your resume
blasting your cv
automate cv submissions
submited your resume to head hunters
```

Make use of generic keyword modifiers. Here comes the part where you can make further keyword combinations. Your imagination is your only limit. However, your keywords should make sense. Here are some examples of using generic keyword modifiers:

```
free resume submission
better resume blaster
easy cv blaster
premium resume submission services
```

Continue by finding related keywords. Related keywords can be synonyms (or semantically related keywords). For example, the site we are building (a resume submission service) might also be talking about:

```
resume tips
resume writing
interview tips
interview preparation
recruiter directory
```

Finding related keywords

You can find related keywords in many ways. For example, you can use Google's ~ operator to find semantically related keywords. Figure 11-11 shows Google's SERP when you search for keywords related to the keyword *resume*.

As shown in Figure 11-11, the keywords related to *resume* are *jobs* and *job*, in addition to their uppercase variations, as the ~operator is case-sensitive. Note that this is only the first page of the Google results. You can find more semantically related words by browsing more Google results pages.

If you look at the SERP closely, you will see many other related terms that you can use. These words are not shown in boldface, like the ones we already talked about, but you can easily realize their relevance. So, we can expand our keyword list to include keywords such as:

```
job leads with resume submission
blast resume to get jobs
reach job recruiters find jobs
```

```
job seeker advice
career boost with resume submission services
resume blaster career tips
cv blaster interview tips
```

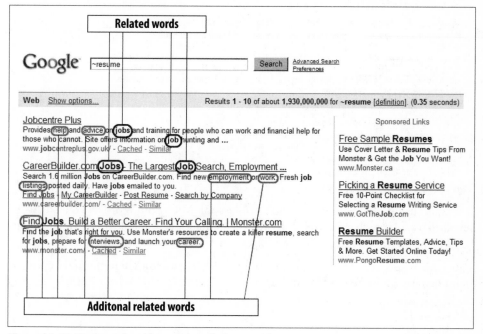

Figure 11-11. Finding related keywords with the ~ operator

You can also use the star operator, *. The star operator is interpreted as any single term preceding or following the specified term. Here is an example:

```
*blast*resume
```

Executing this in Google will return results that contain the term *blast* preceded and followed by any term, then followed by the term *resume*. Figure 11-12 shows what we get in the Google results.

If you look closely, we have now found a synonym for the term *blast*, which is *distribution*. We have also found another keyword modifier: *instantly*. You can use many different combinations of the * operator to learn more related words. This exercise is also about seeing your competitors' keyword permutations.

Make use of Microsoft Word. Yes, you read it correctly! Microsoft Word offers a great built-in keyword research tool in its thesaurus and the Microsoft Encarta Encyclopedia. These tools are helpful when building your keyword list. The Word thesaurus is especially good when searching for synonyms and related words. Figure 11-13 shows the kinds of things you can do within Word.

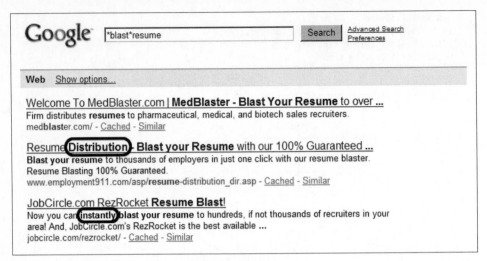

*Figure 11-12. Using the * operator to find related terms*

If you are using Microsoft Office, do not overlook Microsoft Word as your keyword research tool. Note that Figure 11-13 illustrates the tools available in Microsoft Office 2003 edition. You may see a different layout or setup in your version.

Using Microsoft Word, I was able to get the following additional terms and keywords that I can use in my keyword combinations:

```
employment
occupation
trade
profession
economic downturn
labor market
job loss
get hired
got fired
looking for work
finding jobs
getting interviews
recession jobs
tough market
innovative jobs
career change
career move
```

When using the Microsoft Word thesaurus, you can get more words of interest simply by clicking on resulting words. For example, when I type in the word *job*, I get about 20 synonyms or other related words. I can then click on any of these to get another set of related words. This drill down is virtually endless.

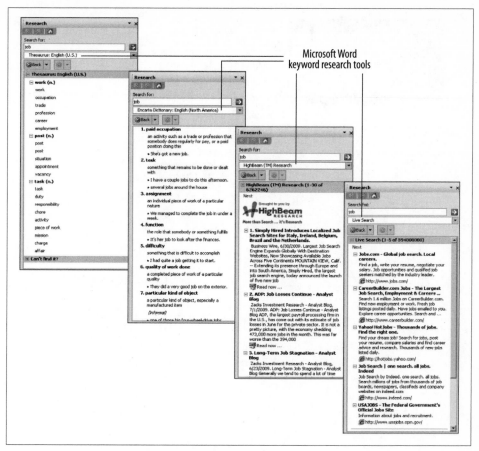

Figure 11-13. Microsoft Word keyword research

Using search engine keyword suggestions and related searches

Search engines provide an endless pool of keyword suggestions. As soon as you arrive at the search box and start typing your keywords, search engines start showing their search suggestion drop-downs with a list of predicted keywords relevant to your currently typed-in text. Figure 11-14 shows how this looks at the time of this writing on Bing, Google, and Yahoo!.

As soon as you get to your results page, you are again given some keyword suggestions. Figure 11-15 illustrates how this looks in the major search engines. As you can see, there are plenty of keywords you can find just by using search engine interfaces.

The examples shown here are for only a single term. You could run all of your terms and keywords through this process to obtain many new keyword suggestions.

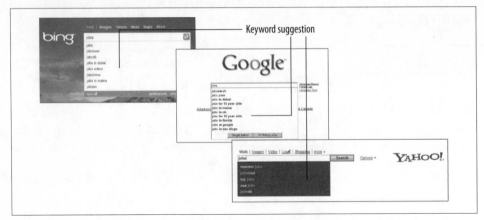

Figure 11-14. Keyword suggestion: Bing, Google, and Yahoo!

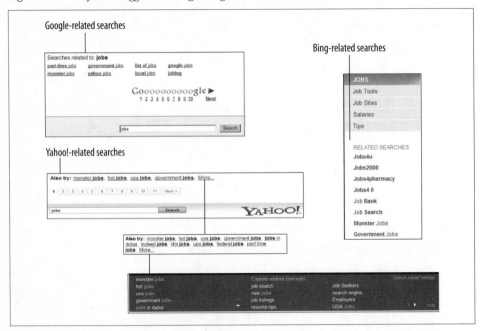

Figure 11-15. Related searches on Bing, Google, and Yahoo!

Google keyword tools and resources

Google provides several keyword-oriented tools that you can use for SEO. These include the Google AdWords Keyword Tool, Google Sets (*http://labs.google.com/sets*), Google Trends (*http://google.com/trends*), and Google Insights for Search (*http://google .com/insights/search/#*). All of these are free and can be quite useful for obtaining keyword suggestions.

Google AdWords Keyword Tool. The Google AdWords Keyword Tool is perhaps the most popular free keyword research tool. What makes this tool particularly useful is that you can use it for your SEM or SEO campaigns. If you are just doing SEO, you do not need to register to use it.

You can search for related keywords in two basic ways. You can use your own (starting draft) keywords, or you can specify a particular URL from which to obtain your ideas. This includes your competitor URLs as well.

Several filters are available with both methods. Note that the results are tailored for U.S. English by default. You can modify this by clicking on the Edit button. One option allows you to tell Google to discard results containing particular words or phrases. Another option tells Google to include adult words in the suggested results.

You also have the option to just use your own keywords, without requesting suggestions. You would do this if you are only interested in related search traffic information. Figure 11-16 shows the two interfaces. In this case, I am using the keyword *jobs* as well as a fictitious competitor URL.

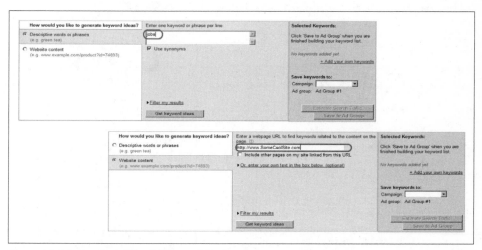

Figure 11-16. Google AdWords Keyword Tool

After you click the "Get keyword ideas" button, the results come up and you have further options on the righthand side of the screen, where you can change the keyword match type from Broad to Phrase, Exact, or Negative. You can also hide particular columns. Figure 11-17 shows the top six suggested terms for the two scenarios (using some of my keywords and a fictitious competitor URL).

The Google AdWords Keyword Tool is one of the best on the market. Think of it this way: Google has access to most searchers' data. The company ought to know keywords better than anyone. Some people just use Google AdWords and nothing else!

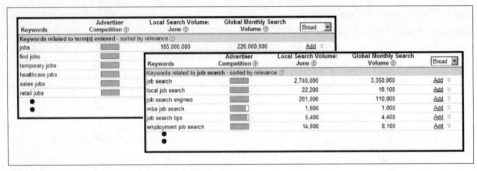

Figure 11-17. Google AdWords comparison

Google Sets. You can use the Google Sets platform to get additional related keywords. The idea behind Google Sets is that Google will expand the list of your provided keywords by finding related keywords collected from related sets found on the Internet.

Google Sets uses probabilities of finding other keywords next to your keywords when compiling results. Figure 11-18 shows sample Google Sets output. Using Google Sets is easy. Simply enter your related terms and Google does the rest.

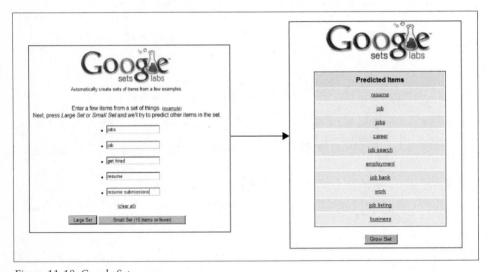

Figure 11-18. Google Sets

Google Trends. The Google Trends platform provides performance timelines for your keywords, as shown in Figure 11-19. You can select particular (world) regions or time frames.

The Google Trends platform also provides the top 100 search queries for a given day. You can see the so-called Google Hot Trends site at *http://www.google.com/trends/hot trends*. Figure 11-20 shows a sample Google Hot Trends screen as of this writing.

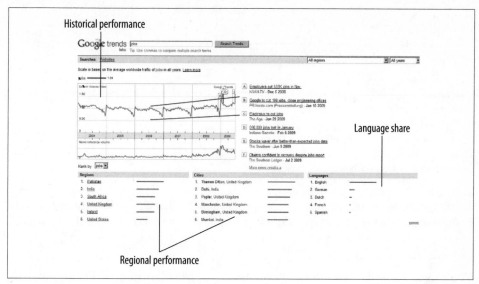

Figure 11-19. Google Trends

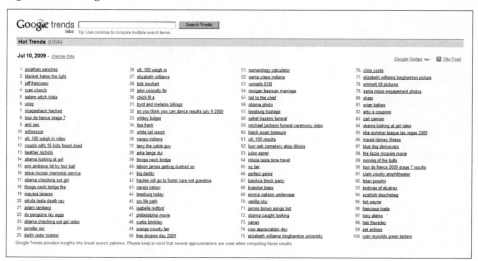

Figure 11-20. Google Hot Trends

You can also scan Hot Trends back in time and see more details of each keyword by clicking on them.

Google Insights for Search. The Google Insights for Search platform is similar to Google Trends, as it too shows geographical data. You can use Google Insights when comparing keyword performance in specific world regions. Figure 11-21 shows the Google Insights for Search entry form.

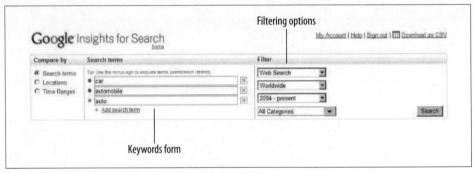

Figure 11-21. Google Insights for Search entry form

When you arrive at the first page of Google Insights for Search, the first thing you want to do is enter your search terms of interest. Next, you may want to modify the default filtering options. For example, you can choose to filter by Web Search, Image Search, News Search, or Product Search.

You can also use Worldwide search or choose a particular country. Finally, you can pick a particular time range. Submitting the form brings up several result sections. These include interest over time (a graph), regional interest (a graph and data), and search terms related to each of your terms. This last item is particularly useful in terms of adding more keywords to your draft keyword list.

Microsoft adCenter Labs

Microsoft is not standing idle while Google continues to produce a new tool every few months. To compete with the Google AdWords Keyword Tool, Microsoft introduced its adCenter Labs platform (*http://adlab.microsoft.com/Keyword-Research.aspx*).

Microsoft's adCenter provides its own keyword suggestion tool similar to Google's AdWords and Yahoo!'s Search Marketing keyword suggestion tools. The only catch is that you need to sign up for an account. There is a $5 fee for a new account. Microsoft also offers free online tools under its adCenter Labs platform.

The adCenter Labs platform comes with many features. The ones specific to keyword research include entity association graph capability, keyword group detection, keyword mutation detection, keyword forecast capability, and search funnels.

Entity association graph. According to Microsoft, the entity association graph is a graphical representation of "co-occurrences of entities in search queries or search sessions". In other words, this tool should be useful for getting additional keyword suggestions. Figure 11-22 shows the entity association graph for the term *jobs*.

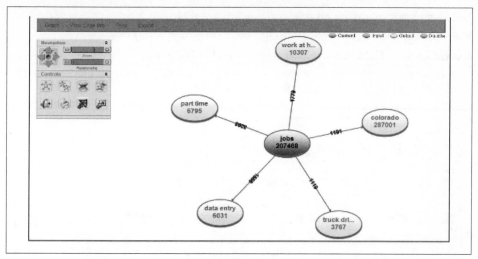

Figure 11-22. Microsoft adCenter Labs: Entity association graph

Keyword group detection. The keyword group detection tool shows words that are related to or similar to keywords entered on the keyword group form. The resulting output shows a long table of related words. At the time of this writing, a search for words related to *jobs* yields the following keywords:

```
job opportunities
job listings
job search
employment opportunities
government jobs
zip codes
employment agencies
phone book
employment
federal jobs
job openings
toyota dealers
nursing jobs
job fairs
phone directory
culinary schools
yellow pages
...
```

Keyword mutation detection. The keyword mutation detection tool produces common misspellings and alternative spellings. When searching for the word *resumes*, I got the following misspellings:

```
reume
resumes
reseme
resum
resume's
```

When it comes to misspellings, if you need to use them, stick them in your meta keywords. Misspellings found on your page copy do not look professional.

Keyword forecast. The keyword forecast tool predicts keyword searches (an impression count) and the associated demographic distributions of entered keywords. Figure 11-23 is a sample illustration for the terms *jobs* and *resume*.

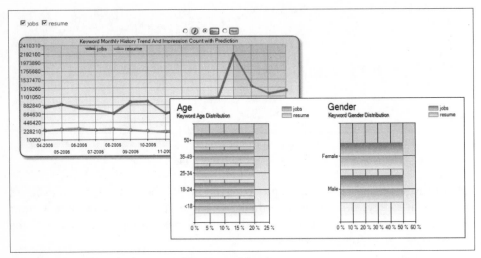

Figure 11-23. Microsoft adCenter Labs: Keyword forecast

Search funnels. You use search funnels to analyze related search sequences. Figure 11-24 shows an example search funnel for the term *jobs*.

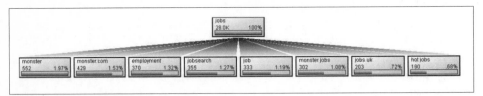

Figure 11-24. Microsoft adCenter Labs: Search funnel

Yahoo! keyword tools

Yahoo! offers a couple of platforms: Yahoo! Research (*http://sandbox.yahoo.com/*) and Yahoo! Search Marketing (the latter being the AdWords Keyword Tool alternative).

Yahoo! Research. Yahoo! Research provides a platform called Sandbox where it runs many different projects. When it comes to keyword-related projects, there are two interesting tools: Correlator and TagExplorer. You can use both to get additional keyword suggestions.

Yahoo! Search Marketing. The Yahoo! Search Marketing platform provides another PPC keyword tool that you can use for SEO work. Its interface is similar to Google AdWords and you can find it at *http://sem.smallbusiness.yahoo.com/searchenginemarketing/*. Figure 11-25 shows keywords that Yahoo! Search Marketing suggested based on the keyword *jobs*.

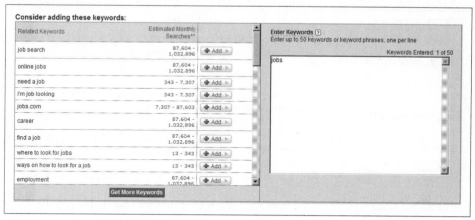

Figure 11-25. Yahoo! Search Marketing: Keyword suggestions

As of this writing, you do not need to register to use Yahoo!'s keyword suggestion tool.

Additional keyword research tools

Many companies provide free and commercially available keyword research tools. This section mentions some of the popular ones. You can try a few tools and find one or two that you like. Then you can use those tools in conjunction with the Google AdWords Keyword Tool for most of your work.

Free keyword research tools. Table 11-1 lists some of the popular free online keyword research tools.

Table 11-1. Popular free keyword research tools

Tool	Description
KwMap (*http://kwmap.net/*)	Generates a visual and textual representation of related keywords
Quintura (*http://quintura.com/*)	Generates a visual tag cloud in addition to its own textual search results
Reference (*http://www.reference.com/*)	Generates dictionary, thesaurus, and reference information
Visual Thesaurus	Generates a visual representation of word relationships

Tool	Description
(*http://www.visualthesaurus.com/*)	
Glossarist	Provides links to glossaries and dictionaries on all subjects
(*http://glossarist.com/*)	
Webmaster Toolkit	Generates related keyword searches using many search engines, including Google
(*http://webmaster-toolkit.com/*)	
Keyword Discovery	Generates up to 100 related keywords and an estimate of their daily search volumes; a paid version is available with no restrictions
(*http://keyworddiscovery.com/search .html*)	
Wordtracker	Generates up to 100 related keywords and an estimate of their daily search volumes; a paid version is available with no restrictions
(*http://freekeywords.wordtracker .com/*)	
Search Forecast	Provides a keyword suggestion tool with the (predicted) number of searches
(*http://searchforecast.com/*)	

Commercially available keyword research tools.   Table 11-2 lists some of the commercially available online keyword research tools.

Table 11-2. Popular commercially available keyword research tools

Tool	Description
Keyword Elite	Provides ways of finding niche keywords for SEM and SEO
(*http://keywordelite.com/*)	
Keyword Discovery	Provides keyword research tools including competitor data
(*http://www.wordtracker.com/*)	
Wordtracker	Provides extensive keyword research features; based on metadata search engine partnerships
(*http://www.wordtracker.com/*)	
KeywordSpy	Provides competitor keyword data along with other standard keyword research features
(*http://www.keywordspy.com/*)	
Wordze	Provides extensive keyword research features including daily keyword trends
(*http://www.wordze.com/*)	
Compete	Provides comprehensive keyword research facilities as well as many other SEO tools
(*http://compete.com/*)	

Evaluate Your Keywords

Assuming you have compiled your draft list of keywords, you should now group your keywords in order of priority. You want to target keywords that have sufficient search volume as well as those you think will convert. To determine keyword priority, you need to do a bit more research.

Estimating keyword competition, revisited

This chapter started with an example of searching for the keyword *trading cards*, which told us that Google indexed more than 37 million related results. This number does not help much, as we know Google does not show more than 1,000 results per search query.

What we really want to know is how many pages (or sites) are targeting our keywords of interest. More specifically, we want to know how many pages are targeting the keywords we compiled on our list. The kinds of pages we are looking for are those that contain keywords in the page title, in the page URL, and in the link anchor text.

Google provides search command (operators) that can help us see how many URLs are targeting our keywords of interest. The three most important keyword operators are `intitle:`, `inurl:`, and `inanchor:`. Table 11-3 shows an analysis for the keyword *trading cards*.

Table 11-3. Size of Google index

Search command	Relative index size
`trading cards`	37,200,000
`intitle:trading intitle:cards`	5,400,000
`inurl:trading inurl:cards`	1,990,000
`inanchor:trading inanchor:cards`	6,270,000
`allintitle: trading cards`	5,400,000
`intitle:trading intitle:cards inurl:trading`	1,840,000
`intitle:trading intitle:cards inurl:trading inurl:cards`	91,000
`intitle:trading intitle:cards inurl:trading inurl:cards inanchor:trading`	75,000
`intitle:trading intitle:cards inurl:trading inurl:cards inanchor:trading inanchor:cards`	37,000
`star wars intitle:trading intitle:cards inurl:trading inurl:cards inanchor:trading inanchor:cards`	5,750
`han solo star wars intitle:trading intitle:cards inurl:trading inurl:cards inanchor:trading inanchor:cards`	738

The point of Table 11-3 is to drill down to the results that are seriously targeting our keyword. Adding the keywords *star wars* and *star wars han solo* brings the Google index down to 738 results.

If we execute similar commands on Yahoo!, we get the results shown in Table 11-4. Note that Yahoo! does not support the `inanchor:` operator.

Table 11-4. Size of Yahoo index

Search command	Relative index size
trading cards	127,000,000
intitle:trading intitle:cards	977,000
inurl:trading inurl:cards	344,000
inanchor:trading inanchor:cards	355,000
intitle:trading intitle:cards inurl:trading	236,000
intitle:trading intitle:cards inurl:trading inurl:cards	219,000
intitle:trading intitle:cards inurl:trading inurl:cards inanchor:trading	85,000
star wars intitle:trading intitle:cards inurl:trading inurl:cards	36,500
han solo star wars intitle:trading intitle:cards inurl:trading inurl:cards	136

As you can deduce from Yahoo!'s numbers, Yahoo! claims to have more results than Google. But when you drill down with additional criteria, the numbers dwindle down much faster, suggesting inflated index counts.

The takeaway from this exercise is to run your keywords through similar commands to spot any interesting opportunities. You want to target keywords that have a relatively low number of indexed URLs—that is, when your keywords are found in the HTML title, the URL path, and the link anchor text in your competitors' pages.

You can utilize a spreadsheet for easier comparison and tracking. Figure 11-26 illustrates one template you can use in your work. This template is just another tab of the same spreadsheet we discussed earlier in the chapter.

You can also automate these tasks by writing an automated script. Be mindful of search engine resources. Strive to emulate regular human clicking behavior in your script.

KEYWORD COMPETITION ASSESMENT

keyword	basic		inurl		intitle		inanchor		inurl & intitle		inurl & intitle & inanchor	
	Google	Yahoo!	Google	Yahoo!	Google	Yahoo!	Google	Yahoo!	Google	Yahoo!	Google	Yahoo!
car dealer	29,000,000	494,000,000	2,380,000	5,990,000	10,200,000	17,400,000	6,360,000	4,390,000	118,000	292,000	83,800	59,100
car dealer toronto	944,000	4,130,000	997	2,460	28,100	4,790	223,000	n/a	620	141	524	n/a

Figure 11-26. Keyword competition assessment

Estimating keyword search volume

The biggest challenge in the keyword research process is making keyword search estimates. Most of the available tools are pretty good at estimating highly popular broad keywords. When it comes to long tail keywords, it may be best to use one- or two-week PPC campaigns to get some real numbers. Remember, PPC platform vendors will provide you with accurate numbers, as that is in their interest. You can always check their stats claims by carefully examining your web server logfiles.

Employing PPC to estimate your search traffic is one thing. You can also test your keywords for particular conversions. You can set up PPC campaigns to target specific keywords and see whether they work. Utilizing PPC techniques to forecast your SEO conversions can save a lot of time and money, as you can get fast feedback that will allow you to adjust your keyword strategy. Taking out the guesswork pays off in the long run. We will discuss PPC in more detail in Chapter 16.

Finalize Your Keyword List

Perhaps you have done your homework. You have spent time researching your business. In the process, you have utilized several keyword research tools to get the best keywords available. You may have also tested your keywords in a small PPC campaign and have found those that work. You are now ready to implement your keyword list within your content.

Implement Your Strategy

Implementing a keyword strategy simply means optimizing your content for your researched keywords. It takes time to see your results, as they depend on many factors, including your site and page age, your site's trust factor, and many others.

Your keyword research strategy could be to push all of the modified or new content at once, or to create a scheduled content strategy—to target additional keywords over time. Once your content is out, all you can do is wait and see. Monitor your web stats using Google Analytics and other tracing software. Perform a current keyword state assessment audit to see your progress. Perform corrective action on your low-performing keywords. Readjust your keyword list. Repeat the process as required.

Summary

Keyword research activities are the foundation of intelligent SEO. Targeting the wrong keywords can be costly. Regardless of whether you are a new or an old site, spend time conducting appropriate keyword research.

Search engines provide many different tools and resources that you can use to create your keyword lists. Gradually increase your targeted keyword base. Diversify over time to build your web presence. Focus on one keyword per page. Stick your keyword misspellings in your meta keyword HTML tags. Study your web logs and web stats extensively.

## CHAPTER 12

Link Building

The link-building process is one of the pillars of SEO. It helps increase your site's public awareness while also helping you attain higher search engine rankings. The number of inbound links to your site is a measure of its popularity. Each backlink is a vote for your site. All votes count, but search engines do not view them in the same way. Focus your efforts on links that will bring in the most value to your site.

The most effective way to build great links is to build great content. Creating open source software, a free service, a browser plug-in, interesting content, a web comic, or any other value-add feature will work.

Internal link-building activities include the creation of link bait. There are many types of link bait. In this chapter, we will explore how to create a sample website widget, which is one type of link bait. You can also use the social bookmarking paradigm to your advantage. Social bookmarks help make it easy for your visitors to remember, bookmark, and share your site's content. Social bookmarks can help bring huge amounts of inbound traffic to your site.

Using website syndication is the norm for any serious site on the Internet today. Whether you want to use RSS or Atom feeds, syndicate as much of your content as possible. You can use services such as FeedBurner to obtain stats about your feeds.

We will also cover submissions to web directories in this chapter. Not all directories are created equal. We will explore several types of directories and how you can find them. Finding web directories on the Internet is easy with the help of search engines.

To round out the chapter, we will explore ways to increase your web presence by building additional complementary sites to fortify your main site. This includes building your own directory, awards, and product or service review sites.

Precursors to Link Building

Link building takes time. You want to make sure your time is not wasted. Before you start your link-building campaign, perform some research to ensure that you invest your time wisely.

Start Building Your Reputation Early

Even if you don't have a site today, you can still help your future business by being a part of various Internet communities. You can start your own blog, contribute articles to authority sites in your niche, and become active in social media sites such as Facebook, Twitter, MySpace, and LinkedIn. When the appropriate time comes, expose your new business website across all of these channels that were cultivated over time.

Granted, not everyone has the time to do this. In you fall into this category, you can use the classic networking approach: stay in touch with your contacts. When you are ready, let them know what you are working on and ask them to help promote your new site by adding links on their sites (and therefore, spreading your news to their contacts).

Assess Your Current Situation

If you are just starting with a new website, assessing your current situation should be fairly straightforward. If your site is not live yet, you may still have some links pointing to it. This may be the case if you bought an expired domain that still has some residual links, or if you have let others know of your site prior to it being officially live.

If you are working with an existing site, it is important to evaluate the current state of your inbound links. Check your web stats logs with Google Analytics, Google Webmaster Tools, Yahoo! Site Explorer, or any other web tracking software that shows your referrals. Aggregate this information in a list so that you can get a baseline before starting your new link-building campaign (this will enable you to properly measure your campaign results).

You can use a spreadsheet document to record your current state assessment. Figure 12-1 shows a sample you can use in your tracking. The spreadsheet is available for download at *http://book.seowarrior.net*.

Emulate Your Competitors

It makes sense to know what link-building strategies your competitors are using. It would be foolish to ignore their linking strategies. As link building takes time, missing out on specific link-building strategies could be costly.

When looking for competitors, you should start with local ones, as that information may be easier to find. Look at your local business listings as well as the Yellow Pages,

LINK BUILDING: Current State Assement									Summary
#	Backlink	Anchor Text	Linked Page	PPR	SPR	TL	TR	NF	# of current links
									# of natural links
									# of paid links
									# of Backlinks (PR=10)
									# of Backlinks (PR=9)
									# of Backlinks (PR=8)
									# of Backlinks (PR=7)
									# of Backlinks (PR=6)
									# of Backlinks (PR=5)
									# of Backlinks (PR=4)
									# of Backlinks (PR=3)
									# of Backlinks (PR=2)
									# of Backlinks (PR=1)
									# of Backlinks (PR=0)

Figure 12-1. Link-building spreadsheet: Current state assessment

specific niche directories, and similar resources. Pick up your local newspapers and see whether you can find some competitors.

Get a good sample of old and new businesses and research their inbound links. Go after sites that link to your competitors. Don't stop at emulation. See whether you can do better than what they have done. Just because your competitors are ranking high in a particular niche does not mean they have done their due diligence. They may just be playing the field by themselves.

Explore different ways to get better inbound links. You can do this in many ways. At a basic level, assess the inbound links your competition uses. Try to figure out their relative worth. Find out how many pages are linking to the page containing the inbound competitor link. Look at the overall site popularity, age, inbound links, estimated traffic, and so forth. Find sites that are better, and get your inbound links placed on those sites. You can also combine multiple competitors' strategies into your own hybrid strategy. In other words, use an aggregate of methodologies found on several high-ranking sites.

After examining your competition and analyzing your current state, you are ready to formulate some link-building goals. Shoot for the stars, but be realistic. Optimize your time by going after links that will provide most of the benefits. Go after reputable, authoritative, and noncompeting sites that are related to your site.

Natural Link Acquisition

Nothing is better than natural link acquisition. This occurs when people who are genuinely interested in your site link to it. Information travels fast on the Internet. As long as your site is of great quality, you will reach a tipping point where it will no longer be necessary to invest much effort in link building. This is something any site owner should desire: having a site that is so infectious that it becomes the buzz.

Link Sources and Link Quality

Although you can certainly let things develop naturally, you can speed things up by placing your links across different sites on the Internet. You need to ensure that your link-building campaigns are targeting many different sites to make your inbound links look more natural. Pursuing only one type of site, such as blogs, directories, or forums, would not be overly effective. Spice it up!

All links carry some value. Some links are worth more than others. How do you tell what the backlink from a particular site is worth? You can use a number of factors when determining potential inbound link quality. High-quality inbound links originate from topically similar pages. The best inbound links appear on pages that rank well for your targeted keywords. High-quality links also appear on pages with few or no ads or other links.

Elements of Link Building

There are countless opportunities for link building. Everything starts on your site. Your site should make it easy and intuitive for anyone wanting to link to it. To increase your chances of people linking to your site, you need to provide something of value.

Basic Elements

The following subsections talk about the rudimentary elements that all sites need to consider.

Take out the guesswork

Take out the guesswork for your web visitors by providing the HTML code fragment(s) for people to link to your site. Create "Link to Us" and "Tell a Friend" links. Most CMS software includes prebuilt forms for handling these simple concepts.

Run a daily, weekly, or monthly email newsletter

Running your own newsletter provides several benefits. First, you get to remind your existing visitors of your new offerings, whether it is content, products, or services. Plus, the recipients of your newsletter are likely to forward it to people they know if they find your newsletter interesting.

Provide registered services

Many sites offer free and members-only content. This model offers several benefits. If your free content is already great, many of your visitors will also be interested in your members-only content. The idea is that the content that is provided to members only is of even greater quality than the public content. Many sites charge for members-only content. Providing registered services helps you build up the email lists that you can use in your marketing campaigns. Be sure to provide members with opt-in and opt-out options if you're using this channel and strategy.

Link Bait

The terms *link bait* and *link baiting* describe the concept of creating interesting content with the intent of creating maximum Internet buzz to get as many people to link to your site as possible. Link bait exists in many forms. Having great content is your most basic link-baiting technique. You can also think of link bait as content "hooks." Table 12-1 shows some of the most common content hooks.

Table 12-1. Types of content hooks

Type	Description
News	Providing timely news information on any topic can be the main catalyst for retaining and gaining visitor traffic
Information	You can provide information in many different formats, including whitepapers, case studies, research, and various statistics
Gifts, contests, awards, sales, discounts	Enticing people with gifts, contests, awards, sales, and discounts are traditional ways to attract attention
Humor, controversy	You can promote your site by using jokes, funny pictures (videos or sounds), and even controversial information
Software and widgets	Providing free software and widgets is another way to promote your online assets
Games	Online games and multiplayer games can be addicting and can bring visitors back to your site time and again

All forms of link bait have one thing in common: they promote your name, site, and brand. Great link bait fosters accelerated link building and site recognition. When done right, link bait can become extremely viral.

Website widgets in detail

Website widgets are simple, self-contained, value-added units of functionality. They are typically confined to small blocks of screen real estate on one or all the pages of your site. Any information that you can package in a way that provides unique value to other sites can be made into a widget.

Popular website widgets. You can see many examples of website widgets at *http://www .widgetbox.com/*, *http://springwidgets.com/*, and *http://glittertools.com/*. Figure 12-2 shows an example widget that you can place on your website to see the latest article headlines from Digg.com.

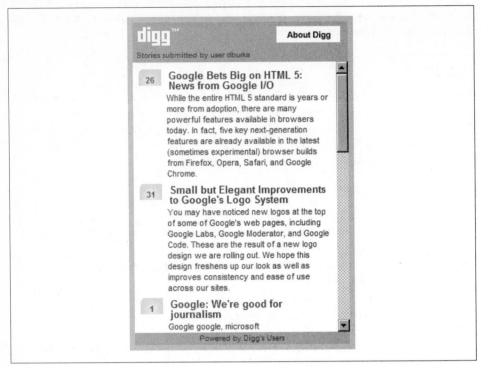

Figure 12-2. Digg.com website widget

Creating custom website widgets. Everything starts with an idea. Creating custom widgets can be as simple or as complex as required. You can create some website widgets by simply creating custom HTML pages. Others you can create by utilizing Atom/RSS feeds, Java applets, and Flash. In this section, we will create a sample HTML-based widget to illustrate the concepts of link baiting and website widgets.

Let's suppose you own a site that sells many different brands of alarm clocks. To promote your site, you want to create your own link bait. Specifically, you want to create a simple digital alarm clock widget (called Wake Up Service) that any site can link to or use. When the widget is used on other sites, you specify the condition that your link must be present to use the widget.

On your site, you also want to ensure that your link bait is highly visible (typically placed at a strategic location for easy recognition). Figure 12-3 shows an example web page layout. You can decide to use a pop-up window widget or one that renders in the same browser window.

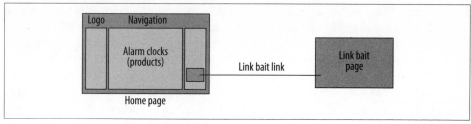

Figure 12-3. Link bait widget web page position

Figure 12-4 shows our Wake Up Service widget as rendered in a web browser. You can find the HTML code at *http://scripts.seowarrior.net/quickpanel/wakeup.html*. For more of my widget examples, please visit *http://scripts.seowarrior.net/quickpanel/*.

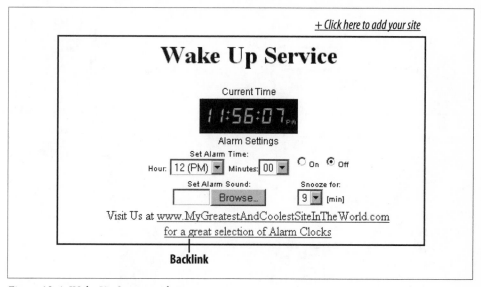

Figure 12-4. Wake Up Service widget

Widget promotion and distribution.   You can proliferate your widgets in many ways. You can do it from your site, you can use a third-party site, or you can employ both methods. Make it easy for your visitors by offering simple cut-and-paste HTML code such as the following:

```
<a href="http://scripts.seowarrior.net/quickpanel/wakeup.html"
target="_new">Wake Up Service</a>
```

This sample code shows the link to our Wake Up Service widget, which will open in a new window. For website widgets such as the one we created in this example, you could also write a small article that will be syndicated along with all of your other articles. People subscribing to your feeds will be able to read about it and propagate the information if they find it interesting.

Let's examine how to use a third-party tool when promoting your widgets. If you're using Widgetbox.com, the process is straightforward. You open an account, import your widget in an appropriate format, submit your widget for approval, and after a day or so your widget becomes public in the Widgetbox.com library. To view usage (installation) stats, come back a few days later. You have the option of hosting all of your widget-related files on your site. A paid account removes widget ads and allows you to create widgets for many of the popular social media sites, including Twitter, YouTube, Flickr, Vimeo, and Hulu. You can also promote your widgets just like you promote your site, using many of the same techniques we discuss in this chapter.

Social Bookmarking

Figure 12-5 shows the basic model of a typical social bookmarking site.

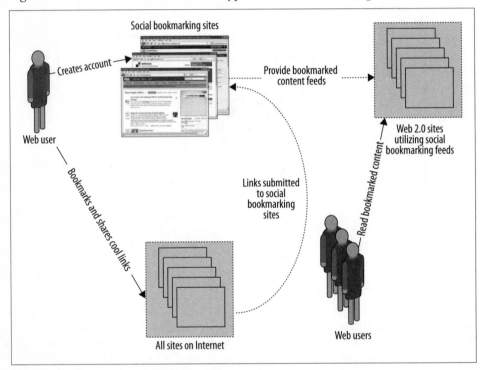

Figure 12-5. How social bookmarking works

Social bookmarking is the concept of adding (typically) article and media bookmarks across various social bookmarking sites. It is a way to store and access bookmarks from anywhere. Everyone benefits in this model. Publishers get a wider audience and web users enjoy fresh, popular content.

Many websites utilize social bookmarking feeds as their additional content. To use social bookmarks, web users need to register with a social bookmarking provider. After users register with a particular provider, they are typically offered the option to install the provider's web browser toolbar. This makes it easier to add bookmarks.

Users surf the Internet while storing and tagging their bookmarks. Provider sites aggregate this social data while showing the most popular links (article leads) on their front page portal. In addition to running portals, social bookmarking sites also provide APIs, tools, and an infinite number of feed types to satisfy any appetite. Millions of other sites leverage these tools when republishing the same content.

The apparent advantage of social bookmarking systems over search engine technology is in the fact that all data is organized by human beings. Social bookmarks employ the concept of collaborative (social) tagging as well as a democratic voting mechanism. Each participant of a social bookmarking system typically tags each bookmark with her custom keywords while also giving her vote to the bookmark. Social bookmarking platforms tabulate these votes when showing the most popular bookmarks.

In terms of SEO, your goal is to utilize social bookmarking to make it easy for everyone to promote your website content. Many social bookmarking providers are available. Some of the popular ones include:

- BlinkList (*http://www.blinklist.com/*)
- Delicious (*http://delicious.com/*)
- Digg (*http://digg.com/*)
- Diigo (*http://www.diigo.com/*)
- Faves (*http://faves.com/*)
- Kaboodle (*http://www.kaboodle.com/*)
- Mixx (*http://www.mixx.com/*)
- Newsvine (*http://www.newsvine.com/*)
- Propeller (*http://www.propeller.com/*)
- Reddit (*http://www.reddit.com/*)
- Simpy (*http://simpy.com/*)
- StumbleUpon (*http://www.stumbleupon.com/*)
- Twine (*http://www.twine.com/*)

Also note that search engines crawl and index pages showing bookmarked content. This includes social bookmarking portals in addition to thousands of sites using customized feeds from these social bookmarking providers. Your links have the potential to be republished on thousands of websites.

Integrating social bookmarks on your site

Each provider will be a bit different when it comes to integrating social bookmarks on your site. But the idea is basically the same. You show an icon next to your content that will allow your visitors to add your link to their preferred social bookmarking site. The most popular links earn the most visibility and value. The following fragment shows example code required to show social bookmarking icons for Digg, StumbleUpon, and Reddit:

```
<!--Digg.com -->
<script src="http://digg.com/tools/diggthis.js"
type="text/javascript"></script>
<script type="text/javascript">
digg_url = 'http://www.YourCoolDomain.com/YourCoolPageLink';
</script>

<!--StumbleUpon.com-->
<a href="http://www.stumbleupon.com/submit?
url=http%3A%2F%2Fwww.yoursite.com%2Farticle.php
%26title%3DThe%2BArticle%2BTitle">
<img border=0
src="http://cdn.stumble-upon.com/images/120x20_su_gray.gif"
alt=""></a>

<!--ReddIt.com-->
<script type="text/javascript"
src="http://www.reddit.com/buttonlite.js?i=2">
</script>
```

Many icon variations are available for you to use. The sample code renders the three icons in a web browser, as shown in Figure 12-6.

Figure 12-6. Sample social bookmarking icons

Tracking your bookmarks

Each social bookmarking platform will have its own interface to track your URLs. For example, if you wanted to track your bookmarked URL on Delicious.com, you could use its URL tracking service at *http://delicious.com/url/*. Figure 12-7 illustrates how to do this. Simply enter your URL in the provided form, submit the form, and observe the results.

The resulting screen (as shown in Figure 12-7) contains four main parts. The header part shows the bookmark count. Moving down the screen you can see details about each bookmark (as saved by each user). At the bottom of the screen, you can also subscribe to this URL's RSS feed. Finally, at the right side of the screen you can see the associated bookmark tags sorted in order of popularity.

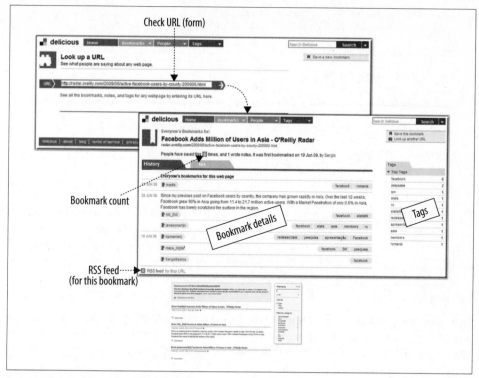

Figure 12-7. Delicious.com URL tracking

Stay away from too many bookmarking icons

Some sites go to extremes. How many of us have seen sites appending too many social bookmarking icons to every single piece of their content on every page, as shown in Figure 12-8? There is no need for this clutter.

Figure 12-8. The "Share and Enjoy" clutter

There is an elegant solution to this problem. You can use a single icon with the ability to post to any social bookmarking site you want. This is what the ShareThis (*http://sharethis.com/*) and AddThis (*http://addthis.com/*) services do.

Both of these providers use website-neutral code. You can add their code to any web page on any site. Here is the code fragment required to create the two icons:

```
<!-- ShareThis Button BEGIN -->
<script type="text/javascript"
```

```
src="http://w.sharethis.com/button/sharethis.js#
publisher=5c02a2bf-4c91-4215-805b-5155b4c52056&amp;type=website">
</script>
<!-- ShareThis Button END -->


<!-- AddThis Button BEGIN -->
<a href="http://www.addthis.com/bookmark.php?v=250" onmouseover="return
addthis_open(this, '', '[URL]', '[TITLE]')" onmouseout="addthis_close()"
onclick="return addthis_sendto()">
<img src="http://s7.addthis.com/static/btn/lg-share-en.gif" width="125"
height="16" alt="Bookmark and Share" style="border:0"/></a>
<script type="text/javascript"
src="http://s7.addthis.com/js/250/addthis_widget.js?pub=xa-
4a256e6f0aeb1299"></script>
<!-- AddThis Button END -->
```

Figure 12-9 shows how these two icons work. Initially, each provider shows only a single icon. When you click on or hover your mouse cursor over the icons, they expand to show you more options. These options include most of the other popular social bookmarking icons. In addition, both providers let you email the current link to your colleagues and friends. The ShareThis icon also allows you to send AIM and SMS messages.

In most cases, you may want to stick to the most popular social bookmarking platforms such as Digg, Delicious, and StumbleUpon. Showing only these three pertinent icons can do the trick for all of your social bookmarking needs.

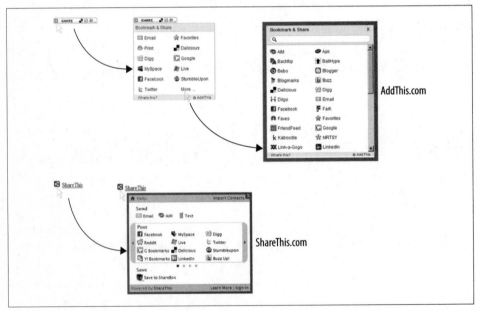

Figure 12-9. Cleaning up social bookmarking clutter

Website Syndication

Website syndication is the de facto standard for content publication. Content publishers publish content in various formats. Syndicated content provides a medium to reach a greater subscriber audience. Subscribers use tools such as Atom and RSS feed readers to stay abreast of newly published content. When users subscribe to your feeds, you have a unique opportunity to keep them interested in your site.

Content syndication provides other benefits as well. You can think of your website feeds as your own broadcast Internet stations. Many sites will republish your content in some fashion. Often, you will want to allow others to publish article leads or teasers. Those who want to read the entire article can visit your site. When they come to your site, they will also see other elements of your site that will hopefully produce additional clicks.

Understanding syndication formats

Two of the most popular syndications types are Really Simple Syndication (RSS) and Atom. The initial goals of the Atom format were to improve on RSS ambiguities in terms of content payload. For example, in RSS feeds you can use plain text or HTML (with no explicit standard to indicate the content format within the feed file). Although RSS feeds are still popular, Atom is gaining traction, as propelled by industry giants Google and Microsoft.

Feed readers

Web users employ a variety of feed readers to read your syndicated content. With the explosion of social media sites, feed readers are now equipped to propagate syndicated content further. Figure 12-10 shows the Google Reader interface. The interface contains many sharing options that all help to propagate interesting articles.

Google Reader also provides the option to share any of the articles you have chosen to share on your website or blog. Simply choose the "Add a clip" option after clicking on the "Shared items" link on the left side of the page. For example, here is the HTML fragment that I can use to share the articles of my choice on any website:

```
<script type="text/javascript"
src="http://www.google.com/reader/ui/publisher-en.js">
</script>
<script type="text/javascript"
src="http://www.google.com/reader/public/javascript/user/
08812256800216401263/state/com.google/broadcast?n=5&
callback=GRC_p(%7Bc%3A%22green%22%2Ct%3A%22John%5C's%20shared%20items
%22%2Cs%3A%22false%22%2Cb%3A%22false%22%7D)%3Bnew%20GRC">
</script>
```

Figure 12-11 shows how this might look when included on a web page.

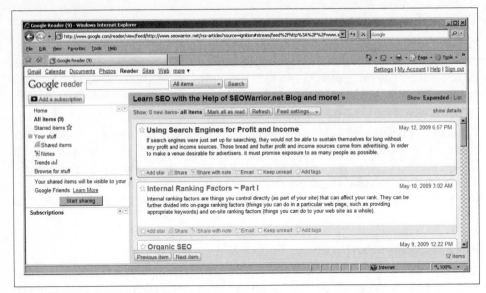

Figure 12-10. Google Reader

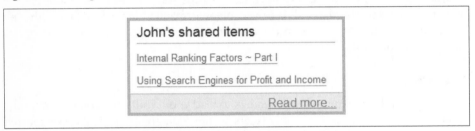

Figure 12-11. Google Reader: Shared Items widget

This should speak volumes about the importance of utilizing website syndication. Sites can disseminate content in many ways, including via social media sites (either natively or via custom add-on options).

Understanding FeedBurner

You can think of FeedBurner as a transparent tracking and management tool for your website feeds. What Google Analytics can do for your web page stats, FeedBurner can do for your website feeds. Figure 12-12 shows Feed Subscribers, one of the most important FeedBurner metrics.

Figure 12-12 shows two colored lines. The green line (the thicker of the two) represents user subscriptions over time, and the blue line illustrates the number of people who have either viewed or clicked on a particular item within your feed. These are not the only metrics FeedBurner provides.

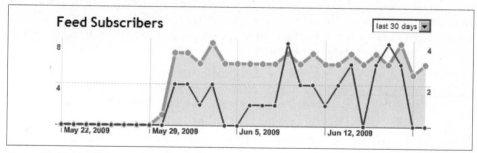

Figure 12-12. FeedBurner subscriber graph

FeedBurner features. The FeedBurner service provides many features. These include services to analyze, optimize, publicize, monetize, and troubleshoot your feeds. Figure 12-13 shows the tabbed options for these features.

Figure 12-13. FeedBurner services

In the Analyze section, you can view your subscriber base in more detail, including seeing specific clicks, a geographical map overlay, and so forth. You also have the option to export the subscriber data as an Excel or CSV file. Here is how an exported file might look:

Date	Subscribers	Reach	Item Views	Item Clickthroughs	Hits
05-30-2009	100	35	88	10	113
05-31-2009	98	32	90	14	268
06-01-2009	97	42	90	13	272
06-02-2009	94	21	78	10	161
06-03-2009	98	42	60	11	263
06-04-2009	92	70	80	10	261
06-05-2009	112	20	55	10	157
06-06-2009	130	80	150	12	358
06-07-2009	147	99	163	14	457
06-08-2009	222	140	320	12	358

In the Optimize section, you can utilize the SmartCast, SmartFeed, and FeedFlare options. The SmartCast option allows you to create a richer, more detailed listing in the iTunes Podcast Directory and in sites using Yahoo! Media RSS. The SmartCast feature allows podcast service providers to optimize their feeds for the iTunes platform. You can specify your podcast category, subcategory, image location, subtitle, summary, search keywords (for Yahoo! MRSS), and author email address. You can also mark your content as explicit in addition to adding a specific copyright message. The SmartFeed feature is disabled by default. Once enabled, it makes your feed compatible with any feed reader. This feature should be enabled for maximum feed propagation. The Feed-Flare feature allows you to spice up your feed with popular social networking features. To quote FeedBurner (*http://bit.ly/BARa3*):

> Give your subscribers easy ways to email, tag, share, and act on the content you publish by including as many or few of the services listed below. FeedFlare places a simple footer at the bottom of each content item, helping you to distribute, inform and create a community around your content.

In the Publicize section, you can use several services:

- Headline Animator, to display rotating headlines
- BuzzBoost, to republish your feed as HTML
- Email Subscriptions, to send email updates
- PingShot, to provide notification on new posts
- FeedCount, to show your feed circulation
- Chicklet Chooser, to generate HTML fragments for popular news aggregators
- Awareness API, to build applications that can display, analyze, and promote your feed's traffic data outside of FeedBurner
- Creative Commons, to attach the appropriate Creative Commons license in your feed's XML
- Password Protector, to implement Basic HTTP authentication for your feed
- NoIndex, to tell search engines not to index your feed

You use the Monetize section of FeedBurner when you want to integrate Google Ad-Sense for your feeds. To implement AdSense for feeds, you must sign in to Google AdSense and click on the "AdSense for feeds" link.

As its name implies, you use the Troubleshootize section to troubleshoot feed problems. FeedBurner calls this service FeedMedic. FeedMedic reports any problems Feed-Burner finds with your feeds.

Integrating FeedBurner with your site. Integrating FeedBurner with your site is relatively simple. You can think of FeedBurner as your website's feed wrapper service to make your feed more compatible, more visible, and more easily tracked. Figure 12-14 illustrates how FeedBurner works.

To redirect your existing feed(s), you can use the *.htaccess* redirect mechanism. The following fragment shows an example of a permanent redirect and a temporary redirect:

```
RewriteEngine On

Redirect 301 /news.rss http://feeds2.feedburner.com/NewsFeed
Redirect 302 /news2.rss http://feeds2.feedburner.com/NewsFeedTemp
```

In addition to FeedBurner, other companies provide website tracking and management services, including PostRank (*http://www.postrank.com/*), FeedBlitz (*http://feedblitz .com/*), Feedity (*http://feedity.com/*), and RapidFeeds (*http://rapidfeeds.com/*).

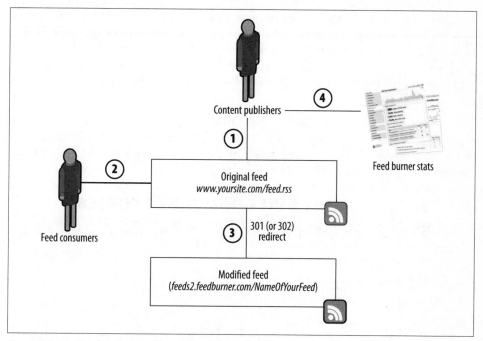

Figure 12-14. Configuring FeedBurner with existing feeds

Future of FeedBurner. FeedBurner is still one of the most popular services for content publishers who want to measure their content syndication subscriber base. After Google acquired FeedBurner, many publishers reported bugs, including a significant drop in their subscribed user base. Google claims to have fixed these bugs in addition to providing more accurate reporting analytics. FeedBurner continues to be a tool of choice for many content publishers. If you wish to use FeedBurner for statistical or marketing purposes, you can redirect your existing feeds to FeedBurner.

As you already saw, FeedBurner is starting to look like the Google Analytics platform. This should only help make FeedBurner easier to use and in line with all of Google's offerings.

Directories

Before you start submitting your sites to directories, you need to ensure that the site titles and descriptions you plan to submit are highly optimized. You should have several variations of these ready before you submit.

Also ensure that your targeted directories will pass link juice. You can double-check by examining several directory listings and searching for the `nofollow` link attribute. If a directory is using `nofollow`, your efforts will be wasted. Only use directories that pass link juice.

Another thing to consider is the directory category. Do you really want to submit your site link to a category page with hundreds or even thousands of links? Look for less crowded categories for optimal link juice transfer. Before you choose your target directories, see what their PageRanks are for their home pages. List your directories in the order of their PageRank values. Ensure that each directory you are planning passes link juice.

Spend your time first on directories with the highest PageRank. Also observe the PageRank value of your targeted category page. You don't want to get a link that is 10 levels deep. Figure 12-15 illustrates how you may want to track this data in an Excel spreadsheet. This is another tab of the same spreadsheet file we discussed earlier.

LINK BUILDING: DIRECTORIES

Directory [URL/Name]	Type [P,F]	Category [Name]	PR [0..10]	Page [URL]	Title [1..N]	Description [1..N]	Submission [date]	Inclusion [date]	Notes
GENERAL DIRECTORIES									
dmoz.org	F		8						
dir.yahoo.com	P		8						
business.com	P		7						
yellowpages.com	FP		7						
botw.org	P		6						
gimpsy.com	P		5						
joeant.com	P		5						
turnpike.net/directory.html	F		5						
directory.v7n.com	P		4						
webworldindex.com	P		3						
NICHE DIRECTORIES									
travelnotes.org	FP		6						
traveltourismdirectory.info	FP		5						

Figure 12-15. Link-building spreadsheet: Directories

The spreadsheet contains several columns, namely "Directory" (the URL address), "Type" (free or paid), "Category" (the name of the category you want to target), "PR" (the Google PageRank value), "Page" (the URL of the page you submitted), "Title" (the title description submitted), "Description" (the description submitted), "Submission" (the date of submission to a particular directory), and "Inclusion" (the date your link was included in the directory).

Start with the top general directories

The Web contains many general directories. Search engines like directories that are not automated (i.e., ones that use human reviewers before sites are included in their listings). Google runs its own directory at *http://directory.google.com/*, which is a copy of Dmoz.org. To get to Google's directory, you have to go through the Dmoz.org submission process. For starters, submit your site to all of the first-tier directories, including Dmoz.org, Yahoo! Directory, Business.com, and YellowPages.com.

Move on to the second-tier directories. They also come in free and paid flavors. Hundreds of second-tier directories charge fees ranging from a few bucks to several hundred dollars. Fees can be one-time or yearly. Some directories let you add your links in exchange for your reciprocal link. Be careful about reciprocal linking.

There are no hard rules as far as how many directories you should submit your site to. You can find general directories in many ways. For instance, you can perform a search query, as shown in the following fragment:

```
directory "submit a link"
general directories
directory of directories
"general directory"
site:dmoz.org inurl:directories
small business "add url"|"add link"
+general +directory add url|link free|paid
```

Continue with niche directories

Go after specific vertical (topic-centric) directories. Finding niche directories is easy. You just need to tweak your search queries. Here are some examples for various niche markets:

```
travel site:dmoz.org inurl:directories
"insurance broker directory"
wine producers directory
electronics manufacturer directory
jewelry stores directory
```

If you are struggling to find directories in your niche, simply use the ones you already have and try doing the following:

```
related:www.travel-directory.org
```

Google's `related:` command lets you find similar sites to the one you supply in the command's argument. In our example, we are looking for related travel directories. You can also use the online service found at *http://www.similicio.us/*. Simply enter your desired URL to get a listing of similar sites.

Consider regional directories

If your target audience is in a specific geographic area, you should go after regional (local) directories. The rules for finding regional directories are similar, except that this time your search query is expanded to your target areas. Here are a few examples:

```
toronto "travel agencies" +directory
ontario "travel agencies" directory
canada "travel agencies" directory
boston "pizza restaurants" directory
new york "shoe stores" directory
los angeles inurl:directory
```

You can visit *http://www.isedb.com/html/Web_Directories/* to find more regional directory listings. You can find another directory repository at *http://www.web-directories .ws/Regional/*.

You should consider submitting your site to Google's Local Business Center (*http:// www.google.com/local/add*), Microsoft's Local Listing Center (*https://ssl.bing.com/list ings/*), and Yahoo!'s Local Listing (*http://listings.local.yahoo.com/*).

Adding Your Links Everywhere

You can do many things outside your site to foster healthy link building. You can write articles, submit blog comments, and post to newsgroup and forum messages. What you want to do is leave your URL within any content you create.

Submitting articles

Many sites let you submit your articles, including ArticlesBase (*http://www.articlesbase .com/*), EzineArticles (*http://ezinearticles.com/*), ArticleGeek (*http://www.articlegeek .com/about_us.htm*), and many others. When you choose your article submission vendor, ensure that your articles are always properly credited.

When your articles are (re)published, you want to make sure they contain appropriate attribution by containing one or all of the following: your name, a link to your biography page, and a URL of your choice. To find more article submission services, simply search for *article submission service*. You may also want to find article submission services for your niche. Simply add your pertinent keywords to the same query to find relevant providers.

Utilizing blog comments, newsgroups, and forum postings

The idea is much the same when posting comments to blogs, newsgroups, and forums as it is when submitting articles. Simply include your signature with your URL every time you post. Note that some sites do not allow URLs. Others employ the `nofollow` attribute to discourage you from placing links in your posts.

The basic rule of thumb is to be relevant to the topic you are posting about. Try to include keywords relevant to your site. Otherwise, your post could look like spam and you might get banned. Here are some search command tips you can use to find relevant discussion sites:

```
"video games" forum
wine producers inurl:forum
"sports apparel" inurl:forum
"fishing gear" forum
```

Build a Complementary Site

This is not a call to create duplicated content. You want to create a complementary content-rich site that targets many other keywords not specifically targeted on your main site. You can utilize a free host or an inexpensive shared host when using this technique. Go easy with cross-linking. Too much or too little is not good. Use a more balanced, natural approach. Host these sites on different IPs as well as different IP range blocks if you can.

Niche directory hubs

You can build your own directories with links to your main site. These directories should be in your niche, and you can list your partner sites, useful tools, and resources. Allow others to submit their links as well. In a sense, you will be creating your own website links hub in addition to your primary (authoritative) site.

Awards websites

Another idea for a complementary site is an awards site. This gives you the opportunity to attract others to link to your site while being able to (shamelessly) promote your own sites of interest.

Site review websites

Thousands of site review websites are on the Web. The number of those that are truly unbiased is, at best, questionable. If others have done this, though, so can you.

Site software

Many scripts are available for you to use to build your directories, awards websites, or site review websites. These scripts are available from HotScripts.com, Tucows.com, ScriptSearch.com, Scripts.com, and Fatscripts.com. You can also use one of the many popular CMS packages that are available. Most CMSs provide modules or add-ons to implement just about any kind of site.

Summary

In this chapter, you learned how to make your site intuitive enough for anyone to link to it. We discussed how to use link bait, social bookmarks, and content syndication, as well as submitting your site to appropriate web directories. We covered the reason you should add a signature to any content you produce outside your site, and we finished the chapter with tips on how to create sites that are complementary to your primary site, and the benefits that social media websites can offer.

It is important to reiterate that the best way to bring in desired links is to create something outstanding. Unique, compelling content is the best way to achieve your link-building strategy. Be creative as you produce content for your target demographic. Be different.

## CHAPTER 13

Competitor Research and Analysis

Competitor research and analysis may seem like a copycat activity, but it is not (at least not entirely). It is about understanding what your competitors are doing. It is about examining their keyword and linking strategies while realizing their current strengths and weaknesses. The bottom line is that you are trying to understand what is making your competitors rank.

This activity may comprise elements of emulation, but what you are really trying to do is be better than your competition. Being better (in a general sense) means providing a site with more value and better perception. In an SEO sense, it means understanding all the things that make your competitors rank.

When learning about your competition, it is good to examine their past and present activities, as well as implement ways to track their future activities. Although many tools are available for you to use to learn about your competition, for most of your work you can get by with the free tools that are available. This chapter emphasizes the free tools and research that you can use in your work.

Finding Your Competition

Before you can analyze your competitors, you need to know who your competitors are. How do you find your biggest competitors? One way to do this is to find sites that rank for your targeted keywords. The sites that sell or provide products and services similar to yours are your competitors.

There is a catch if you're relying only on keywords, though. How do you know whether you are targeting the right keywords? What if you miss important keywords? You may be starting off in the wrong direction. This makes it all the more important to do your keyword research properly. No tool or activity will ever be perfect. You have to start somewhere.

When starting your competitor research, you will almost always want to start with your local competition. Visit the local online business directories in your niche to find potential competition. Research the Yellow Pages (Local Directory) or your area equivalent. Use your local version of Google to find businesses in your area by using your targeted keywords. Also visit the Google Local Business Center to find current advertisers. Visit the Yahoo! Directory, Dmoz.org, and BBB.org to find more competitors in your niche. Note their directory descriptions and analyze the keywords they use in these descriptions. Create a list of your top 10 to 20 local competitors.

If you have global competitors, see whether you can learn anything from their online presence. Just focusing on your local competition can be a mistake, especially if you will be providing products and services globally.

Even if your business or clients are all local, you can still pick up tips from your global equivalents. Chances are someone is doing something similar somewhere else in the world. Create a list of 10 to 20 global competitors.

You can find your competitors using a variety of online tools as well. Later in this chapter, we will explore several tools and methods that can help you identify your competitors.

Keyword-Based Competitor Research

When researching your competitors, you will likely be doing many things at once. Figure 13-1 depicts the basic manual process of competitor research. You also have the option of using some of the online tools that are available to help you along the way—not only to find your competitors, but also to save you time.

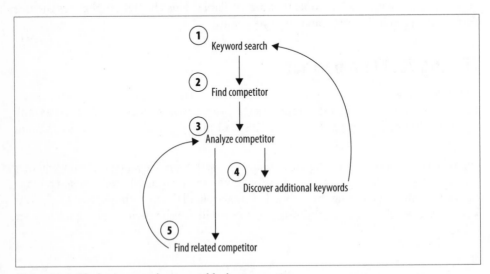

Figure 13-1. The basic manual process of finding competitors

The manual approach

With the manual approach, you run all the keywords on your keyword list through at least two of the major search engines (Google, Yahoo!, or Bing). Of course, not all of the search results will be those of your direct competitors. You will need to browse and research these sites to make that determination.

You might need to browse through several SERPs to get to your competition. If you do, this may mean the keywords you are targeting may not be good. If you find no competitor sites, you may have hit the right niche.

While going through your keyword list, analyze each competitor while finding any new keywords you may have missed. For each competitor URL, run Google's `related:` command to find any additional competitors you may have missed. Repeat this process until you have run out of keywords.

Analyze your competitors' sites using the information we already discussed regarding internal and external ranking factors. When analyzing each competitor site, pay attention to each search result and to the use of keywords within each result. Expand your research by browsing and analyzing your competitor's site.

You can determine the kind of competitor you have just by doing some basic inspections. For starters, you may want to know whether they are using SEO. Inspect their HTML header tags for keywords and description meta tags, as these can be indications of a site using SEO.

Although the use of meta keyword tags is subsiding, many sites still use them, as they may have done their SEO a long time ago when meta keyword tags mattered. The meta description tag is important, though, as it appears on search engine search results. The same can be said of the HTML `<title>` tag. Examine those carefully.

Continue by inspecting the existence or the lack of a *robots.txt* file. If the file exists, this could indicate that your competitor cares about web spiders. If your competitor is using a *robots.txt* file, see whether it contains Sitemap file definition.

Sites syndicating their content will typically expose their RSS link(s) on many pages within their site. You may also subscribe to those feeds to learn of any new developments so that you can keep an eye on your competition. If a site contains a Sitemap (HTML, XML, etc.), scan through it, as it typically will contain a list of your competitor's important URLs as well as important keywords.

For each competitor URL you find, you should do more research to determine the URL's Google PageRank and Alexa rank, the age of the site and the page, the page copy keywords, the meta description, the size of the Google index, and the keyword search volume.

As you can see, doing all of this manually will take time. There ought to be a better (easier) way! And there is.

Utilizing SEO tools and automation

Automation cannot replace everything. You still need to visit each competitor's site to do proper research and analysis. But automation does help in the collection of data such as Google PageRank, Google index size, and so forth. This is where tools such as SeoQuake (*http://seoquake.com/*) can be quite beneficial.

You can install SeoQuake in either Firefox or Internet Explorer. It is completely free and very easy to install. It comes preconfigured with basic features, as shown in Figure 13-2.

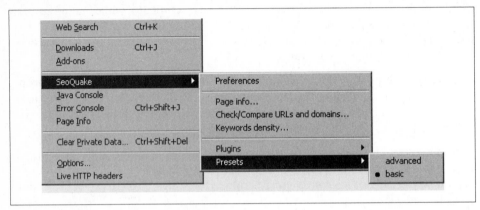

Figure 13-2. SeoQuake Firefox menu options

The best way to learn about SeoQuake is to see it in action. For this small exercise, we'll search for *winter clothes* in Google using the basic method as well as with the help of SeoQuake. Figure 13-3 shows how the Google SERP looks with and without SeoQuake.

SeoQuake augments each search result with its own information (at the bottom of each search result). This includes the Google PageRank value, the Google index size, the cached URL date, the Alexa rank, and many others.

When running SeoQuake, you will see the SERP mashup with many value-added bits of information, which SeoQuake inserts on the fly. You can easily change the SeoQuake preferences by going to the Preferences section, as shown in Figure 13-4.

The beauty of the SeoQuake plug-in is in its data export feature. You can export all of the results in a CSV file that you can then view and reformat in Excel.

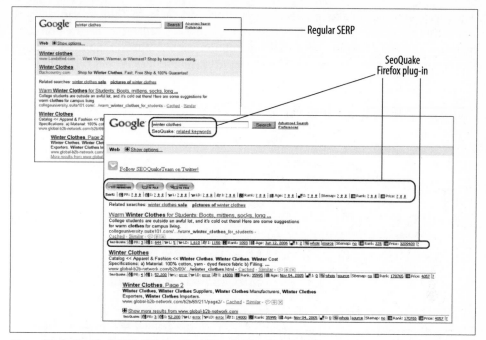

Figure 13-3. Google SERPs: With and without SeoQuake

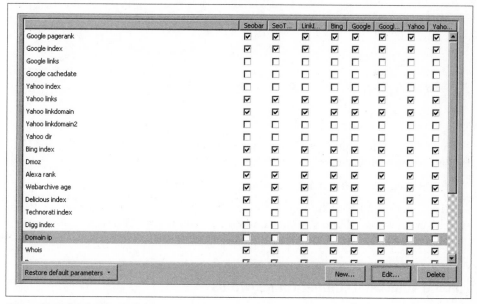

Figure 13-4. SeoQuake preferences

The creators of SeoQuake are also the creators of SEMRush (*http://semrush.com*). SEMRush provides competitor intelligence data that is available either free or commercially. You can find lots of useful information via SEMRush. Figure 13-5 shows sample output when browsing *http://www.semrush.com/info/ebay.com*.

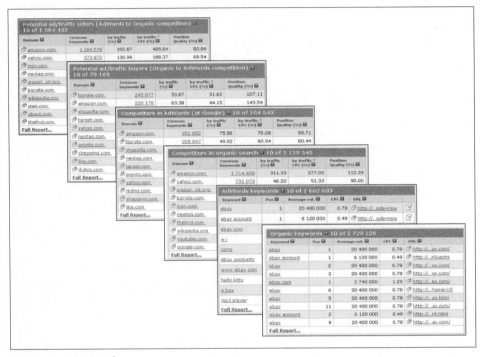

Figure 13-5. SEMRush

You can do the same thing with your competitor URLs. Simply use the following URL format in your web browser:

> *http://www.semrush.com/info/CompetitorURL.com*

SEMRush provides two ways to search for competitor data. You can enter a URL or search via keywords. If you search via keywords, you will see a screen similar to Figure 13-6.

Finding Additional Competitor Keywords

Once you have your competitor list, you can do further keyword research. Many tools are available for this task.

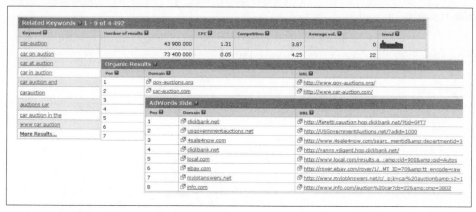

Figure 13-6. SEMRush: Keyword search mode

Using the Google AdWords Keyword Tool Website Content feature

Google offers a Website Content feature in its free AdWords Keyword Tool. Using this feature, you can enter a specific URL to get competitive keyword ideas based on the URL. So far, I have found this feature to be of limited use.

Using Alexa keywords

You can also use Alexa to find some additional keyword ideas. More specifically, Alexa can give you keywords driving traffic to a particular site. Figure 13-7 shows a portion of the results of a keyword search for *oreilly.com*. The actual Alexa screen shows the top 30 keyword queries (as of this writing).

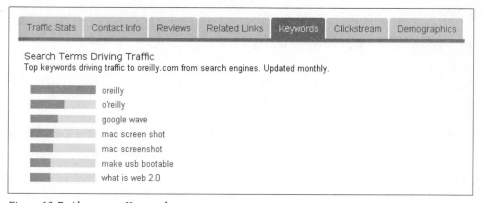

Figure 13-7. Alexa.com: Keywords

Using Compete keywords

You can use Compete (*http://compete.com*) to get similar data. The professional version gets you all of the data in the report. Figure 13-8 shows similar keyword data when searching for *oreilly.com*.

Report Overview

Domain / Category	oreilly.com
Time frame	2009-04-24 to 2009-07-23
Available results	1,227 terms
Displaying	1 - 5	Access: all 1,227 terms

Volume Rank ⑦	Keyword ⑦	% of Site's Search Traffic ⑦	Average Time Index ⑦	Total Time Index ⑦
1	oscon	1.56%	100.00	100.00
2	oreilly	1.42%	69.30	63.23
3	o'reilly	1.05%	38.72	26.13
4	where 2.0	0.90%	72.59	41.98
5	oreilly webcasts	0.88%	4.37	2.47

Figure 13-8. Compete keywords

The free version of Compete gives you the top five keywords based on search volume. Although you can get by with free tools for obtaining competitor keyword data, if you do SEO on a daily basis you will need to get professional (paid) access to Compete.com. You may also want to consider using Hitwise (*http://hitwise.com/*).

Additional competitive keyword discovery tools

In addition to free tools, a variety of commercial tools are available for conducting competitor keyword research. Table 13-1 lists some of the popular ones.

Table 13-1. Commercially available competitor keyword research tools

Name	Description
KeywordSpy (*http://www.keywordspy.com*)	Provides keyword research, affiliate research, and real-time data tracking for Google, Yahoo!, and Bing
SpyFu (*http://www.spyfu.com*)	Allows you to download your competitors' keywords, AdWords, and much more
KeyCompete (*http://www.keycompete.com*)	Allows you to download your competitors' keywords, AdWords, and more
HitTail (*http://www.hittail.com*)	A writing suggestion tool to boost your position in search results

Many other tools are available that focus on keyword research. Refer to Chapter 11 for more information.

Competitor Backlink Research

Backlinks are a major key ranking factor. Finding your competitors' backlinks is one of the most important aspects of competitor analysis. The following subsections go into more details.

Basic ways to find competitor backlinks

The most popular command for finding backlinks is the `link:` command, which you can use in both Google and Yahoo! Site Explorer.

In addition, you can use many other commands to find references to your competitor links. The following commands may be helpful:

```
"www.competitorURL.com"
inurl:www.competitorURL.com
inanchor:www.competitorURL.com
intitle:www.competitorURL.com
allintitle:www.competitorURL.com
allintitle:www.competitorURL.com site:.org
site:.edu inanchor:www.competitorURL.com
site:.gov inanchor:www.competitorURL.com
```

You can also use variations of these commands. Although some of these commands may not yield backlinks per se, you will at least be able to see where these competitors are mentioned. The more you know about your competition, the better. To expedite the process of finding your competitors' backlinks, you can use free and commercially available backlink checker tools.

Free backlink checkers

Some of the free backlink checker tools available today are just mashups of Yahoo! Site Explorer data. With the latest agreement between Yahoo! and Microsoft, it will be interesting to see what happens to Yahoo! Site Explorer, as Bing will become the search provider for Yahoo!'s users.

Table 13-2 provides a summary of some of the most popular backlink checker tools currently available on the Internet. When choosing a tool, you may want to make sure it shows information such as associated Google PageRank, use of `nofollow`, and link anchor text.

Table 13-2. Free backlink checkers

Tool	Description
Yahoo! Site Explorer (*http://siteexplorer.search.yahoo.com/*)	Provides a robust interface with the ability to export the first 1,000 backlinks to a spreadsheet
Alexa (*http://www.alexa.com/site/linksin/URL*)	Provides a backlink interface with up to 100 backlinks displayed (hint: change the "URL" to the actual competitor URL)
Link Diagnosis (*http://www.linkdiagnosis.com/*)	Provides an online backlink report; allows CSV export
Backlink Watch (*http://www.backlinkwatch.com/*)	Provides an online backlink report with several additional features including outbound link counts
Backlink Checker (*http://www.iwebtool.com/*)	Provides basic backlink checker functionality with associated Google PageRank values

Commercially available backlink checkers

Free tools may be sufficient for what you are looking for. However, the best of the commercially available tools give you the bigger picture. You get to see more data. You also save a lot of time. However, no tool will be perfect, especially for low-volume keywords. Table 13-3 lists some of the popular commercially available backlink checkers.

Table 13-3. Commercially available backlink checkers

Tool	Description
Compete (*http://compete.com/*)	Provides the Referral Analytics platform with a breakdown of sites bringing traffic to you or your competitors
Hitwise (*http://hitwise.com/*)	Provides the Hitwise Clickstream platform with a breakdown of sites bringing traffic to you or your competitors
SEO SpyGlass (*http://www.link-assistant.com/*)	Provides many valuable features including detailed backlink analysis

Analyzing Your Competition

You can use many tools to analyze your research data. Many of these tools provide similar information. It is best to use several tools to gauge your competitors. Even Google's AdWords Keyword Tool is not perfect.

It will take some time for you to find what works and what doesn't (especially with the free tools). Whatever the case may be, make sure you use several tools before drawing your conclusions. Try out the free tools and see whether you find them to be sufficient.

Historical Analysis

After you know who some of your competitors are, you will be ready to roll up your sleeves and conduct a more in-depth competitor analysis. We'll start by examining how your competitors got to where there are, by doing some historical research.

The Internet Archive site (*http://www.archive.org/index.php*) provides an easy way to see historical website snapshots. You can see how each site evolved over time, in addition to being able to spot ownership changes. Figure 13-9 shows an example.

Web archives do not store entire sites. Nonetheless, they can help you spot significant changes over time (at least when it comes to a website's home page).

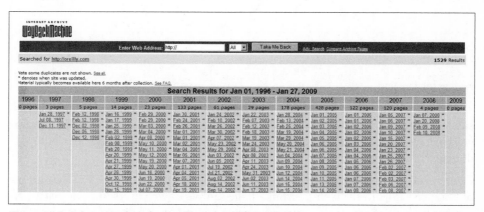

Figure 13-9. Internet archive for "oreilly.com" (1997–2009)

To find historical Whois information, you can use the free Who.Is service at *http://www.who.is/*. Alternatively, you can use the paid service offered by Domain Tools (*http://whois.domaintools.com/*).

Web Presence and Website Traffic Analysis

To scope your competitors' web presence, you need to determine how many websites and subdomains they are running. Additional tools are available for estimating this traffic.

Number of sites

Using the domain lookup tool available from LinkVendor (*http://www.linkvendor.com/*), you can enter a domain name or IP address to get all domains running on that IP address. Figure 13-10 shows partial results from a search for all domains running on the Oreilly.com IP address (208.201.239.36).

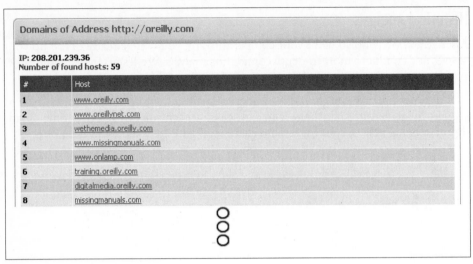

Figure 13-10. LinkVendor results for Oreilly.com

Finding subdomains

The method we discussed in the preceding section covered both domains and subdomains. If you are interested only in subdomains, you can visit the Who.Is page at *http://www.who.is/website-information/*. Figure 13-11 shows a portion of all the sub-domains of Oreilly.com.

Figure 13-11 also shows the *reach percentage*, which is calculated based on the number of unique visitors to the website from a large sample of web users; the *page view per-centage*, which represents the number of pages viewed on a website for each 1 million pages viewed on the Internet (these numbers are based on a large sample of web users); and the number of page views per user. As this data is aggregated by analyzing web usage from a large user pool, these are only approximated values. For more information, visit *http://www.whois.is*. The benefit of these numbers is that you can compare each subdomain in terms of popularity and relative importance.

Hosting and ownership information

By looking at IP-related data, you can deduce several things. For instance, you can make educated guesses as to the type of hosting your competitors are using. If your compet-itors are running on shared hosts, this should give you a good indication of their web budget and what stage of the game they are in. There is nothing wrong with hosting sites on shared hosts. However, the big players will almost always use a dedicated host.

Figure 13-12 illustrates the two extremes. Utilizing the Registry Data section of the service provided at *http://whois.domaintools.com/*, we can see that the top screen frag-ment belongs to a shared hosting site, as its parent DNS server is also home to another

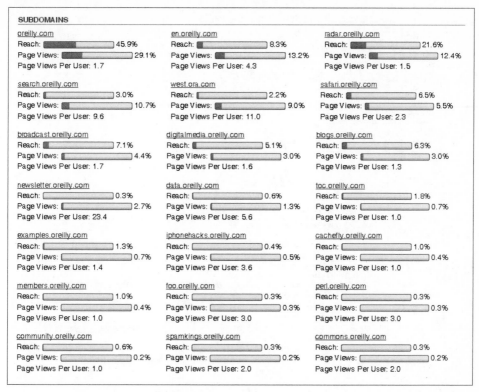

Figure 13-11. Subdomains of Oreilly.com

70,646 domains. In the bottom part of the figure, we can see the Oreilly.com information. In this case, even the DNS name servers are of the same domain (Oreilly.com), which indicates a more serious intent and, probably, dedicated hosting. Most big players will have their own DNS servers.

Geographical location information

Using the same (free) Whois.domaintools.com site, you can find out your competitor's hosting location. Figure 13-13 is a portion of the Server Data section of the results.

Estimating domain worth

Estimating the net worth of a domain is not an exact science. Many companies conduct domain name appraisals. These appraisals are typically based on a subjective formula that takes into account several factors, including the number of inbound links, Google PageRank, domain trust, and domain age.

When using this sort of data, you may be interested in seeing which websites are getting the highest appraisal (giving you another way to rank your opponents). Although these

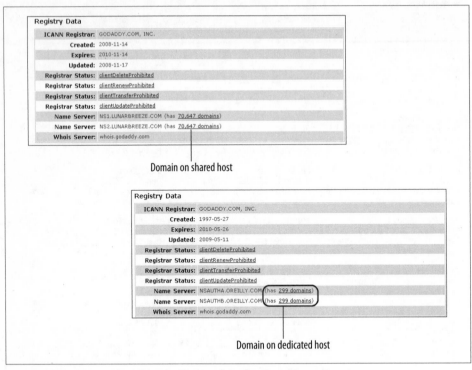

Figure 13-12. Registry data section of http://whois.domaintools.com/

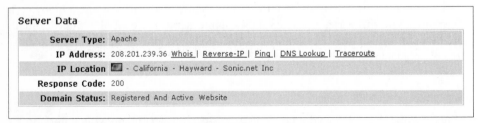

Figure 13-13. Server Data section of http://whois.domaintools.com/

numbers are likely off, at the very least you should compare competitor domains using the same vendor to ensure that the same formula is used. Unless you are trying to buy your competitor, there is no significance in knowing the competitor's relative worth other than to use these numbers to help you support other competitor data and findings. Both free and paid domain name appraisers are available. You can see what's available by visiting the sites we already discussed in Chapter 3.

Determining online size

If you are dealing with small competitor sites, you can download these sites using any offline browser software, including HTTrack Website Copier (*http://www.httrack .com*), BackStreet Browser (*http://www.spadixbd.com/backstreet/*), and Offline Explorer Pro (*http://www.offlineexplorerpro.com*). You can also find their relative search engine index size by using the `site:` command on Google.com, Yahoo.com, and Bing.com.

Estimating Website Traffic

The following subsections discuss details of using Alexa and Compete to estimate competitor traffic.

Alexa Reach

Although some people question the accuracy of data provided by Alexa, you can get some comparative data from Alexa. Figure 13-14 compares Google.com, Yahoo.com, and Bing.com. As you can see in the figure, Alexa provides several different tools. It collects its data from users who have installed the Alexa toolbar. In this example, we are showing the Reach functionality. According to Alexa (*http://bit.ly/3b1no6*):

> Reach measures the number of users. Reach is typically expressed as the percentage of all Internet users who visit a given site. So, for example, if a site like *yahoo.com* has a reach of 28%, this means that of all global Internet users measured by Alexa, 28% of them visit *yahoo.com*. Alexa's one-week and three-month average reach are measures of daily reach, averaged over the specified time period. The three-month change is determined by comparing a site's current reach with its values from three months ago.

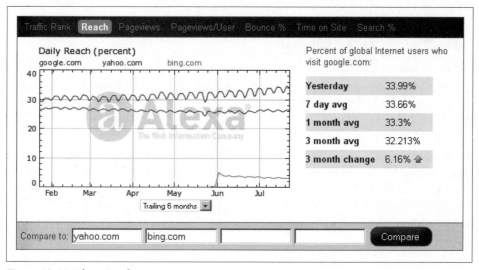

Figure 13-14. Alexa Reach statistics

Compete traffic estimates

Compete provides several free and commercially available tools for competitor research. It is one of the top competitor research tools available on the Internet. When comparing the sites of Google, Yahoo!, and Bing, we get a graph similar to Figure 13-15.

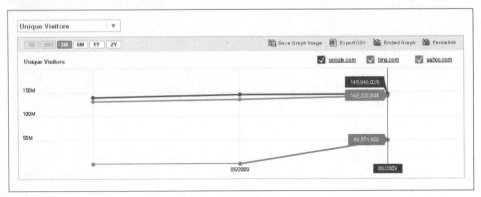

Figure 13-15. Compete: Comparing sites by unique visitors

As you can see, the data is much different as compared to Alexa's graph. This highlights the need to use several tools when doing your research to make better estimates.

Estimating Social Networking Presence

The social web is a web of the moment. What is hot now may not be hot one day, one week, or one year from now. You should examine the major social networking sites to see whether your competitors are generating any buzz.

Technorati blog reactions and Authority

You can visit the Technorati website (*http://technorati.com/*) and enter your competitor's URL in the search box to see whether your competitor received any blog reactions. Technorati defines blog discussions as "the number of links to the blog home page or its posts from other blogs in the Technorati index." Figure 13-16 illustrates the concept of blog reactions.

Technorati also offers an Authority feature, which it defines as "...the number of unique blogs linking to this blog over the last six months. The higher the number, the more Technorati Authority the blog has." You can see the Technorati Authority number in Figure 13-17 just under the blog thumbnail. This number will almost always be lower than the number of blog reactions.

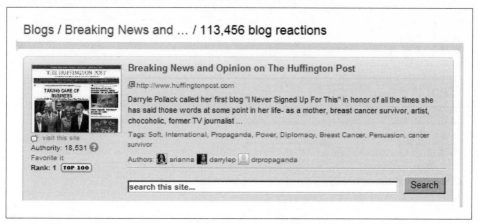

Figure 13-16. Sample blog reactions on Technorati

Digg.com (URL history)

You can also go to *http://digg.com* and search for your competitor URLs to find URLs that got "dugg." To simplify things, you can search for the root (competitor) domain URL to get multiple results (if any). Figure 13-17 illustrates the concept.

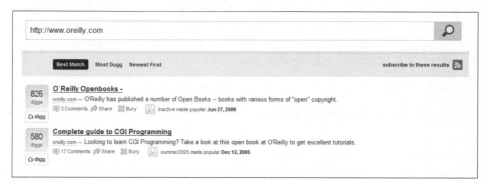

Figure 13-17. Digg.com: Search

Additional tips

In addition to using Technorati and Digg, you can also go to URL shortener sites (e.g., *http://bit.ly/*) and search for your competitor root domain URL. You will get results similar to those shown in Figure 13-18 (if any). From there, you can see the popular links that were shortened by anyone interested.

Go to *http://search.twitter.com/* and enter the base URL. See whether you get any tweet results. Continue your search on Facebook, MySpace, and others.

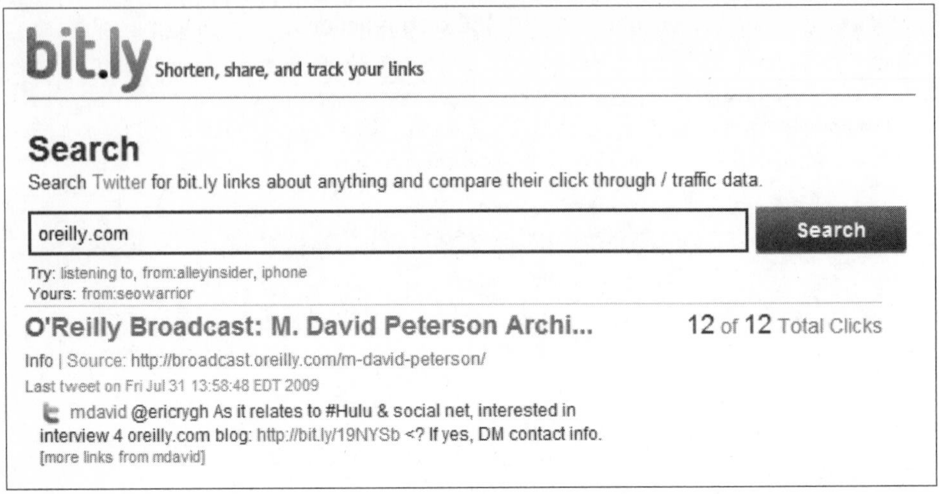

Figure 13-18. Bit.ly search

Competitor Tracking

In the previous sections, we discussed the different tools and methodologies of researching and analyzing your competitors. In this section, we'll discuss how to track your competitors. You can track your competitors in many ways. First we'll address how you may want to track a competitor's current state, and then we'll talk about future tracking.

Current State Competitor Auditing

When collecting current state competitor data, it helps to use an Excel spreadsheet. For example, you can create a spreadsheet to capture keywords alongside the top URLs and other related metrics. Figure 13-19 shows one such example.

Keyword-based Research Template

#	Keyword	URL	IP	Yahoo! Inlinks #	PR	Google Index	AdWords Est.Vol.	inurl	intitle	inanchor
1										
2										
3										
4										
5										

Figure 13-19. Keyword-based basic research template

In this template, you can enter the keyword, URL, IP address, Yahoo! inlinks, Google PageRank, Google index size, AdWords estimated monthly volume, "inurl" index count, "intitle" index count, and "inanchor" index count. Note that the URL would be the top URL for a particular keyword on a particular search engine. You can reuse this template for all of the major search engines.

You can also take a much more detailed approach by using the template shown in Figure 13-20. In this case, you are using similar information with several major differences. You are recording the top 10 or 20 competitors for every keyword. You are also recording the number of backlinks (BLs) as well as the number of other backlinks (OBLs) found on the same backlink page. You would have to replicate this form for all of the keywords, and that would take much more effort.

Keyword-based Research Template

#	URL	Yahoo! Inlinks #	SITE IP inanchor	PR intitle	BLs inurl	OBLs inanchor intitle	Google Index inanchor intitle inurl	AdWords Est.Vol.
	Keyword	abcde						
1								
2								
3								
4								
5								

Figure 13-20. More detailed keyword-based research template

To make your research tracking more complete, you should also spend some time analyzing each competitor manually (in more detail). Figure 13-21 shows an example template you could use in this case. The spreadsheet contains several major areas, each detailing different aspects of a particular competitor.

You don't have to follow this exact format; you can make many different permutations when documenting competitor data. Once you become familiar with your chosen tool, you can customize these templates to your own style.

Competitor-based Research Template

Competitor:

	Details	Top Backlinks	Main Site-wide Keywords			
Root/Main URL:		url1 (pr 8)				
Domain IP		url2 (pr5)				
Additional Sites [Y/N]:						
Using SEO [Y/N]						
Google Index:						
Bing Index:						
Technorati Blog Reactions:						
Twitter Presence [Y/N] or URL				Top URL 1	Top URL 2	Top URL 3
Home Page Google PageRank:			Keyword 1			
Site Alexa Rank:			Keyword 2			
Yahoo Inlinks:			Keyword 3			
Site Age:			kw in <title>			
Site Sitemap [Y/N] or URL:			kw in meta desc			
Robots.txt [Y/N]			kw in <h1..6>			
Site Feeds [Y/N] or URL			kw in <strong>			
Relative Site Worth:			kw in <b>			
			kw in images			
		urlN (pr4)	kw in <body>			

Figure 13-21. Competitor-based research template

You should be familiar with the metrics in Figure 13-21, as we already covered all of them throughout the chapter. The spreadsheet is available for download at *http://book .seowarrior.net*.

Future State Tracking

Performing regular competitor audits should be your homework. You should watch your existing competitors, but also any new ones that might show up unexpectedly. The more proactive you are, the faster you can react.

Existing competitor tracking

So, you've done your due diligence and have documented your (current state) competitor research. At this point, if you want to be proactive, you should think of ways to follow your competition. You want to be right on their tail by watching their every move.

As we already discussed, you could subscribe to their feeds. You could also set up a daily monitor script to watch for changes in their home pages or any other pages of interest. You could alter the monitor script (as we discussed in Chapter 6) by checking for content size changes or a particular string that could signal a change in a page.

New competitor detection

Typically, you can detect new competitors by performing competitor research and analysis again and again. You can also monitor social networking buzz by setting up feeds that key off of particular keywords of interest.

For example, you can use custom feeds from Digg.com to monitor newly submitted URLs based on any keyword. The general format is:

http://digg.com/rss_search?s=keyword

So, if you want to subscribe to a feed on the keyword *loans*, you could add the Digg.com feed to your feed reader by using the following link:

http://digg.com/rss_search?s=loans

The sky is the limit when it comes to competitor tracking and detection. All you need is a bit of creativity and the desire to be proactive. Digg.com is only one of the available platforms; you can do similar things on all the other tracking and detection platforms we discussed in this chapter.

Automating Search Engine Rank Checking

We'll end this chapter by designing a simple automated rank-checking script. Other programs on the Internet can accomplish the same thing. Most of them will stop working anytime search engines change their underlying HTML structure, however.

A few years ago, Google provided the SOAP API toolkit to query its search index database. To use this service, webmasters had to register on the Google website to obtain their API key, which would allow them to make 1,000 queries per day. This service is no longer available.

But all search engines are not the same, and finding rankings on several search engines for specific keywords and URLs can be a tedious exercise if done manually. Fortunately, there is an easier way: web scraping. To do this, it is necessary that you understand the underlying HTML structure of SERPs.

If you try to view the HTML code of Google and Bing, you will see something similar to Figure 13-22. As you can see, this is barely readable. You need to reformat this code so that you can analyze it properly. Many applications can accomplish this. One such application is Microsoft FrontPage.

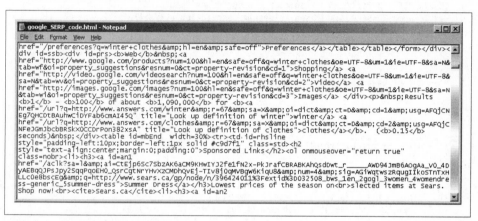

Figure 13-22. Google SERP HTML code

Microsoft FrontPage has a built-in HTML formatter that is available in Code view by simply right-clicking over any code fragment. After you format the HTML code, things start to make sense. Identifying HTML patterns is the key task. At the time of this writing, Google's organic search results follow this pattern:

```
<!-- start of organic result 1 -->
<li class="g">
<h3 class="r">
<a href="http://www.somedomain.com/" class="l" onmousedown="return
  clk(this.href,'','','res','7','')">
Some text <em>Some Keyword</em> </a></h3>
<!--some other text and tags-->
</li>
<!--end of organic result 1 -->
...
...


<!-- start of organic result N -->
<li class="g">
<h3 class="r">
<a href="http://www.somedomain.com/" class="l" onmousedown="return
  clk(this.href,'','','res','7','')">
Some text <em>Some Keyword</em> </a></h3>
<!--some other text and tags-->
```

```
</li>
<!--end of organic result N -->
```

The HTML comments (as indicated in the code fragment) are there only for clarity and do not appear in the actual Google search results page. Similarly, the Bing search results page has the following pattern:

```
<!-- start of organic result 1 -->
<li>
<div class="sa_cc">
<div class="sb_tlst">
<h3><a href="http://somedomain.com/" onmousedown="return
  si_T('&amp;ID=SERP,245')">search result description...</a></h3>
<!--other code-->
</div>
</div>
</li>
<!-- end of organic result 1 -->

...
...

<!-- start of organic result N -->
<li>
<div class="sa_cc">
<div class="sb_tlst">
<h3><a href="http://somedomain.com/" onmousedown="return
si_T('&amp;ID=SERP,246')">search result description...</a></h3>
<!--other code-->
</div>
</div>
</li>
<!-- end of organic result N -->
```

Taking all these patterns into consideration, it should now be possible to create scripts to automate ranking checking. That is precisely what the *getRankings.pl* Perl script does, which you can find in Appendix A.

Before running this script, ensure that you have the *wget.exe* utility in your execution path. You can run the script by supplying a single URL and keyword, or by supplying a keyword phrase as shown in the following fragment:

```
perl getRanking.pl [TargetURL] [Keyword]
                OR
perl getRanking.pl [TargetURL] [Keyword1] [Keyword2] ...
```

Here are real examples:

```
perl getRanking.pl www.randomhouse.com best books
perl getRanking.pl en.wikipedia.org/best-selling_books best books
```

If you run the first example, the eventual output would look like the following:

```
perl getRankings.pl www.randomhouse.com best books

Ranking Summary Report
```

```
~~~~~~~~~~~~~~~~~~~~~~~~~~~~~~~~~~~~~~~~~~~~~~
Keyword/Phrase: best books
Target URL: www.randomhouse.com
~~~~~~~~~~~~~~~~~~~~~~~~~~~~~~~~~~~~~~~~~~~~~~

  Google.....: 1,2
  Bing.......: 40

Note: Check with specific SE to ensure correctness.
```

The output of the script provides the rankings summary. The summary information should be self-explanatory. The *http://www.randomhouse.com* URL shows up on Google in positions 1 and 2, while on Bing it shows up in position 40.

It should be clear that search engine algorithms vary among search engines. Also note that the script uses the top 100 search results for each of the two search engines. You can expand the script to handle 1,000 results or to parse stats from other search engines using similar web scraping techniques.

 Do not abuse the script by issuing too many calls. If you do, Google and others will temporarily ban your IP from further automated queries, and you will be presented with the image validation (CAPTCHA) form when you try to use your browser for manual searches.

The intent of this script is to simplify the gathering of search engine rankings. Depending on the number of websites you manage, you may still be hitting search engines significantly. Consider using random pauses between each consecutive query. Also, search engine rankings do not change every second or every minute. Running this script once a week or once a month should be more than plenty in most cases. Use common sense while emulating typical user clicks.

Summary

This chapter focused on competitor research and analysis and many of the tools you can use to perform these tasks properly and efficiently. First we examined ways to find your competitors. We talked about the manual approach, and then explored ways to automate some of the manual tasks. We explored the SeoQuake plug-in in detail.

We also examined ways to find competitor keywords as well as competitor backlinks. In addition, we talked about different ways to analyze your competition. We discussed historical analysis, web presence, and website traffic analysis.

The last section covered competitor tracking. We explored different ways to audit your competitors, and at the end of the chapter we discussed a script that can automate the process of checking competitor search engine rankings for specific keywords.

## CHAPTER 14

Content Considerations

One of the most basic obstacles that any site can face is lack of unique, compelling, quality content. Good content is planned, researched, copyedited, relevant, and long lasting. Good content is also current, unique, interesting, and memorable.

Producing lots of content does not guarantee the success of your website. Producing little or no new content is not the answer either. Striking the right balance between short- and long-term content will help make your site stand out from the crowd.

Content duplication is one of the most common SEO challenges. With the introduction of the canonical link element, webmasters now have another tool to combat content duplication.

Optimizing your sites for search engine verticals can help bring in additional traffic besides traffic originating from standard organic results. In this chapter, we will discuss all of these topics in detail.

Becoming a Resource

If you had to pick one thing that would make or break a site, it would almost always be content. This does not automatically mean that having the most content will get you the rankings or traffic you desire. Many factors play a role. The best sites produce all kinds of content. Website content can be classified into two broad areas: short-term content and long-term content. You should also be aware of the concept of predictive SEO.

Predictive SEO

Depending on your niche, you can anticipate future events in your keyword strategy. Some events occur only once per year, once every few years, once in a lifetime, once every day, once every week, and so forth. You can leverage this knowledge to foster content development to accommodate these future events.

Future events, buying cycles, and buzz information

You can use Google Trends to see what's happening in the world of search as well as in realizing past trends or keyword patterns that you can leverage when planning for future events.

Future events. Many sites are being built today that will see the light of day only when certain events occur in the future. For example, the Winter Olympic Games occur only every four years. If you are running a sports site, you could start creating a site (or a subsite) specifically for the next Winter Games. This way, you can be ready when the time comes. In the process, you will be acquiring domain age trust from Google and others as you slowly build up your content and audience in time for the Winter Games.

Buying cycles. In the Western world, there are certain known buying cycles throughout the year. For example, the money modifier *gift* starts to spike from early November. It reaches its peak a few days prior to Christmas, only to go back to its regular level by the end of December. Figure 14-1 shows this concept.

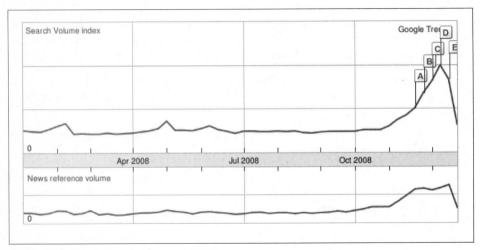

Figure 14-1. Google Trends: Keyword "gift"

Online retailers know this sort of information and are always looking to capitalize on these trends. From an SEO perspective, site owners are typically advised to optimize their sites well before their anticipated shopping surge event, as it takes some time for search engines to index their content.

Buzz information. Search engines are in a race to come up with better live search algorithms. Many sites effectively act as information repeaters. This includes many well-respected (big player) media news sites. They repackage news that someone else has put forth. Some clever sites employ various mashups to look more unique.

The idea of content mashups is to create content that is effectively better than the original by providing additional quality information or compelling functions. In this competitive news frenzy, sites that can achieve additional (value add) functionality benefit from a perceived freshness relevance.

Content mashups are everywhere. Some sites employ commonly available (popular) keyword listings, including those at the following URLs:

- *http://www.google.com/trends/hottrends*
- *http://buzzlog.buzz.yahoo.com/overall/*
- *http://hotsearches.aol.com/*
- *http://buzz.yahoo.com/*
- *http://www.google.com/intl/en/press/zeitgeist2008/*

These types of content mashup schemes employ scraped links to build new (mixed) content by using these popular keywords.

Short-Term Content

Short-term content is the current Internet buzz. Sites producing such content include blogs, forums, and news sites. Short-term content is important, as it aids webmasters by providing a freshness and relevancy boost to their websites. Many legitimate and unethical sites use this to their advantage.

Unexpected buzz

The trick when creating short-term content is to do it while the specific topic is still "hot." Better yet, if you can anticipate the future buzz the content will generate, you will be a step ahead of your competition. Figure 14-2 illustrates search and news article volume trends for the keyword *susan boyle* (the unexpected frontrunner on the televised singing competition, "Britain's Got Talent").

From Figure 14-2, it should be easy to see what transpired over the past few years. From the beginning of 2004 to about April 2009, this keyword was not even on the map. Everything changed after the show was televised. News sites and blogs alike were in a frenzy to cover this emerging story.

Just a few months later, search volumes tumbled. And when you look closely at the graph in Figure 14-2, you can see another pattern. Figure 14-3 shows the same graph, but on a 12-month scale. You can see that in terms of search volume, interest in *susan boyle* was highest at the start of the graph (point A in the figure). When you look at the news reference volume graph, you can see how the news and blog sites scrambled to cover the news, as indicated by the first peak in the graph.

Shortly thereafter, the search volume plummeted (between points B and C in the figure), which is also reflected in the number of news articles generated during that time. By the time the second search volume peak appeared around mid-May (point C), many more news sites were competing for essentially the same story (and the same content).

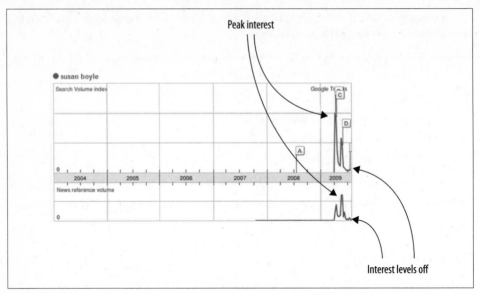

Figure 14-2. Short-term content: Google Trends

By July 2009 (point D), the search volume index and news reference volume were nearly identical.

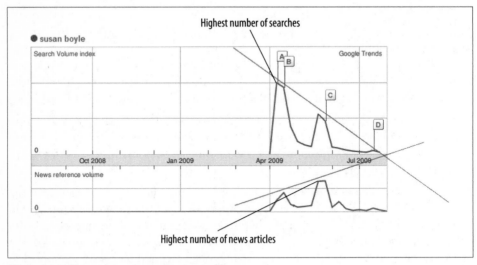

Figure 14-3. Short-term content: Unexpected buzz

Although I am not going to go into detail on TV headlines that produce search volume peaks, this discussion should reinforce the importance of being ready to produce content so that you are one of the first sites to capture any unexpected buzz. You want to catch the first peak, as in this case, so that your content will be unique and fresh and you won't have to deal with a large number of competitor sites in the same news space. You want to capture the search frenzy at its earliest.

Expected buzz

Now let's examine what happens when you can anticipate a certain event. For example, the most popular tennis tournament takes place every year at Wimbledon. Figure 14-4 shows a Google Trends graph for the keyword *wimbledon*.

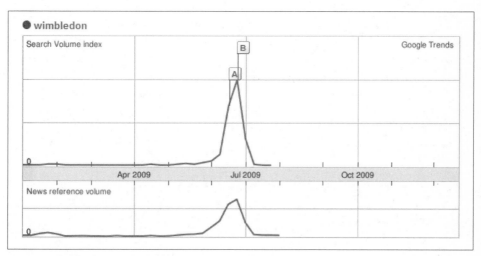

Figure 14-4. Short-term content: Expected buzz

Several things should be clear when you look at Figure 14-4. The two peaks—indicating search volume index and news reference volume—are very much in sync. This should speak loudly about the preparation and production of content that mimics the buzz coming out of the tournament.

The high peak occurs around the tournament finals at the end of June; hence the highest news coverage during that time frame. Creating short-term content of expected events is much easier than doing the same for unexpected events. However, you will be facing a lot more competition for the same storylines.

Long-Term Content

Long-term content is content that sticks. It is the type of content that people bookmark and come back to many times. This type of content has a greater lifespan than short-term content. Its relevancy does not diminish much over time.

Long-term content can be anything from online software tools to websites acting as reference resources. Let's take a look at some examples.

If you use Google to search for any word that appears in the English dictionary, chances are Google will provide among its search results a result from Wikipedia. The English dictionary does not change much over time. Sites containing English language dictionary definitions, such as Wikipedia, are well positioned to receive steady traffic over time.

Most computer programmers use Google to find answers to their development problems. Sites providing answers to such problems can also benefit from this, as they will receive a steady flow of traffic. Figure 14-5 illustrates search volume based on the keyword *html tutorial*.

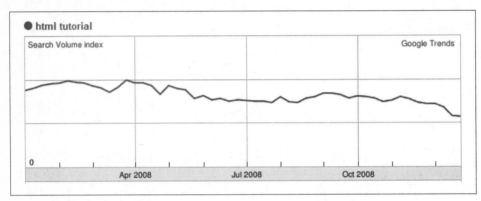

Figure 14-5. Long-term content

You can see that the overall search volume is more or less the same month after month. If your site hosts the best "HTML Tutorial" around and is currently getting good traffic, you can be pretty certain that your site will be getting steady traffic in the future (assuming no other variables are introduced). When people are looking for reference information, they will continue searching until they find exactly what they are looking for. Searching several SERPs is not uncommon.

Content Balance

Both short- and long-term content have their advantages. How much of your content is short term or long term depends on your line of business. If you are in the news or blog business, you will do well by continuously producing new content. If you are providing technical information, you may wish to offer a mix of new articles and technical reference articles, which you can package into a different article category that is easy to access from anywhere on your site.

Organic content

If you are producing lots of semantically similar content, you should consider making it easy for people to add comments to that content. Each comment helps make your associated content page more unique. Content uniqueness is something to strive for, especially if you are in a competitive niche.

Content Creation Motives

At the most basic level, your content is your sales pitch. You create content to make a statement. Compelling content is content that provides newsworthy information, answers to questions, reference information, and solutions to searchers' problems.

The ultimate motive of any website content is to provide information to visitors so that they can accomplish a particular business goal.

Engaging your visitors

Modern sites try to make it easy for their visitors to comment on and share their content. Engaging visitors adds an element of trust when people can say what they wish to say about your products, services, ideas, and so forth. This is mutually beneficial, as you can use your visitors' feedback to improve your products and services.

Fortifying your web authority

Staying ahead of the competition requires continual work. You cannot just design your site and leave. Creating a continuous buzz and interest is necessary to foster and cultivate your brand or business.

Updating and supplementing existing information

All things change. You need to ensure that your site is on top of the latest happenings in your particular niche. Using old information to attract visitors will not work.

Catching additional traffic

Creating additional content to get more traffic is one of the oldest tricks in the book. Search engines are getting smarter by day, so to make this work, your content will need to be unique.

Make no mistake: the fact that content is unique does not automatically say anything about its quality. However, search engines can get a pretty good idea about the quality of your content based on many different factors, such as site trust, social bookmarking, user click-throughs, and so on.

Content Duplication

Content duplication is among the most talked about subjects in SEO. With the advances we have seen in search engine algorithms, the challenge of content duplication is no longer as big as it used to be. Duplicate content can occur for many different reasons. Some common causes include affiliate sites, printer-friendly pages, multiple site URLs to the same content, and session and other URL variables. This section talks about different ways to deal with content duplication.

Canonical Link Element

Content duplication is one of the most common challenges webmasters face. Although you can deal with content duplication in many different ways, the introduction of the canonical link element is being touted as one of the resolutions to this issue. As of early 2009, the canonical link element was officially endorsed by Google, Yahoo!, and Microsoft. Microsoft's blog site (*http://bit.ly/lIVY0*) stated that:

> Live Search (Bing) has partnered with Google and Yahoo to support a new tag attribute that will help webmasters identify the single authoritative (or canonical) URL for a given page.

Ask.com has also endorsed the canonical link element. Needless to say, many popular CMSs and blogging software packages scrambled to produce updated versions of their code or plug-ins to support canonical URLs. These include WordPress, Joomla, Drupal, and many others.

What is a canonical link?

A canonical link is like a preferred link. This preference comes to light when we are dealing with duplicate content and when search engines choose which link should be favored over all others when referring to identical page content.

Matt Cutts, Google search quality engineer, defines canonicalization on his blog site (*http://www.mattcutts.com/blog/seo-advice-url-canonicalization/*) as follows:

> Canonicalization is the process of picking the best url when there are several choices, and it usually refers to home pages.

Canonical link element format

You place the canonical link element in the header part of the HTML file, within the <head> tag. Its format is simply:

```
<link rel="canonical" href="http://www.mydomain.com/keyword.html" />
```

Let's say you have a page, *http://www.mydomain.com/pants.html*, which you want to be the preferred page, as it points to the original (main) document. But you also have three other pages that refer to the same content page, as in the following:

- *http://www.mydomain.com/catalog.jsp?part=pants&category=clothes&*
- *http://www.mydomain.com/catalog.jsp;jsessio-nid=B8C2341GE57FAF195DE34027A95DA3FC?part=pants&category=clothes*
- *http://www.mydomain.com/catalog.jsp?pageid=78234*

To apply the newly supported canonical link element, you would place the following in each of the three preceding URLs, in the HTML header section:

```html
<html>
<head>
<!-- other header tags/elements -->
<link rel="canonical" href="http://www.mydomain.com/pants.html" />
</head>
<body>
<!--page copy text and elements -->
</body>
</html>
```

The Catch-22

Although the introduction of the canonical link element certainly solves some duplication problems, it does not solve them all. In its current implementation, you can use it only for pages on the same domain or a related subdomain.

Here are examples in which the canonical link element *can* be applied:

- *http://games.mydomain.com/tetris.php*
- *http://mydomain.com/shop.do?gameid=824*
- *http://retrogames.mydomain.com/tetris.com*

Here are examples in which the canonical link element *cannot* be applied:

- *http://games.mydomain.net/tetris.php*
- *http://myotherdomain.com/shop.do?gameid=824*

The reason the big search engines do not support cross-domain canonical linking is likely related to spam. Imagine a domain being hijacked, and then hackers using the canonical link element to link the hijacked domain to one of their own in an attempt to pass link juice from the hijacked domain. Although the canonical link element is not a perfect solution, it should be a part of your standard SEO toolkit when dealing with content duplication.

Possibility of an infinite loop

Take care when using canonical link elements, as you could run into a situation such as this:

```html
<!-- Page A -->
<html>
<head>
<link rel="canonical" href="http://www.mydomain.com/b.html" />
</head>
<body><!-- ... page A text ... -->
</html>

<!-- Page B -->
<html>
```

```
<head>
<link rel="canonical" href="http://www.mydomain.com/a.html" />
</head>
<body><!-- ... page B text ... -->
</html>
```

In this example, Page A indicates a preferred page, Page B. Similarly, Page B indicates a preferred page, Page A. This scenario constitutes an infinite loop. In this situation, search engines will pick the page they think is the preferred page, or they might even ignore the element, leaving the possibility of a duplicate content penalty.

Multiple URLs

The canonical link element is only one of the tools you should have in your arsenal. There are other methods for dealing with content duplication.

Trailing slash

There is certainly a debate as to the use of the trailing slash (/) in URLs. The implied meaning of a trailing slash in URLs is that of a directory. A URL with no trailing slash implies a specific file. With the use of URL rewriting, this meaning has become somewhat blurry in a sense. URLs that you see in web browsers may or may not be their true (unaltered) representations when interpreted at the web server.

From an SEO perspective, URL consistency is the only thing that matters. Google Webmaster Tools does report duplicate content URLs. For example, Google will tell you whether you have two URLs, as in the following fragment:

```
http://www.mysite.com/ultimate-perl-tutorial
http://www.mysite.com/ultimate-perl-tutorial/
```

You can handle this scenario by using the following URL rewriting (.htaccess) fragment:

```
RewriteEngine on
RewriteCond %{REQUEST_FILENAME} !-f
RewriteCond %{REQUEST_URI} !(.*)/$
RewriteRule ^(.*)$ http://www.mysite.com/$1/ [R=301,L]
```

All requests will now be redirected (using the HTTP 301 permanent redirect) to the URL version with the trailing slash. If you prefer not to use a trailing slash, you can use the following:

```
RewriteEngine on
RewriteCond %{REQUEST_FILENAME} !-d
RewriteCond %{REQUEST_URI} ^(.+)/$
RewriteRule ^(.+)/$  /$1 [R=301,L]
```

The notable difference in this example is in the second line of code, which checks to make sure the resource is not a directory.

Multiple slashes

Sometimes people will make mistakes by adding multiple slashes to your page URLs in local or external inbound links. To eliminate this situation, you can use the following URL rewriting segment:

```
RewriteEngine on
RewriteCond %{REQUEST_URI} ^(.*)//(.*)$
RewriteRule . %1/%2 [R=301,L]
```

WWW prefix

You do have the time and control to enforce how people link to your site. Suppose you own a domain called SiteA.com that can be reached by either *http://siteA.com* or *http://www.siteA.com*. You've decided to use the *http://www.siteA.com* version. You can easily implement this with the following URL rewriting (*.htaccess*) fragment:

```
RewriteEngine On
RewriteCond %{HTTP_HOST} ^siteA\.com$
RewriteRule (.*) http://www.siteA.com/$1 [R=301,L]
```

Domain misspellings

If you purchased a few misspelled domains, you can use a similar method to redirect those misspelled domains. The following is the URL rewriting (*.htaccess*) fragment to use:

```
RewriteEngine On
RewriteCond %{HTTP_HOST} ^www.typodomain.com$
RewriteRule ^(.*)$ http://www.principaldomain.com$1 [R=301,L,NC]

RewriteCond %{HTTP_HOST} ^typodomain.com$
RewriteRule ^(.*)$ http://www.principaldomain.com$1 [R=301,L,NC]
```

In this example, we are redirecting both *http://typodomain.com* and *http://www.typodomain.com* to *http://www.principaldomain.com*.

HTTP to HTTPS and vice versa

Sometimes you may want to use secure web browser–to–web server communications. In this case, you will want to redirect all of the pertinent HTTP requests to their HTTPS counterparts. You can do this by using the following (*.htaccess*) fragment:

```
RewriteEngine On
RewriteCond %{HTTPS} off
RewriteRule (.*) https://%{HTTP_HOST}%{REQUEST_URI} [R=301,L,NC]
```

If you have an e-commerce store, you may want to redirect users back to HTTP for all pages except those containing a specific URL part. If all of your billing (payment) pages need to be run over HTTPS and all of the billing content is under the *https://mywebstore.com/payments* path, you can use the following (*.htaccess*) fragment:

```
RewriteEngine On
RewriteCond %{HTTPS} on
RewriteRule !^payments(/|$) http://%{HTTP_HOST}%{REQUEST_URI} [R=301,L,NC]
```

Fine-Grained Content Indexing

Sometimes (apart from the case of content duplication) you may want to exclude certain pages from getting indexed on your site. This applies to any generic pages with no semantic relevancy and can include ad campaign landing pages, error message pages, confirmation pages, feedback pages, contact pages, and pages with little or no text.

We already discussed ways to prevent search engines from indexing your content pages. This includes utilization of the *robots.txt* file, the `noindex` meta tag, the X-Robots-Tag, and the `nofollow` attribute. These methods will work for pages at the site level or at the individual page level.

You can also apply some filtering to each page. You can make generic (semantically unrelated) parts of your page invisible to web spiders. There are several ways to do this, including JavaScript, iframes, and dynamic `DIV`s.

External Content Duplication

External content duplication can be caused by a few different things, including mirror sites and content syndication.

Mirror sites

There are two types of site mirroring: legitimate and unethical. We will discuss the legitimate case. For whatever reason, website owners might need to create multiple mirror sites of essentially the same content. If one site was to go down, they could quickly switch the traffic to the other site (with the same or a different URL).

If this is the case with your site arrangement, you want to make sure you block search engines from crawling your mirror sites. For starters, you can disallow crawling in *robots.txt*. You can also apply the `noindex` meta tag or the X-Robots-Tag equivalent.

Content syndication

If you happen to syndicate your content on other sites, Google advises the following (*http://bit.ly/20IhDm*):

> If you syndicate your content on other sites, Google will always show the version we think is most appropriate for users in each given search, which may or may not be the version you'd prefer. However, it is helpful to ensure that each site on which your content is syndicated includes a link back to your original article. You can also ask those who use your syndicated material to block the version on their sites with robots.txt.

You may also want to consider syndicating just the article teasers instead of the articles in their entirety.

Similar Pages

Similar pages can also be viewed as duplicates. Google explains this concept as follows (*http://bit.ly/20IhDm*):

> If you have many pages that are similar, consider expanding each page or consolidating the pages into one. For instance, if you have a travel site with separate pages for two cities, but the same information on both pages, you could either merge the pages into one page about both cities or you could expand each page to contain unique content about each city.

Deep-Linked Content

Blogs, forums, and article-driven sites will often experience indexing problems due to pagination. Pagination does not play a significant role if you have only a few articles on your site. If you are a busy site, however, this becomes an indexing and duplication issue if you do not handle it properly.

Some sites try to deal with this scenario by increasing the number of articles shown per page. This is not the optimal solution. Let's look at a typical blog site. At first, each new blog entry is found in multiple places, including the home page, the website archive, and the recent posts section, all of which have the potential for duplicate content URLs.

Once the blog entry starts to age, it moves farther down the page stack. At some point, it is invisible from the home page. As time passes by, it takes more and more clicks to be reached, and then at some point it gets thrown out of the search engine index. You can deal with this so-called deep-linked content in several ways.

Sitemaps

You can list all of your important pages in your Sitemaps, as we discussed in Chapter 10. Although search engines do not provide guarantees when it comes to what they index, you can try this approach. If you have many similar pages, you might want to consolidate them as per Google's advice.

Resurfacing

Another way to bring your important pages back to the forefront is to link to them from your other internal pages. You can do the same with any external backlinks.

In addition, you could bundle important long-term content pages in another hotspot reference area for easy finding. One example of this concept is with sticky posts in forums that include posts, such as forum guidelines and forum rules. For other types of sites, you might have a top-level page that links to these important links.

Navigation structure

Many newer CMSs also provide an article subcategory view. This approach takes advantage of the semantic relationships between different articles. This provides for better semantic structure of the site.

If you're changing your custom code, ensure that you block duplicate paths to your content. Even if you are using a free or paid CMS, chances are you will need to make some SEO tweaks to minimize and eliminate content duplication.

Protecting Your Content

Any content you create becomes your intellectual property as soon as it is created. With so many people on the Internet today, someone will want to take advantage of your content.

On October 12, 1998, then-President Clinton signed the Digital Millennium Copyright Act (DMCA), after approval from Congress. This act contains provisions whereby Internet service providers can remove illegal copyrighted content from users' websites. You can view the entire document at *http://www.copyright.gov/legislation/dmca.pdf*. For more information on copyrights, visit *http://www.copyright.gov*.

Google takes action when it finds copyright violations. You can read more about how Google handles DMCA at *http://www.google.com/dmca.html*. If you find that your content is being copied on other sites, you can file a complaint to let Google know. The process comprises several steps, including mailing the completed form to Google.

You can also use the service provided by Copyscape (*http://copyscape.com/*). Copyscape provides free and premium copyright violation detection services. The free service allows you to enter your URLs in a simple web form that then returns any offending sites. The premium service provides many more detection features.

If you do find people using your content, you can try to contact them directly through either their website contact information or their domain Whois information. If that does not work, you can contact their IP block owner (provider) by visiting *http://ws .arin.net/whois/*. If that doesn't work, you should consult a local lawyer who is knowledgeable in Internet copyright laws.

Preventing hot links

Hot link prevention is one of the oldest ways webmasters can prevent other sites from using their bandwidth. You can implement hot link prevention with a few lines of code in your *.htaccess* file:

```
RewriteEngine On
RewriteCond %{HTTP_REFERER} !^$
RewriteCond %{HTTP_REFERER} !^http://(www\.)?mycoolsite.com/.*$ [NC]
RewriteRule \.(gif|jpg|png|vsd|doc|xls|js|css)$ - [F]
```

When you add this code to your site, no one will be able to directly access any of the document types as specified in the rewrite rule.

Content Verticals

Your website traffic does not always come from the main search engines. All major search engines provide vertical search links (or tabs) found at the top of the search box. People can find your site by searching for images, news, products, maps, and so forth.

Vertical Search

Each search engine vertical is run by specialized search engine algorithms. In this section, we'll examine Google Images, Google News, and Google Product Search. Bing provides similar, albeit smaller, functionality.

Google Images

The psychology of image search is different from regular searches. Image searchers are usually more patient. At the same time, they are pickier. Therefore, optimizing your images makes sense. The added benefit of image optimization is that your images will show up in the main search results blended with text results. They also appear on Google Maps.

Images need to be accessible. Ensure that your *robots.txt* file is not blocking your image folder. Make sure X-Robots-Tags are not being used on your server (sending the `noindex` HTTP header). You can see whether any of your existing images are indexed by Google by issuing the following commands (when in the Images tab):

```
site:mysite.com
site:mysite.com filetype:png
```

You can do the same thing in Bing by issuing the following command:

```
site:mysite.com
```

The image filename should contain keywords separated by hyphens. Ideally, the full path to the image will contain related keywords. All images should have the `ALT` text with specified width and height parameters.

Consider making images clickable, surrounded by relevant descriptive copy. If an image is clickable, the destination page should be on the same topic and should include the same or a larger version of the image. When linking to images, use descriptive anchor text with pertinent keywords.

Google News

To include your site's articles in Google News (*http://news.google.com/*), you will need to submit your link to Google for approval, as described at *http://bit.ly/1UeZHp*.

Google will review the link to ensure that it meets its guidelines. There is no guarantee of inclusion.

When approved, utilize the Google News Sitemaps when submitting your news content. We already talked about creating news Sitemaps in Chapter 10. In early 2009, Google published several tips for optimizing articles for Google News (*http://bit.ly/ 4xXQ3Y*). Here are the eight optimization tips Google recommends:

- Keep the article body clean.
- Make sure article URLs are permanent and unique.
- Take advantage of stock tickers in Sitemaps.
- Check your encoding.
- Make your article publication dates explicit.
- Keep original content separate from press releases.
- Format your images properly.
- Make sure the title you want appears in both the title tag and as the headline on the article page.

With the Google News platform, the more clicks your articles produce, the better. Google is tracking all of the clicks on its Google News portal. As of this writing, the following is the HTTP header fragment when clicking on one of the articles:

```
GET /news/url?sa=t&ct2=ca%2F0_0_s_0_0_t&usg=AFQjCNFjVmWpHfAZj–
UVnmQA6HjxXyuYg&cid=1292192065&ei=cqR7SsD5Fqjm9ASm_p-
OAw&rt=HOMEPAGE&vm=STANDARD&url=http%3A%2F%2Fwww.cbc.ca%2Fhealth%2F
story%2F2009%2F08%2F06%2Fswine-flu-vaccine.html HTTP/1.1
```

This request is then followed by a 302 (temporary) HTTP redirect to the (news) source site:

```
HTTP/1.x 302 Found
Cache-Control: private
Content-Type: text/html; charset=UTF-8
Location: http://www.cbc.ca/health/story/2009/08/06/swine-flu-vaccine.html
Date: Fri, 07 Aug 2009 03:50:21 GMT
Server: NFE/1.0
Content-Length: 261
http://www.cbc.ca/health/story/2009/08/06/swine-flu-vaccine.html
```

In this way, Google can easily test and promote articles that are getting the most clicks.

Google Product Search

The Google Product Search platform allows sellers to create product feeds. Sellers can increase their website traffic and sales. The platform setup is free of charge. You can create your account by registering for an account with Google Base. According to Google (*http://bit.ly/3s8XKI*):

Google Base is a place where you can easily submit all types of online and offline content, which we'll make searchable on Google (if your content isn't online yet, we'll put it there). You can describe any item you post with attributes, which will help people find it when they do related searches. In fact, based on your items' relevance, users may find them in their results for searches on Google Product Search and even our main Google web search.

Currently, Google Base supports the following product feed formats: tab delimited, RSS 1.0, RSS 2.0, Atom 0.3, Atom 1.0, and API. When constructing your feeds, pay special attention to the product title and description fields. These are the fields that will appear in the Google Product Search results. Make use of your targeted keywords with a call to action.

It is believed that Google favors older feeds just like it favors older domains. Also note that Google Product Search lists seller ratings as well as product reviews in its search results. Products with better reviews are favored in the search results. Figure 14-6 shows a sample Google Product Search results page.

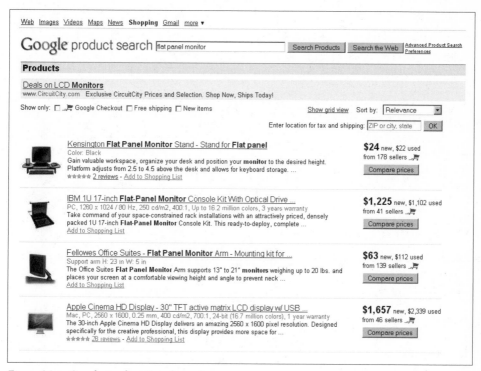

Figure 14-6. Google Product Search results page

Summary

As we discussed in this chapter, content is king. Depending on your site, you will want to have both short- and long-term content. Short-term content helps you capture traffic associated with current Internet buzz. Long-term content helps bring more consistent traffic volumes over time.

Content duplication is one of the most talked about issues in SEO. Using the canonical link element along with existing content duplication elimination methods is part of sound SEO.

Utilizing search engine verticals helps bring in additional website traffic. Companies selling products should explore using Google Base and its Google Product Search platform.

## CHAPTER 15

Social Networking Phenomenon

This chapter looks at some of the most popular social media sites and how they relate to SEO. Social networking is not new. It existed—albeit in a primitive manner—prior to the mainstream Internet, in the form of bulletin board systems, newsgroups, and IRC chats. Even in those days, people were able to share all kinds of information and files, including media files. The only catch at that time was that you had to be a computer geek to use these services effectively.

Although those days are long gone, the idea is still the same in the sense of social networking and information sharing. As the mainstream Internet matured, so did its users. The Web as we know it is changing, with an emphasis on self-expression. This is what the social web is all about.

Why is social networking important? Social networks give you other sites on which you can place your URL and attract hits. You are in control—you don't have to hope someone else will link to you. Simply put, social networks provide you with additional channels of inbound website traffic. Optimizing your site with social media in mind is referred to as *SMO*, or social media optimization.

Rohit Bhargava coined the term SMO. Wikipedia defines it as follows (*http://en.wiki pedia.org/wiki/Social_media_optimization*):

> Social media optimization (SMO) is a set of methods for generating publicity through social media, online communities and community websites. Methods of SMO include adding RSS feeds, social news buttons, blogging, and incorporating third-party community functionalities like images and videos. Social media optimization is related to search engine marketing, but differs in several ways, primarily the focus on driving traffic from sources other than search engines, though improved search ranking is also a benefit of successful SMO.

We covered some SMO methods in Chapter 12. In this chapter, we will look at the top social networking sites in detail as well as ways to develop and implement a sound SMO strategy.

We will also look at ways to streamline and control your social web presence. We'll create a skeleton application to illustrate the concepts of social media automation. And we'll create a Twitter scheduler application in PHP and MySQL.

At the end of the chapter, we'll look at the concept of real-time search. We'll compare Twitter with Google and take a look at a newcomer, OneRiot.

Social Platforms and Communities

The rules of social networking are defined by each social networking community. Each platform or social site will have its own user community or set of subcommunities. Each community helps define and cultivate its own rules, culture, and online etiquette. The following subsections discuss various social platforms and their associated communities.

Blogs

Companies need corporate blogs to strengthen their brands and their clients' perception of them. Blogs provide interactive ways for clients to learn about your company's products and services. They also provide a means by which clients can help you gauge your offerings. Blogs can be helpful in attaining additional targeted website traffic. The Technorati community measures a blog's importance with its so-called blog reactions rating. The more blog reactions you have, the more important your blog is perceived to be.

Technorati provides easy ways for webmasters to submit their blog URLs as well as ping their search service anytime they update their blogs. To register your blog with Technorati, go to *http://technorati.com/*, click the Blogger Central menu item, and choose Claim Your Blog. Anytime you update your blog, you may also want to ping Technorati to let the company know of your new content. You can do this manually through the Technorati interface. Select Blogger Central→Ping Your Blog.

Marketers can utilize Technorati Media (the Technorati parent company) to post ads on participating blog sites and social media sites. Technorati is not the only player when it comes to blogs. Other blog directories, blog search engines, and news aggregator sites are interested in your blogs. These include Bloglines (*http://www.bloglines.com/*), Weblogs.com (*http://weblogs.com/*), NewsIsFree (*http://newsisfree.com/*), and News-Gator (*http://www.newsgator.com/*). Most of the popular blog software allows you to ping multiple blog directories and blog search engines.

You can create your own scripts, or you can use some of the free scripts that are readily available on the Internet. You can download the Weblog_Pinger script (*http://work bench.cadenhead.org/weblog-pinger/*), which supports Technorati and others utilizing XML-RPC services. This is yet another way to get inbound links. For a list of ping URLs, see Appendix B.

The most popular blogging software is WordPress. Companies big and small use WordPress for their blogs. WordPress comes with many SEO plug-ins that take care of many on-page and on-site search optimization factors.

Twitter

The concept of microblogging is similar to traditional blogging, but with some exceptions, including the size of each blog. In the case of Twitter, each message can be no more than 140 characters in length and should be answering one simple question: what are you doing? Microblogging is well suited for wireless devices that can send SMS messages or emails.

As of April 2009, Twitter was used by more than 17 million people in the United States alone (*http://blog.comscore.com/2009/05/twitter_traffic_quadruples.html*). At the time of this writing, it is the most talked about social networking site on the Internet. Some people hate it while others love it. Many people are just not interested in knowing when other people go to work or when they go to sleep. They find this sort of information a big waste of their time as well as a big distraction. Proficient Twitterers use mobile phones to tweet several times a day.

Many celebrities have joined the Twitter bandwagon as of late. This includes the current and former presidents, actors, and others. The top 100 Twitter accounts (according to *http://twitterholic.com*) in terms of the number of followers are littered with celebrity names.

Twitter has many practical uses. You can use Twitter to find a job or business partner, advertise a new business, discuss politics, and debate sports. You can use it for just about anything. Although many people use Twitter just for fun, companies are constantly looking for ways to monetize their Twitter presence. For instance, news corporations tweet their news headlines, and companies selling products tweet announcements of their new offerings.

Twitter tips

If you're going to use Twitter, you may want to heed the following tips.

Open an account to safeguard your potential future presence should you want to use it later. Somebody may have already taken your name. Spend some time optimizing your profile. Pay special attention to the Name, Username, More Info URL, and One Line Bio fields. Try to use relevant keywords.

Twitter started using the `nofollow` link attribute to discourage tweet link spam. This, of course, means any search engines adhering to the `nofollow` standard will not pass any link juice for the link labeled with the `nofollow` link attribute.

As of this writing, the mobile version of Twitter (*http://m.twitter.com*) is still passing link juice. Search engines crawl and index both versions of Twitter. Figure 15-1 shows some sample Google results when searching for *oreilly site:twitter.com*.

Twitter Launches New Homepage Design | **WebProNews**
Jeremy Muncy has been a part of the **WebProNews** team and the iEntry Network since 2003.
Follow him on Twitter @jmuncy. ...
twe.ly/oib - Cached - Similar

WebProNews (WebProNews) on Twitter
WebProNews is using Twitter. Twitter is a free service that lets you keep in touch with ... Name
WebProNews; Location Lexington, KY; Web http://www.webpro. ...
twitter.com/**WebPronews** - Cached - Similar

Figure 15-1. Sample Twitter results on Google

Showing up in search engine results is a good enough reason to use Twitter. Anyone clicking on the Twitter search result has, after being directed to Twitter, access to your profile information, including your website link.

You can think of this concept as an indirect way to build links. People who see your tweets will be able to spread your message by bookmarking your site, adding a backlink on their sites, or retweeting.

Google and Bing also index redirected destination links from their short URL equivalents. For example, you can check the size of the Google index for the Bit.ly URL shortener by issuing the `site:bit.ly` command.

Start tweeting about your area of interest and stick to it. You want to establish yourself as an authority on the subject matter while gaining a large following. Start following people who have common interests and people in your industry or community. Become a resource. Get mentioned in #FollowFridays (*http://followfridays.com/*) by someone who is well known. This is how more people will follow you.

Also add your Twitter link in your signatures in any offline and online marketing campaigns. Make it easy on your site for people to follow you on Twitter. Cross-promote your friends' tweets and have them do the same. Make use of various Twitter tools to optimize your time spent on Twitter.

You can do many things with Twitter. Explore the Twitter API documentation at *http://apiwiki.twitter.com/* for ideas. You can find an example of Twitter API programming toward the end of this chapter.

See whether your competitors are on Twitter. Read your competitors' tweets and see how many followers they have. As you tweet, use relevant keywords without looking spammy.

Twitter tools

Literally hundreds of Twitter tools are available online. This can be attributed to Twitter's API resources that make it easy to tap into the Twitter database. Table 15-1 lists some of the popular Twitter tools and resources as of this writing.

Table 15-1. Twitter tools and resources

Tool/resource	Description
Twitter Search (*http://search.twitter.com*)	Twitter search engine (formerly Summize)
TweetGrid (*http://tweetgrid.com/*)	Twitter search dashboard in real time
Hashtags (*http://hashtags.org/*)	Directory of hash tags on Twitter
GroupTweet (*http://grouptweet.com/*)	Tool to send private messages to a group
TweetBeep (*http://tweetbeep.com/*)	Site that sends you alerts when people are tweeting about you or your company
TweetDeck (*http://tweetdeck.com/beta/*)	Application that allows integrated Twitter and Facebook activities
TweetMeme (*http://tweetmeme.com/*)	Tool that tracks most popular links on Twitter
Twellow (*http://www.twellow.com/*)	Twitter directory, search, and Yellow Pages
Twitpic (*http://twitpic.com/*)	Site for sharing photos on Twitter
Bit.ly (*http://bit.ly/*)	One of the best URL shorteners
TinyURL (*http://tinyurl.com/*)	Another good URL shortener

Overcoming limitations

Microblogging with Twitter has its limitations. You can do only so much with a single tweet. You have only 140 characters to describe what you are doing. Anytime you want to share a long URL, you may run over the 140-character limit.

To create the most efficient tweets, make them even shorter than the 140-character limit. This way, anyone wishing to retweet your tweets can do so more easily. This is your way of ensuring that your tweets can propagate to their fullest potential.

To solve this character limitation problem, you can use URL shortening services. In addition to Bit.ly and TinyURL, you can also use BudURL (*http://budurl.com/*).

Most of the popular URL shortening providers offer live stats (including geolocations) and a history of clicks on your shortened URLs. For example, suppose you want to shorten the following URL:

> *http://www.seowarrior.net/search-engine/search-engine-and-internet-censorship
> -not-every-country-is-open/*

Here is how this URL looks when converted to its short version using the Bit.ly service:

> *http://bit.ly/ne8HX*

URL shortening providers utilize the HTTP permanent redirect (301) when redirecting traffic to the destination URL.

Twitter is a popular topic. For additional Twitter tips, you may wish to read *The Twitter Book (http://oreilly.com/catalog/9780596802813/)* by Tim O'Reilly and Sarah Milstein (O'Reilly).

Content-Sharing Sites

The big players in content sharing have made it relatively simple for anyone to leverage their platforms in the creation of media-rich content.

YouTube

Three former employees of PayPal created YouTube in 2005. They sold YouTube to Google in 2006. YouTube is by far the most visited video sharing site on the Internet. In January 2009, YouTube enjoyed an audience of 100+ million people in the United States alone (*http://bit.ly/11Xxcu*).

You can post a video on YouTube.com and then embed the same video on your website by following a relatively painless process. You can simply insert the Embed code as supplied by YouTube (and highlighted in Figure 15-2) within your HTML page. You can also download many custom YouTube widgets to do the same thing.

Uploading your videos to YouTube is also easy. Make sure you optimize your video title, description, and associated tags. Also, specify in the privacy setting that you want to make your video public.

Once you upload your video, you can share it by connecting your YouTube account with Facebook, MySpace, and Google Reader. Take advantage of these opportunities to spread your news.

You may also consider using YouTube's video annotations and AudioSwap features. Video annotations allow you to add pop-up speech bubbles, pop-up boxed notes, textual spotlights that are shown when the mouse moves over a predefined video area, and video pauses. The AudioSwap feature lets you add background music to spice up your videos.

As of this writing, YouTube does not allow you to make your videos clickable (to go to a destination URL of your choice). Nonetheless, you can use a watermark image to show your URL in your video as well as to use a call to action during your video presentation. YouTube does allow you to create links to your other YouTube videos.

Figure 15-2. YouTube.com: The most popular content-sharing site

If you plan to create a lot of videos, you may also want to consider creating your own YouTube channel. Many sites have successfully used YouTube videos in their marketing campaigns. Viral videos can be a great asset to your link-building campaigns. Some of the most viral videos get downloaded by millions of people.

If you've got good-quality videos, YouTube users will begin to subscribe to your content. Anytime you upload a new video, your subscribers will be notified. For more information on creating YouTube videos, refer to the YouTube Handbook (*http://www .youtube.com/t/yt_handbook_home*).

YouTube Insight provides granular reporting capabilities, including geostats. It also offers a paid Promoted Video option (*https://ads.youtube.com/*). When users search for specific keywords, promoted videos show up at the top of the search results.

YouTube videos show up in the blended Google search results as well. For a video to show up on either Google search results or YouTube's front page, it has to be popular and highly rated. Google uses a special algorithm when deciding what videos to show and in which order. It uses multiple ranking factors including video title, video description, video tags, number of views, and user ratings. When including YouTube videos on your site, you may wish to place them on their own HTML page with the appropriate relevant copy and text transcripts.

Utilizing YouTube's videos is a good way to increase the popularity of your site. Modern Internet users prefer videos over text. Using YouTube is free. You do not have to pay to embed your videos seamlessly into your site's pages.

YouTube tools and resources. Many tools and resources are available for the YouTube platform. Table 15-2 lists some of the popular tools and resources.

Table 15-2. YouTube tools and resources

Tool/resource	Description
YouTube APIs and Tools (*http://code.google.com/apis/youtube/overview.html*)	Official YouTube APIs
iDesktop.tv (*http://www.idesktop.tv/index.html*)	Desktop YouTube application
Mappeo.net (*http://www.mappeo.net/*)	Mashup of Google Maps and YouTube videos
YouTube API Extraction Tool (*http://tinyurl.com/4v2aly*)	API extraction tool for YouTube
Viral Video Chart (*http://viralvideochart.unrulymedia.com*)	Top viral videos (from YouTube and others)
TimeTube (*http://www.dipity.com/mashups/timetube*)	Video timeline mashup

Flickr

Ludicorp, a Canadian company, created Flickr in 2004. Only a year later, Flickr was acquired by Yahoo!. Flickr is still the most popular photo sharing site on the Internet. The basic Flickr idea is about sharing and organizing photos. You can upload multiple photos at once, group photos in sets and collections, and make them either private or public.

What YouTube is for video, Flickr is for photos and images. From a marketing perspective, the objective is still the same: engage people with your shared media. If you are in the business of producing pictures or graphical images (e.g., photography), Flickr is your natural choice among all of the social media sites. Flickr is more than just a picture sharing service. You can participate in discussions, let others comment on your pictures, and join groups in your niche.

Flickr tips. When uploading your photos, make sure you optimize your photos with rich keywords. Each picture can be described by several fields, including title, description, and tag fields.

When searching through Flickr, find people who are ranked the highest for a particular keyword of your choice. Post favorable comments to their photos while telling them to see your picture(s). Also make sure you optimize your profile with keyword-rich and relevant links and information.

It is possible for your Flickr page to rank higher than your site pages for a particular keyword. Join groups pertinent to your niche. Use the Flickr map feature to place your photos to specific geolocations. Flickr also offers a video sharing service. It was first offered to paid accounts, but is now available to everyone for free. The only catch is that the videos must be no more than 90 seconds long.

Flickr tools and resources. Many Flickr tools and resources are available on the Internet. They come in free and paid flavors. Table 15-3 lists some of the popular Flickr tools and resources.

Table 15-3. Flickr tools and resources

Tool/resource	Description
Flickr Tools (*http://www.flickr.com/tools/*)	Mobile, desktop, email, and Mac photo uploaders
Flickr Search (*http://www.flickr.com/search/*)	Flickr search capability
Batch Organize (*http://flickr.com/photos/organize/*)	Organizer tool for creating photo sets
Flump (*http://tinyurl.com/6zwswz*)	Downloads public photos for specific accounts
Foldr Monitr (*http://rebeleos.com/FoldrMonitr/*)	Freeware utility that monitors a folder for new images
Earth Album (*http://www.earthalbum.com/*)	Flickr mashup of the most beautiful pictures from around the world
FlickrSync (*http://flickrsync.freehostia.com/*)	Flickr file synchronization tool

Podcasts

You can think of a podcast as a taped radio show available for download. Typically, podcasts are syndicated via RSS feeds. Podcasts are usually stored in the MP3 or AAC sound format, which you can play on your computer or on any modern portable media player. Content publishers often choose the AAC format due to its smaller size and enhanced features, such as chapter markers that can include images and captions.

You can find podcasts in many ways. You can use Apple's iTunes player, Audible.com, Podcast.com, Podcast Alley (*http://www.podcastalley.com/*), and many other resources. If you are using iTunes, simply go to the Podcast menu item to find desired podcasts.

You can do several things in terms of podcast SEO. You should have text transcripts of all your MP3 files. All your MP3 files should use keyword-rich filenames. You should also consider submitting your podcasts to specialized directories. Announce all your new podcasts on your site.

Podcasts provide another channel for marketing your products or services. The next subsection talks about Podcast.com, which ties the world of podcasts to the social networking paradigm.

Podcast.com. When you go to the Podcast.com website, you should first register for an account. After registration, you may want to set up your profile, as you are automatically assigned your own home page at *http://my.podcast.com/userid/*, as well as its mobile equivalent at *http://my.podcast.com/seowarrior/mobile/*. Your home page is visible to the public, and you are allowed to add your website link to your profile. As of this writing, Google is indexing more than 130,000 user home pages.

Search for podcasts in your niche. Pick the ones you like and subscribe to them. Add friends (using the Add Buddy option) and see what other people are listening to. Share your selections by email or via social bookmarks available on the site.

Add your own podcasts. Use *http://ping.podcast.com/ping.php* to inform Podcast.com of your new content. Creating podcasts is relatively simple. You can use the Windows Sound Recorder and an inexpensive microphone to create your own sound recordings. Most people use more advanced audio editors and recorders. One of the most popular programs is Audacity (*http://audacity.sourceforge.net/*). Audacity is free and comes in Windows, Mac, and Linux versions.

iTunes podcast publishing. You can publish your podcast to the iTunes podcast distribution service. The steps involved include the creation of your RSS podcast feed. For more information, visit *http://bit.ly/4P3n4*.

Social Bookmarking Sites

A variety of social bookmarking sites are on the Internet. Content publishers should make it easy for users to bookmark their content by placing social bookmarking icons on their sites. We covered social bookmarking in detail in Chapter 12. The following subsections talk about the most popular players in the social bookmarking domain.

Digg

According to Compete, Digg was visited by more than 38 million unique visitors in May 2009 (*http://siteanalytics.compete.com/twitter.com+digg.com/?metric=uv*). Digg is the current leader in the social bookmarking domain. Digg is also a community of social bookmarking people.

Digg users can bookmark and share articles, images, videos, or any other interesting content. The more "diggs" a URL gets, the better. Most popular URLs get surfaced on the front page of Digg.com. The links on Digg's home page are not using `nofollow` (as of this writing).

As with any social media site, register your Digg account. Complete your profile with keyword-rich profile information. Upon registration, you will have your own home page at *http://digg.com/users/userid*. You can share your Digg activities on Facebook, and you can synchronize your personal profile information on both sites.

Start to "digg" stories. Anything you post to Digg will be seen by the Digg community. As a result, spam will not work. For best results, you will need to become an active participant in the Digg community. Participation is crucial. Digg a few articles per day. Write comments. Build friendships. Be consistent.

You can install a Digg web browser toolbar to submit new content, or you can use social bookmarking icons found on other sites. Alternatively, you can take the more manual approach of going to the Digg website. Before submitting anything new, use the Search function to check whether the URL has already been submitted.

When submitting your new content, be sure to use keyword-rich content titles and descriptions. Also, try to pick the most appropriate topic (category). Ask your friends (contacts) to digg your content. Visit *http://digg.com/tools/* and *http://apidoc.digg.com/* for various Digg tools and the Digg API, respectively.

StumbleUpon

As of this writing, StumbleUpon has more than seven million users. Upon registering with StumbleUpon, users choose their interests and are prompted to install the StumbleUpon toolbar. You can import your friends from Hotmail or other email accounts when creating your account and setting up your profile. Note that StumbleUpon creates your home page as *http://userid.stumbleupon.com*.

Once your toolbar is installed, you can click the Stumble button to channel-surf pages in your area of interest. Upon viewing different pages, you have an option to approve the page by clicking on the thumbs-up icon or disapprove it by clicking on the thumbs-down icon. StumbleUpon uses its recommendation engine as follows (*http://www.stumbleupon.com/technology/*):

> StumbleUpon integrates peer-to-peer and social networking principles with one-click blogging to create an emergent content referral system. Our patent-pending Toolbar system automates the collection, distribution and review of web content within an

intuitive social framework, providing users with a browsing experience which resembles "channel-surfing" the web. This architecture has easily scaled to millions [of] users.

StumbleUpon does not use the `nofollow` link attribute on its home page as of this writing. The more thumbs-up icons you get, the more views your site will get.

Social Networking Sites

In this section, we will discuss three of the most popular social networking sites: Facebook, MySpace, and LinkedIn. Each of these sites has a counterpart mobile site: *http://m.facebook.com*, *http://m.myspace.com*, and *http://m.linkedin.com*.

Facebook

As of this writing, Facebook is the absolute frontrunner of all sites in the social media market. According to some, it may eventually become more important than Google. From the user perspective, Facebook's concepts are not much different from other social networking sites.

The growth of Facebook is astounding. It is one of the most visited websites on the Internet. According to Alexa's traffic rank, Facebook is currently ranked fourth (*http://www.alexa.com/siteinfo/facebook.com*). According to Compete, Facebook gets 8% less traffic than Google and 17% more traffic than Yahoo (*http://siteanalytics.compete.com/facebook.com+google.com+yahoo.com/*).

Facebook account types. There are two types of Facebook accounts: regular user accounts and business accounts. To open a regular user account, register your account, fill in your profile, and you are ready to connect with your friends, share your photos, share information, and provide your current status. After registration, Facebook provides you with your very own home page with the following format: *http://www.facebook.com/userid*.

Companies should almost always use a Facebook Pages account. This type of account allows you to build your own branded page on Facebook. Facebook users can become fans of your company. Company pages have a similar user interface as regular Facebook user pages. When users search Facebook, they get mixed results with Facebook user links and company (page) links. Companies can post their website links for everyone to see.

When companies update their Facebook pages, their fans get notified. Use these notifications to your advantage. Use Facebook events to organize real social events and parties with your friends or your organization. Use Facebook discussions to talk about your products and services. One example of a Facebook Pages profile is that of the Starbucks franchise (*http://www.facebook.com/Starbucks*). Figure 15-3 shows the Starbucks page in Facebook as of this writing.

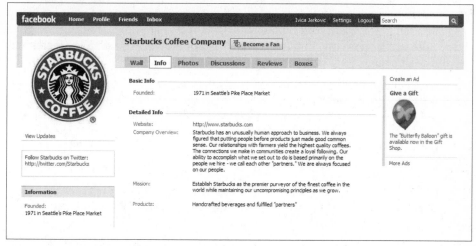

Figure 15-3. Facebook Pages: Starbucks

Facebook tips.   The major search engines do not fully index Facebook's content, thereby limiting your SEO efforts. The basic public profile page links are indexed and do show up in search results. Sometimes even these basic Facebook profile pages will show up on Google before the principal site links do. For that reason, it is worth creating your Facebook account and placing relevant keywords in your public profile page.

There are three basic forms of Facebook marketing. The first is the community-based approach, in which you build, connect, and cultivate relationships. The second type comes in the form of building Facebook applications. To see how you can develop social applications for Facebook, visit *http://developers.facebook.com/*. The last type of marketing comes in the form of using Facebook Ads. Facebook Ads allow you to target specific demographics when building your ad campaigns.

MySpace

MySpace is no longer as important as it once was, but it's still very important, particularly for media companies, bands, and so forth. Over the past two years, MySpace has made several changes in a bid to reclaim its top spot in the social networking domain. So far it hasn't worked.

Traditionally, MySpace was geared toward the music crowd. MySpace rose to its heights in part thanks to a large teenage audience. MySpace allowed musicians to upload their albums, which were sold through the MySpace Records label.

After registering your MySpace account, you should complete your profile information. Add some photos and videos. Many people refuse the Add a Friend request if a profile is not accompanied by a picture. Search for and add your friends. Make posts to your bulletin board. All your friends get to see your posts. You can also add videos to your bulletin posts.

Stay away from spam on MySpace. Use your profile real estate to add your company links. You can also update your mood (status) settings. Participate in forums in your niche. Add your own events. Join other events. Reconnect with former classmates and find out what's happening with your school.

The Search functionality of MySpace.com is still handled by Google. Marketers can leverage the MySpace advertising program by placing ads on MySpace. Developers can leverage developer tools at *http://developer.myspace.com/community/* to create engaging MySpace applications and more.

LinkedIn

LinkedIn is another social networking platform, geared toward professionals. It is a way for people to get in touch with their former, present, and perhaps future colleagues, coworkers, managers, and friends.

After you register, LinkedIn will remind you to complete your profile information. You can upload your picture, join different groups (associations), and start communicating with your contacts. After finishing your profile, start building your network by using (importing) your existing email account contacts. You can ask questions and be part of discussions. If you need to hire resources, you can post your hiring requirements.

LinkedIn lets you receive updates on your existing connections (and they get to see yours). See who they have connected with recently. Find out what they are doing and more. You can also link with your former classmates. You can recommend your contacts, and they can recommend you. You can join, browse, and follow many groups on LinkedIn. You can also create your own groups.

Update your current status to let everyone know what you are doing or working on. LinkedIn is a great tool for building and cultivating contacts.

Social Media Strategy

When forming a social media strategy, start by understanding the benefits and associated risks. Continue by building a tangible strategy, which you can use to get your company's buy-in. Start implementing your strategy. If your goals are not met, consider revising your strategy. Take corrective steps along the way and evaluate your benefits against your costs.

Do Some Research

Try to figure out which social media platform is suitable for your company. The answer to that should be linked to where your audience is. On what platforms do you see the most engaging audience in your niche? Whichever platform you choose, you will need to invest your time. There is no other way around it. You cannot be in it this month, skip the next month, and then come back to it again the following month. Social networking is a daily chore.

Understand the benefits

SMO is not just about your website visibility or your company brand. SMO allows for many other benefits. Fostering open dialogs with your clients allows for faster product or service feedback loops. Obtaining instant feedback can be an empowering prospect when developing new products or services.

You can also use these discussions to improve your current offerings. SMO can help you build your perceived trust, influence, and authority. The byproduct of all this is a greater power to influence your clients. When done correctly, SMO can bring huge amounts of traffic and profit. Achieving great social media traction allows for natural link building from an SEO perspective.

Understand the risks

It is important to understand that social media campaigns come with certain risks. All content is scrutinized by your web audience. If you're not careful, you could ruin your entire brand and image.

Another potential risk is in wasting your time and resources. Marketing departments do not have infinite budgets. It is possible that the costs will outweigh the perceived benefits. Nobody can forecast the exact results. Account for known and unknown risks.

Understand the process

All social media platforms have some things in common. All platforms, to be used to their full potential, require their users to register for an account. After this comes creating and optimizing your profile. Be sure to include your business or website links.

The next steps include finding and building your friends network, participating in various outlets such as comment posting, forums, and discussions, sharing your content including links and website feeds, and more. While doing all of this, it is important to continue creating media-rich, engaging experiences as well as focusing your work effort on your specific niche.

Formulate Your Strategy

With your research out of the way, present your information to the key stakeholders to get their buy-in as well as budget and resource commitments. After you know your budget and resources, start defining your short-, medium-, and long-term goals.

Define (audit) check points to track your progress and to allow for corrective actions. Determine how you will report and measure your progress. Also define your exit points and any contingency plans should you run out of money or in case of unexpected problems.

Implement Your Strategy

At first, do not try to do too much. Pick a couple of the top social bookmarking sites (e.g., Delicious, Digg), and then optimize your current site with their icons. Next, register with one or two of the top social networking sites (e.g., Facebook, Twitter). Take some time to fully learn these platforms. Also, consider creating viral videos on YouTube.

Reevaluate your strategy

Create monthly progress reports. Analyze your current costs and benefits. Determine whether you have to make adjustments. Determine what is working and what is not producing desired results. Try to replicate things that work to amplify their cumulative effects.

Using Automation

Many tools and vendor-specific APIs are available to do custom development for just about any social networking site. You can also design custom scripts. Before you go this route, check what's currently available online. Sometimes you may have no choice but to create an in-house design to fit your requirements.

Some of the pitfalls of custom design include the need to continuously monitor and modify the scripts when the host site changes its site structure (in case of scraper scripts). When creating automated agent scripts, be mindful of the target site. Create your scripts to emulate regular user behavior with appropriate pauses between clicks. Otherwise, the host sites might ban your account.

Creating a Twitter Scheduler

Many complementary tools, sites, and services are available for most of the social media sites. It is wise to explore what can help you achieve your social media strategy. You can also automate some tasks.

For example, if you are implementing a strategy for Twitter, instead of worrying about the steady flow of your tweets, you can create a simple application to send prerecorded scheduled tweets. Imagine a simple application as described in the use case diagram in Figure 15-4.

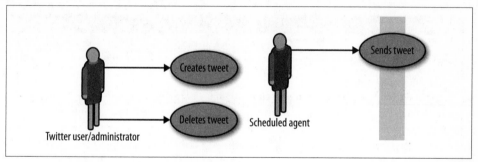

Figure 15-4. Twitter scheduler: Use case diagram

Creating the database

You can use PHP and MySQL to create a simple Twitter scheduler application to send your tweets. To create such an application, we will use a single database table (queue) to store some tweets. Here is how the queue table will look when created in MySQL:

```
+---------+--------+------+-----+---------+----------------+
| Field   | Type   | Null | Key | Default | Extra          |
+---------+--------+------+-----+---------+----------------+
| id      | int(6) | NO   | PRI | NULL    | auto_increment |
| message | text   | NO   |     | NULL    |                |
| status  | int(1) | NO   |     | 0       |                |
+---------+--------+------+-----+---------+----------------+
```

The queue table will contain only three fields: id, message, and status. The id (integer) field auto-increments by default. The message (text) field contains your tweets. The status (integer) field indicates whether the tweet was sent. A status value of 0 indicates that a tweet was not sent. A status value of 1 indicates that a tweet was sent. Here is the SQL fragment required to create the queue table:

```
CREATE TABLE `mytest`.`queue` (
`id` INT( 6 ) NOT NULL AUTO_INCREMENT PRIMARY KEY ,
`message` TEXT NOT NULL ,
`status` INT( 1 ) NOT NULL DEFAULT '0'
) ENGINE = MYISAM ;
```

With the database out of the way, we can create a simple HTML/PHP interface.

Building the interface

All we need for our interface is a simple HTML form that submits future tweets to our MySQL database. It would also be nice to have a visible list of future tweets already stored in the database. Finally, there should be a way to delete unwanted tweets. Figure 15-5 shows how our *index.php* file will look when rendered in a web browser.

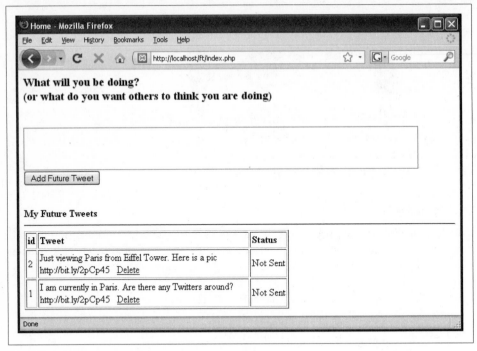

Figure 15-5. Twitter scheduler: Graphical user interface

As you can see in Figure 15-5, the index page is relatively simple. A database query is always called to show stored tweets, just below the new tweet entry form.

When you click on the Add Future Tweet button, the form submits the new tweet to the database, bringing you back to the same screen as the screen in which your newly added tweet appears on the top of the My Future Tweets list.

Sending tweets

We can send Twitter updates using the Twitter API. We can use PHP and `curl` to send our tweet by visiting *http://twitter.com/statuses/update.xml*. The following code fragment (*sendTweet.php*) is used to send a single tweet:

```php
<?php

include("config.php");

mysql_connect(localhost,$username,$password);
@mysql_select_db($database) or die( "Unable to select my database");

### get the tweet
$result = mysql_query("select id, message from queue where status=0
order by id asc LIMIT 1");

$row = mysql_fetch_array($result);
```

```
### send the tweet
$curl_handle = curl_init();
curl_setopt($curl_handle, CURLOPT_URL, "$tURL");
curl_setopt($curl_handle, CURLOPT_CONNECTTIMEOUT, 2);
curl_setopt($curl_handle, CURLOPT_RETURNTRANSFER, 1);
curl_setopt($curl_handle, CURLOPT_POST, 1);

$message = $row['message'];

curl_setopt($curl_handle, CURLOPT_POSTFIELDS, "status=$message");
curl_setopt($curl_handle, CURLOPT_USERPWD, "$tusrid:$tpasswd");

$response = curl_exec($curl_handle);

curl_close($curl_handle);

// get the status message
if (empty($response)) {
    echo 'tweet not delivered';
} else {
    echo 'tweet delivered';
    ###update db status
    $mid = $row['id'];
    mysql_query("UPDATE queue SET status = 1 WHERE id = $mid");
}

mysql_close();

?>
```

We used a POST request coupled with the user credentials necessary to handle the basic authentication used at *http://twitter.com/statuses/update.xml*. Note that this link is stored in an external configuration file and is referenced by the $tURL variable.

Scheduling tweets

The web part of the application does not submit the tweet(s). We leave that to a scheduled job. Now we come to the part that actually initiates the tweet uploads. In a Linux-flavored environment you can use crontab to create your schedule.

Let's suppose we want to send five tweets per day at 7:00 a.m., 9:00 a.m., 11:00 a.m., 1:00 p.m., and 3:00 p.m. Execute crontab -e to edit the crontab list, and enter the following:

```
# Tweet 5 times a day at  7am, 9am, 11am, 1pm and 3pm
* 8,10,12,14,16 * * * php sendTweet.php
```

You can also send tweets manually by using the same command (php sendTweet.php) in your shell window.

Extending the application

We can extend the application we have built to do many more things. We can add custom authentication and RSS integration, among other things. See Appendix A for the full source code, or visit *http://book.seowarrior.net* to download the code.

Google and Social Media Sites

Google is not sitting on the sidelines of the social media playing field. With its acquisitions of YouTube (the most popular video sharing site), FeedBurner (the most popular web feed tracker), and Jaiku (a microblogging site similar to Twitter), Google is making a statement regarding its interest in the social media domain. YouTube is by far Google's most popular social media property, with tens of millions of daily video downloads.

Google indexes hundreds of millions of pages from its competing social media sites. Table 15-4 lists the Google index size for certain sites as of this writing. Facebook is currently by far the most popular social media site, followed by MySpace, Flickr, YouTube (owned by Google), and Twitter.

Table 15-4. Google index size of major social media sites

Site	Type	Indexed pages
MySpace.com	Social networking	217 million
Facebook.com	Social networking	378 million
Twitter.com	Microblogging	89.3 million
Digg.com	Social bookmarking	16.8 million
Technorati.com	Blogs	9.67 million
StumbleUpon.com	Social bookmarking	4.04 million
YouTube.com (Google)	Video sharing	144 million
Flickr.com (Yahoo!)	Picture sharing	169 million

In mid-2009, there was a lot of speculation about Google acquiring Twitter. A custom search engine called Twoogle is just fueling the speculations. Figure 15-6 shows its current interface. Searches in Twoogle produce mixed results, including results from Twitter.com and Jaiku.com as well as the regular Google results.

Where Google is currently behind is in the real-time search realm.

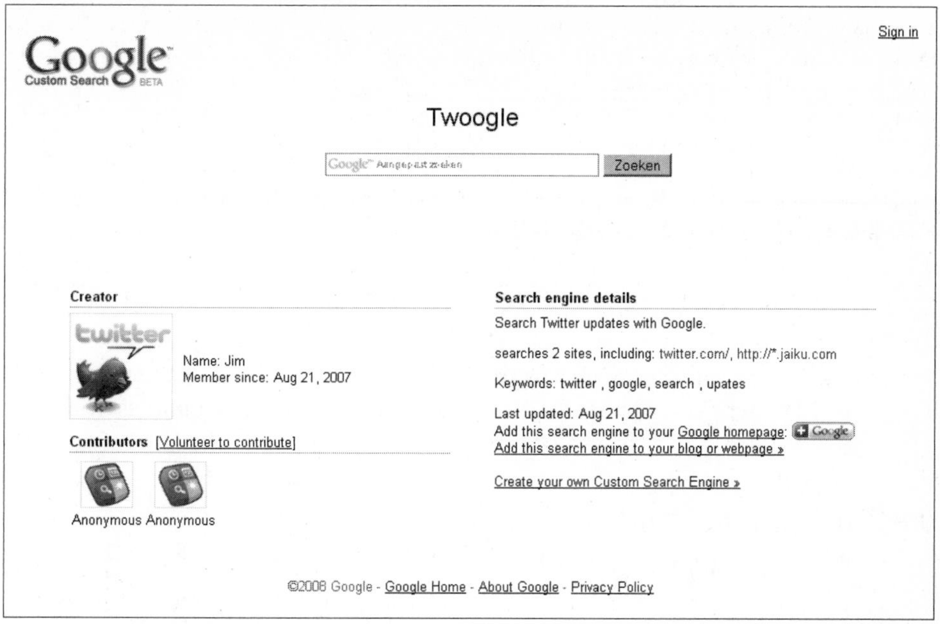

Figure 15-6. Twoogle

Real-Time Search

Theoretically speaking, real-time search across the Internet is virtually impossible. What is possible is collecting a subset of newly posted information across an array of sites and making this available relatively quickly.

For real-time search to be viable, it has to address many different factors but answer one basic question: what is relevant at this moment? The viability of real-time search relies on its heavy use of the social networking community sites as well as in designing algorithms to filter junk versus relevant, important content on the fly.

Nonetheless, live search seems to be the next big thing. Twitter already has "real-time" search capabilities from its acquisition of Summize (*http://search.twitter.com*). There are many up-and-coming real-time-search contenders, including Scoopler (*http://www .scoopler.com/*), OneRiot (*http://www.oneriot.com/*), Topsy (*http://topsy.com/*), and TweetMeme (*http://tweetmeme.com/*), among others.

Twitter Real-Time Search

Twitter is the frontrunner when it comes to real-time search. Tweets are searchable instantly. If you create a page, Google does not index it until its crawler finds it. So, in that sense, Twitter has a head start when compared to Google.

When it comes to Twitter's real-time search, tweet keyword relevancy is the top-ranking factor. Twitter uses a different kind of keyword matching when producing its search results. If you search for *watching TV*, you will get results that contain both terms.

Twitter search produces up to 1,500 tweet search results broken down to 15 tweets per page (as of this writing). Even the last search result out of the 1,500 can be only a few minutes old, depending on your search keyword. For hot topics, this may even go down to a few seconds. Twitter's search is case-insensitive. Twitter does not have any fancy search commands like Google does, but in time it is expected that Twitter will catch on in that department.

Tweet scheduler applications (such as the one we developed in this chapter) will play a big role in Twitter search. What matters now will not matter a few minutes from now or one hour from now; this is what the Twitter paradigm is all about.

OneRiot Real-Time Search

OneRiot is one of the frontrunners in real-time search. OneRiot uses the concept of a Pulse Rank to rank real-time content. Tobias Peggs (of OneRiot) states the following (*http://bit.ly/3cZdzy*):

> We have invented a new ranking algorithm—Pulse Rank—to drive the realtime ordering of our search results. Think of Pulse Rank as PageRank for the realtime web. If PageRank reflects historical dependability, then Pulse Rank reflects current social buzz. Pulse Rank is the ranking algorithm for the 40% of searches that traditional search engines struggle with.

Some of the factors used in OneRiot's indexing algorithms include freshness, domain authority, people authority, and acceleration. For more information, read the full article at *http://blog.oneriot.com/content/2009/06/oneriot-pulse-rank/*.

Summary

In this chapter, we discussed the importance of coordinating all of your online marketing and SEO efforts. Once you know your site is in order, optimize it for social bookmarking. Make it easy for people to share your site by using linkable social bookmarking icons.

Don't go overboard, however. Use just a few of the big social bookmarking sites. Expand your campaign by participating in social media sites. Explore the creation and sharing of viral content. Before spending too much time on any particular social networking platform, know your audience. Sites such as *http://www.DandyID.com/cmn/claimmyname* make it easy to reserve your name or brand across multiple social networking sites.

As you learned from reading this chapter, it is easy to see how powerful a Twitter presence can be. Just think about its paradigm. Write useful tweets. Get people to follow you. Show up in search engine results. Cultivate many followers over time. People are typically genuinely interested in those they follow. Those who are followed therefore have a great influence. A Twitterer with a large following is perceived as an authority. Becoming an authority is the key to monetizing your Twitter presence.

Finally, be ready for the real-time search. Strategize with scheduled tweets.

## CHAPTER 16

Search Engine Marketing

You can use search engine marketing (SEM) platforms to benchmark your SEO efforts. This chapter is a brief overview of two important Google SEM platforms: Google Ad-Words and Google AdSense.

Google AdWords is the number one SEM platform on the Internet today, and is the subject of many books. Although we cannot cover every single detail of AdWords in this chapter, we will spend some time on the most important features of the platform.

Google AdSense is the extended arm of AdWords. Whereas you can use AdWords to test, validate, and improve your keyword research, you can use AdSense to earn income from Google by showing contextual ads. You can also use AdSense ads on your target web pages to see whether relevant ads will show up to further validate your targeted keywords.

We'll start this chapter by covering the major SEM players and the basics of the pay-per-click (PPC) paradigm. We'll talk about the factors and variables influencing visitor conversion, and the associated conversion rate. We'll also discuss common PPC terminology.

Before we discuss AdWords in detail, we'll cover the fundamentals of the SEM process. Our coverage of AdWords includes basic campaigns, ad groups, and ad setup. In between, we'll cover the important topics of keyword match types, including broad match, phrase match, exact match, and negative match.

We'll also spend some time discussing AdWords testing, including A/B testing and multivariate testing, which can help you increase your conversion rates and lower your advertising costs.

Next, we'll cover the basics of AdSense, including installation, ad types, and more. We'll end the chapter by examining ways to use SEM for SEO purposes.

The World of SEM

By SEM I am primarily referring to underlying PPC platforms. The introduction of the first PPC platform in 1996 is credited to Bill Gross, the founder of Idealab and Goto.com. SEM is really the main tool that keeps search engine companies in business. Holding the biggest search market share, Google has made a fortune with its AdWords platform. Although the lion's share of the advertising dollar is spent on Google, four additional players—Yahoo!, Microsoft, Yandex, and Baidu—also have a stake in the PPC realm, across the globe and in specific ethnic regions. According to Wikipedia (*http://en.wikipedia.org/wiki/Pay_per_click*):

> Pay per click (PPC) is an Internet advertising model used on search engines, advertising networks, and content sites, such as blogs, in which advertisers pay their host only when their ad is clicked. With search engines, advertisers typically bid on keyword phrases relevant to their target market. Content sites commonly charge a fixed price per click rather than use a bidding system. Websites that utilize PPC ads will display an advertisement when a keyword query matches an advertiser's keyword list, or when a content site displays relevant content. Such advertisements are called sponsored links or sponsored ads, and appear adjacent to or above organic results on search engine results pages, or anywhere a web developer chooses on a content site.

PPC Platforms

Google AdWords is not the only player in the world; many other viable PPC platforms exist. Table 16-1 lists some of the major players in the PPC domain. Note that not all PPC platforms are built around underlying search engines.

Table 16-1. Major PPC platforms

Platform	Details
Google AdWords (*http://adwords.google.com*)	Offers the widest reach and the largest number of impressions of all the platforms (boasts 80% of the entire global search audience). Extends its reach with the Google AdSense platform.
Yahoo! Search Marketing (*http://searchmarketing.yahoo.com*)	Offers similar (albeit fewer) features as Google AdWords. Boasts 53 million daily unique searches and 2.8 billion monthly searches. Supports its own content network.
Microsoft adCenter (*http://adCenter.microsoft.com*)	Offers similar features as Yahoo! Search Marketing and Google AdWords. Ads appear on their own content network, including MSN, MSNBC, the *Wall Street Journal*, and Fox Sports.
Ask.com Sponsored Listings (*http://sponsoredlistings.ask.com*)	Provides a large ad distribution network reaching more than 73 million unique users. Has a partnership to show AdWords ads on Ask.com in addition to its own PPC network.
Miva (*http://miva.com*)	Offers two PPC networks: core and precision. Targets verticals across myriad content sites.
7Search (*http://7search.com*)	Partners with many lesser-known search engines.

Platform	Details
Kanoodle	Provides many tools, including those for ad scheduling and contextual ads.
(http://kanoodle.com)	

PPC platform selection

Click fraud refers to unethical (usually) competitor ad clicks designed to increase competitors' marketing costs. All of the big players are paying special attention to click fraud and taking action against offenders. To avoid click fraud, stick with reputable SEM platforms. If you are just starting with PPC, you may want to concentrate on only one major platform. Figure 16-1 depicts the AdWords platform.

Most click fraud is now automatic—using bot networks that spoof IP addresses—and is unlikely to be competitor-driven. Most click fraud occurs in the content network by AdSense publishers looking to unethically drive up their AdSense revenues.

As shown in Figure 16-1, advertisers create ads in AdWords that Google uses on its search result pages as well as on its content and search partner sites. Website owners use AdSense to generate Google income by showing Google ads. Web searchers and the partner site visitors click on Google AdWords ads, generating a revenue stream for Google and its associated partner sites.

Having the biggest reach has its advantages. If you have to decide among the biggest players, stick with Google AdWords. In a nutshell, AdWords provides by far the most comprehensive set of tools and features when compared to any of its competitors.

PPC Fundamentals

In this section, we will look at the PPC paradigm in a general sense, which should be applicable to any platform. We'll focus on the kinds of variables you will face in your PPC campaigns.

Know your variables

Let's start by looking at an example. Say you have a website selling one product. Let's assume the following information is true about the product:

```
Product A
======================
Total Cost with S&H: $20
Online Sale Price: $50
Total Margin: $30
Acceptable Margin: $15
```

Your problem is that you have little or no traffic coming to your site, so you are now entertaining the possibility of using a PPC platform to help you with the lack of visitors coming to your site by way of organic search results.

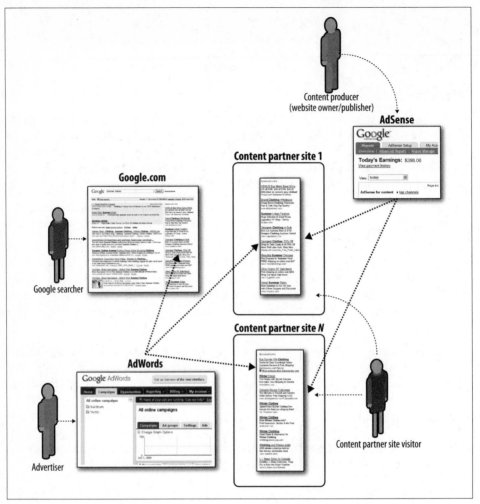

Figure 16-1. Google AdWords platform

Before spending your advertising money, you will do better by doing some basic math and research. Given the information in relation to Product A, it should be clear that to keep a part of your profit you will need to have a sufficient conversion rate so that the net margin is greater than zero (once you subtract the costs of your PPC campaign).

Beating the breakeven point is really not the objective here. You need to consider other associated costs, such as your time. Therefore, you will need to conduct a more detailed cost analysis before coming up with your acceptable margin. For the sake of this example, let's assume your acceptable margin is $15.

In our example, many other (unknown) variables are also at play, as shown in Figure 16-2.

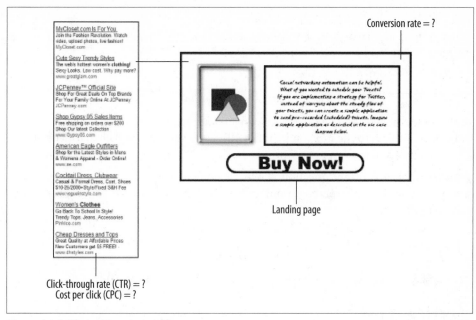

Conversion rate = ?

Landing page

Click-through rate (CTR) = ?
Cost per click (CPC) = ?

Figure 16-2. The unknown variables

Since you are not getting any organic traffic, you may not know much about your eventual landing page conversion rate. Conversion rates vary per keyword, which makes your situation even more interesting (and complicated).

Let's assume you have done all of your research. You estimate that your cost-per-click (CPC) will be $1 (for the sake of simplicity). This means you will need at least 1 visitor out of 30 to buy your product so that you can break even. This also means that to keep your acceptable margin in your pocket, you will need exactly 1 sale for every 15 visitors (or ad clicks).

Another unknown variable is your click-through rate (CTR). You do not know how many people will be clicking on your ad and at what frequency. Although PPC platforms will estimate your traffic, there is no guarantee that these numbers will come true. Your CTR depends on many factors, including the current keyword demand, your ad copy, and your relative ad position.

Let's look at another example. Suppose you are selling another product with the following details:

```
Product B
=======================
Total Cost with S&H: $10
Online Sale Price: $20
Total Margin: $10
Acceptable Margin: $5
CPC: $0.50
```

```
CTR: 0.5%
Landing Page Conversion Rate: ?
```

What is your required landing page conversion rate to break even? Here is how we could calculate the breakeven point:

```
Number of Clicks = Margin/CPC
                 = $10/0.50
                 = 20 clicks (absorbs entire margin)
```

In this case, the required landing page conversion rate is 1/20, or 5%. When you add multiple keywords to the mix, most (if not all) of the variables will change. The goal of all campaigns is to make a net profit.

Another, more important question is what is your required landing page conversion rate to reach your acceptable profit margin? Here is how we can calculate this information:

```
Number of Clicks = Margin/CPC
                 = $5/0.50
                 = 10 clicks (absorbs allowable margin)
```

In this case, the required landing page conversion rate is 1/10, or 10%.

The SEM Process

The SEM process comprises several phases: planning and research, content creation, campaign creation, campaign monitoring and analysis, and campaign refinements.

The SEM process looks similar to the SEO process. Figure 16-3 illustrates the various phase relationships. The process is highly iterative and contains two logical loops, as indicated by the double arrows.

As you can see in Figure 16-3, a minor loop occurs between the campaign monitoring and analysis phase and the campaign refinements phase. A major loop occurs between the campaign monitoring and analysis phase and the planning and research phase. Let's go over the details of each phase.

The planning and research phase

The planning and research phase of the SEM process is similar to the first two phases of the SEO process. In this phase, you are learning about the products and services you are about to advertise, or you are performing additional research and analysis based on your existing campaigns.

The input to this phase includes allocated advertising budgets, product and service information, existing campaign information, and any other information necessary to formulate a new SEM campaign. A large part of this phase is concentrated on keyword research and planning for content creation. In other words, you are brainstorming your keywords and content ideas, and creating your PPC landing pages and ad copy.

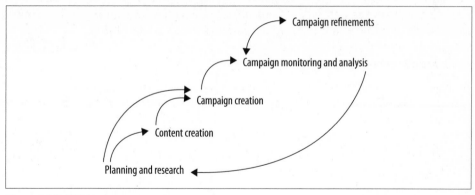

Figure 16-3. SEM process

Chapter 11 covered many different ways to find keywords. In our coverage of Google AdWords, we'll discuss additional keyword topics in a PPC context. The output of this phase can include a keyword list(s) and content requirements.

The content creation phase

The input to the content creation phase includes defined content requirements from the preceding phase as well as any defined (targeted) keywords. Before your PPC campaign can begin, you must have appropriate (actionable) content. Unless you are using PPC for your brand or company awareness, you will almost always point your PPC links to some sort of landing page, and almost never to your home page, as it is too generic.

For example, retail sites selling lots of products may redirect visitors to a specific product page. Sometimes this page may already exist in a satisfactory form. In other cases, the advertiser will create a special landing page if the product page is not converting.

Big established retailers do not need to create fancy landing pages, as visitors usually know who they are and know what to expect, which speaks to the power of brand trust. All landing pages have one thing in common: their main objective is to capture visitors' attention to such an extent that they complete the presented call to action. A call to action can be anything, including completing a survey, purchasing a product or service, or registering on the site.

The output of this phase includes any content required to support the PPC campaign. This can include ad copy, landing pages, and URL information. At the completion of this phase, you should be ready to start your PPC campaign.

The campaign creation phase

The campaign creation phase uses the output of the previous two phases as its campaign input. In this phase, you do two things. You upload the files necessary to support your landing pages to your web server. Soon after, you create your campaigns, ad groups, and ads while utilizing your planned keywords, budgets, and so forth.

The campaign monitoring and analysis phase

In this phase, you monitor your campaign while analyzing the need for any corrective action. You should also be looking for ways to improve your existing campaign. Your competition is not standing still.

The output of this phase could be an assessment/audit from which you can take further action. This action could be making small refinements or improvements, or something as drastic as pausing your campaign and starting all over again.

The campaign refinements phase

The campaign refinements phase is when you take care of the minor and major corrective actions you identified in the preceding phase.

Google AdWords

By far the biggest Google profit maker, AdWords is responsible for Google's meteoric rise. This section provides an overview of the AdWords platform. Although each PPC platform has its own partner sites network, none of them come close to the market penetration of Google AdWords. You can check out Google's partner sites network at *http://www.google.com/adwords/contentnetwork/index.html*.

AdWords Setup

Setting up AdWords is fast and easy. If you already have a Google account, the process is even easier. Let's assume you do not have a Google account.

Creating a Google account

To create a Google account for AdWords, browse to *http://adwords.google.com*. Figure 16-4 shows screenshots of the main steps.

Your screens may not look the same as those shown in Figure 16-4, but the registration process should be straightforward. In one of the initial registration screens, you are presented with a choice between using the Starter Edition or the Standard Edition. Choose the Starter Edition if you are completely new to PPC. Otherwise, choose the Standard Edition.

After you fill out the registration form, you will be instructed to log in to your account to provide your billing information. With AdWords, you can choose to pay either after you get clicks or in advance of future clicks. You can pay either by credit card or a bank

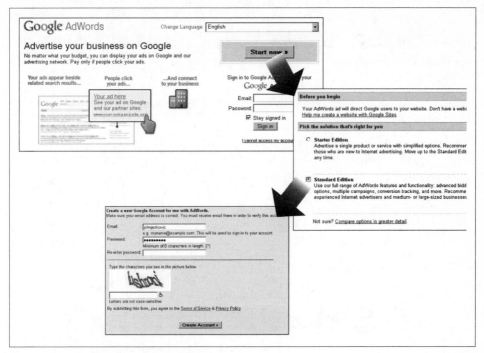

Figure 16-4. Google AdWords installation

transfer. As of this writing, Google charges a one-time activation fee of $10 on the creation of a new account.

By default, the first thing you see when you log in to AdWords is the Account Snapshot home page. You are presented with your account summary information as well as the menu shown in Figure 16-5. Note the menu options. If you hover your mouse pointer over each menu item, additional menu options will appear.

Navigating through AdWords

Navigating through AdWords takes some time to get used to. Figure 16-6 shows all of the current options on the main menu.

Clicking on the Home button brings you back to the Account Snapshot page, which provides a Dashboard-type view of your account. You will find various sections, including alerts, account status, announcements, keyword performance, active campaigns, campaign performance, help, and tips.

Clicking on the Campaign button brings you to the Campaign Summary page. On this page you can set up and modify your campaigns, campaign ad groups, and ads for each of your ad groups. This section of AdWords uses the menu structure shown in Figure 16-7.

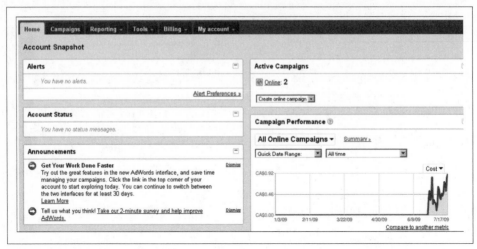

Figure 16-5. Account snapshot

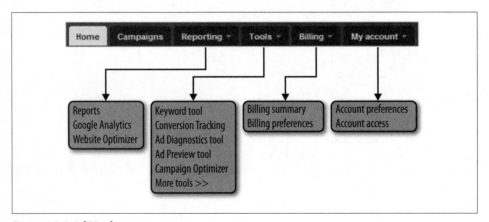

Figure 16-6. AdWords main menu

The Reporting menu item allows you to create and run custom performance reports, use Google Analytics, and use the Website Optimizer tool to increase your conversions. The Tools menu item allows you to go to specific AdWords tools, including the Keyword tool, the Conversion Tracking tool, the Ad Diagnostics tool, the Campaign Optimizer, and more.

The last two main menu buttons are labeled Billing and My Account. In the Billing section, you can see your click and cost summary. You can also change your billing information. In the My Account section, you can change many account settings in addition to letting others manage campaigns associated with your account.

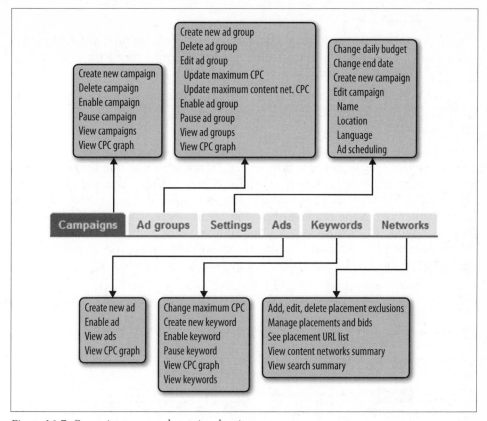

Figure 16-7. Campaign menu and associated actions

You can use three access levels or user roles: administrative, standard, and reports.

Campaign Setup

Assuming you have successfully registered and updated your billing information, you are ready to go. Once you create your ads, they will be displayed in a matter of minutes on the Google search engine. Ads may not show up on Google content and search partner sites unless they are reviewed. Google content partner sites are sites participating in the AdSense program.

Although ads may appear almost immediately, they will not receive full exposure for all potential search matches until they have passed editorial review. In addition, new accounts may experience delayed ad delivery while quality and relevance are established.

Creating a campaign

Creating your campaigns is a straightforward process. From the AdWords home page, select Campaigns→New campaign, which should bring up a page with a rather large form that you need to fill out.

In Figure 16-8, you can see several sections of this form. On the Settings page, in the General section under the "Campaign settings" heading, type your campaign name in the "Campaign name" text box.

Move down the form to the Audience section. For Locations, choose the geographical location in which you want your ads to appear. Do not select the "Bundle: All countries and territories" radio button unless you really do want to target the entire world. Most people will select their own country or countries whose inhabitants speak the same language they do. In the example shown in Figure 16-8, AdWords preselected the Country option, which in my case is Canada. If you click on the "Select one or more other locations" link, AdWords opens another window, giving you all your possible options while showing your selection on a dynamically generated map.

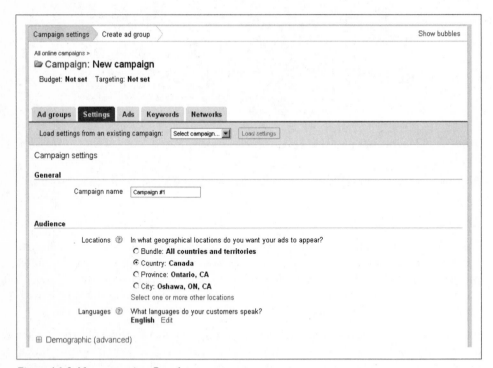

Figure 16-8. New campaign: Part 1

Moving to the bottom of the portion of the form shown in Figure 16-8, you can see the Languages section. AdWords automatically selects your default language (in my case,

English). You can change that by clicking on the Edit link. At the time of this writing, AdWords allows users to select the languages shown in Table 16-2.

Table 16-2. New campaign: Language options

Languages				
Arabic	Dutch	Hindi Hungarian	Norwegian	Spanish
Bulgarian	English	Icelandic	Polish	Swedish
Catalan	Estonian	Indonesian	Portuguese	Thai
Chinese (simplified)	Filipino	Italian Japanese	Romanian	Turkish
Chinese (traditional)	Finnish	Korean	Russian	Ukrainian
Croatian	French German	Latvian	Serbian	Urdu
Czech	Greek	Lithuanian	Slovak Slovenian	Vietnamese
Danish	Hebrew			

Figure 16-9 shows the remainder of the form you need to fill out to start a new campaign. If you expand the "Demographic (advanced)" section, you can set bidding preferences for specific demographics on eligible content network sites. As of this writing, Google allows you to choose demographic options based on gender and age. For age demographics, you can choose among several age groups, including 0–17, 18–24, 25–34, 35–44, 45–54, 55–64, and 65+.

Moving down the form, we reach the "Networks, devices and extensions" section. The default option is "All available sites and devices." You can customize this by clicking on the "Let me choose" radio button. If you choose to customize, you are presented with several options divided into three sections: Search, Content, and Devices.

The Search option allows you to include or exclude Google Search as well as sites using Google Search. In most cases, you want to keep this option on. The Content option allows you to include or exclude the Google Content Network. It is unwise to have the Content and Search options "on" in the same campaign, as preferred ad group structure, ad copy, and budgeting will likely need to be different for the Google Content Network and the Search network. If you are just starting and you are in an English-speaking country, you may want to exclude these options. Finally, the Devices option allows you to include or exclude different Internet devices, such as PCs, notebooks, iPhones, and so forth.

The next section of the form is labeled "Bidding and budget." For "Bidding option" you can choose either "Basic options" or "Advanced options." If you choose "Basic options" (the default), you can choose to perform manual bidding whereby you set up your maximum CPC, or automatic bidding to let AdWords choose an optimal price for you. Most people choose manual bidding, which is also the default. In the Budget section, you are asked to enter your daily budget. If you are not sure what that is, start with the lowest possible amount.

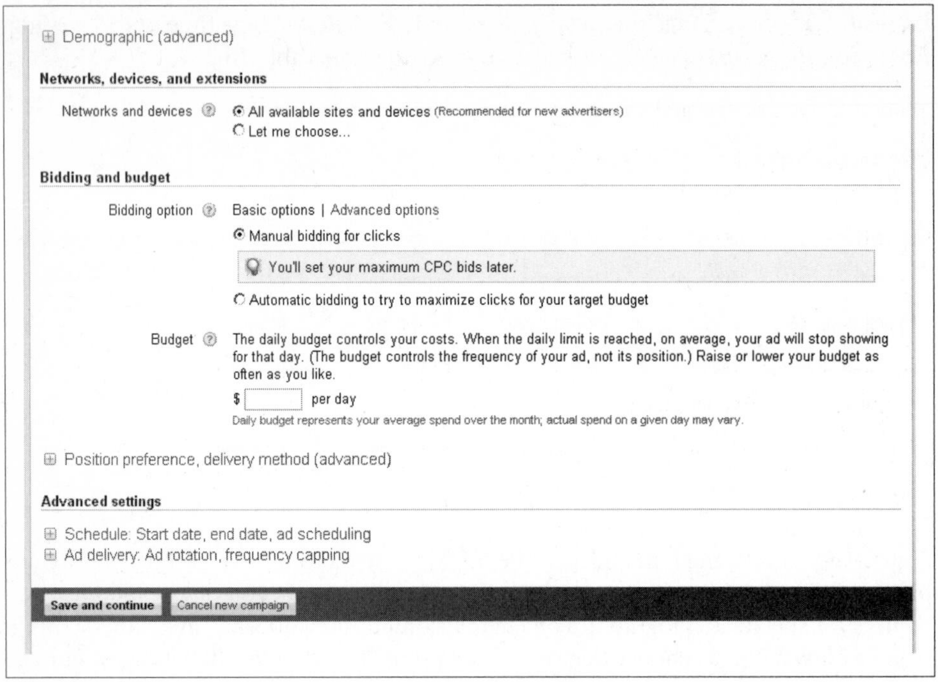

Figure 16-9. New campaign: Part 2

If you choose "Advanced options" for your "Bidding option," you are presented with additional options, including "Focus on conversions" (based on the cost per action, or CPA, model) and "Focus on impressions" (based on the cost per 1,000 views, or CPM, model).

The "Focus on impressions" option is good if you are targeting ad visibility. Ad costs are calculated based on 1,000-impression bundles. The "Focus on conversions" option allows you to set maximum costs you are willing to pay for each conversion. To quote Google (*http://adwords.google.com/support/aw/bin/answer.py?answer=113240*):

> Using historical information about your campaign, the AdWords system then automatically finds the optimal cost-per-click (CPC) bid for your ad each time it's eligible to appear. You still pay per click, but you no longer need to adjust your bids manually to reach your CPA goals.

Any conversion-focused automation in AdWords requires use of AdWords conversion tracking. It is imperative that the accuracy of the tracking be confirmed prior to using any CPA-based automation.

More advanced campaign options are also available. These include ad scheduling, ad delivery, ad rotation, and frequency capping. If you are just starting out, you may wish to ignore these advanced settings.

Once you're done with all of your form entries, click on the "Save and continue" button. If you have any form errors, AdWords will not let you continue and will ask you to make corrections.

Creating an ad group

After creating your campaign, you are ready to create your ad groups. Each campaign can have multiple ad groups, and each ad group can contain multiple ads. Figure 16-10 shows the "Ad groups" screen. You may wish to create ad groups based on different keywords.

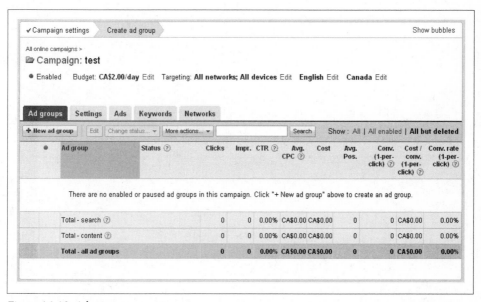

Figure 16-10. Ad groups

To create an ad group, simply click on the "New ad group" button. You should see a form similar to the one shown in Figure 16-11. This form presents many options. Figure 16-11 shows only the top part of the form.

You do not need to complete this form at this point if you are not ready. You can simply enter the name of your ad group, add a small bid amount at the bottom of the form, and save the form, effectively setting this ad group in "pending" mode.

If you decide to fill out the form, start by entering the ad group name. Moving down the form, you can enter your first ad followed by your targeted keywords. You are also presented with an option to obtain a detailed traffic estimate report.

The last two sections of the form are labeled Placements and "Ad group default bids (Max, CPC)." The Placements section allows more granular control of ad placement at Google Content Network sites. The "Ad group default bids (Max, CPC)" section

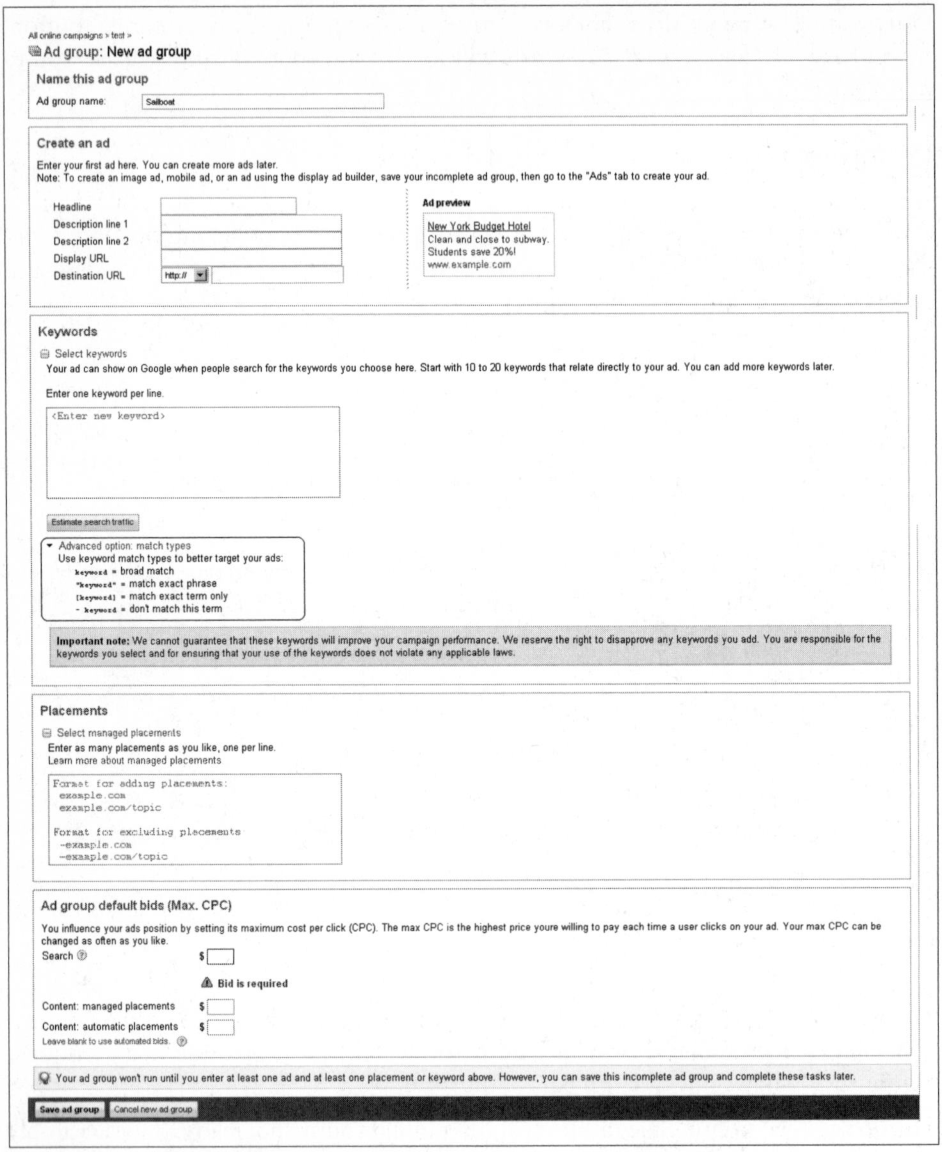

Figure 16-11. Ad group entry form

allows you to specify your default CPC as well as managed and automatic Google Content Network placement bids.

Before we start creating AdWords ads, let's talk about how you specify keywords within AdWords.

Keyword Match Types

AdWords uses four basic match types: broad match, phrase match, exact match, and negative match. The following subsections go into more detail on each.

Broad match

Broad match keywords get more traffic than the other types, as they try to catch similar (semantically related) word variations. According to Google:

> With broad match, the Google AdWords system automatically runs your ads on relevant variations of your keywords, even if these terms aren't in your keyword lists. Keyword variations can include synonyms, singular/plural forms, relevant variants of your keywords, and phrases containing your keywords.

Using the broad matching method allows you to discover additional converting keywords that you may have missed in your keyword research. Table 16-3 illustrates the concept of broad matching.

Google's expanded matching for broad match means terms not explicitly in the keyword list may be matched based on Google's history of user behavior. For example, it is possible that an ad for prom dresses may match a query for *evening gowns* if Google determines that the terms *prom dresses* and *evening gowns* are interchangeable from a user's point of view. This is a relatively recent addition to Google matching and makes a negative keyword strategy incredibly important if broad matching is being used.

Table 16-3. Broad match examples

Keyword	Ads will show for the following keywords
basketball hoops	basketball
	hoops
	portable basketball hoops
	kids basketball hoops
	lifetime basketball hoops
	huffy basketball hoops
	basketball hoops reviews
	indoor basketball hoops
	basketball rims
	sports authority
prom dress	prom
	dress
	prom night accessories
	short prom dress

Keyword	Ads will show for the following keywords
	prom dress 2009
	jovani *prom dress*
	plus size *prom dress*
	homecoming *dress*
	prom hair
	formal *dress*
	buy a *dress* for *prom*

You can use the Conversion Optimizer feature of AdWords to highlight your broad match keywords with the highest conversions. Using broad match keywords is a good idea when you do not have too many keywords to start with.

Phrase match

Quoted keywords represent an exact phrase match. In other words, the order of words found in quotation marks must be honored. A phrase match is more conservative than a broad match, as you are specifically looking for a particular keyword phrase in a specific word order.

With a phrase match, you are telling AdWords to show your ads for any keyword queries containing the phrase plus any other terms before or after the phrase. Table 16-4 illustrates the concept of phrase match conditions.

Table 16-4. Phrase match examples

Keyword	Ads may show up for related searches such as
"basketball hoops"	*basketball hoops* online
	shop *basketball hoops*
	portable *basketball hoops*
	outdoor *basketball hoops*
	basketball hoops for kids
"prom dress"	buy a *prom dress*
	prom dress store
	prom dress
	designer *prom dress*

Exact match

To specify an exact match condition, you surround your keywords with square brackets. This is the strictest and most conservative of the matching option. Table 16-5 illustrates the concept of exact keyword matching.

Table 16-5. Exact match examples

Keyword	Ads may show up (only) for the following searches
[basketball hoops]	basketball hoops
[prom dress]	prom dress

Using the exact match method allows you to conduct highly targeted (narrow) keyword matching. The search volume will be lower, but it tends to generate highly qualified converting traffic.

Negative match

The negative keyword match operator, -, helps you prevent showing your ads for irrelevant searches. Let's suppose you are selling apples at your online grocery delivery shop. If you type in the word *apple* in Google, most of the results that come up are related to Apple Inc. In this case, you need to weed out all the searches that are related to the computer maker. Table 16-6 illustrates this example in more detail.

You should spend some time finding relative negative matches. The more precise you are, the more you save by eliminating your money-wasting clicks. You can find negative keywords in many ways. Let's examine two of the most basic methods.

The first method involves using a search engine. Go to Google and search for your targeted keyword. Note any irrelevant results and their associated terms (words). Use those as your negative keywords.

The second method involves doing some in-house inspections. You can look at your current web server stats and see which keywords are completely irrelevant to your website. Add those to your negative keyword list.

Table 16-6. Negative match examples

Targeted keywords	Negative keywords	Searches with ads showing up	Searches with ads not showing up
buy apples	-used	buy apples	used apples
buy apple	-iphone	buy fresh apples	buy iPod
	-mac	apples producer	buy mac apple computer
	-computer	McIntosh apples	
		fresh apples	

You can classify the examples in Table 16-6 as negative broad matches. You can also use the negative match operator with the phrase and exact match operators. For example, let's say you want to post ads for people searching for a paid PHP script, but not a CGI script. You could use the following negative keywords (phrase matches):

```
-"cgi script"
-"cgi program"
```

Similarly, you could use the negative exact matches as follows:

```
-[cgi script]
-[cgi program]
```

You can be very creative when picking your negative keywords. Negative keywords save you money, so use them liberally.

Let's move on and explore how to create ads.

Ad Setup

You have four options when creating ads in AdWords: standard text ad, image ad, display ad builder, and mobile ad. A regular text ad is created in a form, as shown in Figure 16-12.

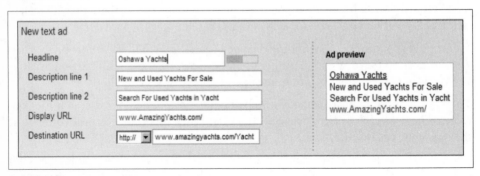

Figure 16-12. Creating a new text ad

Anatomy of a text ad

In Figure 16-12, you can see that there are five fields that every ad must have: a headline, two description lines, a display URL, and a destination URL. Also note that the fifth field (the destination URL) is invisible when shown on the search results page. Table 16-7 lists the basic text ad field limits for Latin and double-byte characters (for China, Japan, and Korea).

Table 16-7. Text ad character limits

Text ad	Headline	Description line 1	Description line 2	Display URL	Destination URL
Latin characters	25	35	35	35	Valid URL
Double-byte characters	12	17	17	35	Valid URL

Google states that the maximum allowable number of characters may be smaller in some cases when using certain Latin wide characters.

Ad copy

Writing Google ads requires creativity. For starters, you may want to use your company name and company brand as parts of your ad. Numbers, initial caps, exclamation points, and question marks are all part of the ad copy mix.

Google has very strict editorial guidelines. For example, using all caps is prohibited. Also, you can use exclamation points only in description lines (not in titles), and you must back up any superlatives with web content supporting your claim.

Use actionable words and let your ad be perceived as the answer to the searcher's question. Probably the easiest way to get ad copy ideas is to look at your competitors' ads. AdWords has some built-in ideas as well. Let's look at the concept of dynamic keyword insertion and keyword capitalization.

Dynamic keyword insertion and keyword capitalization. The idea behind dynamic keyword insertion is in the creation of dynamic ad copy based on searchers' keywords. It is based on the following piece of code:

```
{keyword:default text}
```

You can place this code into the actual ad fields. If the keyword is too long to be inserted in the ad, Google will automatically use the default text. Let's look at some examples. Suppose you are an online retailer of handbags and you carry many brands, including Radley, Linea, and Kenneth Cole Reaction. Table 16-8 illustrates the resulting ads for the following ad setup:

```
Headline.: {Keyword:Handbags} for Sale
Line 1...: Only 10 Units Left in Our Stock
Line 2...: Find Deals on New and Used {Keyword:Handbags}
Disp. URL: www.tophandbags.ca
Dest. URL: http://www.tophb.ca/c.do?kw={keyword:nil}
```

Table 16-8. Dynamic keyword insertion

Search keywords	Resulting ads
Radley	Headline: Radley for Sale
	Line 1: Only 10 Units Left in Our Stock
	Line 2: Find Deals on New and Used Radley
	Disp. URL: *http://www.tophandbags.ca*

Search keywords	Resulting ads
	Dest. URL: *http://www.tophb.ca/c.do?kw=radley*
linea	Headline: Linea for Sale
	Line 1: Only 10 Units Left in Our Stock
	Line 2: Find Deals on New and Used Linea
	Disp. URL: *http://www.tophandbags.ca*
	Dest. URL: *http://www.tophb.ca/c.do?kw=linea*
kenneth cole reaction	Headline: Handbags for Sale
	Line 1: Only 10 Units Left in Our Stock
	Line 2: Find Deals on New and Used Handbags
	Disp. URL: *http://www.tophb.ca*
	Dest. URL: *http://www.tophbg.ca/c.do?kw=kenneth%20cole%20reaction*

Note that capitalization of every letter of the word *keyword* carries different implications or effects. For example, using *Keyword* instead of *keyword* tells Google to capitalize the first term of the search keyword (for more information, see Google's dynamic keyword insertion guide at *http://adwords.google.com/support/bin/answer.py?hl=en&answer= 74996*). You must carefully review any dynamic keyword insertion ad groups to avoid grammatically incorrect or nonsensical ads.

AdWords Testing

AdWords provides a comprehensive set of tools to help you increase your conversions and ROI. In this section, we'll talk about conversions or goals and what you can do to help improve them.

Conversion and conversion rate

Website conversion can be defined as a set of predetermined actions or clicks performed by each web visitor. The set of actions could be as simple as signing up for your newsletter. Every conversion can be thought of as having a predetermined starting point and an equivalent predetermined ending point.

In web marketing, conversion means a user coming to a particular landing page, viewing and executing the provided call to action (CTA), and arriving at the final converting page. In that sense, the conversion rate is the number of conversions divided by the total number of page views for that particular landing page. You can also define this type of conversion as the number of people who reach the end point page divided by the total number of people who view the particular starting point landing page. Multiply the resulting number by 100 to get the percentage rate.

Marketing folks typically use conversion data when showing campaign sales data. In this case, the starting point could be a product landing or selling page. The call to action would be the "Add to cart" button. Finally, the conversion is realized upon showing the purchase confirmation (or thank-you) page.

Improving conversions and ROI

A lousy campaign equals lousy sales. As they say, perception is everything! Even if you are selling mediocre products, people will buy them if you create the right perception. With the advent of PPC platforms, marketers have the benefit of real-time testing and fine-tuning their online campaigns. Sometimes all it takes is changing one variable for the campaign to be profitable. The world of online marketing is not easy. There is much competition. It also does not help that there are so many variables to consider.

Consider AdWords text ads. You have about 130 characters to make an impression. This sounds easy, but it is not. When you add landing pages to the mix, things get even more complicated. Figure 16-13 shows the kinds of permutations and variations that exist.

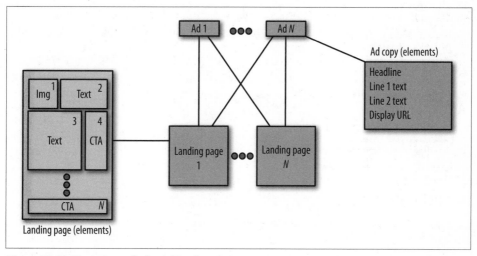

Figure 16-13. Variations of ads and landing pages

Starting from the top, you can have from 1 to *N* number of ads. Each ad has several ad copy elements, as shown in the top right of the figure. Each ad will show 1 to *N* landing pages. Each landing page could have a number of elements that all play a role in the ultimate conversion rate.

Improving conversion rates is not a one-time deal. To stay competitive, always look for ways to improve on your existing conversion numbers. To do that, you will need to continuously experiment. Starting with AdWords ads, you should try to create different ad variations using all four of the visible fields.

The next thing you can do is try to test entirely different landing pages optimized for the same ads. You want to see whether you can get a better landing page. You can also try to change specific page elements such as images, page copy, and the call to action.

Doing all of this takes time. When making these changes, it is important to have an established baseline. Having a baseline can help you gauge your progress. AdWords provides a tool called Website Optimizer that you can use to perform A/B testing as well as multivariate testing.

A/B testing

The A/B testing method is the simpler of the two forms of testing, as it tests the conversion performance of one or more entirely different landing pages. Google advises A/B testing for sites receiving fewer than 1,000 page views per week.

A/B testing in AdWords is straightforward. Pick your baseline landing page (it could be one of your current landing pages). Create a few alternative pages that effectively perform the same function. Add references to these pages in Website Optimizer. Finally, add references to your conversion page (the end point page) and you are set.

Google suggests a 100-conversions-per-page variation before making any judgments as to the success or failure of your new landing page. Figure 16-14 shows how the entry form looks in Website Optimizer.

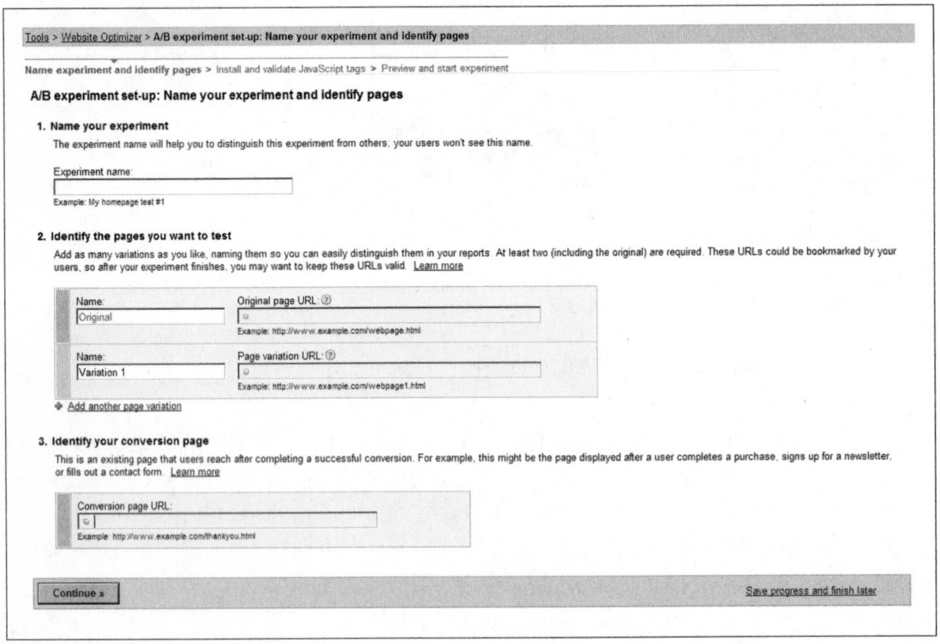

Figure 16-14. A/B testing form

After filling out the form, you will be prompted to install the required HTML/JavaScript code. You must install the code in all the URLs for Google to track your conversions.

After you add the code, Google will try to validate that everything is in place. Once your code has been validated, you are ready to test. After starting your testing, come back in a few hours to see how each variation is performing.

Multivariate testing

Figure 16-15 shows the multivariate testing entry form. There is only one test page to work with. In multivariate testing, you are testing the effects of changing the different sections of a particular page. Google advises multivariate testing for sites receiving more than 1,000 page views per week.

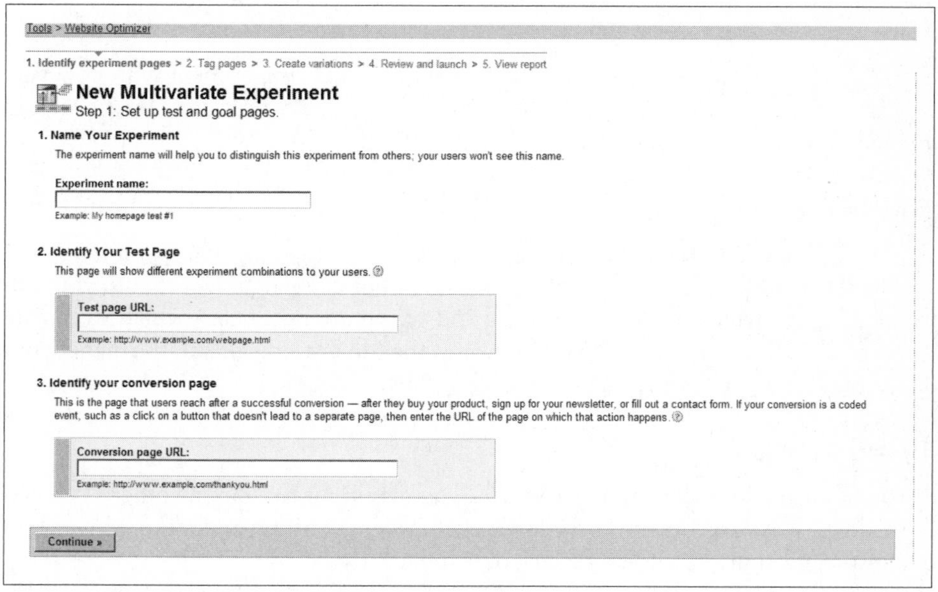

Figure 16-15. Multivariate testing form

A better metric is to use 10 actions per day. The rate of data acquisition on actions, not views, determines the speed of the test. And even at this point, you would only want to do a 2 × 2 test and not something more complicated, as the length of the test could double (or worse) for every additional variable being tested.

After completing the form, you will need to update your test page and the conversion page with the specific HTML/JavaScript code provided by Google. Validate your code, and you are ready to test.

Because of the higher volume of traffic, multivariate testing allows for more precise analysis, which can lead to identification of elements producing higher conversions.

Come back to AdWords in a few hours to start observing the performance of your testing variations.

AdWords Tips

The following subsections provide several tips you can use when managing your Ad-Words campaigns.

Observe and track your competition

Observe the competition. Write a script to track ads of your targeted keyword list. Record competitor ads for several weeks. Note changes in ads. Analyze ads that changed. If the ads are not changing, this could mean they are working.

Experiment

Don't stop with weeding out the nonworking keywords. Experiment with new keywords. Learn of any new competitors. Learn what their keywords are. Don't be afraid to gradually lower your bid prices to see the effects on your CTR.

Refine your ad copy

A poor CTR usually means bad ad copy, bad keyword targeting, and bad timing. You can easily create several versions of your ads for your campaign. Use that to your advantage. Learn which ads are converting and which are not. Learn which words are being used in the ads that work and in the ads that do not. In general, the higher your CTR, the lower your average cost-per-click will be.

Try other platforms

If you have stiff competition on AdWords, you may want to examine other PPC platforms. Yes, search volumes may be lower, but less competition and more keywords of interest could compensate for the lack of volume.

If you score a successful campaign with ads producing clicks and, ultimately, profits, you may want to consider replicating the campaign across the other platforms—especially Yahoo! and Microsoft. Replicating your winning formula is smart marketing.

Bidding

Spend your money wisely. You can tell how many competitors are bidding for your keyword simply by clicking on the More Sponsored Links link in Google. You can also use the tools we discussed in Chapter 13 to determine who is bidding for which keywords.

If fewer than eight competitors are competing for specific keywords, in some cases there is no reason to pay more than the minimum. Google gives preference to better-performing ads. Start with the lowest bid and see what position your ad is averaging. Increase your bid a bit and see whether there are any differences in your CTR.

Stay away from high bids. You don't need to be located at the top of the ladder to achieve a good ROI or a high CTR. People who are serious about finding what they are looking for will skim through all of the ads, especially if the organic results are not giving them what they want. Pay more attention to your ad copy and your landing page copy.

Keywords

The total number of clicks does not say much regarding the number of targeted clicks. Think like your potential visitor. Make sure the keywords you target are specific enough and are those you would use to find a particular product, service, or piece of information.

Provide answers to your site visitors' problems. Make that obvious in your ad copy. Make your keywords actionable and straight to the point. Make your ad copy be perceived as the answer to their question.

As we discussed in Chapter 11, utilize common misspellings to capture cheap clicks.

Google Content Network or Google SERPs

The Google Content Network comprises all participating sites showing Google ads. Using the Google Content Network is not good in all cases. You would be better off to start advertising on Google's results pages first. Placing ads across the Google Content Network brings in many variables that you do not need to deal with, especially if you are just starting out.

Google ads can appear in all kinds of places that may be detrimental to their respective CTRs. Imagine a news portal site with thousands of unrelated keywords. What Google shows on such sites is not overly predictable.

If you are targeting small exotic countries, you may do better by using the Google Content Network than you would by using Google SERPs (for specific keywords). If you are not sure where to place your ads, run them on all platforms and take corrective action for poorly performing content sites or platforms.

Conversion rate

A low conversion rate can mean any number of things, including misleading ad copy, irrelevant keywords, and bad landing pages. You may want to use A/B testing or multivariate testing to examine and improve your poorly performing ads.

Google AdSense

Google AdSense allows webmasters to make money by showing AdWords content-targeted ads. AdSense comes in several different flavors, including AdSense for Content, AdSense for Search, AdSense for Feeds, AdSense for Domains, and AdSense for Mobile Content. Figure 16-16 illustrates the AdSense offerings.

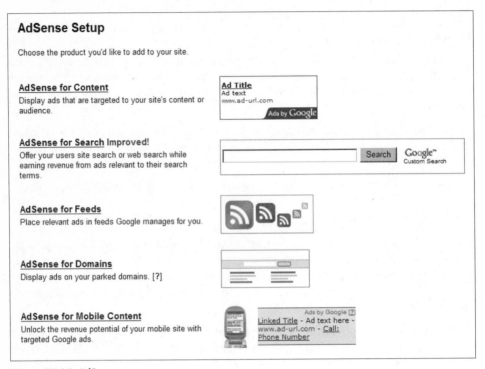

Figure 16-16. AdSense setup

AdSense Setup

The steps for setting up an AdSense account are similar to any other Google account. Simply go to *http://google.com/adsense* and sign up for your account. When you get to the AdSense sign-up form, you will be asked to provide your site's URL and language. You will also be asked not to place ads on porn sites and sites that provide incentives to click on ads.

You will have an option to register as an individual or as a company. Farther down the form you will be asked to enter payee information (name and address) as well as your contact information. You should be done filling out the form within a couple of minutes. Once you open one AdSense account, you do not need to open additional accounts for placing ads on your additional sites.

AdSense Earnings

Google does not disclose how much you will earn per click on its ads. Here is how Google explains it (*http://bit.ly/2aJaFd*):

> The Google ads you are able to display on your content pages can be either cost-per-click (CPC) or cost-per-1000-impressions (CPM) ads, while AdSense for search results pages show exclusively CPC ads. This means that advertisers pay either when users click on ads, or when the advertiser's ad is shown on your site. You'll receive a portion of the amount paid for either activity on your website. Although we don't disclose the exact revenue share, our goal is to enable publishers to make as much or more than they could with other advertising networks.

Typically, Google sends checks about one month behind if your earnings pass Google's payment threshold ($10 in the United States). You are responsible for paying any taxes as required in your country. Let's look at example earnings you can make with AdSense.

Suppose you have a site that shows 1,000 AdSense impressions per day. Assuming that your CTR is at 1% and that the average click worth is $0.10, we get the following:

```
Daily AdSense Earnings =
1000 (impressions) × 0.01 (CTR) × 0.10 (click worth)
= $1
```

So, if you have a busy site, you can do the math and see what you can earn. It sounds pretty simple, but to make it work you need to put in the time to create good content. A lot depends on your visitor levels as well as how you integrate AdSense within your site(s).

AdSense Website Setup

Once your account is created and approved, you can set up AdSense on your site in a matter of minutes. For example, if you are going to be using AdSense for Content, you will see screens similar to those in Figure 16-17.

You can choose among many types of AdSense ads. Some will be textual, and some will be image ads. After completing the form, you will be presented with Google AdSense JavaScript code that you can place in your website. Here is how the code might look:

```
<script type="text/javascript"><!--
google_ad_client = "pub-2543652322383302";
/* 120x600, created 7/18/09 */
google_ad_slot = "0138057722";
google_ad_width = 120;
google_ad_height = 600;
//-->
</script>
<script type="text/javascript"
src="http://pagead2.googlesyndication.com/pagead/show_ads.js">
</script>
```

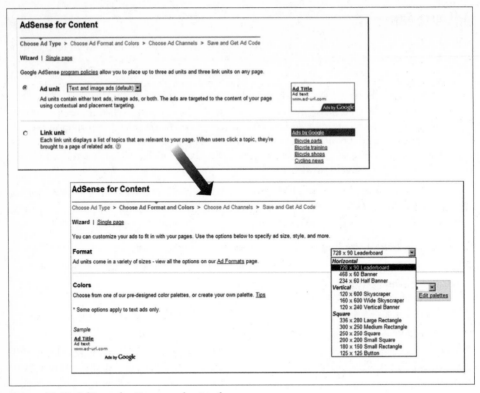

Figure 16-17. AdSense for Content selection form

In case you are wondering, this code will create a vertical AdSense ad area measuring 120 × 600 pixels.

AdSense Tips

The following subsections provide some tips if you decide to use AdSense on your site.

Unique content

Stick with niche content. If you want to have a chance at a successful AdSense site, the rules of content uniqueness apply. You want to drive targeted relevant traffic.

Seamless blending

Most people become AdSense-blind sooner or later. The more your AdSense ads look like they're part of your content, the better. Spend time choosing color schemes that will help with this effect. You want to make it harder for visitors' eyes scanning your AdSense pages to tell the difference between your page elements and the ads. One way to achieve this is by using the same text colors and text size.

Strategic placement

The basic idea behind strategic ad placement is that of forcing the visitor's eye to scan the ads while looking for specific web page actions. For example, placing ads next to the navigational elements is one of those ways. You could also make your navigation links look similar to the AdSense ad links for added confusion. This approach may be viewed as being against basic website usability principles, however.

According to Google, placing AdSense ads near the top left and middle of a page seems to work best. You can read more about Google's research at *https://www.google.com/adsense/support/bin/answer.py?answer=17954*.

SEM and SEO Unison

The following subsections cover things you can do with PPC platforms to validate and refine your SEO efforts.

SEO Keyword Tuning with PPC Testing

The PPC paradigm allows for fast, real-time feedback loops. You do not need to wait several weeks or months to realize whether your SEO is working.

Say you have a list of pages with specific targeted keywords. You can create an equivalent PPC test campaign using exact keyword matching to see whether your pages perform as expected. You can also use broad keyword matching to see whether there are other keywords that you may have missed but are producing good conversion rates.

Finding mistakes quickly can save you a ton of money and time in the long run. Use PPC platforms as your SEO testing ground.

Choosing Better Keywords

When it comes to choosing keywords, you should generally be interested in high-volume, low-competition keywords. The Google AdWords Keyword Tool shows you relative keyword search volume numbers. Although the accuracy of this data is questionable, it should give you a relative baseline when comparing different keywords. If you take this information together with the number of derived competitors by using Google's `intitle:`, `inurl:`, and `inanchor:` commands, as we discussed in Chapter 11, you can make better keyword quality estimates.

Summary

As we discussed in this chapter, the AdWords platform is useful for many reasons. You can use its Keyword Suggestion tool to find additional keywords in your keyword research. Other times, its built-in testing facilities can be very helpful in your SEO efforts.

Using SEM in conjunction with SEO is a smart choice. SEM is especially useful for new sites with little or no web presence or public awareness. Setting up an AdWords campaign is not a one-time thing. Your challenge is in making continual campaign improvements. Campaigns producing solid results will not do so forever. The competition will eventually catch up to you. There is always room to improve in terms of creating converting ads, ad groups, and campaigns. Challenge yourself to outperform your current best ad, campaign, and so on.

If your site produces lots of content or has lots of traffic, employing Google AdSense can earn you cash from Google. Before you implement AdSense, ensure that you have enough existing content or visitors. Don't bother with AdSense if you are just starting out.

## CHAPTER 17

Search Engine Spam

Search engine users search to find relevant content. And search engines try to deliver links to relevant content. Unethical SEO, referred to in the industry as spam, attempts to boost page rank by abusing the idea of relevant content—that is, improving page rank by doing something other than delivering quality, relevant pages. So, for example, getting a page about Viagra to come up in a search for sports results would be considered search engine spam.

If you are an established brand or company, your image is everything and you will do everything to protect that image. If you are struggling to get to the top of the SERPs, you might be tempted to use artificial, or black hat, SEO. Artificial SEO strives for immediate benefits—usually to make a quick profit. Its sole focus is in tricking search engines by finding loopholes in the search engine algorithms. It is this "tricking" component that makes it unethical SEO. Nevertheless, black hat SEO practitioners are always looking for ways to manipulate search engine results.

What exactly are such SEO practitioners trying to do? Simply put, they are trying to use search engines to get much more traffic. The goal is as simple as the law of large numbers. Suppose a site gets 50 search engine referrals per day. On average, it takes about 200 referrals to make a sale. This means it takes four days to make only one sale. Some people need better sales results than that, and they are easily tempted by unethical techniques to attain the results they desire.

You may even hire SEO practitioners who will employ unethical methods without your prior knowledge or consent. Many companies have found this out the hard way (usually after being blacklisted on Google and others). It is therefore imperative that you understand both ethical and unethical SEO methods. This chapter focuses on unethical methods.

Before going down the unethical SEO path, consider this. If your goal is simply to obtain immediate website traffic, there are ethical methods that will not hurt you in the long run. This includes the use of PPC campaigns.

Understanding Search Engine Spam

Many different search engine spam techniques have sprung up over the years. Some techniques are more effective than others. Techniques that target related traffic typically have higher returns (number of sales) if undetected. They include keyword stuffing, hidden or small text, and cloaking. Techniques targeting any traffic include blog and forum spam, domain misspellings, and site hacking.

Low-end spam techniques are typically broadly targeted. For example, many people want to be number one on Google for the keywords *viagra* and *sex*. This is the case even when their website has nothing to do with those two keywords. The premise is that because the two keywords are so popular, enough of the referred traffic will end up buying the product that the spam site is selling.

Similarly, how many times have you seen adult SERP spam when searching for seemingly innocent keywords? The bottom line is that spammers seek traffic for an immediate benefit. Spammers will sometimes use any means necessary to achieve their goals—often at the expense of legitimate website owners.

What Constitutes Search Engine Spam?

Search engine spam is also known as *web spam* or *spamdexing*. Using any deceptive methods to trick search engines to obtain better search engine rankings constitutes search engine spam. According to *http://www.wordspy.com/words/spamdexing.asp*:

> There's also "spamdexing," which involves repeatedly using certain keywords—registered trademarks, brand names or famous names—in one's Web page. Doing this can make a Web site move to the top of a search engine list, drawing higher traffic to that site—even if the site has nothing to do with the search request.

All of us have seen search result spam. After searching for a particular term, you click on one of the results, believing it to be relevant to your query, only to get something completely different, usually annoying ads.

Google guidelines

Google is very vocal when it comes to search engine spam. Google is not shy about taking action against spammy sites; websites big and small can be removed from Google's index if they are found to be guilty of search engine spam. In its Quality Guidelines, Google spells out some of the most common spam techniques (summarized in Table 17-1). Google also states the following (*http://bit.ly/3KJpND*):

> These quality guidelines cover the most common forms of deceptive or manipulative behavior, but Google may respond negatively to other misleading practices not listed here (e.g. tricking users by registering misspellings of well-known websites). It's not safe to assume that just because a specific deceptive technique isn't included on this page, Google approves of it.

Table 17-1. Google Quality Guidelines: Search engine spam

Spam technique	Description
Hidden text	Using invisible text specifically tailored to search engine spiders
Cloaking	Presenting different content for the same URL to the web user and the search engine spider
Sneaky redirects	Using JavaScript to redirect web users to a page they did not expect, usually one that is unrelated to their search query
Irrelevant keywords	Employing techniques such as keyword stuffing
Duplicate content	Using the same content on numerous domains or subdomains
Badware	Using malicious tactics including phishing (pretending to be another site) and malware software (installable on the victim's PC)
Doorway pages	Pages designed specifically for search engines to rank for certain search terms. Typically, doorway pages include a redirect to the target page of interest

Yahoo! guidelines

Yahoo! sees unique content as paramount. It wants to see pages designed for humans with links intended to help users find quality information quickly. Yahoo! also wants to see accurate meta information, including title and description meta tags.

Yahoo! does not want to see inaccurate, misleading pages or data, duplicate content, automatically generated pages, and other deceptive practices (many of which are in line with the Google Quality Guidelines). For more information on Yahoo!'s guidelines, visit *http://help.yahoo.com/l/us/yahoo/search/basics/basics-18.html*.

Bing guidelines

Bing wants to see well-formed pages, no broken links, sites using *robots.txt* as well as Sitemaps, simple (and static-looking) URLs, and no malware. Microsoft is vocal about shady tactics as well.

The company also advises against the use of artificial keyword density (irrelevant words including the stuffing of ALT attributes), use of hidden text or links, and link farms. For more information on Bing search guidelines, visit *http://bit.ly/8bJZp*.

Search Engine Spam in Detail

It is possible to violate search engine guidelines without even knowing it! There are a lot of gray areas, and lots of clever ideas that sound good but are easily abused. You could be blacklisted for doing something that would be considered ethical by any philosopher, but that uses techniques associated with unethical behavior.

Search engines know about these techniques, but they don't know about your intentions. This section explores many of the common scenarios that might be considered search engine spam. These are the kinds of things to avoid to ensure a steady flow of free visitors.

Keyword stuffing

Keyword stuffing is the mother of all spam. The idea is to acquire higher search engine rankings by using an artificially high keyword count in the page copy or in the HTML meta tags. In the early days of the Internet, all you had to do was stuff the keywords meta tag with enough of the same or similar keywords to get to the top of the SERPs on some search engines.

Keyword stuffing increases page keyword density, thereby increasing perceived page relevance. For example, suppose you have an online store selling basketball apparel. Here is how reasonable SEO copy might look:

```
MJ Sports is your number one provider for all your basketball needs.
We are your one stop location for a great selection of basketball
apparel. At MJ sports we know basketball. Basketball experts are at
your fingertips, please call us at 1-800-mjsports.
```

In this example, we have a keyword density of about 10% for the keyword *basketball*. The keyword-stuffed version might look as follows:

```
Basketball at MJ Sports. Basketball apparel, basketball shoes,
basketball shorts, basketball. We play basketball and we know your
basketball needs.  Best basketball shoes in town. MJ Sports basketball
apparels. Why go anywhere else for basketball? Shop basketball now!
```

A keyword density of 29% for the keyword *basketball* hardly looks "natural." Remember to write your page copy for the web visitor first. The page copy should be readable.

Keyword stuffing no longer works for most search engines. This has been the case for some time. Furthermore, the use of the keywords meta tag has lost its meaning in SEO. Google and others do not pay attention to keyword meta tags for rankings. They do use meta (description) information for search result display text.

Hidden or small text

The purpose of hidden text is to be perfectly visible to web crawlers but invisible to web users. Search engines do not like this and consider this as spam or deception. The goal of using hidden text is the same as in keyword stuffing. It is to artificially increase page rank by artificially stuffing targeted keywords via hidden text. Hidden text can be deployed in several different ways, including via the <noscript> element, the text font color scheme, and CSS.

The <noscript> element. The <noscript> element is meant to be used as alternative content in cases where scripting is not enabled by the web browser or where the browser does not support scripting elements found within the **script** tag. According to W3C (*http://www.w3.org/TR/REC-html40/interact/scripts.html#h-18.3.1*):

> The NOSCRIPT element allows authors to provide alternate content when a script is not executed. The content of a NOSCRIPT element should only be rendered by a script-aware user agent...

The overwhelming majority of people use browsers that have client scripting enabled. The <noscript> element is used to display alternative text in a browser where scripting is disabled. Since very few users disable scripting, very few, if any, will see the text. But the search engines will still discover it. Here is an example:

```
<SCRIPT>
// some dynamic script (JavaScript or VBScript)
function doSomething() {
// do something
}
</SCRIPT>
<NOSCRIPT>
sildenafil tadalafil sildenafil citrate uprima impotence caverta
apcalis vardenafil generic softtabs generic tadalafil vagra zenegra
generic sildenafil citrate pillwatch generic sildenafil buy sildenafil
buy sildenafil citrate little blue pill clialis lavitra silagra
regalis provigrax kamagra generic pills online pharmacy
</NOSCRIPT>
```

The text found within the <noscript> element would appear only to a very small number of people (a number that is negligible for all intents and purposes).

The text font color scheme. This technique involves strategically formatting text to be of the same color as the page background color. The rationale behind this technique is that the hidden text will "show up" to both the search engine crawler and the web user.

The problem, of course, is that the text appears invisible to the web user, unless it is highlighted by a mouse selection. This is clearly deception. Here is an example:

```
<html>
<head>
<meta http-equiv="Content-Language" content="en-us">
<title>Page X</title>
</head>

<body bgcolor="white">
<div>
<font color="white">sildenafil tadalafil sildenafil citrate uprima impotence
caverta
apcalis vardenafil generic softtabs generic tadalafil vagra zenegra
generic sildenafil citrate pillwatch generic sildenafil buy sildenafil
buy sildenafil citrate little blue pill clialis lavitra silagra
regalis provigrax kamagra generic pills online pharmacy
</font>
</div>

<!--Regular Text Goes Here -->
<p>Discount Satellite Dishes... Buy Viewsonic for $199...</p>
...
</body>
</html>
```

The text contained within the DIV tags is enclosed within the `<font>` tag. The `<font>` tag is using a `color` attribute value of `white`. Since the default body background usually renders white, the text will blend in with the default white background perfectly—effectively becoming invisible.

Even ethical SEO practitioners can fall victim to this form of spam. Use care when picking font colors and using CSS. It is relatively easy to make a mistake and make your text invisible.

CSS. A more discreet way to hide text is with Cascading Style Sheets (CSS). Here is the example from the preceding section, but rewritten using CSS:

```html
<html>
<head>
<meta http-equiv="Content-Language" content="en-us">
<title>Page X</title>
<style>
.special {
color:#ffffff;
}
</style>
</head>

<body>
<div class="special">
sildenafil tadalafil sildenafil citrate uprima impotence caverta
apcalis vardenafil generic softtabs generic tadalafil vagra zenegra
generic sildenafil citrate pillwatch generic sildenafil buy sildenafil
buy sildenafil citrate little blue pill clialis lavitra silagra
regalis provigrax kamagra generic pills online pharmacy
</div>

<!--Regular Text Goes Here -->
<p>Beast deals on Hockey Cards...</p>
...
</body>
</html>
```

Another way to do the same thing is to place all CSS content in an external file, or use absolute positioning coordinates—effectively placing the optimized text out of the viewable screen area.

Don't be foolish and attempt to use these hiding techniques. If your site employs CSS, be careful not to make mistakes that might appear as search engine spam. Consider the following example:

```css
<style>
.special {
color:#000000;
padding:2px 2px 2px 2px;
margin:0px;
font-size:10px;
background:#ffffff;
font-weight:bold;
```

```
line-height:1px;
color:#ffffff;
}
</style>
```

Note that the `color` attribute is defined twice—the second time as `#ffffff` (white). The second definition overrides the first, so any text rendered inside a tag with this special CSS class will be rendered in white. If the background is white, as is usually the case, the text will be invisible. Some people will attempt to augment this approach by placing all of the CSS in external files blocked by *robots.txt*.

Tiny text

Tiny text strives for the same end goals as the preceding methods: higher search engine rankings via a higher keyword density. Tiny text is visible to both search engine spiders and web users. The only catch is that it is (for all practical purposes) unreadable by web users due to its size. Here is an example:

```
<p><font style="font-size:1px;">keyword keyword</font></p>
```

Rendering this text in a modern browser produces output that is only 1 pixel high, which would be impossible to read.

Cloaking

You can think of cloaking as the bait and switch technique on steroids! Typically, smaller sites employ this method in an attempt to be perceived as big sites by search engine spiders. Figure 17-1 shows how cloaking works.

On the arrival of any web visitor (agent), a website that employs cloaking checks the originating IP address to determine whether the visitor is a human or a web spider. Once this is determined, the page is served according to the type of visitor. Pages prepared for web spiders are usually nonsensical collections of targeted keywords and keyword phrases.

There are some legitimate reasons to serve different content to different IP addresses. One involves the use of geotargeting. For example, if you are running an international website, you may want to serve your images from the server node that is closest to the requesting IP address to improve your website performance. Akamai (*http://www.aka mai.com*) is one company that does this.

Sometimes you may want to show a page in French as opposed to English if the originating IP is from France. Other times, you may want to show pages specifically optimized for particular regions of the United States. Google advises that you treat search engine spiders the same way you would treat regular (human) users. In other words, serve the same content to all visitors.

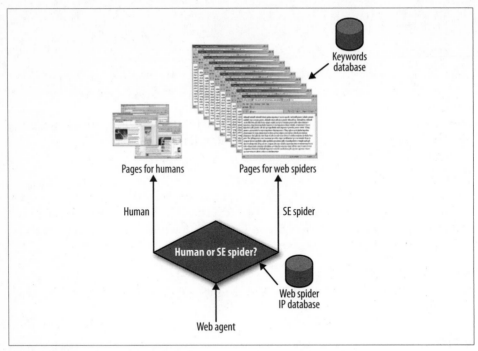

Figure 17-1. Search engine spam: Cloaking

Doorway pages

A doorway page is a page completely optimized for web spiders. Usually sites employ hundreds or even many thousands of doorway pages, each optimized for the specific term or phrase.

Doorway pages are usually just a conduit to one or several target pages. This is accomplished by a redirect. Most common redirects are implemented via JavaScript or meta refresh tags. The following fragment shows the meta refresh version:

```
<!-- META refresh example-->
<html><head><title>Some Page</title>
<meta http-equiv="refresh" content="0;url=http://www.somedomain.com">
</head>
<body>
<!-- SE spider optimized text -->
</body>
</html>
```

The key part of the meta refresh redirect is the numerical parameter specifying the number of seconds after which to execute the redirect. In this case, the parameter is 0 seconds (which is in boldface in the code fragment). The next fragment uses JavaScript to accomplish the same thing:

```
<!-- JavaScript redirect example-->
<html>
```

```
<head>
   <title>Some Page</title>

<script type="text/javascript">
function performSpecial(){
  window.location = "http://www.somedomain.com/";
}
</script>

</head>

<body onLoad="performSpecial();">

<!-- SE spider optimized text -->
</body>
</html>
```

In this example, after the HTML page loads, the `onLoad` page handler calls the `performSpecial` JavaScript function, which then uses the `window` object to issue the redirect. One of the most famous cases of doorway page spam involved BMW, as it was allegedly using this technique on its German language site. The site was eventually reindexed after removal of the spammy content.

Scraper sites

Many malicious sites are lurking on the Internet. Often, these sites will crawl your site and copy its entire contents. Usually, they will post your content on their sites in an attempt to get the ranking benefits of your site.

With the use of offline browsers, anyone can copy your site. After slurping all of the contents, some black hat SEO practitioners could convert all of these pages to act as doorway pages to their target site, simply by inserting a few lines of JavaScript code or the meta refresh equivalent.

Link farms, reciprocal links, and web rings

The concept of link farms is fairly old. Free For All (FFA) sites are a thing of the past. In their heyday, a site could get thousands of useless backlinks with the click of a button. The concept was based on the idea that link farms would boost the popularity of the submitted URL. If you are caught using an FFA site, it can harm your rankings.

Reciprocal links fall in the category of link exchange schemes. Sometimes reciprocal links can occur naturally for topically related websites. For sites with high authority (trust), this is not a big concern. For smaller (newer) sites, be careful to not overdo it. Google has penalized sites using reciprocal links in the past.

A web ring is a circular structure composed of many member sites—approved by the web ring administrator site. Each member site of the ring shares the same navigation bars, usually containing "Next" and "Previous" links.

The web ring member sites share a common theme or topic that would be something desirable in terms of SEO. Having relevant inbound and outbound links is a good thing. However, most web rings (at best) are just a collection of personal sites. Using web rings can be perceived as an endorsement of all associated sites in the web ring. Web rings can also fall into the trap of using too many reciprocal links, which are likely to be penalized.

Hidden links

There are many scenarios for placing hidden links. Say a black hat SEO consultant is working on two new sites, A and B, while also having access to an existing (popular) site, X. All three sites are completely unrelated, but to improve the new sites' rankings, he creates hidden links from site X to sites A and B, so both sites are credited with having more links, even though there's no reason for the relationship.

Hidden links are typically used to boost the link popularity of the recipient site. The assumption is that the victim site is compromised by an unethical SEO practitioner (or hacker) working on the site. The following example uses a 0-pixel image to employ a hidden link:

```
To protect your PC, <a href="http://www.domaintobeboosted.com"><img
src="1pixel.gif" width="0" height="0" hspace="0" alt="deals on jeans"
border="0"></a>use antivirus programs.
```

The code fragment using the 0-pixel image will render nothing in relation to the actual image. But search engine crawlers would still pick it up. The next example uses the `<noscript>` element to accomplish the same thing:

```
<script>
//do something
</script>
<noscript>
<a href="http://www.domaintobeboosted.com">For a great deal on jeans
visit www.domaintobeboosted.com</a>
</noscript>
```

In this example, we are using the `<noscript>` element (as we discussed in "Hidden or small text" on page 364). Unethical SEO practitioners can easily place these hidden links in their clients' web pages, with their clients not noticing anything.

Paid links

Search engines know that paid links are essentially one of the biggest noise factors in their ranking algorithms. To minimize this noise, Google actively encourages webmasters to report paid links (*https://www.google.com/webmasters/tools/paidlinks*). Google is interested in knowing about sites that either sell or buy paid links.

Using paid links will not necessarily get your site penalized. Google cares about paid links that distribute PageRank. So, if you are worried about being penalized, you can do two things: use the `nofollow` link attribute or use an intermediary page that is blocked by *robots.txt*. To obtain further information, visit *http://www.google.com/support/web masters/bin/answer.py?hl=en&answer=66736*.

Some sites sell links in more discrete ways. You can "rent" an entire page to point to your site or to buy custom ad space (that does not follow any ad patterns). Nonetheless, as they say, the truth gets out eventually. For some, it may be just what they need to get enough net traction in the beginning, which by then would allow them to clean up their act by employing strictly white hat practices.

Regardless of what search engines think, using paid links could be a legitimate strategy (if you use them in ethical ways, as discussed earlier) and a viable alternative to organic SEO. Use caution and make sure you do it correctly. This depends on many factors, including budget, reputation, and brand.

Blog, forum, and wiki spam

How many times have you seen comment spam? This could range from legitimate users posting comments to automated nonsensical comments submitted by black hat SEO practitioners. Legitimate comments can also include URLs. The ultimate goal in this case is much the same as in spam comments: passing link juice to the site of choice. The only difference is that legitimate comments add some value to the page.

With the introduction of the `nofollow` link attribute, the big search engines have united in the fight against comment spam. The idea of the `nofollow` link attribute is to disallow the passing of link juice from the blog or forum site to the destination URLs found in the web user comments.

By placing the `nofollow` link attribute with all of the link tags found in the comments, you are simply telling search engines that you cannot vouch with confidence as to the value, accuracy, and quality of the outbound link. The intent was to discourage SEO black hats from utilizing comment spam.

This method can never be a catchall solution. The problem lies in the fact that a majority of sites are not using this attribute. In addition, most sites are not even using SEO. Furthermore, not all search engines treat the `nofollow` link attribute equally. Google is the most conservative, followed by Yahoo!. Ask.com completely ignores the attribute.

In the case of wikis, it is relatively easy to see how abuse can unfold. Unethical editors can be deliberately passing link juice to site(s) of their own interest, or worse yet, be paid to do so.

Acquiring expired domains

People acquire expired domains in an attempt to acquire the domains' link juice. Although Google has said it would devalue all backlink references to expired domains, it may still be helpful to buy expired domains, especially if they contain keywords that are pertinent to your website.

Buying expired domains has other benefits, even if the domain is completely removed from the search engine index. Valuable backlinks may still be pointing to expired domains. In addition, some people may have bookmarked the domain. These residual references may also merit the effort to acquire these domains.

In another sense, knowing that search engines will erase all of the acquired benefits of an expired domain means it is important to stay on top of your domain expiry administration. Domain registrars allow for a certain grace period, typically up to 60 days, to renew a domain. Depending on your hosting provider, your site may or may not be visible during this grace period. Technically speaking, it should be visible. Some hosting providers might block your site entirely to remind you that you need to renew your domain.

Acquiring misspelled domain names

Many times web users typing in your domain name will make mistakes. Webmasters or content publishers may also make typing mistakes in your backlinks. These situations can be viewed as opportunities to gather additional traffic.

There is nothing wrong with buying misspelled domain names—when it comes to your own domain name misspellings. They can become a part of your SEO strategy. In these cases, using the permanent HTTP 301 redirect from the misspelled domain to the main domain is the correct approach.

When you buy a misspelling of a known (brand name) domain name, you could get into legal trouble. This black hat technique is troublesome, as it is trying to capitalize on the known brand while also confusing the web searcher.

Site hacking

Many sites get hacked every day. Once vulnerability is discovered within particular (mostly popular) software, hackers can have a field day in terms of wreaking havoc on all sites employing this software. Staying up-to-date with software patches and performing regular database and content backups is extremely important.

Depending on the severity of the damage, it could take quite some time to get your site up and running again once hackers have compromised it. Chances are, web crawlers have already visited your site and are likely giving link juice to the hacker's site if referenced on the compromised site. Sometimes your site can be hacked without your knowledge. It is possible for hackers to continuously exploit your site by installing hidden links or other sorts of spam.

You can detect hacker activities at the file or system level in many ways. If your website contains mostly static files and content, you can utilize software versioning control (such as CVS). If you have a dynamic website, you can utilize an offline browser to periodically download your site and then perform a comparison on the file level. You can also compare the contents of your database to past versions in order to detect any differences/anomalies.

What If My Site Is Penalized for Spam?

Sometimes search engines can make a mistake and mark your site as spam. Other times you are knowingly or unknowingly being deceptive. If you are caught conducting search engine spam, any other sites that you own might come under scrutiny and be considered part of a bad neighborhood. Whatever the case, if you want to "come clean," you can submit your site for reconsideration.

Requesting Google site reevaluation

You can request that Google reconsider your site in Google Webmaster Tools. Before you submit your site for reconsideration, remove any shady pages or practices, submit a truthful report, and then wait for your site to reappear in the SERPs. This can take several weeks or more, so patience is required.

Here is what Google says when you are submitting your website's reconsideration request (*https://www.google.com/webmasters/tools/reconsideration?hl=en*):

> Tell us more about what happened: what actions might have led to any penalties, and what corrective actions have been taken. If you used a search engine optimization (SEO) company, please note that. Describing the SEO firm and their actions is a helpful indication of good faith that may assist in evaluation of reconsideration requests. If you recently acquired this domain and think it may have violated the guidelines before you owned it, let us know that below. In general, sites that directly profit from traffic (e.g., search engine optimizers, affiliate programs, etc.) may need to provide more evidence of good faith before a site will be reconsidered.

Use caution before you submit your site for reconsideration. Keep your request straight to the point. In the worst case, creating a new domain may be your only option, provided you are sure that none of your pages are employing search engine spam.

Requesting Yahoo! site reevaluation

Yahoo! provides a web form (*http://help.yahoo.com/l/us/yahoo/search/urlstatus.html*) you can use to initiate a reevaluation request. You should fill out and submit this form after you have cleaned up your site. What I said regarding Google reconsideration requests also applies to Yahoo!. Simply be honest, fix any spam, and then contact Yahoo! using the form.

Requesting Bing site reevaluation

Bing is no different from Google and Yahoo!. It also provides an online submission method for submitting site reevaluations. You can find the online form at *http://bit.ly/1NgzUo*. Use the same advice I gave regarding Google and Yahoo! when submitting Bing reevaluation requests.

Summary

All search engines regularly post and update their webmaster guidelines. Google's webmaster guidelines talk about "illicit practices" and possible penalties (*http://bit.ly/PFen*):

> Following these guidelines will help Google find, index, and rank your site. Even if you choose not to implement any of these suggestions, we strongly encourage you to pay very close attention to the "Quality Guidelines," which outline some of the illicit practices that may lead to a site being removed entirely from the Google index or otherwise penalized. If a site has been penalized, it may no longer show up in results on Google.com or on any of Google's partner sites.

Basically, if you break the rules and use any sneaky tactics, your site will eventually be penalized. Often, it does not take more than a few days before you are caught. Even if search engines cannot detect a particular deception through their underlying algorithms, your site (or sites) is still likely to be caught, thanks to web users reporting spam results. All major search engines provide easy ways for the public or (often angry) webmasters to report search engine spam. Here are links to forms for reporting SERP spam:

Yahoo!
> *http://add.yahoo.com/fast/help/us/ysearch/cgi_reportsearchspam*

Google
> *http://www.google.com/contact/spamreport.html*

Bing
> *http://support.msn.com/feedbacksearch.aspx*

As we discussed in this chapter, understanding search engine spam is important. It is a road map of all the things you should avoid. Although certain black hat SEO practitioners in the industry boast of their black-hat-style successes, this is not the way to go.

The question then becomes: is it worth it to explore the use of shady tactics for short-term benefit? Black hat techniques are focused only on short-term benefits and are increasingly easy for the big search engines to spot. Once you are caught in a deceptive tactic, it is very hard to be trusted again. It is best to stay clear of any and all deceptions. Invest your time in building legitimate content that inspires people to link to your site.

## CHAPTER 18

Industry Buzz

Search engines never stand still, and if they did, their competitors, black hat SEO practitioners, and hackers would run them over. The SERPs would become spam wastelands of irrelevant search results.

Search quality is the most important area search engines need to worry about. Although search engines can and will continue to improve their algorithms, they are increasingly relying on webmasters to adopt new web crawler standards. It is also easy to see how search engines will continue to develop tools and associated platforms to further filter and refine their algorithms.

Other areas of advancements or changes are related to search results pages. Google is the leader in this area with its introduction of Blended Search (also known as Universal Search). Google also introduced a service called SearchWiki that has raised some questions in the Internet community.

SEO blogs go into a state of frenzy as soon as the search engine leaders announce anything. Many times this excitement is filled with theories and false information or information that is not really important in the core SEO practice.

In this chapter, we will examine three of the most talked about SEO topics as of this writing: Bing, SearchWiki, and the `nofollow` link attribute. At the end of the chapter, I'll provide a list of some of the most popular sites where you can read the latest news as it relates to SEO.

Bing

The Bing search engine arrived on the scene with a lot of buzz and fanfare. Microsoft sees Bing as "the better way to search" and calls it the "decision engine" that will save searchers time by helping them find information faster.

Microsoft made Bing available to the general Internet audience a few days before its scheduled launch. At the time, many people in the SEO community rushed to learn more about Bing.

Bing is clearly different from Google in many ways. Its search engine interface is the same as its predecessor (Live Search), but its search results pages feel and act different. Also, its search engine algorithms have changed.

One side of the community thinks Bing is only a more advanced version of Live Search, with similar ranking factors. Others go on to say that Bing is the most advanced search engine today—even better than Google.

With Microsoft getting ready to serve Yahoo! search results, one thing comes to mind. For Yahoo! to abandon its search engine technology in favor of Bing suggests that Bing does bring a lot to the table.

As far as making any conclusions in terms of Bing's ranking factors, I prefer doing my analysis on a site-by-site basis. You can take out the guesswork by utilizing the tools we covered in this book.

The Keyword Dashboard Tool

To help you compare the different search results pages, I have designed a tool called the Keyword Dashboard. The Keyword Dashboard allows you to see the search results of the major search engines side by side. Figure 18-1 shows how the Keyword Dashboard looks as of this writing.

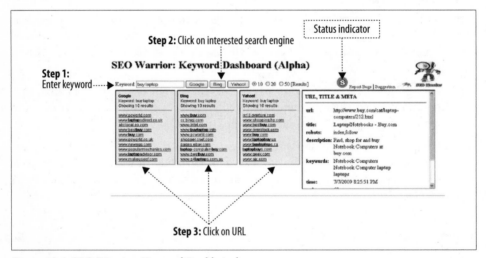

Figure 18-1. SEO Warrior: Keyword Dashboard

To run the Keyword Dashboard, all you need is a web server supporting PHP. There are no database requirements. In the search form at the top of the page, enter a keyword to compare. Click on the search engine button of choice (Google, Bing, or Yahoo!) and observe the results.

Results containing your keyword are also highlighted. If you click on each result, you will see the preview pane change on the far right. The preview pane contains additional information for the selected site, including the full URL, title and meta tags, and so forth.

You can download the latest version of the Keyword Dashboard at *http://book.seowar rior.net*. I plan to add additional features in time. I welcome any suggestions as well as any bug reports.

SearchWiki

The premise of SearchWiki is to let you rank search results just the way you like them (*http://googleblog.blogspot.com/2008/11/searchwiki-make-search-your-own.html*):

> ...SearchWiki ... [is] a way for you to customize search by re-ranking, deleting, adding, and commenting on search results. With just a single click you can move the results you like to the top or add a new site. You can also write notes attached to a particular site and remove results that you don't feel belong. These modifications will be shown to you every time you do the same search in the future. SearchWiki is available to signed-in Google users. We store your changes in your Google Account. If you are wondering if you are signed in, you can always check by noting if your username appears in the upper right-hand side of the page.

According to Google, the changes you make affect only your own searches. You can also use SearchWiki to share your insights with other searchers.

SearchWiki in Action

To see how SearchWiki works, you need to have a Google account. If you don't have an account, you can sign up for one at *https://www.google.com/accounts/NewAccount*. Once you log in to your Google account, you should start noticing three icons that are a part of every search result. Figure 18-2 highlights the SearchWiki icons.

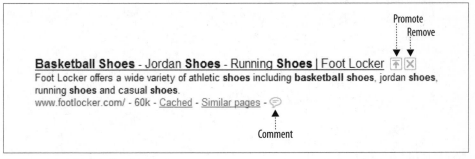

Figure 18-2. SearchWiki icons

Figure 18-2 shows the first search result on Google when searching for the keyword *basketball shoes* from Toronto. When you click on a result and then click the "promote" icon, you are effectively moving the result up one place.

Clicking on the "remove" icon hides the search result. Once you move any item up, the "remove" icon changes to a down arrow that still shows a "remove" tool tip. This is a bug in the tool tip text, since when you click on the down arrow it just moves the result down as opposed to removing the search result.

When you click on the "comments" icon, a small text box opens where you can add your comments. Now, what if you made a mistake or changed your mind? You can fix this by clicking on the "See all my SearchWiki notes" link at the bottom of the Google results page, as shown in Figure 18-3.

Figure 18-3. SearchWiki options

On the "See all my SearchWiki notes" page, you can simply click on the Restore link to get the result you want back on the SERP. To add another URL to the current SERP, simply click on the "Add a result" link.

The most interesting part of SearchWiki is the fact that your comments are made public and your username is displayed next to your comments. For an example, see Figure 18-4.

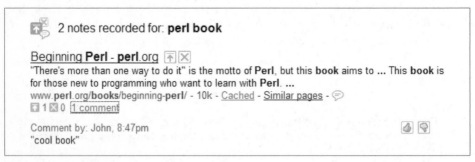

Figure 18-4. SearchWiki comments

Benefits of SearchWiki

It remains to be seen whether SearchWiki will be used by the masses. Most people, when searching Google or other search engines, are there to find information quickly and don't have time to add comments or reorder search results.

Where SearchWiki might come in handy is in academic research projects. Other than that, it looks like a tough sell in the age of instant search gratification.

Addressing SearchWiki Concerns

In November 2008, when SearchWiki was publicly announced, many people in the SEO industry were propagating the false rumor that SearchWiki would spell certain doom to SEO as we know it.

The fear was that since users can essentially grade and rerank each search result, Google would somehow use the SearchWiki data as one of its ranking factors. Since users can grade each search result, this would seem like a conceivable proposition.

The problem with Google using SearchWiki data is multifold. Just as some people will use it for what it's meant to be used for, others will abuse it by adding the sites they want to see for particular search queries.

The nofollow Link Attribute

The nofollow link attribute is not new, but it is still a fairly popular topic in SEO forums and blogs, and there still seems to be confusion about the use of this link attribute. In early 2005, Google introduced the nofollow link attribute to "prevent comment spam" in blogs, message boards, and so forth (*http://bit.ly/4wNpLa*):

> If you're a blogger (or a blog reader), you're painfully familiar with people who try to raise their own websites' search engine rankings by submitting linked blog comments like "Visit my discount pharmaceuticals site." This is called comment spam, we don't like it either, and we've been testing a new tag that blocks it. From now on, when Google sees the attribute (rel="nofollow") on hyperlinks, those links won't get any credit when we rank websites in our search results. This isn't a negative vote for the site where the comment was posted; it's just a way to make sure that spammers get no benefit from abusing public areas like blog comments, trackbacks, and referrer lists.

The major search engines support the nofollow attribute, but in different capacities. Whereas Google will honor the attribute in its most conservative form—by not indexing or passing PageRank—other search engines might index the link or even pass the link juice.

Mere seconds (literally!) after Google introduced this attribute, popular blog, CMS, and forum software packages started to implement it as part of their released software. The premise of nofollow was to combat comment spam. But in reality, it just promoted laziness. Does it make sense to punish all links just because some are spam? All serious site owners already moderate their site's comments in addition to minimizing spam by implementing the CAPTCHA technique.

A perfect example of the misuse of the `nofollow` attribute is on pretty much every page of Wikipedia. Wikipedia indiscriminately uses `nofollow` on almost all outbound links, including *.gov* and *.edu* links.

Format

If a regular link looked like the following:

```
<a href="http://www.mydomain.com/page.html">Great Site</a>
```

the link that should be "not followed" would be in this form:

```
<a href="http://www.mydomain.com/page.html" rel="nofollow" >
Great Site</a>
```

According to the W3C (*http://www.w3.org/TR/html401/struct/links.html#adef-rel*):

> [The rel] attribute describes the relationship from the current document to the anchor specified by the href attribute. The value of this attribute is a space-separated list of link types.

So, it is entirely possible to have mixed `rel` values separated by a space, as shown in the following code fragment:

```
<a href="http://www.mydomain.com/page.html" rel="next nofollow" >
Great Site</a>
```

Further Thoughts

If you use the `nofollow` attribute, ensure that your comments are either moderated or submitted through the CAPTCHA mechanism. If your comments are automatically approved when submitted, ensure that your site has a clearly defined "acceptable use policy" document. Also make sure to check that your policy is honored by inspecting your comments.

One easy way to check your comments is to run some queries in your database, such as:

```
SELECT userid, comment FROM comments WHERE comment LIKE '%sex%'
SELECT userid, comment FROM comments WHERE comment LIKE '%viagra%'
SELECT userid, comment FROM comments WHERE comment LIKE '%buy%'
SELECT userid, comment FROM comments WHERE comment LIKE '%great site%'
SELECT userid, comment FROM comments WHERE comment LIKE '%http%'
SELECT userid, comment FROM comments WHERE comment LIKE '%www%'
SELECT userid, comment FROM comments WHERE comment LIKE '%.com%'
```

The idea is to obtain user IDs and their comments containing poison words such as the ones in the examples. In addition, you also want to see all comments with embedded links. The SQL used here is for the MySQL database.

Utilizing the `nofollow` attribute can also send signals to search engines and your competitors that your site is using SEO. This is especially the case if your site does not exhibit URL patterns of commonly known CMS, blog, or forum software. The main reason for this is that the `nofollow` link attribute is mostly known to the SEO community.

Finding the Buzz

Thousands of sites around the world discuss SEO. The first place to look for SEO-related information is the big search engines. They are the search service providers, and they are to be trusted the most when it comes to any development.

SEO-Related Sites Provided by Search Engines

Search engines also make statements about SEO. Google is the most vocal and provides the most information. Read what the big search engines are saying on their sites:

- Google Webmaster Central Blog (*http://googlewebmastercentral.blogspot.com/*)
- Bing Search Community Blog (*http://blogs.msdn.com/webmaster/*)
- Yahoo! Search Blog (*http://ysearchblog.com/*)
- Ask.com (*http://about.ask.com/en/docs/about/webmasters.shtml*)

Blog Sites

There are many SEO blog sites. One of the most popular is run by Google search quality engineer Matt Cutts. Here is a list of the most popular SEO blogs on the Internet:

Matt Cutts (http://www.mattcutts.com/blog/)
Matt's blog site is not just about SEO. Matt shares his thoughts on many other things, including food, personal information, and Google's Chrome web browser. Nonetheless, the site does contain more than 400 posts related to SEO—enough to keep you reading for a few days!

Search Engine Land (http://www.searchengineland.com/)
This blog provides news and information about SEM, SEO, and how search engines work.

SEOBook (http://www.seobook.com/)
This is one of the most popular SEO sites, providing online (free and paid) training and information.

Graywolf's SEO Blog (http://www.wolf-howl.com/)
This is an informative, thought-provoking SEO blog.

SEO by the Sea (http://www.seobythesea.com/)
This blog provides marketing and SEO information and services.

SEOmoz (http://www.seomoz.org/blog/)
Boasting more than 60,000 members, this blog provides free and paid SEO information and services.

Search Engine Watch (http://blog.searchenginewatch.com/)
> The Search Engine Watch blog offers tips on SEM and SEO and the latest news about search engines.

SEO Chat (http://www.seochat.com/)
> This blog provides information on SEO and other search engine–related news.

Search Engine Roundtable (http://www.seroundtable.com/)
> This blog provides the latest information on SEO, SEM, and search engines.

Search Engine Journal (http://www.searchenginejournal.com/)
> This blog provides the latest search engine news, including SEO news.

WebProNews (http://www.webpronews.com)
> You can read news coverage on many SEO topics and events on this blog.

All of these sites provide lots of SEO information. However, not all of the information will be useful. Ultimately, finding the "buzz" is relatively easy; deciphering between quality, factual information and hype that carries no weight can be time-consuming.

Summary

In this chapter, we discussed several topics, including Bing, SearchWiki, and the `nofollow` link attribute.

The Bing search engine is here to stay. Both Microsoft and Yahoo! will be showing Bing results for the next 10 years. SearchWiki can be helpful when conducting academic research. It has no known ranking effects nor does it require any SEO methodology adjustments.

You should use the `nofollow` attribute sparingly, and only in cases where it really makes sense. Staying abreast of search engine and SEO news is important. Check with authoritative search engine sites first.

Script Listings

Chapter 2

Please note that some of these scripts are used to query search engines. Take extra caution before using these scripts in particular.

spiderviewer.php

```
<html>

<head>
<title>Search Engine Web Page Viewer</title>
</head>

<body>

<form name=mainform action="" method="get">
<table border="0" width="100%" align=center>
    <tr>
        <td>Enter URL: <br>
        <input type="text" name="url" size="20"></td>
    </tr>
    <tr>
        <td>
        <input type="submit" value="Click to See Search Engine View" name="submit">
        </td>
    </tr>
</table>
</form>
<hr>

<?php

$myurl = $_GET['url'];

if (isset($myurl)) {
   print spiderViewer($myurl);
}
```

```php
?>

</body>
</html>

<?php

function spiderViewer($url) {
    $finalHTML='';
    if($url) {
      $originalHTML=get_content($url);
      if($originalHTML) {
        $finalHTML.='<table border="0" align="center" width="75%">';
        $finalHTML.='<tr><td align="center" valign="top">';
        $finalHTML.='<b>Search Engine View for URL:'  . $url .
'</b></tr>';
        $finalHTML.='<tr><td align="left" valign="top">';
        $originalHTML=preg_replace('/<script.*?>.*?<\/script.*?>/sim'
,'', $originalHTML);
        $originalHTML=preg_replace('/<object.*?>.*?<\/object.*?>/sim'
,'', $originalHTML);
        $originalHTML=preg_replace('/<applet.*?>.*?<\/applet.*?>/sim'
,'', $originalHTML);
        $originalHTML=preg_replace('/<style.*?>.*?<\/style.*?>/sim'
,'', $originalHTML);
        $originalHTML=preg_replace('/<.*?>/sim','',$originalHTML);
        $originalHTML=preg_replace('/&[#]{0,1}.[^ ]*;/sim',' '
,$originalHTML);
        $stopWordsArray=explode("<br />",
file_get_contents('stopwords.txt'));

        for($tmploop=0;$tmploop<count($stopWordsArray);$tmploop++) {
            $originalHTML=preg_replace('/[\W]{1,1}' .
$stopWordsArray[$tmploop] . '[\W]{1,1}/sim','',$originalHTML);
        }

        $originalHTML=preg_replace('/[^A-Z0-9a-z\.\?\!\;\,\-\r\n ]*/sim',''
,$originalHTML);
        $originalHTML=preg_replace('/[\r\n ]{2,1000}/sim',' '
,$originalHTML);
        $finalHTML.= $originalHTML . '</td></tr></table>';
      } else {
        $finalHTML='Please check your URL.';
      }
    } else {
      $finalHTML='The url you entered was invalid.';
    }
    return $finalHTML;
}

function get_content($url)
{
   $ch = curl_init();
   curl_setopt ($ch, CURLOPT_URL, $url);
```

```
        curl_setopt ($ch, CURLOPT_HEADER, 0);
        curl_setopt($ch, CURLOPT_FAILONERROR, 0);
        curl_setopt($ch, CURLOPT_FOLLOWLOCATION, 1);
        curl_setopt($ch, CURLOPT_USERAGENT,'Mozilla/4.0 (compatible;
MSIE 8.0; Windows NT 6.0)');
        curl_setopt($ch, CURLOPT_TIMEOUT, 30);
        if(preg_match('/^https:\/\//sim',$url)==true) {
            curl_setopt($ch, CURLOPT_SSL_VERIFYPEER, false);
            curl_setopt($ch, CURLOPT_SSL_VERIFYHOST, false);
        }
        ob_start();
        curl_exec ($ch);
        curl_close ($ch);
        $string = ob_get_contents();
        ob_end_clean();
        return $string;
}
```

Chapter 3

layout1.html

```
<html>
<head>
<style>
#navigation {
position: absolute;
top: 10px;
left: 50%;
width: 800px;
margin-left: -400px;
text-align: left;
}

#content {
position: absolute;
top: 150px;
left: 50%;
width: 800px;
margin-left: -400px;
text-align: left;
}

body {
    text-align: center;
    min-width: 600px;
}
</style>
</head>
<body>

<div id="content">content<!-- SEO optimized content text goes here.--></div>
```

```
<div id="navigation">navigation<!-- navigational elements, ads go here--></div>

</body>
</html>
```

layout2.html

```
<html>
<head>

<style>
#navigation {
position: absolute;
top: 0px;
left: 400;
width: 200px;
margin-left: -400px;
text-align: left;
}

#content {
position: absolute;
top: 0px;
left: 600;
width: 600px;
margin-left: -400px;
text-align: left;
}

body {
    text-align: center;
    min-width: 800px;
}
</style>
</head>
<body>

<div id="content">
SEO optimized content text goes here.</div>

<div id="navigation">navigational elements, ads go here</div>

</body>
</html>
```

layout3.html

```
<html>
<head>
<style>

#top {
position: absolute;
top: 10px;
```

```
left: 50%;
width: 800px;
margin-left: -400px;
text-align: left;
}

#left {
position: absolute;
top: 150px;
left: 50%;
width: 200px;
margin-left: -400px;
text-align: left;
}

#main {
position: absolute;
top: 150px;
left: 50%;
width: 600px;
margin-left: -200px;
text-align: left;
}

#right {
position: absolute;
top: 150px;
left: 50%;
width: 200px;
margin-left: 0px;
text-align: left;
}

body {
    text-align: center;
    min-width: 800px;
}

</style>
</head>

<body>

<div id="main">optimized main body</div>

<div id="left">left panel</div>

<div id="top">top panel</div>

<div id="right">right panel</div>

</body>

</html>
```

Chapter 4

rankingfactors.pl

```perl
#!/usr/local/bin/perl
###########################################################
# File: rankingfactors.pl                                 #
# Description: This script performs analysis on several   #
#              ranking factors including:                 #
#  1) Keywords in Page Titles                             #
#  2) Keywords in Domain Names                            #
#  3) Keywords in Page Copy                               #
#  4) Keywords in Headings                                #
#  5) Keywords in Meta description                        #
#  6) Keyword Proximety                                   #
#  7) Keywords in Outbound Links                          #
#  8) Page Size                                           #
#  9) Words per Page                                      #
# 10) Website Size                                        #
# and more...                                             #
#                                                         #
# Format: perl rankingfactors.pl 10|100 keyword(s)        #
###########################################################

use LWP::Simple;
use LWP::UserAgent;
use HTML::TokeParser;
use HTML::TreeBuilder;
use File::Path;
use Math::Round qw(:all);

my $keyphrase = "";

my @googleLinks  = ( );
my @googleTitles = ( );
my @yahooLinks   = ( );
my @yahooTitles  = ( );
my @bingLinks    = ( );
my @bingTitles   = ( );

#buid keyphrase/keyword if necessary
foreach $argnum (1 .. $#ARGV) {
    $keyphrase = $keyphrase . "$ARGV[$argnum] ";
}
my $numres = $ARGV[0];
$keyphrase =~ s/^\s+//;
$keyphrase =~ s/\s+$//;
$keyphrase =~ s/'//g;
$keyphrase =~ s/"//g;


print "\nStarting..";
#cleanup temp files
rmtree( './serptemp', {keep_root => 1} );
```

```perl
print "\n..cleanup done";
#initialize variables
initializeKeyVariables($keyphrase,      \@googleLinks,
                       \@googleTitles, \@yahooLinks,
                       \@yahooTitles,  \@bingLinks,
                       \@bingTitles);

#let's store all destination links found on SERPs
print "\n..getting SERPs";
getSERPResults($#googleLinks, \@googleLinks, "google");
getSERPResults($#yahooLinks,\@yahooLinks, "yahoo");
getSERPResults($#bingLinks,\@bingLinks, "bing");
print "\n..got the SERPs";

#------------------TITLE Analysis----------------------
#get real titles
my @googleRealTitles = ( );
my @yahooRealTitles  = ( );
my @bingRealTitles   = ( );
getRealTitles($#googleLinks, \@googleRealTitles, "google");
getRealTitles($#yahooLinks,\@yahooRealTitles, "yahoo");
getRealTitles($#bingLinks,\@bingRealTitles, "bing");
print "\n..got the real titles";

#compare real titles with titles on SERPs
my @googleTitleComp = ( );
my @yahooTitleComp  = ( );
my @bingTitleComp   = ( );
my $percentMatchTitlesGoogle = compareArrays($#googleTitles,\@googleRealTitles,
\@googleTitles,

\@googleTitleComp);
my $percentMatchTitlesYahoo = compareArrays($#yahooTitles,\@yahooRealTitles,
\@yahooTitles, \@yahooTitleComp);
my $percentMatchTitlesBing = compareArrays($#bingTitles,\@bingRealTitles,
\@bingTitles, \@bingTitleComp);
print "\n..finished partial title comparisons";

#find keyword title matches
my @googleKeywordTitleMatch = ( );
my @yahooKeywordTitleMatch  = ( );
my @bingKeywordTitleMatch   = ( );
getKeywordsTitleMatch($keyphrase, \@googleRealTitles,$#googleRealTitles,
\@googleKeywordTitleMatch );

getKeywordsTitleMatch($keyphrase, \@yahooRealTitles, $#yahooRealTitles,
\@yahooKeywordTitleMatch);
getKeywordsTitleMatch($keyphrase, \@bingRealTitles, $#bingRealTitles,
\@bingKeywordTitleMatch);
print "\n..finished keyword title comparisons";

#find if keyword in title found in page copy
my @googleKeywordTitlePageCopy = ( );
my @yahooKeywordTitlePageCopy  = ( );
my @bingKeywordTitlePageCopy   = ( );
```

```
compareTitlePageCopy($#googleRealTitles,\@googleRealTitles,
\@googleKeywordTitlePageCopy, "google");
compareTitlePageCopy($#yahooRealTitles,\@yahooRealTitles,
\@yahooKeywordTitlePageCopy, "yahoo");
compareTitlePageCopy($#bingRealTitles,\@bingRealTitles,
\@bingKeywordTitlePageCopy, "bing");
print "\n..finished title page copy comparisons";


#------------------Domain Name Analysis-----------------------

#exact match
my @googleDomainKeywordExactMatch = ( );
my @yahooDomainKeywordExactMatch  = ( );
my @bingDomainKeywordExactMatch   = ( );
my $percentDomainKeywordExactMatchGoogle =  keywordDomainExactMatch($keyphrase,
\@googleLinks, $#googleLinks,

\@googleDomainKeywordExactMatch);
my $percentDomainKeywordExactMatchYahoo = keywordDomainExactMatch($keyphrase,
\@yahooLinks, $#yahooLinks,

\@yahooDomainKeywordExactMatch);
my $percentDomainKeywordExactMatchBing = keywordDomainExactMatch($keyphrase,
\@bingLinks, $#bingLinks,

\@bingDomainKeywordExactMatch);
print "\n..finished domain name exact keyword analysis";


#partial match
my @googleDomainKeywordPartialMatch = ( );
my @yahooDomainKeywordPartialMatch  = ( );
my @bingDomainKeywordPartialMatch   = ( );
$percentDomainKeywordPartialMatchGoogle =  keywordDomainPartialMatch($keyphrase,
\@googleLinks, $#googleLinks,

\@googleDomainKeywordPartialMatch);
$percentDomainKeywordPartialMatchYahoo = keywordDomainPartialMatch($keyphrase,
\@yahooLinks, $#yahooLinks,

\@yahooDomainKeywordPartialMatch);
$percentDomainKeywordPartialMatchBing = keywordDomainPartialMatch($keyphrase,
\@bingLinks, $#bingLinks,

\@bingDomainKeywordPartialMatch);
print "\n..finished domain name partial keyword analysis";



#------------------Page Copy Analysis--------------------------
my @googleKeywordDensity = ( );
my @yahooKeywordDensity  = ( );
my @bingKeywordDensity   = ( );
```

```perl
my $googleAvgDensity = keywordDensity($#googleLinks, $keyphrase,
\@googleKeywordDensity, "google");
my $yahooAvgDensity = keywordDensity($#yahooLinks, $keyphrase,
\@yahooKeywordDensity, "yahoo");
my $bingAvgDensity = keywordDensity($#bingLinks, $keyphrase,
\@bingKeywordDensity, "bing");

#------------------Description META Tag Analysis------------------
my @googleDescriptionMetaExact = ( );
my @yahooDescriptionMetaExact  = ( );
my @bingDescriptionMetaExact   = ( );

checkExactDescriptionMeta($#googleLinks, \@googleDescriptionMetaExact,
$keyphrase, "google");
checkExactDescriptionMeta($#yahooLinks, \@yahooDescriptionMetaExact,
$keyphrase, "yahoo");
checkExactDescriptionMeta($#bingLinks, \@bingDescriptionMetaExact,
$keyphrase, "bing");


my @googleDescriptionMetaPartial = ( );
my @yahooDescriptionMetaPartial  = ( );
my @bingDescriptionMetaPartial   = ( );

checkPartialDescriptionMeta($#googleLinks, \@googleDescriptionMetaPartial,
$keyphrase, "google");
checkPartialDescriptionMeta($#yahooLinks, \@yahooDescriptionMetaPartial,
$keyphrase, "yahoo");
checkPartialDescriptionMeta($#bingLinks, \@bingDescriptionMetaPartial,
$keyphrase, "bing");
print "\n..finished description META analysis";

#------------------Header Tag Analysis----------------------------
my @googleNumberOfHeaderTags = ( );
my @yahooNumberOfHeaderTags  = ( );
my @bingNumberOfHeaderTags   = ( );
my @googleHeaderTagsKeywords = ( );
my @yahooHeaderTagsKeywords  = ( );
my @bingHeaderTagsKeywords   = ( );

checkHeaderTags($#googleLinks, \@googleNumberOfHeaderTags,
\@googleHeaderTagsKeywords, "google", $keyphrase);
checkHeaderTags($#yahooLinks, \@yahooNumberOfHeaderTags,
\@yahooHeaderTagsKeywords, "yahoo", $keyphrase);
checkHeaderTags($#bingLinks, \@bingNumberOfHeaderTags,
\@bingHeaderTagsKeywords, "bing", $keyphrase);
print "\n..finished header tags analysis";


#------------------Keyword Proximity Analysis--------------------
my @googleKeywordPositions = ( );
my @yahooKeywordPositions  = ( );
my @bingKeywordPositions   = ( );
my @googleKeywordPositionsList = ( );
my @yahooKeywordPositionsList  = ( );
```

```perl
my @bingKeywordPositionsList  = ( );
analyzeKeywordPositions($#googleLinks, \@googleKeywordPositions,
\@googleKeywordPositionsList, "google",

$keyphrase);
analyzeKeywordPositions($#yahooLinks, \@yahooKeywordPositions,
\@yahooKeywordPositionsList, "yahoo", $keyphrase);
analyzeKeywordPositions($#bingLinks, \@bingKeywordPositions,
\@bingKeywordPositionsList, "bing", $keyphrase);
print "\n..finished keyword proximity analysis";


#------------------Outbound Link Analysis-------------------------
my @googleOutboundLinkKeywords = ( );
my @yahooKOutboundLinkKeywords = ( );
my @bingOutboundLinkKeywords   = ( );
outboundLinkKeywordAnalysis($#googleLinks, \@googleLinks,
\@googleOutboundLinkKeywords, "google", $keyphrase);
outboundLinkKeywordAnalysis($#yahooLinks, \@yahooLinks,
\@yahooKOutboundLinkKeywords, "yahoo", $keyphrase);
outboundLinkKeywordAnalysis($#bingLinks, \@bingLinks,
\@bingOutboundLinkKeywords, "bing", $keyphrase);
print "\n..finished outbound links analysis";


#------------------Outbound Link PR Analysis-------------------------
my @googleOutboundLinksPR = ( );
my @yahooKOutboundLinksPR = ( );
my @bingOutboundLinksPR   = ( );
outboundLinkPRAnalysis($#googleLinks, \@googleLinks,
\@googleOutboundLinksPR, "google", $keyphrase);
outboundLinkPRAnalysis($#yahooLinks,  \@yahooLinks,
\@yahooKOutboundLinksPR, "yahoo", $keyphrase);
outboundLinkPRAnalysis($#bingLinks,  \@bingLinks,
\@bingOutboundLinksPR, "bing", $keyphrase);
print "\n..finished outbound link PR analysis";

#------------------Average Page Size Analysis-------------------------
my @googlePageSize = ( );
my @yahooPageSize = ( );
my @bingPageSize   = ( );
my $googleAvgPageSize = averagePageSize($#googleLinks, \@googlePageSize, "google");
my $yahooAvgPageSize = averagePageSize($#yahooLinks,  \@yahooPageSize, "yahoo");
my $bingAvgPageSize = averagePageSize($#bingLinks,  \@bingPageSize, "bing");
print "\n..finished average page size analysis";


#------------------Optimum Number of Words Analysis--------------------
my @googleWords = ( );
my @yahooWords = ( );
my @bingWords = ( );
my $googleWordsPerPage = optimumWordsPerPage($#googleLinks, \@googleWords, "google");
my $yahooWordsPerPage = optimumWordsPerPage($#yahooLinks,  \@yahooWords, "yahoo");
my $bingWordsPerPage = optimumWordsPerPage($#bingLinks,  \@bingWords, "bing");
print "\n..finished optimum number of words analysis";
```

```perl
#-------------------Website Size Analysis-----------------------------
my @googleResultsWebsiteSizes = ( );
my @yahooResultsWebsiteSizes = ( );
my @bingResultsWebsiteSizes = ( );
my $googleAverageWebSize = analyzeWebsiteSize($#googleLinks, \@googleLinks,
\@googleResultsWebsiteSizes);
my $yahooAverageWebSize  = analyzeWebsiteSize($#yahooLinks, \@yahooLinks,
\@yahooResultsWebsiteSizes);
my $bingAverageWebSize   = analyzeWebsiteSize($#bingLinks, \@bingLinks,
\@bingResultsWebsiteSizes);
print "\n..finished website size analysis";

#-------------------Page Age Analysis----------------------------------
my @googlePageAge = ( );
my @yahooPageAge = ( );
my @bingPageAge = ( );
pageAgeAnalysis($#googleLinks, \@googleLinks, \@googlePageAge);
pageAgeAnalysis($#yahooLinks, \@yahooLinks, \@yahooPageAge);
pageAgeAnalysis($#bingLinks, \@bingLinks, \@bingPageAge);



#-------------------Create HTML Report---------------------------------

#create index file
createIndexHTML($keyphrase);

my $numberOfLinesGoogle = $#googleLinks;
my $numberOfLinesYahoo = $#yahooLinks;
my $numberOfLinesBing = $#bingLinks;

createGoogleHTMLReport();
createYahooHTMLReport();
createBingHTMLReport();


#--------------------------SUBROUTINES--------------------------
# Subroutine:
#    createGoogleHTMLReport
# Description:
#    This subroutine creates google.html file
#    which summerizes Google SERP findings
# Inputs:
#    None
# Outputs:
#    Creates google.html
# Returns:
#    Returns nothing
sub createGoogleHTMLReport {
   #create summary table first
   my $googleFile = "<html><head><title>Detailed Summary for Google</title>";
   $googleFile   .= "<style>";
   $googleFile   .=
```

```
        "body, td, tr{font-family: \"Trebuchet ms\", verdana, sans-serif; font-size:9px;}";
        $googleFile   .=
"b{font-family: \"Trebuchet ms\", verdana, sans-serif;font-size:10px;}";
        $googleFile   .= "</style>";
        $googleFile   .= "</head>";
        $googleFile   .= "<body><h1>Ranking Report Summary</h1>";
        $googleFile   .= "<br>";
        $googleFile   .=
"<table border=\"1\" width=\"500\" cellspacing=\"2\" cellpadding=\"2\">";
        $googleFile   .= "<tr><td colspan=2><b>Averages</b></td>";
        $googleFile   .= "</tr>";
        $googleFile   .= "<tr>";
        $googleFile   .= "<td><b>% Title Match</b></td>";
        my $tmp = sprintf "%.1f", $percentMatchTitlesGoogle;
        $googleFile   .= "<td>$tmp</td>";
        $googleFile   .= "</tr>";
        $googleFile   .= "<tr>";
        $googleFile   .= "<td><b>% Keyword Domain Exact Match</b></td>";
        $tmp = sprintf "%.1f", $percentDomainKeywordExactMatchGoogle;
        $googleFile   .= "<td>$tmp</td>";
        $googleFile   .= "</tr>";
        $googleFile   .= "<tr>";
        $googleFile   .= "<td><b>% Keyword Domain Partial Match</b></td>";
        $tmp = sprintf "%.1f", $percentDomainKeywordPartialMatchGoogle;
        $googleFile   .= "<td>$tmp</td>";
        $googleFile   .= "</tr>";
        $googleFile   .= "<tr>";
        $googleFile   .= "<td><b>% Keyword Density</b></td>";
        $tmp = sprintf "%.1f", $googleAvgDensity;
        $googleFile   .= "<td>$tmp</td>";
        $googleFile   .= "</tr>";
        $googleFile   .= "<tr>";
        $googleFile   .= "<td><b>Page Size [bytes]</b></td>";
        $tmp = sprintf "%.0f", $googleAvgPageSize;
        $googleFile   .= "<td>$tmp</td>";
        $googleFile   .= "</tr>";
        $googleFile   .= "<tr>";
        $googleFile   .= "<td><b>Words Per Page</b></td>";
        $tmp = sprintf "%.0f", $googleWordsPerPage;
        $googleFile   .= "<td>$tmp</td>";
        $googleFile   .= "</tr>";
        $googleFile   .= "<tr>";
        $googleFile   .= "<td><b>Website Size [of base url]</b></td>";
        $tmp = round($googleAverageWebSize);
        $googleFile   .= "<td>$tmp</td>";
        $googleFile   .= "</tr>";
        $googleFile   .= "</table><br><br>";
        $googleFile   .= "<b>Detail Table</b> <br>";
        $googleFile   .= "<table border=1 cellpadding=2 cellspacing=2>";
        $googleFile   .= "<tr>";
        $googleFile   .= "<td nowrap>#</td>";
        $googleFile   .= "<td width='100'><b>URL</b></td>";
        $googleFile   .= "<td nowrap width='150'><b>Google Title</b></td>";
        $googleFile   .= "<td nowrap width='150'><b>Page Title</b></td>";
        $googleFile   .= "<td nowrap><b>Keyword(s) found<br> in Title? [Y|N]</b></td>";
```

```perl
$googleFile    .= "<td nowrap><b>Title Keywords <br>In Page Copy [%]</b></td>";
$googleFile    .= "<td nowrap><b>Domain name <br>Exact Match</b></td>";
$googleFile    .= "<td nowrap><b>Domain name <br>Partial Match</b></td>";
$googleFile    .= "<td nowrap><b>Keyword Density</b></td>";
$googleFile    .= "<td nowrap><b>META Description<br> Exact Match</b></td>";
$googleFile    .= "<td nowrap><b>META Description<br> Partial Match</b></td>";
$googleFile    .= "<td nowrap><b>Header Tags</b></td>";
$googleFile    .= "<td nowrap><b>Header Tag <br>Keywords</b></td>";
$googleFile    .= "<td nowrap width='350'><b>Keyword Positions in Page</b></td>";
$googleFile    .= "<td nowrap><b>Keyword Prominence Map</b></td>";
$googleFile    .= "<td nowrap><b>Outbound Links with Keywords</b></td>";
$googleFile    .= "<td nowrap width='150'><b>Outbound Link<br> PRs</b></td>";
$googleFile    .= "<td nowrap><b>Page Size <br>[bytes]</b></td>";
$googleFile    .= "<td nowrap><b>Words in<br> Page</b></td>";
$googleFile    .= "<td nowrap><b>Website Size</b></td>";
$googleFile    .= "<td nowrap><b>Page Age</b></td>";
$googleFile    .= "</tr>";

for (my $i=0; $i < $numberOfLinesGoogle; $i++) {
    $googleFile    .= "<tr>";
    $googleFile    .= "<td align=left>$i </td>";
    $googleFile    .= "<td align=left>$googleLinks[$i] </td>";
    $googleFile    .= "<td align=left>$googleTitles[$i] </td>";
    $googleFile    .= "<td align=left>$googleRealTitles[$i] </td>";
    $googleFile    .= "<td align=left>$googleKeywordTitleMatch[$i] </td>";
    $tmp = sprintf "%.1f", $googleKeywordTitlePageCopy[$i];

    $googleFile    .= "<td align=left>$tmp </td>";
    $googleFile    .= "<td align=left>$googleDomainKeywordExactMatch[$i] </td>";
    $googleFile    .=
"<td align=left>$googleDomainKeywordPartialMatch[$i] </td>";
    $tmp = sprintf "%.3f", $googleKeywordDensity[$i];
    $googleFile    .= "<td align=left>$tmp </td>";
    $googleFile    .= "<td align=left>$googleDescriptionMetaExact[$i] </td>";
    $googleFile    .= "<td align=left>$googleDescriptionMetaPartial[$i] </td>";
    $googleFile    .= "<td align=left>$googleNumberOfHeaderTags[$i] </td>";
    $googleFile    .= "<td align=left>$googleHeaderTagsKeywords[$i] </td>";
    $tmp = $googleKeywordPositionsList[$i];
    $tmp =~ s/\|/\, /g;
    $googleFile    .= "<td align=left>$tmp </td>";
    $googleFile    .=
"<td align=left><a href='./maps/google".$i.".html'>Map</a></td>";
    printIndividualKeywordProminenceMap($i, \@googleKeywordPositions, "google");
    $googleFile    .= "<td align=left>$googleOutboundLinkKeywords[$i] </td>";
    $googleFile    .= "<td align=left>$googleOutboundLinksPR[$i] </td>";
    $googleFile    .= "<td align=left>$googlePageSize[$i] </td>";
    $googleFile    .= "<td align=left>$googleWords[$i] </td>";
    $googleFile    .= "<td align=left>$googleResultsWebsiteSizes[$i] </td>";
    $googleFile    .= "<td align=left>$googlePageAge[$i] </td>";
    $googleFile    .= "</tr>";
}
my $filename = "./report/google.html";
open FILE, ">", "$filename" or die $!;
print FILE $googleFile;
close FILE;
```

```
    }


    # Subroutine:
    #    createYahooHTMLReport
    # Description:
    #    This subroutine creates yahoo.html file
    #    which summerizes Yahoo SERP findings
    # Inputs:
    #    None
    # Outputs:
    #    Creates yahoo.html
    # Returns:
    #    Returns nothing
    sub createYahooHTMLReport {
       #create summary table first
       my $yahooFile = "<html><head><title>Detailed Summary for Yahoo</title>";
       $yahooFile    .= "<style>";
       $yahooFile    .=
    "body, td, tr{font-family: \"Trebuchet ms\", verdana, sans-serif; font-size:9px;}";
       $yahooFile    .=
    "b{font-family: \"Trebuchet ms\", verdana, sans-serif;font-size:10px;}";
       $yahooFile    .= "</style>";
       $yahooFile    .= "</head>";
       $yahooFile    .= "<body><h1>Ranking Report Summary</h1>";
       $yahooFile    .= "<br>";
       $yahooFile    .=
    "<table border=\"1\" width=\"500\" cellspacing=\"2\" cellpadding=\"2\">";
       $yahooFile    .= "<tr><td colspan=2><b>Averages</b></td>";
       $yahooFile    .= "</tr>";
       $yahooFile    .= "<tr>";
       $yahooFile    .= "<td><b>% Title Match</b></td>";
       my $tmp = sprintf "%.1f", $percentMatchTitlesYahoo;
       $yahooFile    .= "<td>$tmp</td>";
       $yahooFile    .= "</tr>";
       $yahooFile    .= "<tr>";
       $yahooFile    .= "<td><b>% Keyword Domain Exact Match</b></td>";
       $tmp = sprintf "%.1f", $percentDomainKeywordExactMatchYahoo;
       $yahooFile    .= "<td>$tmp</td>";
       $yahooFile    .= "</tr>";
       $yahooFile    .= "<tr>";
       $yahooFile    .= "<td><b>% Keyword Domain Partial Match</b></td>";
       $tmp = sprintf "%.1f", $percentDomainKeywordPartialMatchYahoo;
       $yahooFile    .= "<td>$tmp</td>";
       $yahooFile    .= "</tr>";
       $yahooFile    .= "<tr>";
       $yahooFile    .= "<td><b>% Keyword Density</b></td>";
       $tmp = sprintf "%.1f", $yahooAvgDensity;
       $yahooFile    .= "<td>$tmp</td>";
       $yahooFile    .= "</tr>";
       $yahooFile    .= "<tr>";
       $yahooFile    .= "<td><b>Page Size [bytes]</b></td>";
       $tmp = sprintf "%.0f", $yahooAvgPageSize;
       $yahooFile    .= "<td>$tmp</td>";
       $yahooFile    .= "</tr>";
```

```perl
$yahooFile    .= "<tr>";
$yahooFile    .= "<td><b>Words Per Page</b></td>";
$tmp = sprintf "%.0f", $yahooWordsPerPage;
$yahooFile    .= "<td>$tmp</td>";
$yahooFile    .= "</tr>";
$yahooFile    .= "<tr>";
$yahooFile    .= "<td><b>Website Size [of base url]</b></td>";
$tmp = round($yahooAverageWebSize);
$yahooFile    .= "<td>$tmp</td>";
$yahooFile    .= "</tr>";
$yahooFile    .= "</table><br><br>";
$yahooFile    .= "<b>Detail Table</b> <br>";
$yahooFile    .= "<table border=1 cellpadding=2 cellspacing=2>";
$yahooFile    .= "<tr>";
$yahooFile    .= "<td nowrap>#</td>";
$yahooFile    .= "<td width='100'><b>URL</b></td>";
$yahooFile    .= "<td nowrap width='150'><b>Yahoo Title</b></td>";
$yahooFile    .= "<td nowrap width='150'><b>Page Title</b></td>";
$yahooFile    .= "<td nowrap><b>Keyword(s) found<br> in Title? [Y|N]</b></td>";
$yahooFile    .= "<td nowrap><b>Title Keywords <br>In Page Copy [%]</b></td>";
$yahooFile    .= "<td nowrap><b>Domain name <br>Exact Match</b></td>";
$yahooFile    .= "<td nowrap><b>Domain name <br>Partial Match</b></td>";
$yahooFile    .= "<td nowrap><b>Keyword Density</b></td>";
$yahooFile    .= "<td nowrap><b>META Description<br> Exact Match</b></td>";
$yahooFile    .= "<td nowrap><b>META Description<br> Partial Match</b></td>";
$yahooFile    .= "<td nowrap><b>Header Tags</b></td>";
$yahooFile    .= "<td nowrap><b>Header Tag <br>Keywords</b></td>";
$yahooFile    .= "<td nowrap width='350'><b>Keyword Positions in Page</b></td>";
$yahooFile    .= "<td nowrap><b>Keyword Prominence Map</b></td>";
$yahooFile    .= "<td nowrap><b>Outbound Links with Keywords</b></td>";
$yahooFile    .= "<td nowrap width='150'><b>Outbound Link<br> PRs</b></td>";
$yahooFile    .= "<td nowrap><b>Page Size <br>[bytes]</b></td>";
$yahooFile    .= "<td nowrap><b>Words in<br> Page</b></td>";
$yahooFile    .= "<td nowrap><b>Website Size</b></td>";
$yahooFile    .= "<td nowrap><b>Page Age</b></td>";
$yahooFile    .= "</tr>";

for (my $i=0; $i < $numberOfLinesYahoo; $i++) {
    $yahooFile    .= "<tr>";
    $yahooFile    .= "<td align=left>$i </td>";
    $yahooFile    .= "<td align=left>$yahooLinks[$i] </td>";
    $yahooFile    .= "<td align=left>$yahooTitles[$i] </td>";
    $yahooFile    .= "<td align=left>$yahooRealTitles[$i] </td>";
    $yahooFile    .= "<td align=left>$yahooKeywordTitleMatch[$i] </td>";
    $tmp = sprintf "%.1f", $yahooKeywordTitlePageCopy[$i];

    $yahooFile    .= "<td align=left>$tmp </td>";
    $yahooFile    .= "<td align=left>$yahooDomainKeywordExactMatch[$i] </td>";
    $yahooFile    .=
"<td align=left>$yahooDomainKeywordPartialMatch[$i] </td>";
    $tmp = sprintf "%.3f", $yahooKeywordDensity[$i];
    $yahooFile    .= "<td align=left>$tmp </td>";
    $yahooFile    .= "<td align=left>$yahooDescriptionMetaExact[$i] </td>";
    $yahooFile    .= "<td align=left>$yahooDescriptionMetaPartial[$i] </td>";
    $yahooFile    .= "<td align=left>$yahooNumberOfHeaderTags[$i] </td>";
```

```perl
        $yahooFile    .= "<td align=left>$yahooHeaderTagsKeywords[$i] </td>";
        $tmp = $yahooKeywordPositionsList[$i];
        $tmp =~ s/\|/\, /g;
        $yahooFile    .= "<td align=left>$tmp </td>";
        $yahooFile    .=
"<td align=left><a href='./maps/yahoo".$i.".html'>Map</a></td>";
        printIndividualKeywordProminenceMap($i, \@yahooKeywordPositions, "yahoo");
        $yahooFile    .= "<td align=left>$yahooOutboundLinkKeywords[$i] </td>";
        $yahooFile    .= "<td align=left>$yahooOutboundLinksPR[$i] </td>";
        $yahooFile    .= "<td align=left>$yahooPageSize[$i] </td>";
        $yahooFile    .= "<td align=left>$yahooWords[$i] </td>";
        $yahooFile    .= "<td align=left>$yahooResultsWebsiteSizes[$i] </td>";
        $yahooFile    .= "<td align=left>$yahooPageAge[$i] </td>";
        $yahooFile    .= "</tr>";
    }
    my $filename = "./report/yahoo.html";
    open FILE, ">", "$filename" or die $!;
    print FILE $yahooFile;
    close FILE;
}


# Subroutine:
#    createBingHTMLReport
# Description:
#    This subroutine creates bing.html file
#    which summerizes Bing SERP findings
# Inputs:
#    None
# Outputs:
#    Creates bing.html
# Returns:
#    Returns nothing
sub createBingHTMLReport {
    #create summary table first
    my $bingFile = "<html><head><title>Detailed Summary for Bing</title>";
    $bingFile    .= "<style>";
    $bingFile    .=
"body, td, tr{font-family: \"Trebuchet ms\", verdana, sans-serif; font-size:9px;}";
    $bingFile    .=
"b{font-family: \"Trebuchet ms\", verdana, sans-serif;font-size:10px;}";
    $bingFile    .= "</style>";
    $bingFile    .= "</head>";
    $bingFile    .= "<body><h1>Ranking Report Summary</h1>";
    $bingFile    .= "<br>";
    $bingFile    .=
"<table border=\"1\" width=\"500\" cellspacing=\"2\" cellpadding=\"2\">";
    $bingFile    .= "<tr><td colspan=2><b>Averages</b></td>";
    $bingFile    .= "</tr>";
    $bingFile    .= "<tr>";
    $bingFile    .= "<td><b>% Title Match</b></td>";
    my $tmp = sprintf "%.1f", $percentMatchTitlesBing;
    $bingFile    .= "<td>$tmp</td>";
    $bingFile    .= "</tr>";
    $bingFile    .= "<tr>";
```

```
$bingFile    .= "<td><b>% Keyword Domain Exact Match</b></td>";
$tmp = sprintf "%.1f", $percentDomainKeywordExactMatchBing;
$bingFile    .= "<td>$tmp</td>";
$bingFile    .= "</tr>";
$bingFile    .= "<tr>";
$bingFile    .= "<td><b>% Keyword Domain Partial Match</b></td>";
$tmp = sprintf "%.1f", $percentDomainKeywordPartialMatchBing;
$bingFile    .= "<td>$tmp</td>";
$bingFile    .= "</tr>";
$bingFile    .= "<tr>";
$bingFile    .= "<td><b>% Keyword Density</b></td>";
$tmp = sprintf "%.1f", $bingAvgDensity;
$bingFile    .= "<td>$tmp</td>";
$bingFile    .= "</tr>";
$bingFile    .= "<tr>";
$bingFile    .= "<td><b>Page Size [bytes]</b></td>";
$tmp = sprintf "%.0f", $bingAvgPageSize;
$bingFile    .= "<td>$tmp</td>";
$bingFile    .= "</tr>";
$bingFile    .= "<tr>";
$bingFile    .= "<td><b>Words Per Page</b></td>";
$tmp = sprintf "%.0f", $bingWordsPerPage;
$bingFile    .= "<td>$tmp</td>";
$bingFile    .= "</tr>";
$bingFile    .= "<tr>";
$bingFile    .= "<td><b>Website Size [of base url]</b></td>";
$tmp = round($bingAverageWebSize);
$bingFile    .= "<td>$tmp</td>";
$bingFile    .= "</tr>";
$bingFile    .= "</table><br><br>";
$bingFile    .= "<b>Detail Table</b> <br>";
$bingFile    .= "<table border=1 cellpadding=2 cellspacing=2>";
$bingFile    .= "<tr>";
$bingFile    .= "<td nowrap>#</td>";
$bingFile    .= "<td width='100'><b>URL</b></td>";
$bingFile    .= "<td nowrap width='150'><b>Bing Title</b></td>";
$bingFile    .= "<td nowrap width='150'><b>Page Title</b></td>";
$bingFile    .= "<td nowrap><b>Keyword(s) found<br> in Title? [Y|N]</b></td>";
$bingFile    .= "<td nowrap><b>Title Keywords <br>In Page Copy [%]</b></td>";
$bingFile    .= "<td nowrap><b>Domain name <br>Exact Match</b></td>";
$bingFile    .= "<td nowrap><b>Domain name <br>Partial Match</b></td>";
$bingFile    .= "<td nowrap><b>Keyword Density</b></td>";
$bingFile    .= "<td nowrap><b>META Description<br> Exact Match</b></td>";
$bingFile    .= "<td nowrap><b>META Description<br> Partial Match</b></td>";
$bingFile    .= "<td nowrap><b>Header Tags</b></td>";
$bingFile    .= "<td nowrap><b>Header Tag <br>Keywords</b></td>";
$bingFile    .= "<td nowrap width='350'><b>Keyword Positions in Page</b></td>";
$bingFile    .= "<td nowrap><b>Keyword Prominence Map</b></td>";
$bingFile    .= "<td nowrap><b>Outbound Links with Keywords</b></td>";
$bingFile    .= "<td nowrap width='150'><b>Outbound Link<br> PRs</b></td>";
$bingFile    .= "<td nowrap><b>Page Size <br>[bytes]</b></td>";
$bingFile    .= "<td nowrap><b>Words in<br> Page</b></td>";
$bingFile    .= "<td nowrap><b>Website Size</b></td>";
$bingFile    .= "<td nowrap><b>Page Age</b></td>";
$bingFile    .= "</tr>";
```

```perl
    for (my $i=0; $i < $numberOfLinesBing; $i++) {
        $bingFile    .= "<tr>";
        $bingFile    .= "<td align=left>$i </td>";
        $bingFile    .= "<td align=left>$bingLinks[$i] </td>";
        $bingFile    .= "<td align=left>$bingTitles[$i] </td>";
        $bingFile    .= "<td align=left>$bingRealTitles[$i] </td>";
        $bingFile    .= "<td align=left>$bingKeywordTitleMatch[$i] </td>";
        $tmp = sprintf "%.1f", $bingKeywordTitlePageCopy[$i];

        $bingFile    .= "<td align=left>$tmp </td>";
        $bingFile    .= "<td align=left>$bingDomainKeywordExactMatch[$i] </td>";
        $bingFile    .= "<td align=left>$bingDomainKeywordPartialMatch[$i] </td>";
        $tmp = sprintf "%.3f", $bingKeywordDensity[$i];
        $bingFile    .= "<td align=left>$tmp </td>";
        $bingFile    .= "<td align=left>$bingDescriptionMetaExact[$i] </td>";
        $bingFile    .= "<td align=left>$bingDescriptionMetaPartial[$i] </td>";
        $bingFile    .= "<td align=left>$bingNumberOfHeaderTags[$i] </td>";
        $bingFile    .= "<td align=left>$bingHeaderTagsKeywords[$i] </td>";
        $tmp = $bingKeywordPositionsList[$i];
        $tmp =~ s/\|/\, /g;
        $bingFile    .= "<td align=left>$tmp </td>";
        $bingFile    .= "<td align=left><a href='./maps/bing".$i.".html'>Map</a></td>";
        printIndividualKeywordProminenceMap($i, \@bingKeywordPositions, "bing");
        $bingFile    .= "<td align=left>$bingOutboundLinkKeywords[$i] </td>";
        $bingFile    .= "<td align=left>$bingOutboundLinksPR[$i] </td>";
        $bingFile    .= "<td align=left>$bingPageSize[$i] </td>";
        $bingFile    .= "<td align=left>$bingWords[$i] </td>";
        $bingFile    .= "<td align=left>$bingResultsWebsiteSizes[$i] </td>";
        $bingFile    .= "<td align=left>$bingPageAge[$i] </td>";
        $bingFile    .= "</tr>";
    }
    my $filename = "./report/bing.html";
    open FILE, ">", "$filename" or die $!;
    print FILE $bingFile;
    close FILE;
}


# Subroutine:
#   createIndexHTML
# Description:
#   This subroutine creates HTML fragment for the index file
#   looking for last modified string
# Inputs:
#   $keyword => keyword
# Outputs:
#   Creates index.html
# Returns:
#   Returns nothing
sub createIndexHTML {
    my $keyword = shift;

    my $indexFile = "<html><head><title>Ranking Report Summary</title></head>";
    $indexFile    .= "<body><center><strong>Ranking Report Summary";
```

```perl
    $indexFile    .= " (for \"$keyword\") <br><br>";
    $indexFile    .=
"<a href=\"#\" onclick=\"document.all.myiframe.src='google.html\'\">";
    $indexFile    .= "Google</a> |";
    $indexFile    .=
"<a href=\"#\" onclick=\"document.all.myiframe.src='yahoo.html'\">";
    $indexFile    .= "Yahoo!</a> |";
    $indexFile    .=
"<a href=\"#\" onclick=\"document.all.myiframe.src='bing.html'\">";
    $indexFile    .= "Bing Search</a><br><br>";
    $indexFile    .= "Click on Links to View Summary..<br><br>";
    $indexFile    .=
"<iframe name=\"myiframe\" width=5000 height=6000 border=\"0\" frameborder=\"0\">";
    $indexFile    .= "</iframe></center></body></html>";

    my $filename = "./report/index.html";
    open FILE, ">", "$filename" or die $!;
    print FILE $indexFile;
    close FILE;
}


# Subroutine:
#    pageAgeAnalysis
# Description:
#    This subroutine scrapes all URLs found on SERPs
#    looking for last modified string
# Inputs:
#    $numberOfElements => number of files to process
#    $destArr => array (reference) to links array
#    $srcArr => array (reference) to links array
# Outputs:
#    none
# Returns:
#    Returns nothing
sub pageAgeAnalysis {
    my ($numberOfElements, $srcArr, $destArr) = @_;

    for(my $i=0; $i<$numberOfElements; $i++) {
        #print "\nprocessing: $srcArr->[$i]";
        my $ua = new LWP::UserAgent;
        $ua->agent("Mozilla/3.0 (compatible)");
        my $request = new HTTP::Request("GET", "$srcArr->[$i]");
        my $response = $ua->request($request);
        my $code=$response->code;
        $destArr->[$i]= scalar(localtime($response->last_modified)),
        #print "\n$destArr->[$i]";
    }
}


# Subroutine:
#    analyzeWebsiteSize
# Description:
#    This subroutine scrapes Google SERPs to pick up size of
```

```
#   different websites
# Inputs:
#   $numberOfElements => number of files to process
#   $destArr => array (reference) to links array
#   $srcArr => array (reference) to links array
# Outputs:
#   none
# Returns:
#   Returns average site size
sub analyzeWebsiteSize {
   my ($numberOfElements, $srcArr, $destArr) = @_;
   # compose "site:" links
   my $ua = new LWP::UserAgent;
   my $res;
   $ua->timeout(25);
   $ua->agent("Mozilla/3.0 (compatible)");
   my $total = 0;

   for($i=0; $i<$numberOfElements; $i++){

      my $filename = "./serptemp/temp.txt";
      my $url = $srcArr->[$i];
      #let's get the base URL first

      if($url =~ /^http/) {
         my @tmparr1 = split (/\/\//,$url);
         my @tmparr2 = split (/\//,$tmparr1[1]);
         my $baseurl = "";
         if($#tmparr2>0) {
            $baseurl = $tmparr2[0];
         }else {
            $baseurl = $tmparr1[1];
         }
         $baseurl =~ s/\/$//;
         $url = $baseurl;
      }

      my $tmpurl =
'http://www.google.com/search?hl=en&q=site%3A' . $url . '&btnG=Search';
      my $randNum = int(rand(5));
      #print "\nSleeping for $randNum seconds.\n";
      sleep($randNum);
      $res = $ua->get("$tmpurl",':content_file' => "$filename");
      #get the google SERP pagecopy variable
      my $pageCopy = "";
      if (-e "$filename"){
         my $p = HTML::TokeParser->new($filename);
         #get pageCopy for this file
         while (my $token = $p->get_tag("body")) {
            $pageCopy = $p->get_text("/body");
         }
      }else {
         print "\nfile does not exist";
      }
      #break it up with "of about <b>"
```

```perl
        my $separator1 = 'of about ';

        my @tempArr1 = split(/$separator1/, $pageCopy);
        my $separator2 = 'b';
        my @tempArr2 = split(/$separator2/, $tempArr1[1]);
        my $separator3 = ' for';
        my @tempArr3 = split(/$separator3/, $tempArr2[0]);

        my $size = $tempArr3[0];

        #remove comma in the number
        $size =~ s/,//g;

        # store it for that URL
        $destArr->[$i] = $size;
        $total = $total + $size;
    }
    #calculate and return the average
    if ($total>0) {
        return ($total/$numberOfElements);

    } else {
        return 0;
    }
}


# Subroutine:
#   optimumWordsPerPage
# Description:
#   This subroutine loops through all files to record
#   page sizes in destination array.
# Inputs:
#   $numberOfElements => number of files to process
#   $destArr => array (reference) to links array
#   $prefix => SE file prefix
# Outputs:
#   none
# Returns:
#   Returns average words per page size
sub optimumWordsPerPage {
    my ($numberOfElements, $destArr, $prefix) = @_;
    my $total = 0;
    for(my $i=0; $i< $numberOfElements; $i++) {
        my $filename = './serptemp/' . $prefix . "$i.txt";
        my $tree = HTML::TreeBuilder->new;
        $tree->parse_file("$filename");
        my $non_html = $tree->as_text();
        $non_html =~ s/^s+/ /g;
        my @tempsizearr = split(/ /,$non_html);
        $destArr->[$i]= $#tempsizearr;
        $total = $total + $#tempsizearr;
    }
    return ($total/$numberOfElements);
}
```

```
# Subroutine:
#    averagePageSize
# Description:
#    This subroutine loops through all files to record
#    page sizes in destination array.
# Inputs:
#    $numberOfElements => number of files to process
#    $destArr => array (reference) to links array
#    $prefix => SE file prefix
# Outputs:
#    none
# Returns:
#    Returns average page size
sub averagePageSize {
    my ($numberOfElements, $destArr, $prefix) = @_;
    my $total = 0;
    for(my $i=0; $i< $numberOfElements; $i++) {
        my $filename = './serptemp/' . $prefix . "$i.txt";
        my $filesize = -s "$filename";
        $destArr->[$i] = $filesize;
        $total = $total + $destArr->[$i];
    }
    return ($total/$numberOfElements);
}


# Subroutine:
#    outboundLinkPRAnalysis
# Description:
#    This subroutine parses PR values from root domains
#    of all outbound links
# Inputs:
#    $numberOfElements => number of files to process
#    $srcLinksArr => array (reference) to links array
#    $prefix => SE file prefix
# Outputs:
#    prints the keyword map
# Returns:
#    No returns
sub outboundLinkPRAnalysis {
    my ($numberOfElements, $srcLinksArr, $destArr, $prefix) = @_;
    my $PRURL = 'http://www.seowarrior.net/scripts/pr.php?pr=';
    my $range = 2;
    #loop through each file
    for(my $i=0; $i< $numberOfElements; $i++) {
        my $filename = './serptemp/' . $prefix . "$i.txt";
        my %linkHash = ();
        my $PRs = "";
        #check for file existence
        if (-e "$filename") {
            my $p = HTML::TokeParser->new($filename);
            while (my $token = $p->get_tag("a")) {
                #get link and anchor text
```

```perl
            my $url = $token->[1]{href} || "-";
            my $text = $p->get_trimmed_text("/a");
            #check if link internal or external
            if($url =~ /^http/) {
                my @tmparr1 = split (/\/\//,$url);
                my @tmparr2 = split (/\./,$tmparr1[1]);
                my $tmpbaseURLChild = $tmparr2[0] . $tmparr2[1];

                my @tmparr3 = split (/\/\//,$srcLinksArr->[$i]);
                my @tmparr4 = split (/\./,$tmparr3[1]);
                my $tmpbaseURLParent = $tmparr4[0] . $tmparr4[1];

                my @tmparr5 = split (/\//,$tmparr1[1]);
                my $baseurl = "";
                if($#tmparr5>0) {
                    $baseurl = $tmparr5[0];
                }else {
                    $baseurl = $tmparr1[1];
                }
                $baseurl =~ s/\/$//;

                if($tmpbaseURLChild ne $tmpbaseURLParent) {
                    #working with external link
                    if( !(exists $linkHash{$baseurl}) ){
                        #obtain PR value / use random sleep
                        my $randNum = int(rand($range));
                        #print "\nSleeping for $randNum seconds.\n";
                        sleep($randNum);

                        my $tmpurl = $PRURL . $baseurl;
                        my $PR = get $tmpurl;
                        #print "$PR:";
                        $PR =~ s/\n//g;
                        $PRs = $PRs . $PR . "|";
                        $linkHash{$baseurl} = 1;
                    }
                }
            }
        }
    }
    else {
            #print "\nFilename: $filename not found!";
    }
    $destArr->[$i] =  $PRs;
    #print "\n$PRs";
    }
}


# Subroutine:
#   outboundLinkKeywordAnalysis
# Description:
#   This subroutine analyzes keywords in outbound links
# Inputs:
#   $numberOfElements => number of files to process
```

```
#    $srcLinksArr => array (reference) to links array
#    $prefix => SE file prefix
#    $keyword => keyword
# Outputs:
#    prints the keyword map
# Returns:
#    No returns
sub outboundLinkKeywordAnalysis {
    my ($numberOfElements, $srcLinksArr, $destArr, $prefix, $keyword) = @_;
    my @keywordFragments = split(/ /,$keyword);
    #loop through each file
    for(my $i=0; $i< $numberOfElements; $i++) {
        my $filename = './serptemp/' . $prefix . "$i.txt";
        my $keywordMatchPercent = "";
        my $foundCount = 0;
        my $total = 0;
        #check for file existence
        if (-e "$filename") {
            my $p = HTML::TokeParser->new($filename);
            while (my $token = $p->get_tag("a")) {
                #get link and anchor text
                my $url = $token->[1]{href} || "-";
                my $text = $p->get_trimmed_text("/a");
                $text =~ s/"//;
                $text =~ s/'//;

                #check if link internal or external
                if($url =~ /^http/) {
                    @tmparr1 = split (/\/\//,$url);
                    @tmparr2 = split (/\./,$tmparr1[1]);
                    $tmpbaseURLChild = $tmparr2[0] . $tmparr2[1];

                    @tmparr3 = split (/\/\//,$srcLinksArr->[$i]);
                    @tmparr4 = split (/\./,$tmparr3[1]);
                    $tmpbaseURLParent = $tmparr4[0] . $tmparr4[1];
                    if($tmpbaseURLChild ne $tmpbaseURLParent) {
                        #external link..process it
                        if($#keywordFragments >0){
                            #handle multi keywords
                            for(my $j=0; $j <= $#keywordFragments; $j++){
                                #check for a match
                                if($text =~ /$keywordFragments[$j]/i) {
                                    #match found
                                    $foundCount++;
                                    last;
                                }
                            }
                        } else {

                            if($text =~ /$keyword/i) {
                                #match found
                                $foundCount++;
                            }
                        }
                    }
                }
```

```perl
            }
            $total++;
        }
    }
    else {
            #print "\nFilename: $filename not found!";


    }
    if($total>0) {
        $destArr->[$i] = ( $foundCount);
    } else {
        $destArr->[$i] = 0;
    }
    #print "\n$destArr->[$i]";
    }

}



# Subroutine:
#    printKeywordProminenceMap
# Description:
#    This subroutine prints each URL map
# Inputs:
#    $numberOfElements => number of files to process
#    $srcArr => array (reference) to result array
# Outputs:
#    prints the keyword map
# Returns:
#    No returns
sub printKeywordProminenceMap {
    my ($srcArr, $numberOfElements) = @_;
    for(my $i; $i<$numberOfElements; $i++){
        print "$srcArr->[$index]\n";
    }
}



# Subroutine:
#    printIndividualKeywordProminenceMap
# Description:
#    This subroutine prints each URL map
# Inputs:
#    $numberOfElements => number of files to process
#    $srcArr => array (reference) to result array
# Outputs:
#    prints the keyword map
# Returns:
#    No returns
sub printIndividualKeywordProminenceMap {
    my ($index, $srcArr, $prefix) = @_;
    my $filename = "./report/maps/$prefix".$index.".html";
    open FILE, ">", "$filename" or die $!;
    print FILE "<html><head><title>\n";
    print FILE "Keyword Prominence Map\n";
```

```
        print FILE "</title></head>\n";
        print FILE "<body><table width=400 cellpading=2 cellspacing=0><tr><td width=400>";
        print FILE $srcArr->[$index];
        print FILE "</td></tr></table></body></html>";
        close FILE;
}


# Subroutine:
#    analyzeKeywordPositions
# Description:
#    This subroutine analyzes relative positions of keywords within a page copy
# Inputs:
#    $numberOfElements => number of files to process
#    $destArr => array (reference) to result array
#    $keyword => keyword to analyze
#    $prefix => file prefix
# Outputs:
#    No outputs produced
# Returns:
#    No returns all work done on arrays


sub analyzeKeywordPositions {
    my ($numberOfElements, $destArr, $destArr2, $prefix, $keyword) = @_;
    my @keywordFragments = split(/ /,$keyword);
    #loop through each file to get
    for(my $i=0; $i< $numberOfElements; $i++) {
        my $pageCopy = "";
        my $tmpMap = ":";
        my $filename = './serptemp/' . $prefix . "$i.txt";
        #check for file existence
        if (-e "$filename"){
            my $p = HTML::TokeParser->new($filename);
            #get pageCopy for this file
            while (my $token = $p->get_tag("body")) {
                $pageCopy = $p->get_trimmed_text("/body");
                $pageCopy = cleanText($pageCopy);
            }
            $pageCopy =~ s/s+/ /g;
            my @tempArr = split(/ /, $pageCopy);
            $totalWords = $#tempArr;
            #print "\ntotal words for this page: $totalWords";
            #loop through all words
            for(my $j=0; $j < $totalWords; $j++){
                my $flag = "N";
                if($#keywordFragments >0){
                    #handle multi keywords
                    for(my $k=0; $k <= $#keywordFragments; $k++){
                        #check for a match
                        if($tempArr[$j] =~ /$keywordFragments[$k]/i) {
                            #update destination variable with index of keyword array
                            $destArr->[$i] .= "$k ";
                            #update destination variable with relative positionposition
                            $destArr2->[$i] = $destArr2->[$i] ."$j" . "|";
```

```perl
                $flag = "Y";
                last;
            } else {
                if( ($k == $#keywordFragments) && ($flag ne "Y") ) {
                    $destArr->[$i] .= "* ";
                }
            }
        }
    } else {
        #handle single keyword
        $tempArr[$j] =~ s/"//;
        $tempArr[$j] =~ s/'//;

        if($tempArr[$j] =~ /$keyword/i){
            $destArr->[$i] .= "O ";
            $destArr2->[$i] = $destArr2->[$i] . "$j" . "|";
            $flag = "Y";
        } else {
            $destArr->[$i] .= "* ";
        }
    }
    if($flag ne "N") {
        $destArr->[$i] .= "* ";
    }
}
#print "\n\n$destArr->[$i]";
    } else {
        print "\nfile does not exist";
    }
}
}


# Subroutine:
#   checkHeaderTags
# Description:
#   This subroutine checks use of heading tags in addition to checking
#   for keyword use in the same tags.
# Inputs:
#   $numberOfElements => number of files to process
#   $destArr1 => array (reference) to result array
#   $destArr2 => array (reference) to result array
#   $keyword => keyword to analyze
#   $prefix => file prefix
# Outputs:
#   No outputs produced
# Returns:
#   No returns all work done on arrays
sub checkHeaderTags {
    my ($numberOfElements, $destArr1, $destArr2, $prefix, $keyword) = @_;
    my @keywordFragments = split(/ /,$keyword);

    for(my $i=0; $i < $numberOfElements; $i++) {
        my $filename = './serptemp/' . $prefix . "$i.txt";
        if (-e "$filename"){
```

```perl
    my $p = HTML::TokeParser->new($filename);
    my $h1Text = "";
    my $h2Text = "";
    my $h3Text = "";
    my $h4Text = "";
    my $h5Text = "";
    my $h6Text = "";
    my $separator = '|s|e|p|a|r|a|t|o|r';
    while(my $token = $p->get_token) {
        if($token->[0] eq 'S' and $token->[1] eq 'h1') {
            $h1Text = $h1Text . $separator . $p->get_text("/h1");
        }
        if($token->[0] eq 'S' and $token->[1] eq 'h2') {
            $h2Text = $h2Text . $separatpr . $p->get_text("/h2");
        }
        if($token->[0] eq 'S' and $token->[1] eq 'h3') {
            $h3Text = $h3Text . $separator . $p->get_text("/h3");
        }
        if($token->[0] eq 'S' and $token->[1] eq 'h4') {
            $h4Text = $h4Text . $separator . $p->get_text("/h4");
        }
        if($token->[0] eq 'S' and $token->[1] eq 'h5') {
            $h5Text = $h5Text . $separator . $p->get_text("/h5");
        }
        if($token->[0] eq 'S' and $token->[1] eq 'h6') {
            $h6Text = $h6Text . $separator . $p->get_text("/h6");
        }
    }
    $h1Text = cleanText($h1Text);
    $h2Text = cleanText($h2Text);
    $h3Text = cleanText($h3Text);
    $h4Text = cleanText($h4Text);
    $h5Text = cleanText($h5Text);
    $h6Text = cleanText($h6Text);

    my @h1Arr = split($separator, $h1Text);
    my @h2Arr = split($separator, $h2Text);
    my @h3Arr = split($separator, $h3Text);
    my @h4Arr = split($separator, $h4Text);
    my @h5Arr = split($separator, $h5Text);
    my @h6Arr = split($separator, $h6Text);

    my $h1Cnt = ($#h1Arr == -1) ? 0 : $#h1Arr;
    my $h2Cnt = ($#h2Arr == -1) ? 0 : $#h2Arr;
    my $h3Cnt = ($#h3Arr == -1) ? 0 : $#h3Arr;
    my $h4Cnt = ($#h4Arr == -1) ? 0 : $#h4Arr;
    my $h5Cnt = ($#h5Arr == -1) ? 0 : $#h5Arr;
    my $h6Cnt = ($#h6Arr == -1) ? 0 : $#h6Arr;

    my $h1Flag = "N";
    my $h2Flag = "N";
    my $h3Flag = "N";
    my $h4Flag = "N";
    my $h5Flag = "N";
    my $h6Flag = "N";
```

```perl
        $destArr1->[$i] =
  "".$h1Cnt."|".$h2Cnt."|".$h3Cnt."|".$h4Cnt."|".$h5Cnt."|".$h6Cnt;
        if($#keywordFragments > 0) {
            #handle multi keywords
            for(my $j=0; $j<=$#keywordFragments; $j++) {

                if( $keywordFragments[$j] =~ /$h1Text/i ) {
                    $h1Flag = "Y";
                }
                if( $keywordFragments[$j] =~ /$h2Text/i ) {
                    $h2Flag = "Y";
                }
                if( $keywordFragments[$j] =~ /$h3Text/i ) {
                    $h3Flag = "Y";
                }
                if( $keywordFragments[$j] =~ /$h4Text/i ) {
                    $h4Flag = "Y";
                }
                if( $keywordFragments[$j] =~ /$h5Text/i ) {
                    $h5Flag = "Y";
                }
                if( $keywordFragments[$j] =~ /$h6Text/i ) {
                    $h6Flag = "Y";
                }
            }
        } else {
            #handle keyword
            if($keyword =~ /$h1Text/i) {
                $h1Flag = "Y";
            }
            if($keyword =~ /$h2Text/i) {
                $h2Flag = "Y";
            }
            if($keyword =~ /$h3Text/i) {
                $h3Flag = "Y";
            }
            if($keyword =~ /$h4Text/i) {
                $h4Flag = "Y";
            }
            if($keyword =~ /$h5Text/i) {
                $h5Flag = "Y";
            }
            if($keyword =~ /$h6Text/i) {
                $h6Flag = "Y";
            }

        }
        $destArr2->[$i] =
  "".$h1Flag."|".$h2Flag."|".$h3Flag."|".$h4Flag."|".$h5Flag."|".$h6Flag;

    } else {
        # no file =>insert defaults;
        $destArr1->[$i] = "0|0|0|0|0|0|";
        $destArr2->[$i] = "N|N|N|N|N|N|";
    }
```

```
        #print "\n".$destArr1->[$i]."\n".$destArr2->[$i];

    }
}


# Subroutine:
#   checkExactDescriptionMeta
# Description:
#   This subroutine checks for exact keyword match in keyword description.
# Inputs:
#   $numberOfElements => number of files to process
#   $destArr => array (reference) to result array
#   $keyword => keyword to analyze
#   $prefix => file prefix
# Outputs:
#   No outputs produced
# Returns:
#   No returns all work done on array
sub checkExactDescriptionMeta {
    my ($numberOfElements, $destArr, $keyword, $prefix) = @_;
    for(my $i=0; $i<$numberOfElements; $i++){
        $filename = './serptemp/' . $prefix . "$i.txt";
        if (-e "$filename"){
            my $p = HTML::TokeParser->new($filename);
            while (my $token=$p->get_tag("meta")) {
                if ($token->[1]{name}=~/description/i) {
                    my $metaDescription = $token->[1]{content};
                    $metaDescription =~ s/"//;
                    $metaDescription =~ s/'//;

                    if($metaDescription =~ /$keyword/i) {
                        $destArr->[$i] = "Y";
                    } else {
                        $destArr->[$i] = "N";
                    }
                }
            }
        }
        if ( !(exists $destArr->[$i])) {
            $destArr->[$i] = "N";
        }
    }
}


# Subroutine:
#   checkExactDescriptionMeta
# Description:
#   This subroutine checks for exact keyword match in keyword description.
# Inputs:
#   $numberOfElements => number of files to process
#   $destArr => array (reference) to result array
#   $keyword => keyword to analyze
#   $prefix => file prefix
```

```perl
# Outputs:
#    No outputs produced
# Returns:
#    No returns all work done on array
sub checkPartialDescriptionMeta {
   my ($numberOfElements, $destArr, $keyword, $prefix) = @_;
   my @keywordFragments = split(/ /, $keyword);

   for(my $i=0; $i<$numberOfElements; $i++){
      $filename = './serptemp/' . $prefix . "$i.txt";
      if (-e "$filename"){
         my $p = HTML::TokeParser->new($filename);
         while (my $token=$p->get_tag("meta")) {
            if ($token->[1]{name}=~/description/i) {
               my $metaDescription = $token->[1]{content};

               if($#keywordFragments >0) {
                  for (my $j=0; $j<=$#keywordFragments; $j++){
                     if($metaDescription =~ /$keywordFragments[$j]/i) {
                        $destArr->[$i] = "Y";
                        last;
                     } else {
                        $destArr->[$i] = "N";
                     }
                  }
               } else {
                  if($metaDescription =~ /$keyword/i) {
                     $destArr->[$i] = "Y";
                     last;
                  } else {
                     $destArr->[$i] = "N";
                  }
               }
            }
         }
      }
      if ( !(exists $destArr->[$i])) {
         $destArr->[$i] = "N";
      }
   }
}


# Subroutine:
#    keywordDensity
# Description:
#    This subroutine calculates keyword density for given keyword.
# Inputs:
#    $numberOfElements => number of files to process
#    $destArr => array (reference) to result array
#    $keyword => keyword to analyze
#    $prefix => file prefix
# Outputs:
#    No outputs produced
# Returns:
```

```
#   No returns all work done on array

sub keywordDensity {
    my ($numberOfElements, $keyword, $destArr, $prefix) = @_;
    my $total = 0;
    #loop through all files

    for(my $i=0; $i<$numberOfElements; $i++) {
        my $pageCopy = "";
        my $filename = './serptemp/' . $prefix . "$i.txt";
        if (-e "$filename"){
            my $p = HTML::TokeParser->new($filename);
            while (my $token = $p->get_tag("body")) {
                $pageCopy = $p->get_trimmed_text("/body");
            }
        } else {
            print "\nFile not found when calculating keyword density.";

        }
        #compare copy and array (sep function)
        $pageCopy =~ s/"//g;
        $pageCopy =~ s/'//g;

        $total = $total + calculateKD($i, $pageCopy, $destArr, $keyword);
    }
    return ($total/$numberOfElements);
}


# Subroutine:
#    calcualteKD
# Description:
#    Helper subroutine to calculate keyword density
# Inputs:
#    $numberOfElements => number of files to process
#    $destArr => array (reference) to result array
#    $keyword => keyword to analyze
#    $prefix => file prefix
# Outputs:
#    No outputs produced
# Returns:
#    No returns all work done on array
sub calculateKD {
    my ($index, $pageCopy, $destArr, $keyword) = @_;

    my @keywordFragments = split (/ /,$keyword);
    if ($#keywordFragments>0) {
        for (my $i=0; $i<= $#keywordFragments; $i++){
            my @tempArr  = split(/$keywordFragments[$i]/,$pageCopy);
            my @tempArr2 = split(/ /, $pageCopy);
            if( ($#tempArr == -1) || ($#tempArr2 == -1)) {
                $destArr->[$index] = 0;
            }else {
                $destArr->[$index] = $destArr->[$index] + ($#tempArr/$#tempArr2)*100;
            }
        }
```

```
        }
        return $destArr->[$index];

    } else {
        my @tempArr  = split(/$keyword/,$pageCopy);
        my @tempArr2 = split(/ /, $pageCopy);
        $destArr->[$index] = ($#tempArr/$#tempArr2)*100;
        return $destArr->[$index];
    }

}


# Subroutine:
#    keywordDomainExactMatch
# Description:
#    This subroutine analyzes keywords in domain names. It looks
#    to see if keyword is part of the domain name.
#    Possible improvement could also consider keyword stemming.
# Inputs:
#    $numberOfElements => number of files to process
#    $linksArr => array (reference) to links array
#    $destArr => array (reference) to result array
#    $keyword => file prefix for the three SEs
# Outputs:
#    No outputs produced
# Returns:
#    No returns all work done on passed array
sub keywordDomainExactMatch {
    my ($keyword, $linksArr, $numberOfElements, $destArr) = @_;
    my $matchCnt=0;
    my @keywordFragments = split(/ /, $keyword);
    my $numberOfKeywordFragments = $#keywordFragments;
    my $total = 0;
    for (my $i=0; $i<=$numberOfElements; $i++) {
        $matchCnt=0;
        my $tmp = $linksArr->[$i];
        $tmp =~ s/^http:\/\///g;
        $tmp =~ s/^https:\/\///g;
        my @linkFragments = split(/\//,$tmp);
        my $link = $linkFragments[0];

        if($numberOfKeywordFragments>0) {
            for(my $j=0; $j<=$numberOfKeywordFragments; $j++) {
                if ($link =~ /$keywordFragments[$j]/i) {
                    $matchCnt++;
                }
            }
        } else {
            if($link =~ /$keyword/i) {
                $matchCnt++;
            }
        }
        if($matchCnt>0) {
            if($numberOfKeywordFragments>0) {
```

```perl
            if($matchCnt == ($numberOfKeywordFragments+1)) {
                $destArr->[$i] = "Y";
            } else {
                $destArr->[$i] = "N";
            }
        } else {
          # single keyword
          $destArr->[$i] = "Y";
        }

    } else {
        $destArr->[$i] = "N";
    }
    if($destArr->[$i] eq "Y") {
      $total++;
    }
  }
  return ( ($total/$numberOfElements)* 100);
}


# Subroutine:
#    keywordDomainPartialMatch
# Description:
#    This subroutine analyzes keywords in domain names. It looks
#    for partial matche between the keyword and the domain name.
# Inputs:
#    $numberOfElements => number of files to process
#    $linksArr => array (reference) to links array
#    $destArr => array (reference) to result array
#    $keyword => file prefix for the three SEs
# Outputs:
#    No outputs produced
# Returns:
#    No returns all work done on passed array
sub keywordDomainPartialMatch {
    my ($keyword, $linksArr, $numberOfElements, $destArr) = @_;
    my $totalNumber = $numberOfElements;
    my $matchCnt=0;
    my @keywordFragments = split (/ /, $keyword);
    my $numOfKeywordFragments = $#keywordFragments;

    my $keywordHyphen = $keyword;
    my $keywordUnderscore = $keyword;
    my $keywordNoSpace = $keyword;
    $keywordHyphen =~ s/ /-/g;
    $keywordNoSpace =~ s/ //g;


    #loop through all links
    if($numOfKeywordFragments >0) {
       for(my $i=0; $i<$numberOfElements; $i++) {
           my $tmp = $linksArr->[$i];
           $tmp =~ s/^http:\/\///gi;
           $tmp =~ s/^https:\/\///gi;
```

```perl
            my @linkFragments = split(/\//,$tmp);
            my $link = $linkFragments[0];
            for(my $j=0; $j<=$numOfKeywordFragments; $j++) {
                if($link =~ /$keywordFragments[$j]/i) {
                    $destArr->[$i] = "Y";
                    $j = $numOfKeywordFragments;
                    $matchCnt++;
                } else {
                    $destArr->[$i] = "N";
                }
            }
        }
    } else {

        for(my $i=0; $i<$numberOfElements; $i++) {
            my $tmp = $linksArr->[$i];
            $tmp =~ s/^http:\/\///g;
            $tmp =~ s/^https:\/\///g;
            my @linkFragments = split(/\//,$tmp);
            my $link = $linkFragments[0];

            if( ($link =~ /$keyword/) ||
                ($link =~ /$keywordHyphen/) ||
                ($link =~ /$keywordNoSpace/) ) {
                $destArr->[$i] = "Y";
                $matchCnt++;
            } else {
                $destArr->[$i] = "N";
            }
        }



    }
    return ( ($matchCnt/$totalNumber)* 100);
}


# Subroutine:
#   compareTitlePageCopy
# Description:
#   This subroutine compares page title to page copy
# Inputs:
#   $numberOfElements => number of files to process
#   $titlesArr => array (reference) to titles array
#   $destArr => array (reference) to result array
#   $prefix => file prefix for the three SEs
# Outputs:
#   No outputs produced
# Returns:
#   No returns all work done on passed arrays
sub compareTitlePageCopy {
    my ($numberOfElements, $titlesArr, $destArr, $prefix) = @_;
    #loop through all files
    for(my $i=0; $i<=$numberOfElements; $i++) {
```

```perl
    #split up current title into token words
    my $title = $titlesArr->[$i];

    $title = cleanText($title);
    $title =~ s/\'//g;
    $title =~ s/\"//g;


    my @titleFragments = split(/ /,$title);
    #get copy of each file
    my $pageCopy = "";
    my $filename = './serptemp/' . $prefix . "$i.txt";
    if (-e "$filename"){
        my $p = HTML::TokeParser->new($filename);
        while (my $token = $p->get_tag("body")) {
            $pageCopy = $p->get_trimmed_text("/body");
            $pageCopy =~ s/\'//g;
            $pageCopy =~ s/\"//g;

            last;
        }
    }
    #compare copy and array (sep function)
    compareTitlePageCopyHelper($i, $#titleFragments,
\@titleFragments, $pageCopy, $destArr);
    }

}


# Subroutine:
#    compareTitlePageCopyHelper
# Description:
#    This subroutine is used by compareTitlePageCopy subroutine
#    to compare page title to page copy
# Inputs:
#    $index => represents numerical index of the array
#    $numberOfElements => number of files to process
#    $titleFragments => array (reference) to title fragments array
#    $pageCopy => page copy text
#    $pageCopyTitleArr => array (reference) to resulting array
# Outputs:
#    No outputs produced
# Returns:
#    No returns all work done on passed arrays

sub compareTitlePageCopyHelper {
    my ($index, $numberOfElements, $titleFragments, $pageCopy, $pageCopyTitleArr) = @_;
    my $foundCnt = 0;
    my $totalTitleFragments = $numberOfElements;

    for(my $j=0; $j<=$numberOfElements; $j++) {
        my $tmpfragment = $titleFragments->[$j];

        if( $pageCopy =~ /$tmpfragment/i ){
```

```perl
               $foundCnt++;
          }
     }
     if($foundCnt == 0){
          $pageCopyTitleArr->[$index] = 0;
     } else {
          $pageCopyTitleArr->[$index] = ( ($foundCnt/($totalTitleFragments+1)) * 100);

     }
}


# Subroutine:
#   compareArrays
# Description:
#   This subroutine compares elements of two arrays to see if they
#   are found in each other.
# Inputs:
#   $numberOfElements => number of files to process
#   $realArr => array (reference) to first source array
#   $foundArr => array (reference) to second source array
#   $destArr => array (reference) to result array
# Outputs:
#   No outputs produced
# Returns:
#   Subroutine returns percentage of found matches
sub compareArrays {
     my ($numOfElements, $realArr, $foundArr, $destArr) = @_;
     my $found = 0;
     my $percentMatch = 0;

     for(my $i=0; $i<$numOfElements; $i++){
          $tmpVar = $foundArr->[$i];
          $tmpVar =~ s/\(/\\\(/g;
          $tmpVar =~ s/\)/\\\)/g;
          $tmpVar =~ s/\-/\\\-/g;
          $tmpVar =~ s/\+/\\\+/g;
          $tmpVar =~ s/\$/\\\$/g;
          $tmpVar =~ s/\^/\\\^/g;
          $tmpVar =~ s/\[/\\\[/g;
          $tmpVar =~ s/\]/\\\]/g;
          $tmpVar =~ s/\}/\\\}/g;
          $tmpVar =~ s/\{/\\\{/g;


          if ($realArr->[$i] =~ /$tmpVar/i) {
               $destArr[$i] = "Y";
               $found++;
          }else {
               $destArr[$i] = "N";
          }

     }
     return ( ($found/$numOfElements)*100);
}
```

```
# Subroutine:
#   getRealTitles
# Description:
#   This subroutine retrieves actual titles
# Inputs:
#   $numberOfElements => number of files to process
#   $titlesArr => array (reference) to array that will contain real titles
#   $prefix => prefix of file name to be used
# Outputs:
#   No outputs produced
# Returns:
#   Subroutine operates on array already defined outside the routine.
#   Subroutine returns nothing.
sub getRealTitles {
    my ($numberOfElements, $titlesArr, $prefix) = @_;
    for(my $i=0; $i<$numberOfElements; $i++){
        $filename = './serptemp/' . $prefix . "$i.txt";
        if (-e "$filename"){
            my $p = HTML::TokeParser->new($filename);
            while (my $token = $p->get_token) {
                if ($token->[0] eq "S" and lc $token->[1] eq 'title') {
                    my $title =  $p->get_text() || "not found";
                    $title =~ s/^\s+//;
                    $title =~ s/\s+$//;
                    $titlesArr->[$i]=$title;
                    last;
                }
            }
        }else {
            $titlesArr->[$i]="not found";
        }

    }
}


# Subroutine:
#   getKeywordsTitleMatch
# Description:
#   This subroutine compares given keyword with entires of array
#   while setting third array with results of this comparison
# Inputs:
#   $keyword => keyword or keyphrase to do analysis on
#   $sourceArr => array (reference) to be used for comparisons
#   $numOfElements => size of referred array
#   $destArr => array (reference) that will contain compariosn results
# Outputs:
#   No outputs produced
# Returns:
#   Subroutine operates on array already defined outside the routine.
#   Subroutine returns nothing.
sub getKeywordsTitleMatch {
    my ($keyword, $sourceArr, $numOfElements, $destArr) = @_;
```

```perl
    $keyword = cleanText($keyword);
    $keyword =~ s/\'//g;
    $keyword =~ s/\"//g;
    @keywordFragments = split(/ /, $keyword);
    my $numberOfKeywordTokens = $#keywordFragments;

    for(my $i=0; $i<= $numOfElements; $i++) {
        my $tmp = $sourceArr->[$i];
        $tmp = cleanText($tmp);
        $tmp =~ s/'//;
        $tmp =~ s/"//;
        my $foundCnt = 0;
        if ($numberOfKeywordTokens >0) {
            for(my $j=0; $j<=$#keywordFragments; $j++){
                if ($tmp =~ /$keywordFragments[$j]/i) {
                    $foundCnt++;

                    last;
                }
            }
        } else {
            if ($tmp =~ /$keyword/i) {
                $foundCnt++;

            }
        }
        if($foundCnt > 0) {
            $destArr->[$i] = "Y";
        } else {
            $destArr->[$i] = "N";
        }
    }
}


# Subroutine:
#   initializeKeyVariables
# Description:
#   Main purpose is to setup link and title arrays that are
#   to be used throughout the script.
# Inputs:
#   $keyword => keyword or keyphrase to do analysis on
#   $googleLinksArr => array (reference) containing Google links
#   $googleTitlesArr => array (reference) containing Google titles
#   $yahooLinksArr => array (reference) containing Yahoo! links
#   $yahooTitlesArr => array (reference) containing Yahoo! titles
#   $bingLinksArr => array (reference) containing Bing links
#   $bingTitlesArr => array (reference) containing Bing titles
# Outputs:
#   No outputs produced
# Returns:
#   Subroutine operates on arrays already defined outside the routine.
#   Subroutine returns nothing.
sub initializeKeyVariables {
```

```
my ($keyword,     $googleLinksArr,$googleTitlesArr,
    $yahooLinksArr, $yahooTitlesArr,   $bingLinksArr,
    $bingTitlesArr) = @_;
#create user agents
my $uaGoogle = new LWP::UserAgent;
my $uaYahoo = new LWP::UserAgent;
my $uaBing = new LWP::UserAgent;

#setup time out to 25 seconds
$uaGoogle->timeout(25);
$uaYahoo->timeout(25);
$uaBing->timeout(25);

#setup user agent
my $useragent = "Mozilla/4.0 (compatible; MSIE 7.0; Windows NT 6.0)";
$uaGoogle->agent("$useragent");
$uaYahoo->agent("$useragent");
$uaBing->agent("$useragent");

#setup & get one hundred results for each SE
my $gurl=
"http://www.google.com/search?num=$numres&hl=en&safe=off&q=$keyword&sa=N";
my $yurl=
"http://search.yahoo.com/search?p=$keyword&ei=UTF-8&fr=sfp&n=$numres&b=1";
my $lurl=
"http://search.bing.com/results.aspx?q=$keyword&first=1&count=$numres&";


my $reqGoogle = new HTTP::Request GET => "$gurl";
my $reqYahoo = new HTTP::Request GET => "$yurl";
my $reqBing = new HTTP::Request GET => "$lurl";

my $resGoogle = $uaGoogle->request($reqGoogle);
my $resYahoo = $uaYahoo->request($reqYahoo);
my $resBing = $uaBing->request($reqBing);

#assign SERPs to special variables
my $ghtml = $resGoogle->content;
my $yhtml = $resYahoo->content;
my $lhtml = $resBing->content;

#get links for each serp
my $streamGoogle = HTML::TokeParser->new(\$ghtml);
my $streamYahoo  = HTML::TokeParser->new(\$yhtml);
my $streamBing   = HTML::TokeParser->new(\$lhtml);

# process google links
my $cnt=0;
my $threeDots = '...';
while (my $token = $streamGoogle->get_token) {
    if ($token->[0] eq 'S' && $token->[1] eq 'a') {
        if( ($token->[2]{'href'} !~ /cache/i) &&
        !($token->[2]{'href'} !~ /^http/i) &&
         ($token->[2]{'href'} !~ /^https/i) &&
         ($token->[2]{'href'} !~ /google/i) &&
```

```perl
                    ($token->[2]{'href'} !~ /aclk/i) &&
                    ($token->[2]{'href'} !~ /youtube/i)&&
                    ($token->[2]{'href'} !~ /wikipedia/i) ) {
                    $googleLinksArr->[$cnt] = $token->[2]{'href'};
                    $googleTitlesArr->[$cnt] = $streamGoogle->get_trimmed_text("/a");
                    $googleTitlesArr->[$cnt] =~ s/$threeDots$//;
                    $cnt++;
                }
        }
}
# process yahoo links
my $cnt2=0;
while (my $token = $streamYahoo->get_token) {
    if ($token->[0] eq 'S' && $token->[1] eq 'a') {
        @tmpurl= split (/\*\*/, $token->[2]{'href'});
        $tmpurl[1] =~ s/%3f/?/g;
        $tmpurl[1] =~ s/%26/&/g;

        if( ($tmpurl[1] !~ /cache/i) &&
            ($tmpurl[1] !~ /^https/i) &&
            ($tmpurl[1] !~ /yahoo/i) &&
            ($tmpurl[1] !~ /wikipedia/i) &&
            ($tmpurl[1] !~ /overture/i) ){
            $tmpurl[1] =~ s/%3a/:/g;
            $tmpurl[1] =~ s/^s+//g;
            if( $tmpurl[1] ne "" ) {
                $yahooLinksArr->[$cnt2] = $tmpurl[1];
                $yahooTitlesArr->[$cnt2] = $streamYahoo->get_trimmed_text("/a");
                $yahooTitlesArr->[$cnt2] =~ s/$threeDots$//;
                $cnt2++;
            }
        }
    }
}
# process bing links
my $cnt3=0;
while (my $token = $streamBing->get_token) {
    if ($token->[0] eq 'S' && $token->[1] eq 'a') {
        if( !($token->[2]{'href'} !~ /^http/i) &&
            ($token->[2]{'href'} !~ /^https/i) &&
            ($token->[2]{'href'} !~ /cache/i) &&
            ($token->[2]{'href'} !~ /wikipedia/i) &&
            ($token->[2]{'href'} !~ /msn/i) &&
            ($token->[2]{'href'} !~ /hotmail/i) &&
            ($token->[2]{'href'} !~ /microsoft/i) &&
            ($token->[2]{'href'} !~ /bing\.com/i) ) {
            $token->[2]{'href'} =~ s/^s+//g;
            if($token->[2]{'href'} ne "") {
                $bingLinksArr->[$cnt3] = $token->[2]{'href'};
                $bingTitlesArr->[$cnt3] = $streamBing->get_trimmed_text("/a");
                $bingTitlesArr->[$cnt3] =~ s/$threeDots$//;
                $cnt3++;
            }
        }
    }
}
```

```
        }
}


# Subroutine:
#   getSERPResults
# Description:
#   This subroutine downloads htmls of all urls specified
#   in the array referenced by $urlArr
# Inputs:
#   $numberOfElements => size of referred array
#   $urlArr => array (reference) containing urls to process
#   $name => prefix of file name to be used
# Outputs:
#   text files contain html from downloaded links
# Returns:
#   Subroutine operates on array already defined outside the routine.
#   Subroutine returns nothing.
sub getSERPResults {
    my ($numberOfElements, $urlArr, $name) = @_;
    my $ua = new LWP::UserAgent;
    my $res;

    $ua->timeout(25);
    $ua->agent("My Crawler");

    for($i=0;$i<$numberOfElements;$i++){
        $filename = "./serptemp/". $name . $i . ".txt";
        $res = $ua->get("$urlArr->[$i]",':content_file' => "$filename");
    }
}


# Subroutine:
#   cleanText
# Description:
#   This is a utility subroutine to clean HTML fragments.
# Inputs:
#   $text => content of text to clean
# Outputs:
#   No outputs produced
# Returns:
#   No returns; all work done on passed array
sub cleanText {
    my $text = shift;
        $text =~ s/\(/ /g;
        $text =~ s/\)/ /g;
        $text =~ s/\[/ /g;
        $text =~ s/\]/ /g;
        $text =~ s/\./ /g;
        $text =~ s/\-/ /g;
        $text =~ s/\=/ /g;
        $text =~ s/\|/ /g;
        $text =~ s/\!/ /g;
        $text =~ s/\,/ /g;
```

```perl
        $text =~ s/\?/ /g;
        $text =~ s/\^/ /g;
        $text =~ s/\:/ /g;
        $text =~ s/\;/ /g;
        $text =~ s/\&/ /g;
        $text =~ s/\*/ /g;
        $text =~ s/\$/ /g;
        $text =~ s/\s+/ /g;
    return $text;
}
```

Chapter 5

linkchecker.pl

```perl
#!/usr/local/bin/perl
#######################################################################
# File: linkchecker.pl                                               #
# Description: Check Links Script                                    #
# Usage: perl linkchecker.pl http://somedomain.net > report.csv     #
use WWW::Mechanize;
use LWP::Simple;
my $baseurl = shift;
my @url=();
my @level=();
my @type=();
my @title=();
my @status=();
my @page=();
my %uniqueURL=();
my %checkedURL=();
my $masterCnt=0;
my $masterLevel=1;
$mech  = WWW::Mechanize->new();
#### Processing Level One
$mech->get( $baseurl );

@links = $mech->links();
foreach $link (@links) {
$tmpurl = $baseurl . '/' . $link->url();
  if ( ($link->url() !~ /mailto/i) &&
       ($link->url() !~ /javascript/i ) ) {
    if ($link->url() !~ /^http/) {
      #collect unique URL
      $uniqueURL{$tmpurl}=$link->text();
      $url[$masterCnt]=$tmpurl;
      $type[$masterCnt]= "relative";
    }else {
      $tmpurl = $link->url();
      $uniqueURL{$link->url()}=$link->text();
      $url[$masterCnt]=$link->url();
      if( $link->url() =~ /$baseurl/ ){
        $type[$masterCnt]= "absolute internal";
```

```
      }else {
        $type[$masterCnt]= "outbound";
      }
    }
    $level[$masterCnt]=$masterLevel;
    $title[$masterCnt]=$link->text();
    $page[$masterCnt]=$baseurl;
    $masterCnt++;
  }
}
$masterLevel++;
$linksOnFirstLevel=$masterCnt;


####Processing Level Two
%levTwoURLs = ();
$masterCnt = processSubLevel(2, $masterCnt, \@url, \@level, \@type,
                    \@title, \@status, \@page, \%uniqueURL,
                    $baseurl,  $masterLevel, \%levTwoURLs);
$masterLevel++;
$linksOnSecondLevel = keys(%levTwoURLs);
####Processing Level Three
%levThreeURLs = ();
$masterCnt = processSubLevel(3, $masterCnt, \@url, \@level,
                          \@type, \@title, \@status, \@page,
                    \%levTwoURLs, $baseurl, $masterLevel,
                    \%levThreeURLs);
$masterLevel++;
$linksOnThirdLevel = keys(%levThreeURLs);
####Processing Level Four
%levFourURLs = ();
$masterCnt = processSubLevel(4, $masterCnt, \@url, \@level, \@type,
                    \@title, \@status,\@page, \%levThreeURLs,
                    $baseurl, $masterLevel, \%levFourURLs);
$linksOnFourthLevel = keys(%levFourURLs);
printReport(\@level,\@page,\@url,\@type,\@title,\@status, $masterCnt);
#### subroutines
sub processSubLevel {
  my ($currentLevel, $mstCnt, $urlArr, $leArr, $tyArr, $tiArr,
          $stArr,  $paArr, $urls, $burl, $mlevel,
          $uniqueHashRef) = @_;

  my %urlHash = ();
  foreach $item (@$urlArr){
    $urlHash{$item} = 1;
  }
  foreach $lURL (keys %$urls) {
    if( ($lURL !~ /.gif$/) && ($lURL !~ /.jpg$/) &&
        ($lURL !~ /.png$/) && ($lURL !~ /.pdf$/) &&
        ($lURL !~ /.doc$/) && ($lURL !~ /.xls$/) &&
        ($lURL !~ /.asf$/) && ($lURL !~ /.mov$/) &&
        ($lURL !~ /.avi$/) && ($lURL !~ /.xvid$/) &&
        ($lURL !~ /.flv$/) && ($lURL !~ /.mpg$/) &&
        ($lURL !~ /.3gp$/) && ($lURL !~ /.mp4$/) &&
        ($lURL !~ /.qt$/) && ($lURL !~ /.rm$/) &&
        ($lURL !~ /.swf$/) && ($lURL !~ /.wmv$/) &&
```

```perl
                (($lURL !~ /.txt$/) && ($lURL !~ /.js$/) &&
                 ($lURL !~ /.css$/) && ($lURL =~ /$burl/) &&
                 ($lURL !~ /mailto/i)&&($lURL !~ /javascript/i)  ) {
            $mech->get( $lURL );
            @sublinks = $mech->links();
            $cnt2=0;
            foreach $link (@sublinks) {
              my $tmpurl ="";
              #assuming relative link creating temp variable
              if ( $link->url() !~ /^http/i ) {
                $tmpurl = $burl . '/' . $link->url();
              }else {
                $tmpurl = $link->url();
              }
              if(!(exists $urlHash{$tmpurl}) ){
                if ( ($link->url() !~ /mailto/i) &&
                     ($link->url() !~ /javascript/i ) ) {
                  #check UNIQUENESS
                  if( !(exists $urls->{$tmpurl}) ) {
                     $urls->{$tmpurl}=$link->text();
                     $uniqueHashRef->{ $tmpurl } = $link->text();
                  }
                  # check if link relative or absolute
                  if ( $link->url() !~ /^http/ ) {
                     ## RELATIVE
                     $urlArr->[$mstCnt]= $tmpurl;
                     $tyArr->[$mstCnt]= "relative internal";
                  }else {
                     ## ABSOLUTE
                     #adjusting temp variable
                     $urlArr->[$mstCnt]=$link->url();
                     if( $link->url() =~ /$baseurl/ ){
                       $tyArr->[$mstCnt]= "absolute internal";
                     }else {
                       $tyArr->[$mstCnt]= "outbound";
                     }
                  }
                  $leArr->[$mstCnt]=$mlevel;
                  $tiArr->[$mstCnt]=$link->text();
                  $paArr->[$mstCnt]=$tmpurl;
                  $mstCnt++;
                }
              }
            }
          }
        }
    }
  return ($mstCnt);
}
sub printReport {
  my ($levelArr, $pageArr, $urlArr, $typeArr, $titleArr,
      $statusArr, $mCnt) = @_;
  %tmpCleanupHash=();
  print "Level\tParent Page or Location\t
Unique URL\tLink Type\tTitle\tStatus Codes";
  for($i=0;$i<$mCnt;$i++) {
```

```
      if ( !(exists $tmpCleanupHash{$url[$i]}) ){
        $tmpCleanupHash{$url[$i]} = 1;
        if ($levelArr->[$i] ne "") {
          print
"\n$levelArr->[$i]\t$pageArr->[$i]\t$urlArr->[$i]\t$typeArr->[$i]\t$titleArr->[$i]\
t".getstore($urlArr->[$i], "temp");
        }
      }
    }
}
```

mymonitor.pl

```
################################################
# File: mymonitor.pl                           #
# Description: This script takes an argument    #
#              reporesenting a web page url     #
# Format: perl mymonitor.pl http://www.xyz.com #
################################################
use threads;
use Benchmark;
use Time::HiRes qw(gettimeofday tv_interval);
use LWP::Simple;
use LWP::UserAgent;
use File::Path;
#get page to monitor
my $pageToMonitor = shift;
my $ua = new LWP::UserAgent;
my $res;
#cleanup temp files
rmtree( './temp', {keep_root => 1} );
# start timer
my $start_time = [ gettimeofday ];
$res = $ua->get("$pageToMonitor",':content_file' => "./temp/temp.dat");
# stop timer
my $end_time = [ gettimeofday ];
my $elapsedtime = tv_interval($start_time,$end_time);
##### CREATING DATA FILES ###################################
my ($sec,$min,$hour,$mday,$mon,$year,$wday,$yday,$isdst)
    = localtime time;
$year += 1900;
$mon++;
# Create today.txt
open OUTPTR, ">>./report/today/today.txt";
print OUTPTR "$mday-$mon-$year $hour:$min:$sec;10;15;20;
$elapsedtime\n";
close OUTPTR;
# Create month.txt
open OUTPTR, ">>./report/month/month.txt";
print OUTPTR "$mday-$mon-$year $hour:$min:$sec;10;15;20;
$elapsedtime\n";
close OUTPTR;
# Create year.txt
open OUTPTR, ">>./report/year/year.txt";
print OUTPTR "$mday-$mon-$year $hour:$min:$sec;10;15;20;
```

```perl
                         $elapsedtime\n";
close OUTPTR;
# Create historical.txt
open OUTPTR, ">>./report/historical/historical.txt";
print OUTPTR "$mday-$mon-$year $hour:$min:$sec;10;15;20;$elapsedtime\n";
close OUTPTR;
```

inlinksAnalysis.pl

```perl
#!/usr/local/bin/perl
###########################################################
# File: inlinksAnalysis.pl                               #
# Description: This script performs analysis on Yahoo!    #
#              inbound links TSD file                      #
###########################################################
use LWP::Simple;
use LWP::UserAgent;
use HTML::TokeParser;
my @URLs = ();
#get the input param name of the file
my $fileToProcess = $ARGV[0];
my $baseurl = $ARGV[1];
print "\nProcessing: $fileToProcess";
my $cnt = 0;
# open the file
if (-e "$fileToProcess"){
    open FILE, "$fileToProcess" or die $!;
    while (<FILE>) {
        my $line = $_;
        my @fragments = split(/\t/, $line);
        my $url = $fragments[1];
        $URLs[$cnt] = $url;
        $cnt++;
    }
} else {
    print "\nfile ($fileToProcess) does not exist";
}
my $ua = new LWP::UserAgent;
my $res;
$ua->agent("My Crawler");
my %linkPopHash = ();
my %anchorPopHash = ();
for(my $i=0; $i<=$cnt; $i++) {
    $res = $ua->get("$URLs[$i]",':content_file' => "temp.txt");
    if (-e "temp.txt") {
        my $p = HTML::TokeParser->new("temp.txt");
        while (my $token = $p->get_tag("a")) {
            #get link and anchor text
            my $url = $token->[1]{href} || "-";
            my $anchorText = $p->get_trimmed_text("/a");
            $url =~ s/^\s+//g;
            $url =~ s/\s+$//g;
            my $text = $p->get_trimmed_text("/a");
            if ($url =~ /$baseurl/i) {
                #print "\n$baseurl URL: $URLs[$i] LINK: $url";
```

```perl
                    if(exists $linkPopHash{$url}){
                        $linkPopHash{$url} = $linkPopHash{$url} + 1;
                        $anchorPopHash{$url} = $anchorText;
                    } else {
                        $linkPopHash{$url} = 1;
                        $anchorPopHash{$url} = $anchorText;
                    }
                }
            }
        }
    }
open (FP, '>report.txt');
foreach my $key ( sort { $linkPopHash{$b} <=> $linkPopHash{$a} }
keys %linkPopHash ) {
    print FP "$key, $linkPopHash{$key}, \"$anchorPopHash{$key}\"\n";
}
close (FP);
```

Chapter 6

searchPhraseReportGoogle.pl

```perl
#!/usr/bin/perl
#---------------------------------#
#  PROGRAM:  Search Phrase Report  #
#---------------------------------#

$numArgs = $#ARGV + 1;

%googleDirCnt = ();

foreach $argnum (0 .. $#ARGV) {
    print "Processing $ARGV[$argnum] file\n\n";
    $LOGFILE = "$ARGV[$argnum]";
    open(LOGFILE) or die("Could not open log file: $ARGV[$argnum].");
    foreach $line (<LOGFILE>) {
      #do Google analysis
      if(($line =~ /q=/) && ($line =~ /google/)) {
          @tmp1 = split ('GET ',$line);
          @tmp2 = split (' ', $tmp1[1]);
          @tmp3 = split ('q=', $tmp1[1]);
          @tmp4 = split ('\&', $tmp3[1]);
          #do some cleanup
          $tmp4[0] =~ s/\+/ /;
          $tmp4[0] =~ s/\%20/ /g;
          $tmp4[0] =~ s/\%3C/\</gi;
          $tmp4[0] =~ s/\%3E/\>/gi;
          $tmp4[0] =~ s/\%23/\#/g;
          $tmp4[0] =~ s/\%22/\"/g;
          $tmp4[0] =~ s/\%25/\%/g;
          $tmp4[0] =~ s/\%3A/\:/gi;
          $tmp4[0] =~ s/\%2F/\//gi;
          $tmp4[0] =~ s/\%2B/\+/gi;
```

```
            @tmp5 =  split ('\"', $tmp4[0]);
            $tmpKey = "<tr><td>".$tmp2[0]." </td><td>".$tmp5[0]."</td>";
            $googleDirCnt{$tmpKey} = $googleDirCnt{$tmpKey} +1;
        }
    }
    close(LOGFILE);
}

open (FP, '>keywordsummary.html');
print FP "<html><head><title>Keyword Summary</title><head>";
print FP "<body><strong>Google Summary</strong>";
print FP "<table width=400><tr><td><b>Resource/URL</b></td><td><b>Keyword</b></td>";
print FP "<td><b>Count</b></td></tr>";
foreach $key (sort hashValueDescendingNum (keys(%googleDirCnt))) {
        print FP $key."<td>".$googleDirCnt{$key}."</td></tr>";
}
print FP "</table></body></html>";
close (FP);


sub hashValueDescendingNum {
    $googleDirCnt{$b} <=> $googleDirCnt{$a};
}
```

Chapter 13

getRankings.pl

```
#!/usr/local/bin/perl

############################################
# File: getRankings.pl                     #
# Description: This script queries SEs      #
#              to produce rankings report  #
############################################

### Basic setup part
$numOfArgs = $#ARGV + 1;
$originalkeywordphrase = "";
$targeturl="";

if ( ($numOfArgs == 0) || ($numOfArgs == 1) || ($numOfArgs < 0)) {
    print ("\n\nUsage: perl getRanking.pl [TargetURL] [Keyword]\n");
    print ("\nOR\n");
    print ("\nUsage: perl getRanking.pl [TargetURL] [Keyword1] [Keyword2] ...
[KeywordN]\n\n");
    exit(0);
}

$targeturl=$ARGV[0];

if ( $numOfArgs == 2){
    $originalkeywordphrase = $ARGV[1];
```

```perl
}else {
    foreach $argnum (1 .. $#ARGV) {
        $originalkeywordphrase =  $originalkeywordphrase . " " . $ARGV[$argnum];

        #remove leading & trailing spaces
        $originalkeywordphrase =~ s/^\s+//;
        $originalkeywordphrase =~ s/\s+$//;
    }
}

$keywordphrase= $originalkeywordphrase;
$keywordphrase =~ s/([^A-Za-z0-9])/sprintf("%%02X", ord($1))/seg;

# define Source Urls
$listingNo=100;

$gurl=
"http://www.google.com/search?num=$listingNo&hl=en&safe=off&q=$keywordphrase&sa=N";
$burl= "http://www.bing.com/search?q=$keywordphrase&first=1&count=100&";

### get SERP pages part
# get google SERP
$gserp = `wget "$gurl"
--user-agent="Mozilla/4.0 (compatible; MSIE 7.0; Windows NT 6.0)"
--output-document="gserp.html" --cookies=off`;
# get Bing SERP
$bserp = `wget "$burl"
--user-agent="Mozilla/4.0 (compatible; MSIE 7.0; Windows NT 6.0)"
--output-document="bserp.html" --cookies=off`;

### analysis part
$googlePositionNumber = getPosition ($targeturl, "google");
$bingSearchPositionNumber = getPosition ($targeturl, "bing");

# report part
##########################
print "\nRanking Summary Report\n";
print   "~~~~~~~~~~~~~~~~~~~~~~~~~~~~~~~~~~~~~~~~~\n";
print   "Keyword/Phrase: $originalkeywordphrase\n";
print   "Target URL: $targeturl\n";
print   "~~~~~~~~~~~~~~~~~~~~~~~~~~~~~~~~~~~~~~~~~\n";
print   " Google.....: $googlePositionNumber\n";

if($bingSearchPositionNumber ne "not found"){
    $cntAdjusted = $bingSearchPositionNumber + 1;
    print   " Bing Search: $cntAdjusted\n";
}else{
    print   " Bing Search: $bingSearchPositionNumber\n";
}
print "\nNote: Check with specific SE to ensure correctness.\n";

##### SUBROUTINES #################################
sub getContent {
    $filename=shift;
    open INPUT, "<$filename";
```

```perl
    undef $/;
    $content = <INPUT>;
    close INPUT;
    #Restore behaviour
    $/ = "\n";

    #substitute new line character with space character
    $content =~ s/\n/ /g;
    #substitute quotes with nothing
    $content =~ s/\"//g;

    #cleanup bing
    $content =~ s/<strong>//g;
    $content =~ s/<\/strong>//g;

    $content =~ s/<cite>//g;
    $content =~ s/<\/cite>//g;

    return $content;
}

sub getPosition {
    $targeturl= shift;
    $se = shift;
    @tokens = ();
    $offset = 0;
    if($se eq "google") {
        $gcontent = getContent("gserp.html");
        @tokens = split(/h3 class=r/, $gcontent);
    } elsif($se eq "bing") {
        $bcontent = getContent("bserp.html");
        @tokens = split(/sa_cc/, $bcontent);
        $offset=2;
    }

    $mastercnt = "not found";
    $cnt=0;
    $foundFlag = "no";
    print "number of tokens:". $#tokens;
    foreach $token (@tokens) {
        #print "\ntoken: $token";
        if ($token =~ /$targeturl/gi) {
            if($foundFlag eq "no") {
                $mastercnt = $cnt - $offset;
            } else {
                $mastercnt = "" . $mastercnt . "," . $cnt;
            }
            #print "\nMATCH: $targeturl cnt: $cnt $mastercnt\n token";

            #got a match return back position number
            $foundFlag = "yes";
        }
        $cnt = $cnt + 1;
    }
```

```
        return $mastercnt;
    }
```

Chapter 15

sql.txt

```
CREATE TABLE `mytest`.`queue` (
`id` INT( 6 ) NOT NULL AUTO_INCREMENT PRIMARY KEY ,
`message` TEXT NOT NULL ,
`status` INT( 1 ) NOT NULL DEFAULT '0'
) ENGINE = MYISAM ;
```

config.php

```
<?
# change all lines but the last line (Twitter status update link)
#database
$username="your-db-username";
$password="your-db-password";
$database="your-database-name";

#twitter
$tusrid = 'your-twitter-userid';
$tpasswd = 'your-twitter-password';
$tURL = 'http://twitter.com/statuses/update.xml';

?>
```

index.php

```
<html>

<head>

<title>Home</title>

<script>
function limitText(limitField, limitNum) {
    if (limitField.value.length > limitNum) {
        limitField.value = limitField.value.substring(0, limitNum);
    }
}
</script>

</head>

<body>

<h3> What will you be doing? <br>(or what do you want others to think you are doing)
```

```
</h3><br>
<form name=mainform method=post action=add.php onSubmit="return checkLength(this)">

<textarea name="message" rows="3" cols="80" onKeyDown="limitText(this,140);"
onKeyUp="limitText(this,140);">
</textarea> <br>
<input type=submit value='Add Future Tweet'>

</form>
<br>


<?php
include("config.php");
mysql_connect(localhost,$username,$password);
@mysql_select_db($database) or die( "Unable to select my database");
$query="SELECT * FROM queue where status=0 order by id desc";
$result=mysql_query($query);

$numOfRecords=mysql_numrows($result);

mysql_close();

echo "<b>My Future Tweets</center></b><br><hr>";

?>

<table border="1" cellspacing="2" cellpadding="2">
<tr>
<td><b>id</b></td>
<td><b>Tweet</b></td>
<td><b>Status</b></td>
</tr>

<?
$i=0;
while ($i < $numOfRecords) {
   $id=mysql_result($result,$i,"id");
   $message=mysql_result($result,$i,"message");
   $status=mysql_result($result,$i,"status");
?>

<tr>
<td nowrap><? echo "$id"; ?></td>
<td width=350><? echo "$message"; ?>

   <?php

   $tmp = "";
   if ($status < 1) {
     $tmp = "Not Sent";
   }

   ?>
  <a href="delete.php?id=<?php echo $id ?>">Delete</a>
```

```
</td><td nowarp><? echo "$tmp"; ?></td>
</tr>
  <?
  $i=$i+1;
}
?>
</table>
</body>
</html>
```

add.php

```
<?
include("config.php");

mysql_connect(localhost,$username,$password);
@mysql_select_db($database) or die( "Unable to select my database");

$message = $_POST['message'];

$query = "INSERT INTO queue (message) VALUES ('$message')";
mysql_query($query);

mysql_close();

?>

<script>
alert('Tweet Added');
window.location.href = "index.php";
</script>
```

delete.php

```
<?
include("config.php");

mysql_connect(localhost,$username,$password);
@mysql_select_db($database) or die( "Unable to select my database");

$myid = $_GET['id'];

$query="UPDATE queue SET status=2 WHERE id=$myid";

mysql_query($query);

mysql_close();

?>

<script>
alert('Tweet Removed');
```

```
window.location.href = "index.php";
</script>
```

sendTweet.php

```php
<?php

include("config.php");

mysql_connect(localhost,$username,$password);
@mysql_select_db($database) or die( "Unable to select my database");

### get the tweet
$result =
mysql_query("select id, message from queue where status=0 order by id asc LIMIT 1");

$row = mysql_fetch_array($result);

### send the tweet
$curl_handle = curl_init();
curl_setopt($curl_handle, CURLOPT_URL, "$tURL");
curl_setopt($curl_handle, CURLOPT_CONNECTTIMEOUT, 2);
curl_setopt($curl_handle, CURLOPT_RETURNTRANSFER, 1);
curl_setopt($curl_handle, CURLOPT_POST, 1);

$message = $row['message'];

curl_setopt($curl_handle, CURLOPT_POSTFIELDS, "status=$message");
curl_setopt($curl_handle, CURLOPT_USERPWD, "$tusrid:$tpasswd");

$response = curl_exec($curl_handle);

curl_close($curl_handle);

// get the status message
if (empty($response)) {
    echo 'tweet not delivered';
} else {
    echo 'tweet delivered';
    ###update db status
    $mid = $row['id'];
    mysql_query("UPDATE queue SET status = 1 WHERE id = $mid");
}

mysql_close();
?>
```

Crontab

```
# Tweet 5 times a day at 7am, 9am, 11am, 1pm and 3pm
* 8,10,12,14,16 * * * php sendTweet.php
```

Chapter 18

The following code listings represent only the main listings. For the full source code please visit *book.seowarrior.com*.

index.html

```
<html>
<head>

<title>SEO Warrior: Keyboard Dashboard (Alfa)</title>
<link rel="stylesheet" type="text/css" href="pagestyle.css" />
<script src="functions.js" type="text/javascript"></script>
<script src="dockablewindow.js" type="text/javascript"></script>
</head>

<body>
<table width=100% cellpadding=0 cellspacing=0 border=0>
<tr>
<td valign=top align=left><h1 style='color=blue'>SEO Warrior:
Keyword Dashboard (Alpha) </h1>
</td>
<td valign=top align=right>
<img border=0 src="http://www.seowarrior.net/images/status.png"
title="SEO Warrior: Keyword Dashboard Status">

<a href="http://www.seowarrior.net/contact/" title="Report Bugs">
<font size=2>Report Bugs</font></a> |
<a href="http://www.seowarrior.net/contact/" title="Make a Suggestion">
<font size=2>Suggestion</font></a>
 <a href="http://www.seowarrior.net"><img border=0
src="http://www.seowarrior.net/images/seowarriormini.png" title="SEO Warrior:
Keyword Dashboard"></a>
</td>
</tr>
</table>

<div id="formdiv">
  <form name="mainform" onSubmit="return false;">
  Keyword: <input type="text" id="keyword" name="keyword" size="20">
  <input type="button" id="phaseGoogleBtn" name="phaseGoogleBtn" value="Google"
onclick="stepOne('google')">
  <input type="button" id="phaseBingBtn" name="phaseBingBtn" value="Bing"
onclick="stepOne('bing')">
  <input type="button" id="phaseYahooBtn" name="phaseYahooBtn" value="Yahoo!"
onclick="stepOne('yahoo')">

    <input type="radio" name="resultLimit" value="10" checked >10
    <input type="radio" name="resultLimit" value="20">20
    <input type="radio" name="resultLimit" value="50">50
    [Results]
  </form>
</div>
```

```
<iframe onLoad="resizeG()" name="responsedivgoogle" id="responsedivgoogle"
scrolling="no"></iframe>
<iframe onLoad="resizeY()" name="responsedivyahoo" id="responsedivyahoo"
scrolling="no"></iframe>
<iframe onLoad="resizeB()" name="responsedivbing" id="responsedivbing"
scrolling="no"></iframe>

<iframe name="detailsframe" id="detailsframe" class="dockclass"></iframe>

<script type="text/javascript">
var dock0=new dockit("detailsframe", 0);
</script>

</body>

</html>
```

bParser.php

```
<html>
<head>


<style>
body {
  font-weight : normal;
  font-size : 12px;
  font-family : helvetica;
  text-decoration : bold;
  background : #f3f3f3;
}

a:hover {
  font-weight : normal;
  font-size : 12px;
  font-family : helvetica;
  background : #989898;
  text-decoration : bold;
}

a:visited, a:link, a:active {
  font-weight : normal;
  font-size : 12px;
  font-family : helvetica;
  color : #000022;
  text-decoration : normal;
}
</style>


</head>

<body>
```

```php
<b>Bing</b>
<br>Keyword: <?=$_GET["keyword"]?>
<br>Showing</b> <?=$_GET["resultLimit"]?> results
<br><hr>
<?

function getBaseURL($url){
    list($part1, $part2) = split("://", $url);
    list($part3, $part4) = split("/", $part2);
#   $baseurl = $part1 . "://" . $part3;
    $baseurl =  $part3;
    return $baseurl;
}


function getBingSERP($mykeyword, $myindex){
    $reg_ex = "[[:space:]]";
    $replace_word = "+";
    $str = $mykeyword;
    $mykeyword = ereg_replace($reg_ex, $replace_word, $str);

    $url = "http://www.bing.com/search?q=".$mykeyword."&first=".$myindex."&";
    $ch = curl_init();
    curl_setopt($ch, CURLOPT_URL, $url);
    curl_setopt($ch, CURLOPT_COOKIEFILE, "c:\cookie.txt");
    $client = $_SERVER['HTTP_USER_AGENT'];
    curl_setopt($ch, CURLOPT_USERAGENT, "$client");
    curl_setopt($ch, CURLOPT_HEADER, 0);
    curl_setopt($ch, CURLOPT_RETURNTRANSFER, true);
    curl_setopt($ch, CURLOPT_TIMEOUT, 10);
    $output = curl_exec($ch);
    curl_close($ch);
    return $output;
}


function processSERP($serp, $masterCnt, $rowLimit) {
    $dom = new DOMDocument();
    @$dom->loadHTML($serp);
    $xpath = new DOMXPath($dom);
    $hrefs = $xpath->evaluate("/html/body//a");
    $sofar = "";
    for ($i = 0; $i < $hrefs->length; $i++) {
        $href = $hrefs->item($i);
        $url = $href->getAttribute('href');

        $baseurl = getBaseURL($url);

        $urlChunks = spliti (" ", $_GET["keyword"]);

        foreach ($urlChunks as $chunk) {
            $highChunk = '<B>'.$chunk.'</B>';
            $baseurl = str_replace("$chunk", "$highChunk", $baseurl);
        }
```

```php
        $anchortext = $href->nodeValue;

        if ( (preg_match("/live.com/i", "$url")) ||
             (preg_match("/msn.c/i", "$url")) ||
             (preg_match("/microsoft.com/i", "$url")) ) {
        }else {
            if (preg_match("/^http/i", "$url") || preg_match("/^ftp/i", "$url")) {
                if (strpos($sofar, $baseurl) !== false) {
                } else {
                    if($masterCnt < $rowLimit){
                        ?>
<a target=detailsframe href='kw.php?url=<?=$url?>&keyword=<?=$_GET['keyword']?>'
title='<?=$anchortext?>'><?=$baseurl?></a><br><?
                        $masterCnt++;
                    }
                }
            }
        }
        $sofar = $sofar . $baseurl;
    }
    return $masterCnt;
}

$rowLimit = $_GET["resultLimit"];

$masterCnt = 0;

$next = 1;
$keyword = $_GET["keyword"];
$serpRes = getBingSERP($keyword, $next);
$masterCnt = processSERP($serpRes, $masterCnt, $rowLimit);
flush();

if($masterCnt<$rowLimit) {
    sleep(rand(1, 3));
    $next = $first+10;
    sleep(rand(2, 6));
    $masterCnt = processSERP($serpRes, $masterCnt, $rowLimit);
    flush();
}

if($masterCnt<$rowLimit) {
    $next = $next+10;
    sleep(rand(1, 3));
    $serpRes = getBingSERP($keyword, $next);
    $masterCnt = processSERP($serpRes, $masterCnt, $rowLimit);
    flush();
}

if($masterCnt<$rowLimit) {
    $next = $next+10;
    sleep(rand(1, 3));
    $serpRes = getBingSERP($keyword, $next);
    $masterCnt = processSERP($serpRes, $masterCnt, $rowLimit);
    flush();
```

```
    }

    if($masterCnt<$rowLimit) {
        $nextRes = $next+10;
        sleep(rand(1, 3));
        $serpRes = getBingSERP($keyword, $next);
        $masterCnt = processSERP($serpRes, $masterCnt, $rowLimit);
    }

    ?>



    </body>
    </html>
```

gParser.php

```
    <html>

    <head>

    <style>
    body {
        font-weight : normal;
        font-size : 12px;
        font-family : helvetica;
        text-decoration : bold;
        background : #f3f3f3;
    }

    a:hover {
        font-weight : normal;
        font-size : 12px;
        font-family : helvetica;
        background : #989898;
        text-decoration : bold;
    }

    a:visited, a:link, a:active {
        font-weight : normal;
        font-size : 12px;
        font-family : helvetica;
        color : #000022;
        text-decoration : normal;
    }
    </style>

    </head>
    <body>

    <b>Google</b>
    <br>Keyword: <?=$_GET["keyword"]?>
    <br>Showing</b> <?=$_GET["resultLimit"]?> results
    <br><hr>
    <?
```

```php
function getBaseURL($url){
    list($part1, $part2) = split("://", $url);
    list($part3, $part4) = split("/", $part2);
#    $baseurl = $part1 . "://" . $part3;
    $baseurl = $part3;
    return $baseurl;
}

function getGoogleSERP($mykeyword){

    $reg_ex = "[[:space:]]";
    $replace_word = "+";
    $str = $mykeyword;
    $mykeyword = ereg_replace($reg_ex, $replace_word, $str);

    $url = "http://www.google.com/search?q=".$mykeyword.".&num=50&";
    $ch = curl_init();
    curl_setopt($ch, CURLOPT_URL, $url);
    $client = $_SERVER['HTTP_USER_AGENT'];
    curl_setopt($ch, CURLOPT_USERAGENT, "$client");
    curl_setopt($ch, CURLOPT_HEADER, 0);
    curl_setopt($ch, CURLOPT_RETURNTRANSFER, true);
    curl_setopt($ch, CURLOPT_TIMEOUT, 10);
    $output = curl_exec($ch);
    curl_close($ch);
    return $output;
}


$rowLimit = $_GET["resultLimit"];

$keyword = $_GET["keyword"];
$serp = getGoogleSERP($keyword);

$dom = new DOMDocument();
@$dom->loadHTML($serp);
$xpath = new DOMXPath($dom);
$hrefs = $xpath->evaluate("/html/body//a");
$sofar = "";
$intCnt = 0;
for ($i = 0; $i < $hrefs->length; $i++) {
    $href = $hrefs->item($i);
    $url = $href->getAttribute('href');

    $baseurl = getBaseURL($url);

    $anchortext = $href->nodeValue;

    $urlChunks = spliti (" ", $keyword);

    foreach ($urlChunks as $chunk) {
        $highChunk = '<B>'.$chunk.'</B>';
        $baseurl = str_replace("$chunk", "$highChunk", $baseurl);
    }
```

```
        if ( (preg_match("/google.com/i", "$url")) ||
            (preg_match("/youtube.com/i", "$url")) ||
            (preg_match("/^\//i", "$url")) ||
            (preg_match("/cache:/i", "$url")) ) {
    }else {
        if (preg_match("/^http/i", "$url") || preg_match("/^ftp/i", "$url")) {

            if (preg_match("/^http/i", "$url") || preg_match("/^ftp/i", "$url")) {
                if (strpos($sofar, $baseurl) !== false) {
                } else {
                    if($intCnt < $rowLimit) {
                    ?>
<a target=detailsframe href='kw.php?url=<?=$url?>&keyword=<?=$_GET['keyword']?>'
title='<?=$anchortext?>'><?=$baseurl?></a><br><?
                    $intCnt++;
                }

            }
        }
        }
    }

    $sofar = $sofar . $baseurl;
}

?>

</body>
</html>
```

yParser.php

```
<html>
<head>


<style>
body {
  font-weight : normal;
  font-size : 12px;
  font-family : helvetica;
  text-decoration : bold;
  background : #f3f3f3;
}

a:hover {
  font-weight : normal;
  font-size : 12px;
  font-family : helvetica;
  background : #989898;
  text-decoration : bold;
}

a:visited, a:link, a:active {
  font-weight : normal;
```

```
  font-size : 12px;
  font-family : helvetica;
  color : #000022;
  text-decoration : normal;
}
</style>


</head>

<body>

<b>Yahoo!</b>
<br>Keyword: <?=$_GET["keyword"]?>
<br>Showing</b> <?=$_GET["resultLimit"]?> results
<br><hr>
<?

function getBaseURL($url){
   list($part1, $part2) = split("://", $url);
   list($part3, $part4) = split("/", $part2);
#   $baseurl =  $part1 . "://" . $part3;
   $baseurl =  $part3;
   return $baseurl;
}


function getYahooSERP($mykeyword){

    $reg_ex = "[[:space:]]";
    $replace_word = "+";
    $str = $mykeyword;
    $mykeyword = ereg_replace($reg_ex, $replace_word, $str);

    $url = "http://search.yahoo.com/search;_ylt=?p=".$mykeyword.".&n=100&";
    $ch = curl_init();
    curl_setopt($ch, CURLOPT_URL, $url);
    curl_setopt($ch, CURLOPT_REFERER, "http://search.yahoo.com/");
    $client = $_SERVER['HTTP_USER_AGENT'];
    curl_setopt($ch, CURLOPT_USERAGENT, "$client");
    curl_setopt($ch, CURLOPT_HEADER, 0);
    curl_setopt($ch, CURLOPT_RETURNTRANSFER, true);
    curl_setopt($ch, CURLOPT_TIMEOUT, 10);
    $output = curl_exec($ch);
    curl_close($ch);
    return $output;
}

$rowLimit = $_GET["resultLimit"];

$keyword = $_GET["keyword"];
$serp = getYahooSERP($keyword);

$dom = new DOMDocument();
@$dom->loadHTML($serp);
```

```php
$xpath = new DOMXPath($dom);
$hrefs = $xpath->evaluate("/html/body//a");
$sofar = "";

$intCnt = 0;
for ($i = 0; $i < $hrefs->length; $i++) {
    $href = $hrefs->item($i);
    $url = $href->getAttribute('href');
    $tmpurl = "";
    list($tmp1, $tmpurl) = split('\*\*', $url, 2);
    $tmpurl = urldecode($tmpurl);
    $baseurl = getBaseURL($tmpurl);

    $urlChunks = spliti (" ", $keyword);

    foreach ($urlChunks as $chunk) {
        $highChunk = '<B>'.$chunk.'</B>';
        $baseurl = str_replace("$chunk", "$highChunk", $baseurl);
    }


    $anchor = $href->getAttribute('title');
    $anchortext = $href->nodeValue;
    if ( preg_match("/\*\*/i", "$url") )  {

        if ( preg_match("/yahoo.com/i", "$baseurl") || preg_match("/cache/i",
"$url") )  {
        } else {
            if (preg_match("/^http/i", "$url") || preg_match("/^ftp/i", "$url")) {
                if (strpos($sofar, $baseurl) !== false) {
                } else {
                    if($intCnt < $rowLimit) {
                        ?>
<a target=detailsframe href='kw.php?url=<?=$tmpurl?>&keyword=<?=$_GET['keyword']?>'
title='<?=$anchortext?>'><?=$baseurl?></a><br><?

                        $intCnt++;
                    }
                }
            }
        }
    }
    $sofar = $sofar . $baseurl;
}

?>
</body>
</html>
```

Ping Servers

Ping Server List

Because services on the Internet change all the time, before using any of these URLs check if they are still operational:

```
http://1470.net/api/ping
http://api.feedster.com/ping
http://api.moreover.com/ping
http://api.moreover.com/RPC2
http://api.my.yahoo.co.jp/RPC2
http://api.my.yahoo.com/RPC2
http://api.my.yahoo.com/rss/ping
http://audiorpc.weblogs.com/RPC2
http://bblog.com/ping.php
http://bitacoras.net/ping
http://blog.goo.ne.jp/XMLRPC
http://blogdb.jp/xmlrpc
http://blogdb.jp/xmlrpc
http://blogmatcher.com/u.php
http://blogpeople.net/ping
http://blogsearch.google.ae/ping/RPC2
http://blogsearch.google.at/ping/RPC2
http://blogsearch.google.at/ping/RPC2
http://blogsearch.google.be/ping/RPC2
http://blogsearch.google.bg/ping/RPC2
http://blogsearch.google.ca/ping/RPC2
http://blogsearch.google.ch/ping/RPC2
http://blogsearch.google.cl/ping/RPC2
http://blogsearch.google.co.cr/ping/RPC2
http://blogsearch.google.co.hu/ping/RPC2
http://blogsearch.google.co.id/ping/RPC2
http://blogsearch.google.com/ping/RPC2
http://blogsearch.google.de/ping/RPC2
http://bulkfeeds.net/rpc
http://bulkfeeds.net/rpc
http://coreblog.org/ping/
http://coreblog.org/ping/
http://mod-pubsub.org/kn_apps/blogchatt
```

```
http://mod-pubsub.org/kn_apps/blogchatt
http://ping.amagle.com/
http://ping.amagle.com/
http://ping.bitacoras.com
http://ping.bitacoras.com
http://ping.blo.gs/
http://ping.bloggers.jp/rpc/
http://ping.blogmura.jp/rpc/
http://ping.blogmura.jp/rpc/
http://ping.cocolog-nifty.com/xmlrpc
http://ping.cocolog-nifty.com/xmlrpc
http://ping.exblog.jp/xmlrpc
http://ping.exblog.jp/xmlrpc
http://ping.feedburner.com
http://ping.myblog.jp
http://ping.namaan.net/rpc
http://ping.rootblog.com/rpc.php
http://ping.syndic8.com/xmlrpc.php
http://ping.weblogalot.com/rpc.php
http://ping.weblogs.se/
http://ping.wordblog.de/
http://pingoat.com/goat/RPC2
http://rcs.datashed.net/RPC2/
http://rpc.blogbuzzmachine.com/RPC2
http://rpc.bloggerei.de/ping/
http://rpc.blogrolling.com/pinger/
http://rpc.icerocket.com:10080/
http://rpc.newsgator.com/
http://rpc.pingomatic.com/
http://rpc.reader.livedoor.com/ping
http://rpc.technorati.com/rpc/ping
http://rpc.technorati.jp/rpc/ping
http://rpc.twingly.com
http://rpc.weblogs.com/RPC2
http://services.newsgator.com/ngws/xmlrpcping.aspx
http://topicexchange.com/RPC2
http://trackback.bakeinu.jp/bakeping.php
http://www.a2b.cc/setloc/bp.a2b
http://www.bitacoles.net/ping.php
http://www.blogdigger.com/RPC2
http://www.bloglines.com/ping
http://www.blogoole.com/ping/
http://www.blogoon.net/ping/
http://www.blogpeople.net/servlet/weblogUpdates
http://www.blogroots.com/tb_populi.blog?id=1
http://www.blogshares.com/rpc.php
http://www.blogsnow.com/ping
http://www.blogstreet.com/xrbin/xmlrpc.cgi
http://www.lasermemory.com/lsrpc/
http://www.mod-pubsub.org/kn_apps/blogchatter/ping.php
http://www.newsisfree.com/RPCCloud
http://www.popdex.com/addsite.php
http://www.snipsnap.org/RPC2
http://www.weblogues.com/RPC/
http://xmlrpc.blogg.de
```

```
http://xmlrpc.bloggernetz.de/RPC2
http://xping.pubsub.com/ping/
http://zhuaxia.com/rpc/server.php
```

Programming Environment

Building Your Own Environment

All of the software used in this book can be downloaded for free. The following subsections provide information in obtaining everything you need to run and modify scripts found in this book or in Appendix A.

Apache Web Server

You can download the Apache Web Server at *http://www.apache.org*. There are many versions of Apache including Windows and Linux.

Perl

Most Linux installations come with Perl. You can also download it manually at *http://www.perl.org*. You can use *http://www.cpan.org* to find any missing Perl modules. If you are using a Windows operating system, you can download Perl from *http://www.activestate.com*.

PHP

You can download PHP from *http://www.php.net*. There are Windows versions as well as binaries for many other systems. Most Linux systems come with PHP.

MySQL

MySQL is now owned by Oracle. You can download the free MySQL Community Server at *http://www.mysql.com*. It comes in many different versions while supporting many different operating systems. You can use PhpMyAdmin (*http://www.phpmyadmin.net*) to administer your MySQL databases.

Utilizing Distribution Packages

If you don't have time to set up your environment from scratch, you can download one of the many distribution packages. These packages include all of the servers as well as PHP and Perl. Here are some of the popular ones:

XAMPP (http://www.apachefriends.org/en/xampp.html)
    Includes Apache, PHP, Perl, and MySQL (runs on Windows, Mac, and Linux)

WAMP (http://www.wampserver.com/en/)
    Includes Apache, MySQL, and PHP for Windows

MAMP (http://www.mamp.info/en/index.html)
    Includes Apache, MySQL, and PHP for Mac OS

The installation process is fairly simple on most operating systems. After a few minutes, you should have a full development environment running. The first thing you may want to do is find out your web root folder so that you know where to place your files. If you have installed Apache using the default HTTP port (80), you should be able to browse to your local site by going to *http://localhost*. If you need further instructions, follow the help available on each site.

Index

Symbols and Numbers

A

We'd like to hear your suggestions for improving our indexes. Send email to *index@oreilly.com*.

authentication
  Basic HTTP, 173
  DNS crawler, 190
Authoring Tool Accessibility Guidelines
      (ATAG), 60
AutoMapIt tool, 195
awards websites, 261
AWStats tool
  overview, 15, 105, 110–112
  user patterns, 119

B

b2evolution open source software, 55
back-order brokers, 42
Backlink Checker tool, 272
backlink checkers, 271–272
Backlink Watch tool, 272
backlinks (see external links)
Backstreet Browser, 277
badware, 363
Baidu.com website, 330
Ballmer, Steve, 96
Basic HTTP authentication, 173
BBB.org website, 264
behavior patterns (see user behavior patterns)
Bhargava, Rohit, 305
Bing search engine
  background, 22
  content verticals, 301
  guidelines for, 363
  industry buzz, 375–377
  meta search engines and, 26
  requesting site reevaluation, 373
Bit.ly URL shortening service, 308, 310
Blended Search results
  popular keywords, 3
  Universal Search model, 25
blogging
  blog sites, 381
  building your reputation, 242
  canonical link element, 294
  deep-linked content and, 299
  free software, 55
  link building via comments, 260
  microblogging, 307, 309
  search engine spam and, 371
  SMO support, 305
  social networking and, 306
  Technorati support, 278

unexpected buzz, 289
Bloglines website, 306
bots (see web spiders)
brainstorming keywords, 223
breadcrumbs, 57
breakeven point (PPC), 332, 334
Brin, Sergey, 20
Brinck, Tom, 56
broken outbound links, 92–93
BudURL URL shortening service, 310
Business.com website, 258
BUST A NAME tool, 39
buying cycles, 288

C

caching, web pages, 165
call to action (CTA), 350
campaigns, creating, 340–343
canonical link element, 294–296
Caphyon graphical tools, 223
CAPTCHA technique, 285, 379, 380
Cascading Style Sheets (CSS), 366
case sensitivity
  keyword capitalization, 350
  robots.txt file, 182
cat system command, 196
ccSLDs (country code second-level domains),
      38
ccTLDs (country code top-level domains)
  assignment regulations, 91
  governance model, 36
  overview, 38
changefreq attribute tag (XML Sitemaps), 197,
      199, 201
click fraud, 331
click-through rate (CTR), 95, 333
Clinton, Bill, 300
CMS (content management system)
  canonical link element, 294
  free software, 54–55
  paid software, 56
  prebuilt forms for link building, 244
  site implementation software, 261
CMS Made Simple open source software, 55
collocation hosting, 48
comanaged hosting, 48
Compete tool
  estimating website traffic, 278
  finding competitor keywords, 270

Disallow directive (robots.txt file)
  code example, 179, 180
  overview, 180, 186
discussion forums
  deep-linked content and, 299
  search engine spam, 371
  submitting postings, 260
DIV tags
  HTML traps, 160
  search engine indexing and, 149
  text font color scheme, 366
Django open source software, 55
DMCA (Digital Millennium Copyright Act),
      300
Dmoz.org web directory, 26, 258, 264
DNS crawler authentication, 190
document security, 173
Dogpile.com search engine, 26
dollar sign ($), 180, 186
domain brokers, 42
domain names
  buying, 39–44
  buying existing, 42
  buying misspellings, 44, 372
  buying via unsolicited approach, 42
  domain resellers, 43
  estimating net worth, 275
  exact keyword matching, 76
  expired, 40–42, 99, 371
  keyword matches for, 75–76
  keyword-rich, 39
  namespaces, 36–39
  nonsensical, 40, 75
  number of registrations, 6
  parking, 44
  partial keyword matching, 76
  redirecting misspellings, 297
  registration period, 40
  renewing, 44
  size considerations, 39
  suggestion tools, 39
  transferring, 44
  vendor discounts, 44
domain parking, 44
domain redemption cycle, 41
domain transfer, 44
DomainsBot tool, 39
DomainTools tool, 39
doorway (splash) pages, 168, 363, 368

double quote ("), 198
Drupal open source software, 55, 294
dynamic keyword insertion, 349
dynamic links
  JavaScript support, 150–152
  <noscript> tags, 152
  URL rewriting and, 53
dynamic websites
  building site skeleton, 52–53
  CMS support, 54
  search engine confusion, 53
dynamic widget traps, 154
  ActiveX controls, 156
  Flash files, 154
  Java applets, 155

E

e107 open source software, 55
.edu domains, 90
EDUCAUSE, 90
emails
  microblogging and, 307
  newsletters via, 244
Enquiro study, 4
entity association graph, 232
entity escape codes, 198
error pages, 166
escape codes, 198
exact keyword matching, 76
expired domain names, 40–42, 99, 371
external links
  age considerations, 91
  anchor text considerations, 88
  assessing current situation, 242
  competitor analysis, 243
  competitor research, 271–272
  deep-linked content and, 299
  defined, 85
  from .edu/.gov domains, 90
  Hilltop Algorithm and, 89
  link anchor text, 72
  managing, 86–88
  quality of, 88–92
  quantity of, 88–92
  relative page position, 91
  relative site popularity, 92
  SEO monitoring phase, 16
  speed of accumulation, 88
  splitting PageRank effect, 92

tracking for competitors, 281
web directories and, 91
external optimization, 15
external ranking factors
broken outbound links, 92–93
defined, 85
external links, 85–92
user behavior patterns, 93–97
website age, 99
website performance, 97
externalFileImport function (JavaScript/Ajax),
153
Eyetools study, 4
eZ Publish open source software, 55
EZineArticles website, 260

F

Facebook website
account types, 316
background, 316
building your reputation, 242
Google index size, 324
usage tips, 317
YouTube support, 310
Fatscripts.com website, 261
feed readers, 253–254
FeedBlitz website, 257
FeedBurner tool
Analyze section, 255
features supported, 255–256
Feed Subscribers metric, 254
FeedFlare option, 255
FeedMedic service, 256
future considerations, 257
Google Analytics and, 257
integrating with sites, 256
Monetize section, 256
Optimize section, 255
overview, 254
Publicize section, 256
SmartCast option, 255
SmartFeed option, 255
social media sites and, 324
Troubleshootize section, 256
Feedity website, 257
FFA (Free For All) sites, 369
Filo, David, 21
filtering data, 120
find system command, 196

first-tier search engines, 23
Flash platform, 154, 246
Flickr website
background, 312
creating website widgets, 248
Google index size, 324
tools and resources available, 313
usage tips, 313
follow directive, 187
<font> tag, 366
formatting
HTML traps, 163
intelligent page, 59
forum postings
deep-linked content and, 299
search engine spam, 371
submitting, 260
frameborder property (iframes), 160
frames as HTML traps, 156–158
<frameset> tags, 157
Free For All (FFA) sites, 369
free hosting, 47
free keyword research tools, 235
funnels
defined, 143
search, 234

G

generic modifiers, 219, 224
generic top-level domains (gTLDs)
governance model, 36
overview, 36–38
sponsored, 37
getRankings.pl script, 284
Glossarist tool, 236
goals, defining, 141–143
Golden Triangle, 4
Google AdSense
click fraud, 331
earnings explanation, 357
news feed support, 256
overview, 329, 356
setting up, 356
usage tips, 358
website setup, 357
Google AdWords
ad setup options, 348–350
campaign setup, 339–344
click fraud, 331

Change of address subsection, 126
Crawl errors page, 131
Crawl stats page, 131
Crawler access option, 126
Dashboard page, 124, 205
Diagnostics section, 131–133
duplicate content URLs, 296
establishing keyword baseline, 222
Google Sitelinks feature, 126
HTML suggestions page, 132
Internal links page, 130
Keywords page, 130
Links to your site option, 129
overview, 123
Settings option, 127
setup, 123
Site configuration section, 124–128
Sitemap submissions, 205–207
Sitemaps option, 124, 206
Subscriber stats page, 130
Top search queries option, 129
validation tools, 177
viewing backlinks, 86
Your site on the web section, 129–130
Googlebot web spider
description, 178
file types supported, 29
showing activity breakdown, 131
signature example, 104
typical request, 28
Googlebot-Image spider, 104, 178
Googlebot-Mobile spider, 178
.gov domains, 90
greater than sign (>), 198
grep system command, 196
Gross, Bill, 330
gTLDs (generic top-level domains)
governance model, 36
overview, 36–38
sponsored, 37

H
<head> tag
canonical link element, 294
HTML meta directives, 187–189
heading tags, keywords in, 69
hidden links, 370
hidden text, 363, 364–367
Hilltop Algorithm, 89

HitTail tool, 270
Hitwise Intelligence study, 4
Hitwise tool, 272
hosting providers
buying services, 43, 44
choosing platforms, 45–46
collocation hosting, 48
comanaged hosting, 48
dedicated server hosting, 48
free hosting, 47
hosting types, 46–49
internal hosting, 49
managed hosting, 48
shared hosting, 47
web page caching, 166
web server compression, 164
hot link prevention, 300
HotScripts website, 261
.htaccess file
document security, 173
error pages, 166
handling website maintenance, 175
hot link prevention, 300
HTTP header directives, 189
redirect mechanism, 256
redirecting domain misspellings, 297
trailing slash, 296
URL variables and, 167
WWW prefix, 297
HTML forms, 59
HTML meta directives, 187–189
HTML reports, 81, 82
HTML Sitemaps, 195–197
HTML tags (see specific tags)
HTML traps
complex HTML, 163
external DIV tags, 160
extremely large pages, 162
formatting problems, 163
frames, 156–158
graphical text, 161–162
iframes, 158–160
HTML validation, 163
.htpasswd file, 174
HTTP header directives, 189
HTTrack Website Copier, 277
Hulu website, 248
hybrid search engines, 25

I

ICANN (Internet Corporation for Assigned
  Names and Numbers), 36
iframes (inline frames), 158–160
iGooMap tool, 204
IIS
  case insensitivity, 183
  NCSA Combined format and, 104
  URL rewriting, 54
implementation phase (SEO process), 14, 15
inbound links (see external links)
index directive, 187
indexing
  crawling comparison, 172, 249
  deep-linked content, 299
  defined, 31, 172
  fine-grained, 298
  frames and, 157
  hidden DIV tags and, 149
  prohibiting, 172–176
  social media sites, 324
  Twitter support, 308
infinite loops, 295
inlinksAnalysis.pl script, 87
inner page invisibility, 78
internal hosting, 49
internal links, 77, 78
internal optimization, 15
internal ranking factors
  analyzing SERPs, 63
  defined, 63
  on-page ranking factors, 64–74
  on-site ranking factors, 74–80
  putting it all together, 80–82
Internet Archive site
  background, 273
  blocking, 183, 185
Internet Corporation for Assigned Names and
  Numbers (ICANN), 36
iProspect survey, 3
iTunes platform, 255, 314

J

Jaiku website, 324
Java applets, 155, 246
JavaScript language
  Ajax and, 152–154
  dynamic links and menus, 150–152

dynamic text within, 147–149
Google Analytics support, 144
sneaky redirects, 363
Joomla! open source software, 55, 294

K

Kanoodle platform, 331
Kartoo.com search engine, 26
KeyCompete tool, 270
Keyword Dashboard tool, 376
Keyword Discovery tool, 236
Keyword Elite tool, 236
keyword forecast tool, 234
keyword group detection tool, 233
keyword modifiers, 219–220
keyword mutation detection tool, 233
keyword prominence, 70
keyword proximity, 70
keyword rankings (see rankings)
keyword research
  additional tools, 235–236
  buying cycles, 288
  buzz information, 288
  compiling targeted draft list, 223–236
  establishing current baseline, 222
  estimating search volume, 238
  evaluating keywords, 236–239
  finalizing keyword list, 239
  finding additional keywords, 268–271
  future events, 288
  implementing strategy, 239
  keyword modifiers, 219–220, 224
  keyword stemming, 217, 224
  Latent Semantic Indexing, 220
  Microsoft Office support, 225
  predictive SEO, 287–289
  process overview, 221
  researching competitors, 264–268
  SEO research phase, 12
  strategy for, 214–216
keyword stemming, 217, 224
keyword stuffing, 363, 364
keywords
  AdWords match types, 345–348
  AdWords tips, 355
  average page densities, 67
  brainstorming, 223
  broad, 215
  capitalization considerations, 350

About the Author

John I. Jerkovic is currently managing a group of IT professionals at a leading mutual funds company in Canada. His team there works closely with the marketing (e-business) team in managing close to 100 internal and external sites. This work includes SEO. He has also had the opportunity to architect (and work with) several enterprise search solutions based on the Google Search Appliance (GSA), IBM OmniFind Yahoo! Edition, and Lucene. In 2009 John won two Web Marketing Association awards for outstanding achievement in website development. He has his own SEO blog at *http://www.seowarrior.net*.

Colophon

The animal on the cover of *SEO Warrior* is an Eleonora's falcon (*Falco eleonorae*). It is named after Eleonor of Arborea (1347–1404), national heroine of the Italian island of Sardinia, who was the first to legislate protection of falcons.

Eleonora's falcon is a medium-sized bird of prey, 14–17 inches long with a 35–40 inch wingspan. It is fast and aerobatic, with pointed wings, a long tail, and a slender body. The species occurs in two different color forms, light and dark, and is distinguished from other falcon species by its unusually dark underwing feathers. It breeds predominantly on Mediterranean islands, as do two-thirds of the world's falcon population. The small Greek island of Tilos is the breeding area for 10 percent, or about 650 pairs, of the total Eleonora's falcon population.

This falcon nests in colonies on coastal cliffs, where it spends much of its time hunting tired migrating birds. It also eats large insects, such as dragonflies, by catching them in its talons and transferring them to its beak in mid-flight. Eleonora's falcon migrates very long distances, typically wintering in Madagascar. Its migration route was once thought to be coastal, but satellite tracking has found that it takes a longer inland route through the Sahara Desert. It can cover up to 5,600 miles on a single one-way trip.

The cover image is from the Dover Pictorial Archive. The cover font is Adobe ITC Garamond. The text font is Linotype Birka; the heading font is Adobe Myriad Condensed; and the code font is LucasFont's TheSansMonoCondensed.

Get even more for your money.

Join the O'Reilly Community, and register the O'Reilly books you own.It's free, and you'll get:

- 40% upgrade offer on O'Reilly books
- Membership discounts on books and events
- Free lifetime updates to electronic formats of books
- Multiple ebook formats, DRM FREE
- Participation in the O'Reilly community
- Newsletters
- Account management
- 100% Satisfaction Guarantee

Signing up is easy:

1. **Go to: oreilly.com/go/register**
2. **Create an O'Reilly login.**
3. **Provide your address.**
4. **Register your books.**

Note: English-language books only

To order books online:

oreilly.com/order_new

For questions about products or an order:

orders@oreilly.com

To sign up to get topic-specific email announcements and/or news about upcoming books, conferences, special offers, and new technologies:

elists@oreilly.com

For technical questions about book content:

booktech@oreilly.com

To submit new book proposals to our editors:

proposals@oreilly.com

Many O'Reilly books are available in PDF and several ebook formats. For more information:

oreilly.com/ebooks

O'REILLY®